THE
AA
KEYGuide

D0230110

The AA KEYGuide
Mallorca

Contents

KEY TO SYMBOLS

- ✚ Map reference
- ✉ Address
- ☎ Telephone number
- 🕐 Opening times
- ✋ Admission prices
- 🚌 Bus number
- 🚉 Train station
- ⛴ Ferry/boat
- 🚗 Driving directions
- ℹ Tourist office
- 🎫 Tours
- 📖 Guidebook
- 🍴 Restaurant
- ☕ Café
- 🍷 Bar
- 🏬 Shop
- 🚻 Toilets
- 🛏 Number of rooms
- 🚭 No smoking
- ❄ Air conditioning
- 🏊 Swimming pool
- 🏋 Gym
- ❓ Other useful information
- 🛍 Shopping
- 🎭 Entertainment
- 🌙 Nightlife
- ⚽ Sports
- ★ Activities
- ❤ Health and Beauty
- ✪ For children
- ★ Walk/drive start point
- ▷ Cross reference

HOW TO USE THIS BOOK

Understanding Mallorca is an introduction to the island, its geography, economy and people. **Living Mallorca** gives an insight into Mallorca today, while **Story of Mallorca** takes you through the island's past.

For detailed advice on getting to Mallorca—and getting around once you are there—turn to **On the Move**. For practical information, from weather forecasts to emergency services, turn to **Planning**.

Out and About gives you the chance to explore Mallorca through walks, drives and bicycle rides.

The **Sights**, **What to Do**, **Eating** and **Staying** sections are divided geographically into four regions, which are shown on the map on the inside front cover. These regions always appear in the same order. Towns and places of interest are listed alphabetically within each region.

Map references for the **Sights** refer to the atlas section at the end of this book or to the individual town plans. For example, Valldemossa has the reference ✚ 212 C3, indicating the page on which the map is found (212) and the grid square in which Valldemossa sits (C3).

UNDERSTANDING MALLORCA

Anyone who thinks that Mallorca is no more than sun, sea and sand has never been there. The island has a well-deserved reputation as a holiday hotspot, whose warm climate and sunny beaches attract millions of visitors, yet there is so much more to Mallorca than that. The diverse landscapes include mountains, valleys, pine woods, marshes, vineyards, orchards and farmland, plus historic towns, sleepy villages and a capital, Palma, which is among the most cosmopolitan cities in Europe. Countless civilizations, from Roman to Moorish and Catalan to Spanish, have left their mark here, and the island continues to absorb outside influences. Outdoors' enthusiasts are drawn to its spectacular scenery; golfers are attracted by the mild winter weather; sybarites flock to its gourmet restaurants and chic hotels; while cultural tourists are discovering the modern art museums of Palma. It is difficult to think of another island of similar size that has such a diverse appeal.

GEOGRAPHY

Mallorca (sometimes still known as Majorca) is the largest of the Balearic Islands (Illes Balears), which are situated off the east coast of Spain around 200km (124 miles) south of Barcelona. The other islands are Menorca, Ibiza and Formentera. Since 1983, the Balearics have been an autonomous region of Spain, with their capital in Palma.

Mallorca measures approximately 100km (62 miles) from east to west and 75km (47 miles) from north to south. The two main mountain ranges, Serra de Tramuntana and Serra de Llevant, are divided by a fertile plain known as Es Pla. The Serra de Tramuntana runs along the north coast from Andratx to Pollença and includes the island's highest peak, Puig Major (1,447m/4,746ft).

The offshore islets of Cabrera (▷ 95) and Sa Dragonera (▷ 75) are nature reserves, which can be visited by boat. There are no rivers in Mallorca, though there are several torrents that rise in the mountains and swell after heavy rain.

PEOPLE

Mallorca has a population of around 700,000, of whom half live in the capital, Palma. The next largest towns are the industrial centres of Manacor (35,000) and Inca (25,000). These figures rise significantly in summer, not just because of the number of visitors but also because of the many Spaniards and others who have second homes on the island. It is estimated that around 10 percent of the permanent population of Mallorca are foreigners, including large numbers of British and German expatriates as well as migrant workers from Ecuador, Morocco and elsewhere.

There are churches, synagogues and mosques serving the various immigrant communities on the island, but the vast majority of the local population is Roman Catholic. However, as elsewhere in Spain, church attendance is in decline and Mallorca is now a largely secular and tolerant society—except at the many village fiestas, most of which are religious in origin if not in practice.

LANGUAGE

The official languages of Mallorca are Catalan and Castilian (Spanish). Most people actually speak Mallorquín, a local dialect of the Catalan language introduced by the Aragonese invaders in the 13th century. Since the death of General Franco in 1975 and the introduction of democracy to Spain, there has been a revival of regional languages and Mallorquín is once again the main language heard on the streets.

Most signposts and official notices are in Catalan, though there is still some inconsistency and you may see signs for both the *playa* (Spanish) and *platja* (Catalan), or for Puerto Pollensa (Spanish) and Port de Pollença

successful tourism infrastructure. In recent years, Mallorca has also led the way in developing alternative forms of tourism.

As the holiday industry has grown in importance, agriculture has declined, though there are still significant crops of potatoes, vegetables and strawberries around Sa Pobla and oranges in the Sóller Valley. Other produce includes almonds, olives, olive oil and wine. There is little heavy industry, though the tourism industry does support a substantial construction sector. Small-scale industries and crafts include the manufacture of leather goods, footwear, pottery, glassware and artificial pearls, much of which is sold at souvenir shops across the island.

Persuasive Mallorca: whether you want to explore the mountains around Deià, see Palma's spectacular cathedral or just laze on a beach in Palma Nova, there are many different reasons to visit Mallorca

COMMON TERMS

English	Catalan	Spanish
avenue	avinguda	avenida
beach	platja	playa
castle	castell	castillo
cave	cova	cueva
church	església	iglesia
market	mercat	mercado
monastery	monestir	monasterio
museum	museu	museo
palace	palau	palacio
square	plaça	plaza
street	carrer	calle

(Catalan). The majority of place names in this book are given in Catalan, except where Spanish is in common use.

POLITICS

In political terms, Mallorca has been consistently out of step with mainland Spain. When José Mariá Aznar's right-wing Partit Popular (PP) was in power, Mallorca's semi-autonomous regional government was led by a coalition of greens and socialists. Shortly before José Luis Zapatero's Socialist party ousted the PP in the national elections of March 2004, Mallorca's local government had swung back to the PP.

ECONOMY

Tourism is the biggest industry on Mallorca, accounting for over two-thirds of jobs and more than 75 percent of GDP (Gross Domestic Product). Over the past 40 years, Mallorca has become a byword for mass package holidays, and emerging leisure destinations often look to the island for guidance on how to create a

MALLORCA TODAY

Mallorca in the 21st century is in a state of flux, with two apparently contrasting trends happening at the same time. On the one hand, the island is being steadily absorbed into the European mainstream, with the development of a multiracial society and the gradual erosion of the siesta in favour of more conventional business hours. The tourism industry is being driven upmarket, and the new hotels, congress centres, golf courses and marinas which have opened in recent years are virtually indistinguishable from their counterparts elsewhere. Alongside this, however, is a revival of island culture, seen in everything from art and music to language and cuisine, but most vividly in the traditional fiestas with their horned devils and giant carnival figures. Although these festivals attract huge numbers of visitors, they remain authentic village events at which everyone— Mallorquíns, foreign residents and tourists— comes together to let their hair down and generally have a great time.

It is often said that the Mallorquíns share the Catalan capacity for exhibiting two conflicting sides to their character known as *seny* (common sense) and *rauxa* (emotion). Perhaps this helps to explain how they can party all night and still go to work in the morning, or how they manage to combine long working hours and one of the highest GDPs in Europe with an ability to find time for the important things in life, such as family, friends and long lunches by the sea. Today's Mallorquín entrepreneurs know how to get things done when they need to, but they are just as likely to shrug you off with a reply of *tanmateix*, an expression best translated as 'oh well' or 'all the same'.

The sights in this book are divided into four geographical regions, though these do not correspond to the island's administrative districts.

Palma includes both the capital, Palma, and some of Mallorca's busiest beach resorts along its bay. Palma is a sophisticated, vibrant, modern city, combining historic buildings with a passion for art and architecture and an energetic street life. This is where you will find the island's best shopping and nightlife, as well as a wide choice of restaurants and a growing number of designer hotels. Fortunately, the city centre is sufficiently compact to be explored on foot. The resorts on either side of the bay, from S'Arenal to the east and Magaluf to the west, were some of the earliest in Mallorca and they are still crowded out with visitors in summer. Alongside these popular resorts are some of Mallorca's most exclusive communities, largely populated by a yachting crowd.

Golf courses such as Marriot's Son Antem, right, are taking over from farmland, but rural scenes still exist around Sa Pobla, left, with wind-powered irrigation. Centre, Mallorca in tiles at Alcúdia

The Serra de Tramuntana is Mallorca's highest mountain range, running the length of the northwest coast. In many people's opinion this is the most enchanting part of the island. It is a region of stark, dramatic landscapes, and a vast outdoor playground offering superb walking and rock-climbing. It contains Mallorca's most sacred site at Lluc (▷ 70–73), one of its prettiest villages, Deià (▷ 67), and a charming town, Sóller (▷ 76–77), nestling in a valley of orange trees. Small, luxurious hotels and excellent restaurants are scattered conveniently throughout the Serra de Tramuntana, making a driving tour of the mountains one of the joys of a Mallorcan holiday. Tourism is the Serra de Tramuntana's principal source of income and its narrow, twisting roads become very busy in summer; the best times to explore are late spring and early autumn.

The Northeast has some of Mallorca's best beaches, along with a trio of historic towns—Alcúdia (▷ 84–85), Artà (▷ 83) and Pollença (▷ 90–93). The coastline is dominated by the great bay of Alcúdia, whose long beaches back onto dunes and marshland, favoured by birdwatchers from across Europe for the variety of birdlife. Among the other attractions of this region are the rugged peninsula of Formentor (▷ 88) and the cave systems at Artà and Campanet (▷ 86). The west of this region, Pollença especially, is popular with British holidaymakers and expatriates, while the east of the region, southward from Cala Rajada, has a high proportion of German businesses.

The South is the rural heartland of Mallorca. The fertile plain at the centre of the island produces most of Mallorca's crops, sold in traditional country markets such as Sineu (▷ 102). Almond orchards blossoming in February are always an impressive sight. Creeks and coves indent the southeast coast, while the south coast is relatively undeveloped, especially around the magnificent dune-backed beach of Es Trenc (▷ 97). The small towns of the south receive few visitors and are ideal for soaking up the atmosphere of everyday Mallorca. Key attractions are the historic town of Petra (▷ 101) and the east coast's caves (▷ 98–99).

Mane attraction: a bronze statue of a winged lion, symbol of Sineu

HOW TO ENJOY MALLORCA

Many people spend their entire holiday in a self-contained beach resort, rarely venturing beyond the hotel pool except perhaps on an organized coach excursion to discover 'the real Mallorca' in the company of a guide. This is fine, but you will get much more out of the island if you explore by yourself, either by hire car, bicycle or public transport (▷ 35–46). Mallorca is easy to get around and its small size means that even on a short visit it is possible to get to know each of its regions, spending your mornings visiting museums and markets or walking in the mountains and your afternoons on the beach. It obviously helps if you can speak some Catalan or Spanish, but most people are happy to help visitors and even in the smallest villages you will usually find someone who speaks English.

The other way to get the most out of your stay is to adopt the local attitude to time. Do not try to cram too much into the day; instead, relax, take things slowly and be spontaneous. You will always find a restaurant willing to serve you at northern European hours, but remember that few locals eat lunch before 1.30pm or dinner before 9pm. The early evening is for strolling, for putting on your smartest casuals and indulging in that delightful Spanish ritual called the *paseo* (*passeig* in Mallorquín). If you want to meet the locals, there's no better way.

Despite the growth of mass tourism at resorts like S'Arenal, left, Mallorcans, such as this smartly dressed horse rider, proudly uphold island traditions. Right, hitting the boutiques on Palma's Avinguda Jaime III

Pollença
Alcúdia
Sóller
Deià
Sa Pobla
Valldemossa
Inca
Artà
Sineu
Petra
Andratx
PALMA
Algaida
Manacor
Llucmajor
Felanitx
Santanyí

Cabrera

THE BEST OF MALLORCA

BEST PLACES TO STAY

Ca's Xorc, Sóller (▷ 187) Make the effort to reach this luxurious celeb hang-out at the top of a mountain.

Es Convent, Alcúdia (▷ 188) It's quiet and minimalist, but there's nothing austere about this small converted convent.

Dalt Murada, Palma (▷ 181) You'll get gorgeous, faded splendour for a bargain price at this townhouse hotel behind Palma's cathedral.

Hotel Born, Palma (▷ 180) Book ahead to get a bed in the capital's best budget hotel.

Illa D'Or, Port de Pollença (▷ 190) Call it old-fashioned, but this hotel still sets high standards and is perfectly placed.

Palacio Ca Sa Galesa, Palma (▷ 182) This palatial townhouse hotel has its own art collection and beautiful rooms.

Mountain views from Ca's Xorc in the Serra de Tramuntana

BEST PLACES TO EAT

La Bodeguilla, Palma (▷ 164) Spanish cuisine is skilfully prepared at this restaurant with its own wine merchant.

La Boveda, Palma (▷ 165) Queues form outside Mallorca's best *tapas* bar on weekend evenings, but it's worth the wait.

Es Cellar, Petra (▷ 175) Watch your meal being barbecued at this traditional *celler* restaurant.

Fabrica 23, Palma (▷ 166) In the heart of buzzy Santa Catalina, Fabrica 23's British chef serves inventive meals.

Es 4 Vents, Algaida (▷ 174) Mallorcan families congregate at this roadside restaurant on Sundays for outstanding cooking.

Make a date for dinner at Read's Hotel

Read's Hotel, Santa Maria del Camí (▷ 169) The British chef at this exclusive hotel creates dishes that live up to the fabulously decorated dining room.

Ses Rotges, Cala Rajada (▷ 172) This French-owned restaurant is a fine-dining favourite with Cala Rajada's German expats and holidaymakers.

BEST BEACHES

Cala Mondragó (▷ 96) A pair of pretty coves are found in a protected natural reserve on the otherwise heavily developed east coast.

Formentor (▷ 88) Once the preserve of a local hotel, this narrow, idyllic stretch of pine-backed sand is open to all now.

Illetes (▷ 51) Locals prefer this small beach in the Bay of Palma to its commercialized neighbours.

Pollença and Alcúdia Bays There's plenty of space and lots of watersports on Mallorca's best long beaches.

Es Trenc (▷ 97) Chill out on Mallorca's most bohemian beach; clothes are optional.

Let your hair down at Es Trenc beach on the south coast

BEST VILLAGES

Deià (▷ 67) Robert Graves put Deià's golden buildings on the tourist trail.

Fornalutx (▷ 77) Regularly voted Spain's prettiest village, Fornalutx doesn't disappoint.

Orient (▷ 74) Orient is a picturesque place for a pitstop on a tour of the Serra de Tramuntana.

Village life at Fornalutx, left, and the mountains around Orient, right

THE BEST OF MALLORCA

BEST MUSEUMS AND GALLERIES

Can Planes, Sa Pobla (▷ 89) Toys are the highlight of this quirky museum in an otherwise unassuming rural town.

Fundació Joan Miró, Palma (▷ 58) This modern museum is dedicated to Mallorca's favourite adopted artist.

Museu de Mallorca, Palma (▷ 60) Head for the impressive prehistory and Islamic galleries in Mallorca's main museum for the story of the island's beginnings.

Museu de Pollença, Pollença (▷ 92) An eclectic account of Pollença's history and residents can be found in this former convent.

Museu Es Baluard, Palma (▷ 59) Modern art is juxtaposed with solid military architecture at this new museum, with the cathedral looming in the background.

The bold Fundació Joan Miró, above, and Es Baluard, right

BEST SHOPS

Camper, Inca (▷ 131) Camper's trendy shoes for men and women can be bought at bargain prices at this factory outlet.

Finca Gourmet, Sóller (▷ 123) Souvenir hunting? Try some of Mallorca's seasonal specialities at this delightful delicatessen.

Frasquet, Palma (▷ 115) Enter an ornate world of chocolate and temptation at Palma's top sweet shop.

Santa Catalina market, Palma (▷ 139) Browse the stalls at this covered market in a lively district of Palma.

Vidrerias Gordiola, Algaida (▷ 130) Watch artisans create Mallorca's famous glassware then buy it at a discount.

Indulge in Mallorca's finest chocolates at Frasquet

BEST NIGHT OUT

Abaco, Palma (▷ 116) Forget the prices, you'll gasp at Abaco's surreal opulence.

Barcelona Jazz Club, Palma (▷ 117) It's small, dark and high-spirited—as a good jazz club should be.

Café Sóller, Sóller (▷ 124) Enjoy *tapas* and drinks at the hub of Sóller's nightlife.

Pacha, Palma (▷ 117) Clubbers dress up for the most stylish nightclub on the island.

Pirates, Palma (▷ 116) Acrobatic pirates host this bawdy show in Magaluf.

Summer concerts at Castell de Bellver (▷ 133) Classical music is showcased at the Castell in this annual summer festival.

Palma has several nightclubs, including one jazz club, right

BEST ACTIVITIES

Cycling You don't have to be a bike racer to enjoy exploring Mallorca on two wheels (▷ 108).

Golf Play a round at one of Mallorca's toughest and prettiest courses, Canyamel Golf (▷ 127).

Sailing Hire a dinghy and learn a new skill with friends or family in Port de Pollença's sheltered bay (▷ 129).

Scuba diving Several operators instruct first-timers or guide qualified divers into Mallorca's underwater caverns (▷ 110).

Walking Complete a section of the Dry Stone route (▷ 109) on foot in the Serra de Tramuntana.

Setting sail in Port de Pollença

Eye up the multi-million-euro yachts bobbing in the harbours during the Copa del Rey when Palma hosts Europe's glitziest sailing regatta (▷ 133).

Watch a demonstration of traditional dancing and crafts at La Granja, a converted farmstead in the mountains that children will love (▷ 68).

Craft shows at La Granja are a hands-on experience

Savour a Mallorcan speciality—*pa amb olí* for a snack, *tumbet* for vegetarians, baked sea bass in rock salt for fish lovers and almond cake for all (▷ 162).

Sample the latest Mallorcan wines at a new-wave *bodega* in Binissalem (▷ 95), where some of Mallorca's best wines are produced.

Go caving, but there's no need to get cold and wet in Mallorca's famous limestone caves, which have sound and light shows in their enormous caverns (▷ 98–99).

Worship the sun on one of Mallorca's many dazzling beaches (▷ 108). You can still find remote, undeveloped stretches of sand.

Beach life: the cove of Portals Vells to the west of Palma

Take a trip back in time and ride the vintage train from Palma to Sóller (▷ 40) through fruit tree plantations, then hop on a tram to Port de Sóller for an afternoon on the beach.

Spot black vultures at the Cuber reservoir (▷ 145), where the rare birds soar on thermals of rising air and scour the mountains for food.

Hunt Palma's Modernist buildings (▷ 137–39), stopping for a pastry from the art deco-fronted Forn de Teatre shop.

Spend a night in a hilltop monastery; the monks at Lluc monastery (▷ 179), and others, welcome respectful overnight guests.

Nose around some of the spectacular hidden courtyards in the back streets of Palma; not all are open to the public but you can peer through the wrought-iron gates.

People-watch on the Passeig Marítim on Saturday night when Palma's party crowd show off on the seafront (▷ 61).

Above, a Modernist bakery. Left, a doorknocker in Palma

Explore the villages of the Tramuntana foothills on a bicycle (▷ 45): a tour of Bunyola, Alaró, Biniamar, Moscari and Campanet makes a challenging day out.

Eat a first-rate meal with an unbeatable view: Ca's Xorc, Es Faro and Bens D'Avall all have stunning vistas.

Find Robert Graves' grave, which bears the simple epitaph 'Poet', in Deià's churchyard (▷ 67).

Deià: home to millionaire expats and a handful of hippies

Follow the twisting road out to the lighthouse at Cap de Formentor (▷ 88), where the Serra de Tramuntana finally drops into the sea.

Go walking (▷ 109) in the craggy mountains of the Serra de Tramuntana and breathe in the aroma of pine woods and wild herbs.

Spend Sunday morning in the market at Pollença (▷ 90–93), then climb the long, cypress-lined staircase to the Calvari chapel above the town.

Combine luxury with rural tranquillity by spending a night at one of the new breed of upmarket country hotels (▷ 178) springing up across the island.

Soak up the vibe of modern Palma with a visit to Museu Es Baluard (▷ 59), then have a drink on the sculpture terrace overlooking the bay.

Sóller is a great base for walking holidays in the Tramuntana

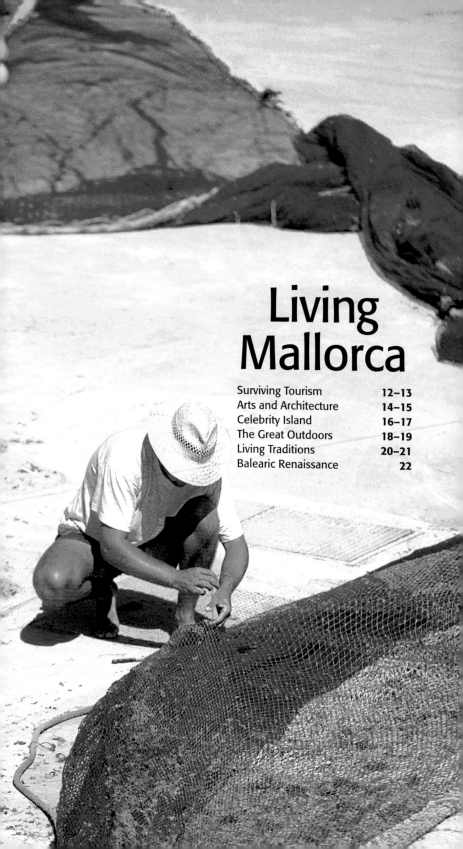

Living Mallorca

The contrast between Magaluf, above, and Valldemossa, below right couldn't be any greater

Above, coach tours hit the roads in summer.
Right, Mallorcan society remains very traditional

Surviving tourism

The boom in package tourism since the 1960s has made Mallorca one of the wealthiest regions in Spain and today tourism accounts for 90 percent of the island's income. Unsurprisingly, such an important source of money has become closely tied to local politics. The government of the Balearic Islands has a degree of autonomy and can introduce measures—such as the eco-tax on tourists—which affect tourism revenue. Islanders have to decide how best to manage the tourist industry and to find a balance between encouraging ever-increasing numbers of visitors and preserving the very things, such as clean beaches and beautiful mountain landscapes, that attract people in the first place.

Tourism also caused a massive social upheaval in Mallorca. For centuries the island's economy was based on agriculture; it was said that in Mallorca's fields 'children worked like women, women worked like men and men worked like Titans'. In landowning families the most fertile and profitable land—always the farmland in the interior—was handed down to the eldest son, whereas the black sheep inherited the worthless coastal land. Within one generation tourism turned society upside down: building on the coastal land yielded huge returns, whereas in comparison farming almonds, olives and oranges inland seemed like hard work for little reward.

Packaging Paradise

In 1960, 250,000 tourists arrived in Mallorca and the advent of affordable package holidays meant that the island was no longer the preserve of the wealthy. Today, more than 7 million people annually take their holidays on the island—and they have to have somewhere to sleep. In 1960 there were around 20,000 hotel beds, but today the figure is nearer 285,000. As befits an island that started the world's first tourist board, Mallorca has been in the vanguard of mass tourism. It's made mistakes, such as piling people into ugly, high-rise hotels, but it's also had the wisdom to rectify those mistakes. As more people book their holidays independently and the package deal loses its appeal, Mallorca is pulling down its cheap, concrete hotels and developing smaller, stylish hotels away from the main resorts.

Charter jets, above, shuttle tourists onto the island in the summer, but away from the resorts farming continues inland, below and bottom left

Above, the yacht-filled harbour at Port d'Andratx and, below, the beach at Palma Nova

Agroturismo

The persistent image of Mallorca as a high-rise hell of concrete beach-front resorts is out of date. Look away from the coast and you'll find that the accommodation Mallorca offers is changing swiftly. The biggest development in recent years has been *agroturismo* (rural tourism): government policies have encouraged farmers and house owners inland to convert their properties to small hotels. There are now more than 120 rural properties in the scheme (▷ 178), from *grand hoteles rurales* to humbler *agroturismos* (often working farms) and renovated townhouse hotels. All offer something special, whether it is sumptuous bedrooms in an old manor house, fantastic Mallorcan cooking, or simply the chance to stay in glorious silence deep in the countryside.

Money, Money

Money talks, and nowhere can you hear it more loudly spoken than in the yacht clubs and marinas of the Bay of Palma. The island has 20,000 yacht moorings and Palma is one of the largest and most prestigious marinas in Europe. Harbours such as Puerto Portals are where the rich and famous park their magnificent yachts for the summer. Here they have all their essential support services: designer boutiques, hideously expensive restaurants and luxury apartments. But what makes Mallorca unusual is that the super-rich and the average holiday-maker co-exist in close proximity. One minute you can be in chic Portals Nous, but walk around the next point and you'll be among the theme pubs and souvenir shops of Magaluf.

Toad in a Hole

There is no more amazing survivor than the critically endangered Mallorcan midwife toad. Long-thought extinct, due to disturbance of its habitat, a pocket of surviving toads was discovered high in the Serra de Tramuntana in 1980. The mountain range is the only place in the world where this diminutive 3.5cm (1.5in) amphibian lives; a tadpole breeding programme by Gerald Durrell's Wildlife Conservation Trust has returned many young *ferrerets* (the toad's local name) to remote mountain-top crevices. The species is unusual because once the female has laid her eggs, the male takes over, winding the strings of eggs around his legs and nurturing them until they hatch. It is hoped that more populations of the Mallorcan midwife toad, a special part of Mallorca's natural heritage, will be established around the island in spite of mass tourism.

Rise and Fall of the Eco-tax

Nobody likes paying tax, but most people admitted that the pioneering eco-tax on tourists introduced in 2002 by the Balearic Government's coalition of Greens and Socialists was for a good cause. The idea was to use the money levied (about €1 per visitor per day of their stay) to offset tourism's impact on the island's environment. Projects would clean up water supplies, support local economies and create eco-friendly initiatives such as walking routes. It didn't last long. In the 2003 elections, the centre-right Popular Party was elected and it promised to scrap the eco-tax. Sure enough the tax was soon phased out, but it funded plenty of worthwhile projects during its short lifetime, when it raised about €35 million.

Above, the Joan Miró Foundation. Left, Casa Olesa. Below, part of *Fundació Palma* by Miró

Arts and
Architecture

There's much more to Mallorca than sunshine and sand: the arts and artists thrive on the island and contemporary culture is as strong now as it has ever been. Two new auditoriums, in Alcúdia and Cala Millor, host theatre, dance and musical productions, and Palma's auditorium attracts high-profile performers to its adventurous seasonal programmes. There are 10 cultural centres in Palma alone, with modern art in the city's galleries and Modernist architecture in its streets. And it's not difficult for culture vultures to sniff out art in other towns throughout the island, from the famous mountain village of Deià to the east coast town of Artà, where several (mainly German) artists have set up art galleries.

Traditional performances at festivals throughout the year (▷ 113) make interesting days out, while crafts such as glass-blowing and the making of clay whistles (*siurells*) are continued for the benefit of tourists. So, if you fancy a break from the beaches, you can always hunt down paintings by Picasso, sculptures by Rodin and buildings by Gaudí.

Miró in Mallorca

You don't have to go far to find evidence of Joan Miró's (1893–1983) impact in Mallorca: the mural in the Parc de la Mar (▷ 61), an urban space in front of Palma's cathedral is based on his art. And, if you use the Spanish or Mallorca tourist boards, you will spot his own work; he designed their logos. The Barcelona-born artist moved to Mallorca in 1956 and the island has claimed him as its own ever since. Prior to settling in Mallorca he had explored Dadaism and Surrealism, but his work post-1960 is characterized by bold, colourful, but precise paintings; he is regarded as a father of Abstract Expressionism. You'll also find sculptures by Miró in the King's Garden and more work at his studio (▷ 58).

Mallorca's *siurells* come in a variety of forms

Above, the façade of
Fundació La Caixa.
Right, Can Forteza
Rey. Below, the artist
Miquel Barceló

Above, a glassblower.
Below, the altar in
Palma's cathedral

Mallorca to Mali

Miquel Barceló is the
most celebrated contem-
porary Mallorcan
artist—and the most
adventurous. He was
born in Felanitx in 1957
and studied at the Arts
and Crafts School of
Palma. Notable for being
the youngest painter to
have exhibited at the
Louvre in Paris, Barceló's
larger paintings can sell
for almost £1 million—
and he also creates
sculptures and pottery.
Clear traces of Spain's
artistic traditions, such as
mysticism and fatalism,
can be seen in his figura-
tive work, but look
closely at the subject
matter—goats, insects
and skulls—and you'll
find clues to his second
home outside Mallorca.
In 1988 Barceló crossed
the Sahara and settled in
Mali, where he built his
own hut in a Dogon
village in the desert.

Shady Dealings

The March family is to
Mallorca what the
Guggenheim family is to
New York: enormously
wealthy, influential phi-
lanthropists. In 2003 the
family mansion, Palau
March, opened to the
public and immediately
dazzled visitors The
linchpin of the March
empire was Joan March,
born in Santa Margalida
in 1880. Having
amassed a huge per-
sonal fortune that made
him one of the world's
richest men during
Franco's regime, he
spent much of it on art
(▷ 64). But there are
increasing indications
that some of his early
wealth was based on
tobacco smuggling and
arms dealing. Accounting
books have been discov-
ered that detail, under
the heading 'Tobacco
Expenses 1902', the
bribes to be paid to
policemen: sergeants
pocketed 150 pesetas.
There are even pay-
ments to spies listed,
some of whom charged
50 pesetas.

Through the Keyhole

The old town of Palma,
the streets around the
cathedral, is the perfect
place for nosing around
other people's houses.
The area is packed with
the mansions of Palma's
movers and shakers, and
when the owners move
on, many of their resi-
dences are opened for
all to see. One of the
most recent houses to
be restored is Can
Marquès (▷ 49), which
opened to the public in
2001. Once the home of
a rich coffee merchant,
you can still appreciate
the owner's taste in
interior design and art.
The wallpaper dates
from the 19th century
and the Modernist stair-
case is marvellous. But
the centrepiece of any
townhouse is its court-
yard, invariably a feast of
graceful sandstone
arches, staircases and
exotic foliage—all of
which you can spy from
the wide doorways on
the street.

Gaudí's Signature

In some respects Palma
is a miniature Barcelona.
Both are attractive cities
with a strong Catalan culture, famous shopping
streets and spectacular
cathedrals by Antoni
Gaudí. In 1904 Gaudí
was commissioned to
restore Palma's Gothic
cathedral and during the
10 years he spent work-
ing on the interior his
presence in the city
undoubtedly helped fire
the imagination of
Mallorcan architects and
designers. Soon
Modernism's motifs—
natural imagery,
elaborate ironwork,
colourful tiling—were
appearing on buildings
everywhere. Gaudí's
assistant Joan Rubió
designed some of the
Modernist landmarks in
Mallorca, while another
Catalan architect, Lluís
Domènech i Montaner,
created the most famous
Modernist building in
Palma—Fundació La
Caixa, previously the
Gran Hotel (▷ 59).

Left, La Residencia hotel in Deià, once owned by the entrepreneur Richard Branson. Above, the grave of Robert Graves in Deià

Right, Antonio Banderas and Melanie Griffiths in Palma. Left, Frédéric Chopin

Celebrity
Island

Mallorca has long been a rich hunting ground for paparazzi. The island attracts an eclectic mix of celebrities and you can see many of their famous haunts today. Australian-born American actor Errol Flynn was arguably the island's first lager lout, raising hell at the Bon Sol hotel in the 1950s. Rock stars, such as Rod Stewart, Annie Lennox and Elton John, have also let their hair down on the island, and Mallorca is even more popular with actors: Alec Guinness, Jack Nicholson, Charlie Chaplin, Peter Ustinov, Grace Kelly and Ava Gardner have all stayed. Michael Douglas liked Mallorca so much he opened a visitor centre in Valldemossa. Couples, from Frédéric Chopin and George Sand to Antonio Banderas and Melanie Griffiths, come and go.

Royalty, racing-car drivers and Richard Branson have all bought property in Mallorca—although the British business tycoon has now sold La Residencia, his exclusive hotel in Deià. Writers make up a significant contingent of visitors to Mallorca. Both Kingsley Amis and Gabriel García Marquez made short pilgrimages to Robert Graves' home in Deià and Agatha Christie was a regular guest at the Hotel Formentor, setting a short story in nearby Pollença Bay. It all adds up to a lot of free publicity for the island.

Sun, Sand and Chopin

George Sand (the pen name of Aurore, Baronne Dudevant) and her lover Frédéric Chopin retreated to Valldemossa (▷ 78–81) in 1838 in the hope of improving the tubercular composer's health. It wasn't successful: his favourite Pleyel piano failed to arrive and he was forced to compose *Preludes, Op. 28* on a ropey local instrument. The Mallorcans were unfriendly to the couple, the relationship foundered and a bitter Sand wrote about the experience in *A Winter in Majorca*, a book that is still proudly sold throughout the island despite being a dispiriting tale of miserable weather, truculent locals and primitive conditions: how it became such a central part of the marketing of Mallorca remains a mystery.

Mallorca

Left, F1 star Michael Schumacher. Right Boris Becker and model Claudia Schiffer

Below, the Costa Nord centre, founded by actor Michael Douglas

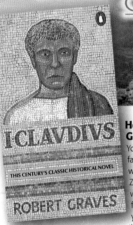

COSTA NORD
de Valldemossa

Below, the King and Queen of Spain, depicted on a poster

Inspiration in Deià

A rather happier literary connection occurred just up the road from Valldemossa in Deià (▷ 67). Having lived briefly in Mallorca with Laura Riding, the poet Robert Graves (1895–1985) moved to the island permanently in 1946 with his second wife, Beryl Hodge (1915–2003). They settled in Deià, in a house called Ca n'Alluny. As readers of Graves' *The White Goddess* know, the prolific writer argued that female muses were essential for a poet's inspiration; while Graves laboured over some of his most distinctive love poems, his wife tolerated the steady stream of muses passing through their house.

Hollywood Glamour

You're a world famous film star, with Catherine Zeta-Jones for a wife, and a young family. What do you do with your spare time? If you're Michael Douglas you represent Mallorca's tourist board. In 2003 he agreed to become the world's most glitzy ambassador, promoting Mallorca at unglamourous travel trade fairs around the world for four years. There's no doubt Douglas loves the island: in the 1980s he bought the S'Estaca estate once owned by Archduke Ludwig Salvator and in 2000 he opened Costa Nord (▷ 81), a cultural centre in Valldemossa devoted to the Serra de Tramuntana, where every summer he hosts the eclectic Mediterranean Nights arts festival. Nevertheless, the £3 million fee he receives for his work must have helped persuade him to take on the job.

Claudia Schiffer

Of the 50,000 Germans who call Mallorca home, supermodel Claudia Schiffer is perhaps the most eye-catching. For several years she has owned a hilltop apartment in the upmarket, celeb-friendly resort Camp de Mar, where neighbouring residents include German racing-car driver Michael Schumacher. One of her favourite haunts is the exclusive and remote hotel-restaurant Ca's Xorc (▷ 187), in the Serra de Tramuntana, where she celebrated her 30th birthday. Should you wish to join Michael, Claudia and the remaining 49,998 Germans and 6,000 Britons with properties in Mallorca, note that prices are almost stratospheric. You won't find many houses for sale under £100,000, and seven-figure sums are not uncommon; Claudia Schiffer is rumoured to have spent £6 million on her apartment.

Royal Retreat

For such a small island, Mallorca has a high concentration of royal visitors. The leader of the pack is King Juan Carlos of Spain. When he was still a prince a group of local businessmen, with admirable foresight for the ongoing publicity opportunities, presented him with the Palau Marivent, a glorious Arab palace next to Palma's cathedral. It has been his summer retreat ever since, and the venue for some of Palma's most elegant soirées. The king, a keen sailor, crosses the road to his favourite hang-out, Palma's Reial Club Náutico. He's a patron of the club's Copa del Rey sailing regatta, one of summer's sporting highlights (▷ 133). He's not the only keen royal sailor: King Harald of Norway is a regular visitor too.

Above, trying a new watersport. Left, exploring S'Albufera natural park by bicycle

Below, a boat trip to Cabrera. Bottom, bird-watching at S'Albufera

The Great
Outdoors

It's no exaggeration to say that whatever your sporting interests, you'll find a way to pursue them in Mallorca. Whether you're into cliff diving or rock climbing, the island has an excellent infrastructure for sports. But it does specialize in a few: golf, cycling and most watersports. Hiking in the mountains is a major activity in autumn, winter and spring. There are 20 top-class golf courses in Mallorca, and a dozen yacht clubs, 10 horse-riding schools, six kayaking schools and one wrestling pavilion.

Perhaps the most visible sport in Mallorca is cycling (▷ 108). Northern European cyclists visit the island for winter training sessions and many hotels provide special facilities for cyclists. Casual cyclists can hire bicycles throughout the island, but shouldn't expect to emulate the professionals, who scarcely seem to notice that the roads of the Serra de Tramuntana mountains have gradients. Yachting is another high-profile sport, with clubs and schools around the coast offering tuition and charters. Dinghies and windsurfers can be hired from most beaches.

Less active pursuits in Mallorca include bird-watching, at places such as the marshes of S'Albufera natural park. Or you can stick to a gentle game of beach volleyball.

Flying High

With a wingspan of 3m (9ft), the black vulture is the largest bird of prey in Europe—and it has a lifespan of 40 years. Impressive it may be, but only a handful remains in existence: some in mainland Spain and about 100 in Mallorca. The birds congregate around Lluc Monastery (▷ 70–73) in the Serra de Tramuntana and you'll probably spot them soaring on the thermals above the Cúber and Gorg Blau reservoirs. Mallorca is one of Europe's best birdwatching locations, so there's plenty of other birdlife worth looking out for, too. Resident and migrant species include Eleonora's falcons, marsh harriers, hoopoes, egrets, bitterns, eagles, greater flamingos and the purple swamp hen.

Right, almond sweets. Below, a hiker in the Boquer Valley. Below right, black vulture numbers are rising

Right, seeing Mondragó from horseback

Bottom, yachts at Palma

Jan Ullrich, right, trains in Mallorca

Walk this Way

One of the beneficiaries of Mallorca's short-lived eco-tax (▷ 13) was the La Ruta de Pedra en Sec, the Dry Stone Route for walkers through the Serra de Tramuntana. The Council of Mallorca-sponsored intention is to construct a path along the length of the mountains and the 90km (56 miles) between Port d'Andratx and Pollença. The route is partially lined by drystone walls and will be paved where necessary through rough terrain. With increasing numbers of walkers arriving in Mallorca every winter to explore the Serra de Tramuntana (▷ 65), demand will be high and the hope is that the walkers will generate income for the quieter mountain villages. Eventually, eight refurbished mountain refuges will accommodate foot-sore travellers, although to date only two, Refugi Muleta and Refugi Tossals Verds near Port de Sóller, have been completed.

Almond, Almond, Everywhere

There's much to thank the humble almond tree for. Mallorca's traditional dessert, almond cake, is on most menus and you'll also be tempted by almond ice cream, almond milk and almond milk liqueur, crushed almonds as garnishes and almond sweets. In fact, although the Moors brought the almond tree to Spain centuries ago, it wasn't until the last 200 years that almond cultivation became widespread in Mallorca. Now, although almond farming has suffered a downturn, the orchards will be preserved. And this is what visitors to Mallorca will be most grateful for, because in January and February white blossom blows in the wind like snowflakes and carpets the country-side.

The King's Cup

Palma's status as the capital of Mediterranean yachting was cemented by the creation of the Copa del Rey competition in 1982. The regatta was founded by the Real Club Náutico and bene-fited from a blend of factors: the offshore sailing conditions were superb; the marina was close to the centre of the handsome city and the Spanish Royal family were fanatical about the club, the city and the sport. The event's royal patronage was key to its success. Fittingly, King Juan Carlos himself was the skipper of the winning yacht, *Bribón IV*, in 1985. By 2001, the Copa del Rey was one of Europe's most famous regattas. The number of teams entering had risen to 125 and spectators could watch awe-inspiring America's Cup yachts being put through their paces. It remains just as popular today.

Pedal Power

Visit Mallorca in winter or spring and you'll find the roads teeming with cyclists, who outnumber drivers on the mountain roads. Professional teams, such as T-Mobile, amateur clubs and keen individuals all come to the island to train on the marvellous terrain. Noticing this rapidly growing group of visitors, the Government of the Balearic Islands stepped in to co-sponsor a Spanish road-cycling team in 2003, putting up most of the multi-million euro budget. Now named Illes Balears-Banesto, the professional team, made up of mainly Spanish and some Mallorcan riders, competes in cycling's top races. It got off to a flying start in its inaugural season, winning the annual five-day Tour of Mallorca in February 2004—which must have been a relief to its new sponsors.

Left, Moors versus Christians in Pollença. Decorations in Petra, right

Right, dressing up as a *dimoni* is an essential part of many festivals. Far left, statues of musicians in the grounds of La Granja

Living
Traditions

One of the most striking aspects of modern Mallorca is the way in which age-old festivals and traditions have survived and adapted in the face of threats from Fascism, global culture and the decline of the Catholic faith. During the Franco dictatorship traditional folk dances were discouraged because of their sensual nature and pagan roots, or sanitized and turned into tourist-oriented folklore performances, yet now they are once again seen at village fiestas.

Many festivals are religious in origin, usually based around a local saint's day, yet as church attendance declines, the fiestas grow in popularity, with bonfires, street parties, pop concerts and sports competitions alongside traditional religious processions. Even the *romería,* an annual pilgrimage to a local shrine, is a jolly community occasion with music, dancing and a picnic. The fact that every town or village in Mallorca outside Palma has a saint's day during the summer months suggests that this is merely a return to the days when each village celebrated the harvest. Other traditions are still deeply religious. At midnight on Christmas Eve in churches across the island, a young boy dressed in a tunic and holding a sword sings the *Cant de la Sibilla,* a medieval chant foretelling the end of the world.

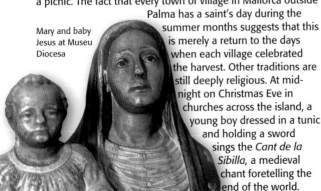

Mary and baby Jesus at Museu Diocesa

Devil of a Time

Horned and masked *dimonis* (devils) are an integral part of many Mallorcan festivals. At one stage, these eye-catching characters were banned by the Catholic Church but they are now tolerated as harmless fun—even if they do occasionally frighten the children. Ironically, their original purpose was probably religious, to symbolize the battle between good and evil. One of the oldest traditions in Mallorca is the *cossiers* dance, performed at Algaida and Montuïri and possibly dating back to Moorish times. Six men and one woman, dressed in white and with bells sewn onto their tights, dance while the devil tries to disrupt them with impudent remarks. The woman, symbolizing virtue, leads the fight against the devil and, of course, triumphs in the end.

Right, a priest blesses a horse and rider at Sant Antoni Abat in Palma. Below, *siurells*

A song and dance: folk music, above right, at La Granja and, below, country dancing at Lluc Monastery

PLAZA DE TOROS MONUMENTAL DE MUR
Empresa: M. Martín-Toros
DOMINGO
22 JUNIO

Tir de Fona

The ancient art of the *foners* (Balearic slingers), banned under Franco, has been revived and the slingshot is now taught in Mallorcan schools—using tennis balls instead of stones. There are active clubs in Palma, Sóller, Lloseta, Sa Pobla and Campanet, and regular competitions are held throughout the year. The leading slinger of the modern era is Joan Guerrero of Lloseta, who was Mallorcan champion 10 times between 1990 and 2002. Antonia Reynes Pons of Campanet has won the women's title eight times. To find out when the slingers are in action, ask at the Bar Espanya, Carrer dels Oms 31, Palma (tel 971 726250), or visit www.tirdefona.com), the Federació Balear de Tir de Fona's website.

A statue of a slinger at Palau de l'Almudaina

Siurells

The miniature earthenware figures known as *siurells* have been made in Mallorca since Moorish times. Painted white with bright flashes of red and green, they typically feature a man on horseback or playing a guitar, though the more unusual designs might include *dimonis* (devils) or even cars and planes. Every *siurell* incorporates a crude whistle at its base, making them great gifts for children. Although you can buy *siurells* in souvenir shops across the island, it is more rewarding to make the trip to the villages of Sa Cabaneta and Pòrtol, where you can still find artists making and painting the figures by hand. While you are there, look into the Museu del Fang (Pottery Museum), which opened in 2002 inside an old windmill in Sa Cabaneta.

Pilgrimage to Lluc

One night in 1974, Tolo Guëll and a group of friends set off from the Bar Guëll in Palma to walk the 48km (30 miles) to Lluc. The following year they made the trip again, joined by more friends, and more the year after that, until the overnight pilgrimage had grown into a mass movement. Some people participate to give thanks for recovery from illness or the birth of a child, while others join in for the camaraderie and sense of fun. All night long, spectators line the route offering food and drink to tired walkers. In 1985 up to 40,000 people took part; in 1993 King Juan Carlos gave the traditional greeting. The pilgrimage takes place on the first Saturday in August, leaving Palma at 11pm.

Toro Toro

There is very little tradition of bullfighting in Mallorca—it has a much greater following in southern Spain than in the Catalan-speaking regions—but bullfights are held once a year during the patronal festivals at Muro and Felanitx. The bullring at Muro is a spectacular sight, chiselled out of the white rock in a former sandstone quarry between 1910 and 1920, with seats for 6,000 spectators. In the past, Muro had its own version of the bullfight, pitting bulls against hounds; these days a more conventional *corrida* takes place during the feast of Sant Joan Baptista on 24 June. Similarly, the bullring at Felanitx is used once a year during the festival of Sant Agustí on 28 August.

Patriotic streamers in Muro, above

Right, art in a vineyard. Below, a multilingual sign in Palma

Port de Palma de Mallorca
Autoritat Portuària de Balears

Molls de trànsit loca
Muelles de Tráfico Loca

Top right, Real Mallorca celebrate winning the King's Cup in 2003

Bodegas in Binissalem, right, offer wine-tasting tours

BODEGA INSCRITA Nº 5
DENOMINACIO
BINI SSA LEM
ORIGEN

VINS NADAL

Balearic
Renaissance

Visca Mallorca!

Reial Club Deportivo Mallorca, also known as Real Mallorca, may only have had 18 seasons in Spain's top football division since being founded in 1916, but, recently, it has become one of Spain's most successful teams. After promotion to the Primera Liga in 1997, Real Mallorca has twice come third in the league, reached the final of the European Cup Winners' Cup in 1999 and won the Copa del Rei (King's Cup) in 2003. Their greatest victory was a 5-1 triumph in 2003 at the Bernabeu, home of formidable Real Madrid.

A football fan's balcony

Ever since the Balearic Islands gained regional autonomy on 22 February 1983, Mallorcans' pride in their island has been resurgent. During General Franco's regime regional identities in Spain were suppressed: local dialects such as Mallorquín were banned and traditional fiestas were cancelled. However, since 1983 the Mallorquín language, a Catalan dialect, has been reinstated as the island's official language and local festivals have returned to the island's calendar. In other areas too, including cuisine, culture and sport, Mallorcans have been incredibly effective in promoting their island's interests.

Language Wars

It may be hard for foreigners to understand, but the difference between *plaça* and *plaza* has become an issue of cultural identity. Since the formation of the Balearic Government in 1983, Catalan has replaced Spanish as the first language in Mallorca, so that you will now see signs to the *platja* rather than *playa* (beach). To add to the confusion, most locals speak Mallorquín, which is essentially a dialect of Catalan with one or two important differences, such as the use of the definite articles *es, sa* and *ses* instead of *el, la* and *els*. Following 2003's elections, bilingualism is in fashion, and it is now common to hear politicians mixing Mallorquín and Castilian.

Winning Wines

Years after the dark days of Franco, Mallorca's wine is finally a sought-after, prize-winning product. And because of the limited land available for growing grapes, it tends to be in short supply and consequently rather expensive. Two wine-producing regions are protected by *Denominació de Origen* (DO) status: Binissalem and neighbouring villages, and the Pla I Llevant covering Algaida, Felanitx, Manacor, Petra and Porreres. As you pass through these areas, look out for a sprig of a vine over doorways: these mean that the place is a *bodega* (wine cellar or maker) with wine to sell. A fresh green cutting indicates that the wine is fresh; a withered old cutting says that it is aged.

The Story of Mallorca

Romans and Moors

The first human beings to arrive in Mallorca were thought to have been fishermen or sailors who came over from the Iberian Peninsula around 5000BC. These early inhabitants lived in caves, hunting with crude tools of flint or stone. By 2000BC the Beaker culture—named after the practice of burying ceramic cups with the dead—had taken hold on the island, but the first organized settlements, such as those at Artà and Capocorb Vell, were built during the Talaiotic era, which flourished between 1400 and 800BC.

Phoenician and Greek traders were attracted to the island and in 123BC the Roman consul Quintus Cecilius Metellus led

a successful invasion—despite an attack on his fleet by the famed Balearic slingers. The Romans established cities at Palmaria (now Palma) and Pollentia (now Alcúdia), named the island Balearis Major and incorporated it into their Mediterranean empire. With the decline of this empire some 500 years later, periods of Vandal and Byzantine rule followed. When the Arabs conquered Mallorca in AD902 the island became part of the Emirate of Córdoba, ushering in three centuries of Muslim rule—the legacy of which can still be seen today.

Prehistory

Myotragus balearicus

In 1909 British palaeontologist Dorothea Bates first discovered evidence that this goat-like mammal, a distant relative of the antelope, with eyes at the front of its head, had inhabited Mallorca. Having probably migrated to the island about six million years ago during a fall in the sea level of the Mediterranean, *Myotragus* continued to thrive until the appearance of the first humans. Evidence from a cave in Sóller suggests that the animal coexisted with man for a time, but domestication and the introduction of goats, sheep and pigs eventually contributed to its demise. Skeletons of *Myotragus balearicus* are displayed at the Museu de Mallorca in Palma (▷ 60) and the Natural Science Museum in Sóller (▷ 76–77).

Above, a ceramic tile showing local history in Calvià. Left, ruins in Roman Pollentia. Below, the Moorish cavalry. Bottom, olives, introduced by the Romans

Talaiotic Life

Archaeologists generally divide the Talaiotic era into three distinct periods. During the pre-Talaiotic period (2000–1400BC) the inhabitants lived in caves and made crude bronze and pottery utensils. The Talaiotic period (1400–800BC) saw the development of sophisticated bronze weaponry, as well as the building of walled villages and fortified stone towers known as *talaiots*. In the post-Talaiotic period (800–123BC) there was greater contact with other Mediterranean civilizations. The Mallorcans traded with the Carthaginians and their pottery began to imitate Roman styles; they also developed a cult of bull worship similar to that found in Sardinia. The bronze statues of warriors seen in the Museu de Mallorca were probably brought back as booty by mercenaries fighting in the Punic Wars.

The Oldest Slingers in Town

The Talaiotic people were renowned for their skill with the slingshot, and it is said that fathers taught their sons to sling by placing their food high in a tree and forcing them to go hungry until they could bring it down with a catapult. The Carthaginian general Hannibal was so impressed by this prowess that he recruited Mallorcan slingers as bodyguards for his epic journey across the Alps on elephant-back, paying them in wine and women rather than in gold. This skill with the sling was praised by the Roman historian Livy, and even gave its name to the islands—Balearic probably derives from the Greek verb *ballein* (to throw).

Roman Remains

Roman settlers planted the first vineyards and olive groves in Mallorca and introduced roads, bridges and aqueducts to the island. Their capital, Pollentia (Alcúdia), was a sophisticated example of town planning, with handsome villas, porticoed streets, a central forum and a theatre. For five centuries the people of Mallorca used Roman currency, spoke Latin and adopted Roman styles of dress; they also worshipped Roman gods until the arrival of Christianity in the second century. With the Vandal invasion of around AD425, however, virtually all traces of Roman Mallorca were wiped out, leaving just wine and olive oil as reminders of their stay.

Medina Mayurqa

From about AD500 to AD1000 Moorish Palma, known as Medina Mayurqa, was a civilized, elegant city with street lights and heated baths. Under Muslim rule the walled city began to take on its present shape, with a castle on the site of the Palau de l'Almudaina and a great mosque on the site of the cathedral. Orchards and market gardens were planted outside the city walls to supply the traders in the souk. The Moors introduced oranges and almonds to Mallorca, both important crops today, along with windmills and irrigation techniques. The rich Moorish legacy also survives in the names of a number of towns and villages, including Alcúdia, Algaida, Binissalem and Deià.

Left, a bronze warrior at the Museu de Mallorca. Right, a slinger

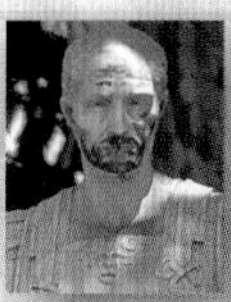

A statue of a Roman in Palma's Via Roma

An image of a Moor in the Museu de Mallorca

1229

Left, a scene that has changed little over the years. Below, Hannibal

The Golden Age

One of the dates etched onto every Mallorcan schoolchild's mind is 31 December 1229—the day Jaume I of Aragón entered Palma to capture the island from the Moors. To reward his nobles for their loyalty, the victorious king divided the island up between them in proportion to the number of men each had supplied, thus populating the island with members of the Catalan nobility and importing the Catalan language.

On his death in 1276, Jaume I bequeathed his kingdom to his sons—the elder son, Pedro, received Aragón and Catalonia, while the younger son, Jaume II, had to make do with Mallorca, Montpellier and Roussillón (today in southern France). However, this arrangement was not to last. Pedro's son Alfonso III captured Mallorca in 1285, forcing Jaume II into exile for 13 years before the restoration of the kingdom in 1298. When Jaume II died in 1311 the crown passed to his asthmatic son, Sancho. Sancho died childless in 1324 and was succeeded by his nine-year-old nephew, Jaume III, but Jaume III's brother-in-law Pedro IV of Aragón felt he had a stronger claim to the throne and seized the island in 1343. When Jaume III, now an adult, tried to return, he was killed at the battle of Llucmajor in 1349, bringing the kingdom of Mallorca to an end.

1229

Jaume the Conqueror

'The best thing man has done for a hundred years past', was how 21-year-old Jaume I described his conquest of Mallorca. In part he was driven by the spirit of the Crusades and the *Reconquista* (Reconquest) of land from the Moors, which was sweeping southwards through Spain; in part, no doubt, by youthful exuberance and greed. His appetite was whetted by a great banquet in Tarragona at which the seafarer Pere Martell served Mallorcan olives and spoke of the bounty of the island; shortly afterwards, the king gathered together his nobles to plan an invasion. He set sail from Salou in September 1229 with a party of 150 ships, 1,500 horses and 16,000 men. Three months later, Mallorca was his.

Top, a cross at Jaume I's arrival at Santa Ponça. Left, his conquest of Palma. Below, Bellver Castle

Pedro the Gigolo

Jaume I's commitments on the mainland meant that he had little time to devote to Mallorca so he entrusted the rule of the island to others. One of those chosen was Don Pedro, Crown Prince of Portugal, who had previously helped the young king out of a difficult situation. In 1228, in an attempt to bring Urgell into his kingdom, Jaume had taken its heiress, the beautiful Countess Aurembiaix, as his mistress. However, having tired of her, he needed to engineer an acceptable way of ending the affair. Don Pedro came to the rescue by marrying the countess and was rewarded after her death with the lordship of Mallorca. He served as lord of Mallorca from 1231 to 1244, playing a key role in the conquest of Ibiza.

Jaume Rules OK

His father may have been the hero of the Reconquest, but it was Jaume II, the first true king of Mallorca, who steered the island into its Golden Age. Jaume ordered the building of the cathedral, Castell de Bellver and the Palau de l'Almudaina, and the construction of Alcúdia's city walls. The finest Gothic churches of Palma, including Santa Eulàlia, Sant Miquel and Sant Francesc, were also begun during his reign. He established royal palaces at Sineu and Valldemossa, and in the French city of Perpignan, and founded new towns at Felanitx, Llucmajor and Manacor. Jaume was an enlightened as well as a visionary ruler, introducing a weekly market at Palma and setting minimum wages for agricultural workers.

Ramón Llull

Although he is now revered as a missionary and scholar, Llull (1235–1315) amounted to little more than a dissolute courtier until a salutary incident changed his life at the age of 40. Chasing a married woman through the streets of Palma on horseback, he followed her into church and down the aisle, whereupon she tore open her bodice to reveal diseased breasts. Much chastened, he took a vow of poverty and retired to Puig de Randa (▷ 102) as a hermit. Recalled to the court by his patron Jaume II, he founded a school of languages at Miramar (▷ 74) and wrote widely on everything from philosophy to poetry. He is said to have been stoned to death while attempting to convert Muslims in Tunisia.

Cheeky Kid

One of the most gruesome episodes in the history of Mallorca is chiefly remembered on the island for the verbal spat it engendered. During his conquest of the island in 1285, Alfonso III met with fierce resistance at Castell d'Alaró (▷ 66), whose commanders remained loyal to Jaume II. The story goes that as the king of Aragón attempted to take the castle, the sentry, Cabrit, asked him his name. When the king replied that his name was Alfonso, Cabrit turned it into an impudent pun. 'We like our *anfós* grilled', he called out, referring to a grouper-like fish. 'And I like my *cabrit* (goat kid) roasted', replied the king, promising to burn Cabrit and his companion Brassa alive on a spit. And he did.

Left, Jaume I of Aragon in Plaça d'Espanya. Below left, the death of Ramon Llull. Below, Jaume I's landing

Porta del Moll, the gateway to Alcúdia

Ramon Llull's statue on Palma's seafront

Mountain views from Castell d'Alaró

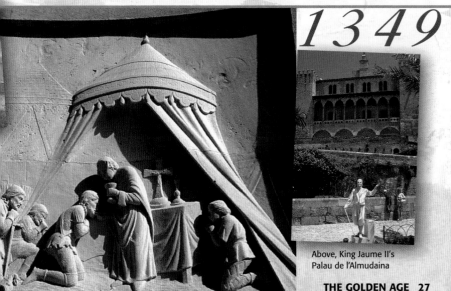

1349

Above, King Jaume II's Palau de l'Almudaina

Catalonia and Spain

Mallorca declined throughout the 14th to 19th centuries as it turned from being an independent kingdom to a poor provincial outpost of Catalonia and Spain. The noble Catalan families who had arrived after the conquest returned to their mainland estates as the kingdom of Aragón grew into a major Mediterranean power incorporating Corsica, Sardinia and Naples. Mallorca's fortunes worsened in 1479 when Fernando V of Aragón married Isabel I of Castile, uniting the two royal houses and paving the way for modern Spain. The defeat of the Moors at Granada in 1492 completed the process; at the same time, explorer Christopher Columbus was setting out on his journeys for the New World, reducing Mediterranean influence and turning attention towards trade across the Atlantic with America.

The 16th century saw renewed attacks on Mallorca from Turkish and North African pirates, which led to watchtowers being built around the coast. Mallorca also picked the wrong side during the War of the Spanish Succession (1701–14), supporting the Hapsburg emperor Charles III against the victorious candidate Felipe V and becoming the last province to surrender in 1715. The island was punished by being stripped of its historic privileges and by the imposition of the Castilian language over Catalan.

1349

Jewish Palma

During the 14th century Jews were active in Palma as merchants, bankers, tailors, dyers, goldsmiths, butchers and bakers. Jewish cartographers Abraham and Jafuda Cresques produced the *Atles Català* here in 1375, a map of the known world now held at the Bibliothèque Nationale in Paris. However, although the Jews of Palma were granted special legal and financial privileges, they were also discriminated against, forced to live in ghettoes and had to wear distinctive dress. An anti-Semitic riot of 1391 led to an attack on the Jewish ghetto in which up to 300 people were killed. This marked the start of the forced conversions to Christianity, which continued with the setting up of an Office of the Inquisition to denounce heretics in 1484.

CARRER
DEL CALL

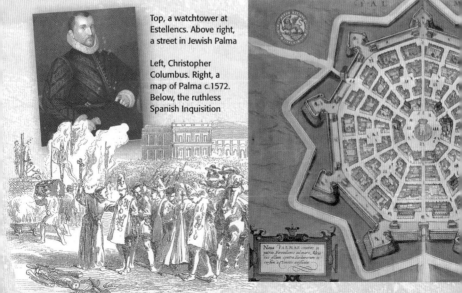

Top, a watchtower at Estellencs. Above right, a street in Jewish Palma

Left, Christopher Columbus. Right, a map of Palma c.1572. Below, the ruthless Spanish Inquisition

Carnival Revolt

In February 1521, during Palma's traditional Carnival celebrations, peasants and traders marched on the capital to protest at high taxes, grain shortages and the concentration of power in a few hands. Forming themselves into a *Germania* (brotherhood), bound together by oath, the protesters quickly occupied the city, forcing many of the nobles to flee to Pollença. Others took refuge in the Castell de Bellver but the rebels soon took the castle by storm. It was two years before Charles V, the Holy Roman Emperor and King of Spain, managed to organize a fleet to recapture Palma from the *Germania*. After agreeing terms for a surrender he reneged on the deal and executed 500 rebels, including their leader, Joan Colom.

A Mallorcan Saint

As you walk around Valldemossa (▷ 78–81) look for the painted tiles on houses with the message *Santa Catalina Thomás pregau per nosaltres* (Santa Catalina Thomás, pray for us). Numerous legends are told about the life of this pious girl (1531–74), who, as a child, preferred long walks with her rosary to toys and games. In the interests of fasting she refused to eat more than one meal a day, going so far as to mix sand with her soup to avoid the sin of gluttony. At the age of 22 she entered the Santa Magdalena convent in Palma, where she was known as a model of humility, chastity and obedience. Beatified in 1792 and canonized in 1930, she is Mallorca's only saint to date.

Junípero Serra

Many people emigrated from Mallorca in the 18th century, but no one from the island had more influence beyond its shores than Serra (1713–84), a farmer's son from Petra, who is honoured in the Capitol in Washington as 'the founder of California'. After studying in convents in Petra and Palma, Serra was ordained as a priest and in 1749 set off for Mexico as a missionary. Two decades later, after an epic trek from Mexico, he established his first Californian mission at San Diego. Over the next 15 years he was to found eight more missions—one of which grew into the city of San Francisco—and baptize more than 5,000 Native Americans into Catholicism. He was beatified in 1988.

Rats!

In 1809 thousands of French soldiers landed on Cabrera (▷ 95), off Mallorca's southern coast, following their defeat at the Battle of Bailén. The Spanish victors needed somewhere to keep their prisoners and this uninhabited island provided the answer. A ruined castle was turned into a prison camp, and meagre rations of bread, beans and oil were delivered every few days by boat. In their desperation, the soldiers foraged for wild food: an account tells how a mouse could be bought for seven or eight beans, and a rat for four times as much. Violence and disease were common. Of the 9,000 men who arrived, barely a third survived; those that did were taken back to France by boat in 1814 and left to die.

In 1521 Bellver Castle was taken by rebels

Santa Catalina, patron saint of Mallorca

Junípero Serra, Petra's favourite son

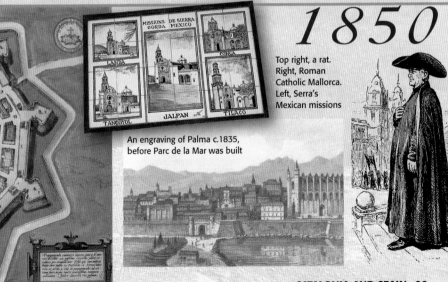

1850

Top right, a rat. Right, Roman Catholic Mallorca. Left, Serra's Mexican missions

An engraving of Palma c.1835, before Parc de la Mar was built

The Modernist Era

In the late 19th century many Mallorcans grew rich on the booming export trade in almonds and wine, which was partly due to the opening in 1875 of a railway line from Palma to Inca and the establishment of a regular steamship service from Palma to Barcelona. Unfortunately this prosperity was short-lived as a phylloxera plague in the 1890s virtually wiped out Mallorca's wine industry, and the loss of Spain's last colonies, Cuba and the Philippines, in 1898 led to a reduction in export markets and widespread emigration.

   Despite these setbacks, the turn of the 20th century was a confident time, fuelled by the *Renaixença*; this Catalan cultural renaissance saw a flowering of the arts, music and literature, and a revival of the Catalan language. One of the products of this was the *Modernista* architectural movement (▷ 137–39). At the same time, adventurous travellers started arriving in Mallorca; the Gran Hotel opened in Palma in 1903; and in the same year Thomas Cook began offering package tours to the island. Authors such as Gordon West (*Jogging Round Majorca*, 1929) and Santiago Rusinyol (*The Island of Calm*, 1922) depicted a tranquil, rural island yet to be disturbed by mass tourism or political upheavals.

1850

The Duke of Mallorca

Of the many foreigners who have been attracted to Mallorca, one in particular has lodged in the hearts of the Mallorcans. Ludwig Salvator (1847–1915), an Austrian archduke, first came to the island at the age of 20 to escape the stuffiness of Viennese court life, and immediately felt at home. An early ecologist (and a renowned womaniser), he bought up most of the land between Valldemossa and Deià, laid out a network of walking trails—which is still in use—and refused to allow any trees on his estates to be cut down. When he wasn't having affairs with local women, he studied Mallorcan history, culture and flora. One of his houses, S'Estaca, built for his lover Catalina Homar, now belongs to the American actor Michael Douglas.

Archduke Ludwig Salvator of Austria

Top left, Joan Rubió's Banco de Sóller. Left, Son Marroig's rotunda

Right, Hotel Formentor and its pretty beach

Below, Rudolph Valentino's clifftop villa on Mallorca

Walls Come Tumbling Down

Until 1902 the outline of Palma had scarcely changed in a thousand years—then the decision was taken to destroy the city walls. Although the walls had stood since the time of the Moors and had been reinforced after the Catalan conquest, the city needed to expand and their destruction was seen as the logical solution. At first it was hoped that the northern gate, through which Jaume I's forces entered the city in 1229, would be saved, but in the name of progress even that had to go. All that remains of the original walls is the bastion of Sant Pere and a section beneath the cathedral; the rest has become a dreary ring road.

Gaudí in the Cathedral

The Modernist architect Antoni Gaudí (1852–1926) is best known for his unfinished Sagrada Família church in Barcelona, and few people realize that he also worked on Palma Cathedral (▷ 54–57). Modernism was a democratic movement, and in 1904 Bishop Campins brought Gaudí in to open up the interior of the cathedral through the careful use of light and space. Among his reforms was the introduction of electric lighting and the moving of the choirstalls from the centre of the nave to their current position in the chancel, thus removing a barrier between congregation and priest. Gaudí worked on the cathedral for 10 years; his assistant Joan Rubió stayed behind in Mallorca and brought Modernist architecture to Sóller (▷ 76–77).

Europe's First Tourist Board

Businessman Enrique Alzamora Goma, the president of Mallorca's chamber of commerce, founded the Fomento del Turismo de Mallorca (Mallorca Tourist Board) in 1905 as a private organization representing hoteliers and transport companies. Initially, it concentrated on promoting Mallorca to the Mallorcans, improving roads and communications and publishing the first guide to the island in 1908. Among its first projects was the construction of a road between Andratx and Estellencs, and the building of *miradors* overlooking the north coast. By the 1930s it was producing tourist brochures and posters, organizing excursions for visitors, and even posting a representative to Paris to market Mallorca as a summer holiday destination.

A Good Tip

In 1929 the opening of the Hotel Formentor was announced to the world with illuminated advertisements on the Eiffel Tower in Paris. The first guests were two English women, who arrived following a storm at sea. They were helped ashore by the Argentinian owner, Adan Diehl. Assuming him to be the porter, they gave him a one-peseta tip; he later joked that this was the only money he ever earned from the hotel. During the 1930s this was the most fashionable address in Mallorca, the haunt of visitors such as statesman Winston Churchill, comic actor Charlie Chaplin and novelist Agatha Christie. The hotel also saw its share of scandal when Edward, Prince of Wales (the future Edward VIII of Britain) stayed there with his lover, Mrs Simpson.

Hitting the wall: what's left of Palma's city wall

The rose window in Palma's cathedral

Winston Churchill. Left, a tourist board poster

Above, Prince Edward and Wallis Simpson

Dictatorship to Democracy

In 1936 General Francisco Franco led a military rebellion that heralded three years of civil war and almost 40 years of Fascist dictatorship across Spain. The army in Mallorca supported Franco's Nationalists from the start, though atrocities were committed on both sides. Despite its support during the Spanish Civil War, Mallorca was not immune from the reprisals unleashed by Franco when he finally took power. The Catalan language was banned, expressions of regional culture were suppressed, and Mallorca was used as a testing ground for mass tourism with little thought given to the impact on the islanders.

Franco's death in 1975 was followed by the restoration of the monarchy and a rapid return to democracy. A new constitution granted limited autonomy to the regions and Spain entered the European mainstream, joining Nato in 1982 and the European Union in 1986. At the same time, the strict Francoist alliance of Church and State gave way to a relaxation of social and sexual mores as the people threw off the enforced power of the Catholic Church. After decades of suppression, Mallorca began to rediscover its own voice—the Mallorquín language was once again heard on the streets and road signs in Spanish were replaced with those in Catalan.

Poor Tourism

At first, Franco was happy to keep foreigners out, fearing an influx of bikini-clad visitors with loose morals, but later he embarked on an aggressive policy of marketing Spain as a tourist destination. Regional identity went out of the window as the clichés of bullfighting, flamenco and sangría—none of which have much relevance to Mallorca—appeared on posters to promote the island. This was the era of 'poor tourism', when high-rise hotels sprung up overnight, transforming fishing villages into concrete resorts and turning property values and the social order upside down. Suddenly, a strip of rocky coastline was worth more than a fertile field and the prime farmland traditionally inherited by the eldest child became worthless in comparison.

1936

Top left, General Franco. Left, the Spanish royal family in Palma. Far left, mass tourism brings sunseekers. Below, clubbers at Tito's in Palma

The Battle for Sa Dragonera

In 1977, two years after Franco's death, there were plans to build a luxury tourist resort on the island of Sa Dragonera (▷ 75). In one of the first protests of its kind, environmentalists from the Grup Ornitològic Balear (GOB), an ornithological group with wider conservation interests, occupied the island. Eventually, the authorities gave in—the Mallorcan government purchased Sa Dragonera and declared it a natural park. The victory for the campaigners is widely seen as a turning point, the moment when Mallorca realized that mass tourism was reaching its limit and that the island's natural heritage had to be protected. The GOB has now become a powerful political voice and an influential member of the Green lobby.

The New Politics

The Statute of Autonomy passed in 1983 gave a degree of self-government to the Balearic Islands, with powers in a wide range of areas including education, transport and the environment. At the same time, Catalan was given equal status to Spanish as an official language of the Balearic Islands, with priority given to Catalan in the areas of education and local government. The Balearic parliament, meeting in Palma, has representatives from Menorca, Ibiza and Formentera, though Mallorcans are in the majority. Each island also has its own ruling council, the Consell Insular. From 1983 to 1999 the Balearic government was controlled by the centre-right Partit Popular; in 1999 it was defeated by a left-wing coalition of socialists, regionalists and Greens.

Multicultural Mallorca

The large number of African traders selling wood carvings and *djembe* drums at street markets in Mallorca might give the impression of a highly integrated society, but in fact this is a very recent phenomenon. For 750 years after the defeat of the Moors, there were few non-white faces in Mallorca and the island is only just coming to terms with its new multi-racial existence. Many immigrants arrived in the late 1990s from Senegal and Morocco to work on the Pla Mirall, a government-funded project to restore the centre of Palma. At first, the workers faced hostility and were forced to live in hostels with alcoholics and drug addicts; only now are they starting to be accepted as equal members of Mallorcan society.

Ich Bin Ein Mallorcan

In 1998 the author Carlos Garrido published *Mallorca de los Alemanes*, a satire about an island populated by Germans in 2013. This was not entirely a joke—it caught the public mood and coincided with a wave of anti-German sentiment on Mallorca. Much of this was directed at rich German landowners, including model Claudia Schiffer, tennis player Boris Becker and racing driver Michael Schumacher, all of whom had houses in Mallorca. The biggest estate agent in Mallorca was a German company and it was estimated that Germans owned 20 per cent of all property, including 80 percent of rural manor houses. There was even talk of launching a German political party. 'Germans are buying up our island', complained Balearic president Jaume Matas.

Sunset over Sa Dragonera

A detail of the regional flag of Mallorca

Equal opportunities arrived late on Mallorca

Certainly not Mallorca's official flag

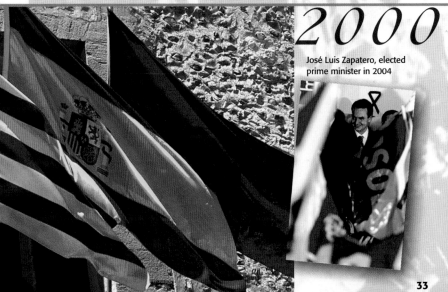

2000

José Luis Zapatero, elected prime minister in 2004

Into the Future

The challenge facing Mallorca in the 21st century is how to maintain its role as Europe's leading tourist destination without destroying its fragile environment. Thanks to tourism, Mallorca has become one of the richest regions of Europe but there is general agreement that the limit has been reached. The introduction of the euro in 2002 has led to inflation and Mallorca is no longer a cheap option, especially when compared to countries outside the euro zone such as Turkey and Tunisia. The buzzwords these days are 'quality' and 'sustainable' tourism—though everybody has a different view of precisely what that means.

Underground Rubbish

As you stroll around the old quarter of Palma, bear in mind that more than the remains of the Roman city lie beneath your feet. An innovative waste disposal system has made refuse sacks and dustcarts a thing of the past. Residents place their rubbish in robotic-looking grey containers on street corners. From here, rubbish is pumped pneumatically along a network of underground pipes to a central collection point outside the city, where it is sorted and compressed for recycling and disposal. This has made Palma's centre a tidier place to live and reduced pollution and damage to historic buildings by keeping lorries out of the old town's narrow lanes.

The Palma Buzz

In the late 1990s a survey by *El País*, a Spanish newspaper, concluded that of all Spanish cities, Palma provided the best quality of life. Of course the people who live there knew this already—from its seaside setting to its vibrant café culture, Palma has all the ingredients of the perfect city. These days, the city has a tangible buzz about it, with new restaurants, bars and designer boutiques opening almost every week. Previously run-down districts, such as Santa Catalina and Sa Gerrería, are being repopulated by young professionals and trendy shops. Low-cost flights from Britain and Germany have made Palma a popular weekend break destination, a trend reinforced by the opening of Museu Es Baluard (▷ 59) and Palau March (▷ 64).

The Return of the PP

Following elections in 2003, the Partit Popular (PP) returned to power in the Balearic Islands under former president Jaume Matas. Its first act was to abolish the tourist eco-tax (▷ 13) introduced by the previous left-wing coalition. Among other policies was a proposal to allow parents to decide whether their children should be taught in Catalan or Spanish. Most controversially, the new government unveiled plans for new roads across the island, including a second Palma ring road and a motorway from Inca to Manacor, which was shelved after widespread protests. Days after the March 2004 bombings in Madrid, the Spanish people elected a Socialist government, so Mallorca once again finds itself politically out of tune with the rest of Spain, as it has been for all but four of the last 22 years.

2000–Today

Left, saturday night fever on the Passeig Marítim. Above, Palma's rubbish is whisked away

Right and far right, street performers and café society in Palma's Plaça Major

On the Move

ARRIVING

ARRIVING BY AIR

Most visitors to Mallorca arrive at Palma's Son Sant Joan airport (code PMI), some 8km (5 miles) east of the city. Once a small provincial airport, this is now one of the busiest in Europe, capable of handling more than 20 million passengers per year. There are daily flights from Palma to Madrid, Barcelona and other Spanish cities, to Menorca and Ibiza, and also to London, Edinburgh and Berlin. During the summer season these are complemented by numerous charter flights bringing tourists from the UK, Ireland, Germany and the rest of northern Europe.

The main terminal at Son Sant Joan is a vast, sprawling place, and the walk from the arrivals gates to the baggage hall can take up to 30 minutes. Once you have collected your luggage, you pass through to the arrivals hall on the ground floor, where there is an information desk, a tourist information office, a newsagent, a café and ATMs (cashpoint machines). A post office is situated on the second floor. There is a larger range of shops, cafés and restaurants in the pre-departure area on the fourth floor, including a branch of La Caixa bank (open 9–2), a pharmacy and shops selling wines and spirits, food, shoes, jewellery, glassware, CDs and electronic equipment.

Palma's airport, 8km (5 miles) from the city, is busy but efficient

These shops are landside and are open to arriving passengers, though to buy certain items you will need a boarding card for a departing flight.

AIRPORT GUIDE

Ground floor: Arrivals, tourist information, car hire.
Second floor: Check-in, post office, first aid.
Fourth floor: Departures, bank, shops, restaurants.
Website: www.aena.es
Telephone numbers:
Son Sant Joan airport tel 971 789000
Tourist information office tel 971 789556

CAR HIRE

The major international car-hire firms have offices at the airport. These are situated inside the baggage hall and inside the arrivals hall (beyond customs).
● It is usually advisable to reserve a car in advance, especially in the peak summer season. You can often get a better deal this way and you can compare rates from different companies.
● Remember to check the small print of the contract, especially with regard to insurance. Most policies include an excess payment of up to €300 for accident damage, though this can sometimes be waived on payment of an

Map showing Mallorca's ferry ports and airports

AIRPORT CAR HIRE FIRMS		
Name	**Telephone**	**Website**
Avis	971 789187	www.avis.com
Centauro	971 789360	www.centauro.net
Europa	971 745390	www.drivespain.com
Europcar	971 789135	www.europcar.com
Hasso	971 789376	www.hasso-rentacar.com
Hertz	971 789670	www.hertz.es
Record	971 743705	www.recordrentacar.com
Serra	971 269411	www.serra-rent.com

additonal premium.

● Local companies may offer more competitive rates than the big international chains. Firms such as Serra (tel 971 269411) can save money by not having an airport office, but they will meet you at the airport or deliver a car to your hotel.

● There are also car-hire companies in all the main towns and resorts. In some cases, these offer very attractive rates, though it is important to check the details of the contract as the cheaper deals are more likely to have exclusions.

● To hire a car, you must be over 21 and you will need a passport, driver's licence and credit card. Keep your passport and driver's licence with you whenever you use the car, as well as the car hire documents. Never leave these documents in the car while it is parked.

● Check the car carefully before you set off, and mark any visible signs of damage on the hire documents.

● Ask about a 24-hour emergency contact number in case of accident or breakdown.

● The majority of rental cars take standard unleaded petrol, though some do take diesel fuel. It is usual to pay for a full tank and return the car full, though some policies vary.

● Most cars hired in Mallorca cannot be taken on ferries to Menorca and Ibiza.

● Never leave any valuable items on display inside the car, and, if possible, remove any obvious signs that indicate it is a hire car as thieves tend to target them.

● Ask about the arrangements for returning the car. Most companies have designated car parking spaces on the ground floor of the car park opposite the terminal. It is essential never to give the keys to anybody other than an authorized employee of the car-hire company. Some foreigners have become targets for car theft by criminals posing as employees of car-hire firms in this way.

LEAVING THE AIRPORT
● Most people arriving on package holidays are taken to their final destination by transfer bus, accompanied by their tour operator's representative.

● The taxi rank is directly outside the terminal. There are fixed fares to destinations across the island and these should be checked in advance. Taxi journeys into central Palma are metered and will usually cost around €20.

● Bus No. 1 leaves for Palma from the bus stop opposite the terminal, between the taxi rank and the multistorey car park. Departures are every 15 minutes from 6.10am to 2.15am. The bus takes around 20–30 minutes to reach central Palma, with a flat fare of €1.80. In Palma, it travels around the Avingudas ring road before continuing along the seafront to the port. The most useful stop is Plaça d'Espanya, which is close to the city centre and has bus and train connections within Palma and across the island. There is a tourist information office close to the bus stop at Plaça d'Espanya, in the Parc de les Estacions (tel 971 754329).

ARRIVING BY SEA
Up to a million people a year arrive in Mallorca by sea, mostly cruise passengers and visitors from the Spanish mainland and the other Balearic Islands.

● Car and passenger ferries from Menorca, Ibiza, Barcelona and Valencia arrive at the commercial port at Palma.

● Balearia and Iscomar operate ferries between Ciutadella on Menorca and Port d'Alcúdia.

● Cruise ships frequently dock at the harbour at Palma.

● There is a taxi rank outside Palma's maritime station. Bus No. 1 runs into the centre and to the airport every 15 minutes from 6.15am to 2.30am. There is a flat fare of €1.10 for journeys to Palma and €1.80 to the airport.

Car and passenger ferries arrive at Palma and Port d'Alcúdia

FERRY COMPANIES		
Name	**Telephone**	**Website**
Balearia	902 160180	www.balearia.com
Iscomar	902 119128	www.iscomar.com
Trasmediterránea	902 454645	www.trasmediterranea.es

GETTING AROUND

BUSES

ON THE MOVE

GETTING AROUND PALMA
Palma's compact city centre is best explored on foot, but there is a good network of buses connecting the city with the outlying suburbs. Buses are operated by EMT (Empresa Municipal de Transports).

INFORMATION

Carrer Josep Anselm Clavé, 5, tel 971 214444; www.a-palma.es

- Buses are blue and are of the low-floor type, making them accessible for passengers in wheelchairs.
- Enter by the front door and buy your ticket from the driver. Disabled passengers may enter via the middle doors. Passengers must leave by the middle doors.
- The standard fare is €1.10 for most journeys though there are a few variations (see box). Children under 5 travel free.
- If you are going to be using the buses a lot, it may be worth getting a *targeta* (card, €7.51), which is valid for 10 journeys. The card must be validated on

Locals and holidaymakers use Mallorca's extensive bus network

PALMA BUS FARES	
Standard tariff	€1.10
10 journeys	€7.51
To Palma Nova	€1.35
To or from airport	€1.80
Children under 5	Free

each trip in the machine behind the driver's cabin.
- Most bus stops have information panels with a full list of timetables and routes, as well as electronic display boards showing waiting times for the next buses.
- The hub of Palma's bus network is at Plaça d'Espanya, where you can transfer between routes and also to island-wide buses and trains.
- Bus No. 1 runs at 15-minute intervals from the airport to the port, via the Avingudas ring road and Plaça d'Espanya.
- Bus No. 2 makes a regular circuit of the old centre. You can pick it up at Plaça d'Espanya, Avinguda Jaume III, or at the foot of Passeig des Born. It does not run on Sundays.

OTHER ROUTES

4 Palma to Gènova
8 Palma to Son Roca (via Son Moix football stadium)
15 Palma to S'Arenal
17 Palma to Can Pastilla
23 Palma to S'Arenal (and to Aquacity in summer)

NIGHT BUS
Bus No. 41 (also known as the Bus de Nit) operates on Friday and Saturday nights from 11pm to 6am. It runs along the seafront

from Parc de la Mar to Porto Pí, with stops outside all the main discos and clubs. There is a flat fare of €1 or a combined ticket for €2, which includes all-night parking in the underground car park beneath Parc de la Mar.

CITY SIGHTSEEING BUS
- The open-top City Sightseeing bus makes a complete circuit of Palma and its outlying sights, including Castell de Bellver.
- The 80-minute tour begins at the port, on the jetty facing the cathedral and Parc de la Mar. You can pick it up at any of 13 stops, including Avinguda d'Antoni Maura, Plaça d'Espanya and Avinguda Jaume III.
- There is a headphone commentary in Spanish, Catalan, English, French, German, Italian, Portuguese and Swedish.
- Tickets are valid for 24 hours and you can get on and off as many times as you like.
- Tickets cost €13 for adults and €6.50 for children aged 5 to 15. Children under 5 travel free.
- The bus runs every 20 minutes from 10am. From November to April the service finishes at 6pm; from March to May and from mid-September to October it finishes at 8pm and from June to mid-September it concludes at 10pm.

Getting Across the Island

All bus services across Mallorca are operated by Transports de les Illes Balears (TIB, www.tib.caib.es), an integrated public transport network that also includes trains. The majority of buses are painted in the red and yellow livery of TIB, though some older buses retain the livery of private companies.

● Buses from Palma to towns and villages across the island depart from the bus station on Carrer Eusebi Estada, which is situated behind the railway station on Plaça d'Espanya. Several information boards here show maps and lists of destinations, together with details of which services depart from which stops. Local buses to Palma Nova, Magaluf, Illetes and Andratx depart from stops on Carrer Eusebi Estada.

● Facilities at Palma bus station include toilets, a café, a newsagent and an information counter (open daily 9–1 and 3–7), which can issue timetables for various routes.

● Many routes, particularly those to and from coastal resorts, operate drastically reduced timetables between November

ON THE MOVE

USEFUL ROUTES		
Route	**Frequency**	**Single fare**
Palma to Cala Rajada	Mon–Fri X5, Sat X3, Sun X2	€8.25
Palma to Coves del Drac	Mon–Sat X2, Sun X1	€6.35
Palma to Port d'Alcúdia	Mon–Sat X16 Sun X5	€4
Palma to Port d'Andratx	Several daily	€3.45
Palma to Port de Pollença	Mon–Fri X7, Sat X6, Sun X3	€4.60
Palma to Port de Sóller (express via tunnel)	Mon–Fri X14 Sat X8, Sun X4	€2.10
Palma to Port de Sóller (via Valldemossa and Deià)	Mon–Fri X5, Sat–Sun X3	€2.25
Palma to Valldemossa	Mon–Fri X9, Sat–Sun X4	€1.20
Pollença to Port de Pollença	Every 15 mins	€1
Port de Sóller to Port de Pollença via Lluc	Mon–Sat X2	€6

and April. In summer, extra buses link all the main resorts with each other and with nearby towns.

● Bus stops across Mallorca are recognizable by the red and yellow colours of TIB.

● Tickets can be bought from the driver on the bus.

● Smoking, eating and drinking are not allowed on board.

ORGANIZED EXCURSIONS

Tour operators offer a range of organized coach trips to popular attractions such as waterparks and caves, as well as shopping trips to Palma and local markets. These tend to be considerably more expensive than using public transport, but they may make a good alternative if you have limited time for exploring the island. Entrance tickets to the attractions are usually included in the price. The majority of tours include a visit to a leather or glass factory, or a gift shop, though be aware that as the tour guide will get a commission on any sales, the prices may be more expensive than in local shops. It is usual to tip the driver at the end of an excursion.

Watch out for slow-moving buses and coaches on mountain roads

TRAINS

Mallorca's modern trains are mainly used by commuters

There are two separate railways in Mallorca. The first, which is publicly owned and operated by Transports de les Illes Balears (TIB), has a fleet of modern trains connecting Palma with the busy commuter towns of Inca, Manacor and Sa Pobla. The second is the privately owned Ferrocarril de Sóller, which has been going over the mountains from Palma to Sóller since 1912 and continues to provide an enjoyable day out for visitors. In Palma, the two railway stations are close to each other on the north side of Plaça d'Espanya, a short walk from the bus station.

THE INCA TRAIN

● Around 30 trains a day run from Palma to Inca, with a journey time of approximately 36 minutes. Between Palma and Inca, there are stops at Marratxí, Santa Maria del Camí, Alaró-Consell, Binissalem and Lloseta.
● Half of the trains continue to Manacor (64 minutes) via Sineu and Petra; the others continue via Llubí and Muro to Sa Pobla (53 minutes).
● An integrated rail-and-bus service provides connections to outlying villages, for example from Santa Maria del Camí to Santa Eugènia and Sencelles.
● Tickets can be bought at Palma railway station, at other main stations or from the conductor on the train.
● There are toilets at Palma and some other stations.
● All trains are accessible for wheelchairs.
● Bicycles may be carried on most trains.
● Smoking is not allowed.

ON TRACK FOR THE FUTURE?

The reopening of the line to Manacor in 2003 has prompted further investment in the rail network and there are plans to open several new routes in the future. These could include the extension of the Sa Pobla line to Alcúdia, the extension of the Manacor line to Artà and Cala Rajada, and a line from Palma to Llucmajor, Campos and Santanyí.

THE SÓLLER TRAIN

The opening of the Sóller tunnel in 1997 means that this train is no longer used by commuters, but it remains viable thanks to its popularity with visitors. Everything about the 27km (17-mile) journey is delightfully old-fashioned, from the hoots and whistles as it pulls out of the station to the vintage walnut carriages and leather upholstery in first-class. The train rattles down Palma's streets before crossing the countryside of the plain and rising gently to Bunyola. After leaving the 3km-long (2 mile) Tunel Major, it twists down the mountainside to Sóller in a dizzying series of gradients, tunnels, viaducts and bends. From Sóller, an antique tram, which began service in 1913, rattles down to the port.
● Five trains run a day in winter and six in summer, with a journey time of one hour. The first departure from Palma is at 8am and at 7am from Sóller.
● The single fare is €2.47 (first class €3.53). A return is €4.94.
● The 10.50am departure from Palma (and also the 12.15pm in summer) is a *tren panoramic,* with an additional stop at a viewpoint overlooking the Sóller Valley. The single fare for this train is €6.
● Bicycles and wheelchairs cannot be taken on the train.
● Smoking is not allowed.
● There are toilets and cafés at Palma and Sóller stations.
● Trams leave Sóller for Port de Sóller every half-hour in summer and every hour in winter. The single fare is €1.

INFORMATION

For timetables, tel 971 752051 or visit www.trendesoller.com.

Continue your journey by tram from Sóller to Port de Sóller

SOME TYPICAL FARES	
Palma to Inca	Single €1.85, return €3.70
Palma to Sa Pobla	Single €2.65, return €4.90
One-day ticket for unlimited travel (Sat/Sun only)	€5.40

ON THE MOVE

BOAT TRIPS

Regular ferries link Mallorca to the Spanish mainland and the other Balearic Islands, and there is a wide choice of pleasure boat trips for summer visitors.

MENORCA AND IBIZA
Fast ferries and catamarans link Mallorca to the islands of Menorca and Ibiza, making it possible to visit either of them for a day. The main services are from Port d'Alcúdia to the port of Ciutadella in Menorca, and from Palma to the Ibizan capital Eivissa. Both these historic cities have several interesting buildings, museums and shops, yet are small enough to explore in a day.

CABRERA AND DRAGONERA
The offshore nature reserves of Sa Dragonera (▷ 75) and Cabrera (▷ 95) can be visited by boat. Depending on weather and sea conditions, it is usually possible to visit Sa Dragonera throughout the year but the trips to Cabrera operate between April and October only. In addition to the regular trips from Cruceros Margarita in Sant Elm, there are

extra departures in summer for Sa Dragonera from Palma Nova, Peguera and Port d'Andratx.

OTHER TRIPS
● Several boat trips operate in summer from beaches, harbours and resorts around the Mallorcan coast. These range from cruises around Palma and Alcúdia bays to 'glass-bottomed' boat trips along the east coast, day trips to remote beaches and coves, and evening 'pirate' cruises with food, drink and entertainment. In most cases, you can simply turn up at the jetty and see what is on offer,

but for the more popular trips it is advisable to book in advance.
● One trip that runs throughout the year is from Port de Sóller to Sa Calobra (▷ 74), operated by Barcos Azules (tel 971 630170). From November to March, there is one departure daily, leaving Port de Sóller at 11.15am and returning from Sa Calobra at 2pm. The return fare is €20 for adults and €10 for children aged 6 to 12; children under 6 travel free. There are extra departures in summer as well as cruises along the coast to Cala de Deià (▷ 67) and Formentor (▷ 88).

There are regular boat trips to Mallorca's outlying islands

SOME POPULAR TRIPS	
Route	**Telephone**
Around Palma Bay	659 636775
Cala Millor to Porto Cristo	971 810600
(optional visit to Coves Del Drac)	
Cala Rajada to Canyamel	971 563622
(optional visit to Coves d'Artà)	
Palma to Sant Elm	971 717190
Palma Nova to Palma	971 131211
Port d'Alcúdia to Formentor	971 545811
Port de Pollença to Formentor	971 864014

TIP
● The sea can be unpredictable and boat trips are always dependent on the weather, which can change suddenly even in summer. It is always worth checking the forecast before setting out.

FERRY COMPANIES				
Name	**Telephone**	**Website**	**Routes**	**Cost**
Baleària	902 160180	www.balearia.com	Fast ferries from Palma to Ibiza (2 hours) and Port d'Alcúdia to Ciutadella (1 hour)	Day return €80
Trasmediterránea	902 454645	www.trasmediterranea.es	Fast ferries from Palma to Ibiza (2 hours)	Day return €75.80
Iscomar	902 119128	www.iscomar.com	Ferry from Port d'Alcúdia to Ciutadella (2.5 hours)	Day return €64
Cape Balear	902 100444	www.capebalear.es	Catamaran from Cala Rajada to Ciutadella (1 hour)	Day return €75

DRIVING

Despite Mallorca's excellent and extensive public transport network, to explore the island thoroughly you will need a car. Bus services are limited in the less populated rural villages, and there is much pleasure to be gained from striking off the beaten track on remote mountain roads. Spanish drivers have a reputation for reckless overtaking and the accident rate in Mallorca is high, but in practice much of the danger comes from visitors in hired cars.

It is possible to take your own car to Mallorca by ferry from mainland Spain, but in most cases it will be easier and cheaper to fly to Palma and hire a car on arrival (▷ 36). If bringing your own car, ensure you have adequate breakdown cover and accident insurance. These can be obtained from your usual insurer or from a motoring organization such as the Automobile Association (www.theAA.com).

You'll need nerves of steel for driving on some mountain routes

RULES OF THE ROAD

● Drive on the right and over-take on the left.
● At roundabouts, give way to traffic coming from the left.
● The minimum age for driving is 18, though you will probably have to be over 21 to hire a car.
● Speed limits are 120kph (75mph) on motorways, 90kph (56mph) on main roads and 50kph (31mph) in built-up areas, unless otherwise indicated.

● The drink-drive limit is 50mg alcohol per 100ml blood, which is lower than in the UK. The only sensible advice is never to drink and drive.
● The Guardia Civil and Policía Nacional have the power to level large on-the-spot fines on speeding motorists and to remove licences from drunk drivers.
● Motorcycle and moped riders must wear a helmet at all times.

MALLORCA'S MAIN ROAD NETWORK

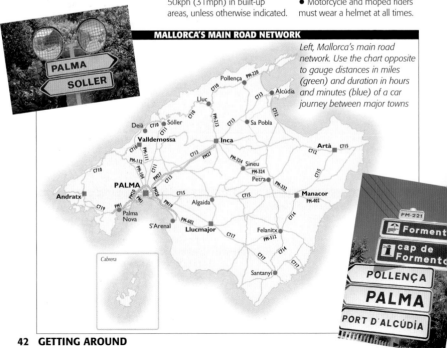

Left, Mallorca's main road network. Use the chart opposite to gauge distances in miles (green) and duration in hours and minutes (blue) of a car journey between major towns

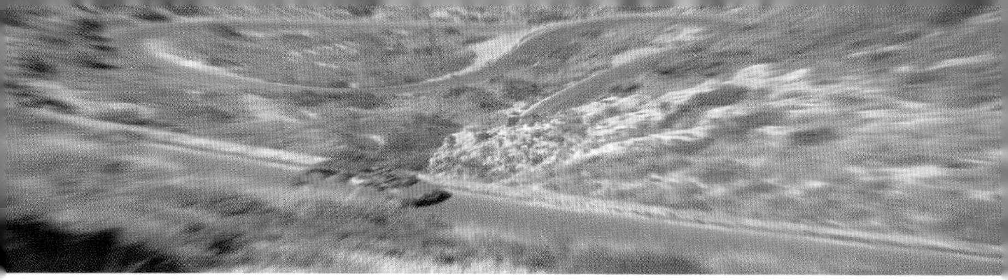

- Car drivers and passengers must wear seat belts at all times.
- Children under 12 may not travel in the front seat of a car; instead they must be strapped into a child seat attached to the rear seat of the vehicle.
- The use of mobile phones while driving is prohibited. It is also illegal to use mobile phones, headlights or car radios while stationary at a petrol station.
- Use dipped headlights in tunnels.
- Drivers are required to carry two warning triangles, a spare set of light bulbs and a reflective vest—which should be worn if you have to get out of the car on the road or the hard shoulder of a motorway. Hire cars should be provided with these items.

MOTORWAYS

- Mallorca has one main stretch of motorway, from Palma to Inca, as well as the Via Cintura (ring road) around Palma and short sections of motorway to Palma Nova and S'Arenal. There are long-term plans for a second, outer, ring road around Palma.
- When joining the motorway from a slip road, give priority to traffic already on the motorway.
- Always overtake on the left.
- Do not exceed the 120kph (75mph) limit, and keep a safe distance from the vehicle in front.
- Do not drive on the hard shoulder except in an emergency.

TOLLS

- Mallorca's only toll road is the Sóller Tunnel, which costs €3.80 for cars and €1.50 for motorcycles, payable by cash or credit card.

FUEL

- All petrol stations sell high-octane unleaded petrol, standard 95-octane petrol and diesel. Most hire cars take 95-octane fuel.
- There are petrol stations on all the main roads and in all the major towns. Many of them are open 24 hours a day and these are listed in the daily newspaper *Diario de Mallorca.*
- Although there are a growing number of self-service stations, the majority still have petrol attendants. Most will accept payment by cash or credit card.

PARKING

- Parking spaces in towns and cities are marked out by blue lines. Never park where you see yellow lines or any other form of markings.
- Most spaces are pay-and-display during working hours, approximately 9–1 and 4–8 on weekdays and Saturday mornings. At these times, buy a ticket from a nearby machine

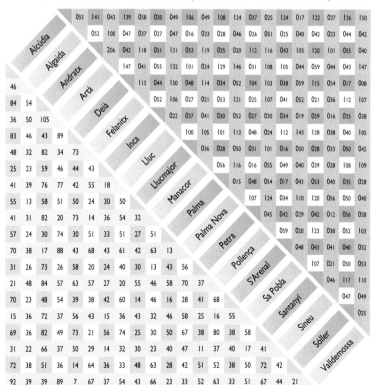

	Alcúdia	Algaida	Andratx	Artà	Deià	Felanitx	Inca	Lluc	Llucmajor	Manacor	Palma	Palma Nova	Petra	Pollença	S'Arenal	Sa Pobla	Santanyí	Sineu	Sóller	Valldemossa
Alcúdia		055	141	043	139	058	030	049	106	049	108	124	037	025	124	017	122	037	126	150
Algaida	46		052	100	047	037	027	047	016	033	028	046	026	051	025	040	042	023	044	042
Andratx	84	54		206	042	118	051	131	053	119	035	020	112	116	043	105	120	101	055	040
Artà	36	50	105		147	041	055	132	101	024	129	146	031	108	105	044	059	044	043	147
Deià	83	46	43	89		113	044	150	048	114	034	052	104	103	038	059	115	054	017	008
Felanitx	48	32	82	34	73		052	106	027	021	053	121	025	107	041	052	021	036	112	107
Inca	25	23	59	46	44	43		022	037	041	030	052	027	030	034	019	059	016	035	038
Lluc	41	39	76	77	42	55	18		100	105	101	113	048	024	112	143	128	038	040	105
Llucmajor	55	13	58	51	50	24	30	50		036	028	050	031	101	016	050	028	033	050	042
Manacor	41	31	82	20	73	14	36	54	32		056	116	016	055	049	040	039	028	108	109
Palma	57	24	30	74	30	51	33	51	27	51		015	048	054	017	043	053	040	035	028
Palma Nova	70	38	17	88	43	68	43	61	42	63	13		107	124	034	110	120	056	050	040
Petra	31	26	73	26	58	20	24	40	30	13	43	56		045	042	029	042	012	056	058
Pollença	21	48	84	57	63	57	27	20	55	46	58	70	37		059	020	123	038	052	103
S'Arenal	70	23	48	54	39	38	42	60	14	46	16	28	41	68		048	043	041	040	032
Sa Pobla	15	36	72	37	56	43	15	36	43	32	46	58	25	16	55		107	021	050	053
Santanyí	69	36	82	49	73	21	56	74	25	30	50	67	38	80	38	58		046	117	110
Sineu	31	22	66	37	50	29	14	32	30	23	40	47	11	37	40	17	41		047	049
Sóller	72	38	51	36	14	64	36	33	48	63	28	42	51	52	38	50	72	42		025
Valldemossa	92	39	39	89	7	67	37	54	43	66	23	33	52	63	33	51	67	44	21	

Parking is restricted in Palma

Mountain roads are much quieter out of the high season

and display it in your windscreen.
● Pay-and-display street parking is usually limited to a maximum of two hours.
● The public car parks in Deià, Valldemossa, Fornalutx and Port de Sóller are pay-and-display at all times.
● Parking in Palma is particularly difficult. There is a large car park on the jetty facing the cathedral and an underground car park beneath Parc de la Mar. This is central and secure, and there are no time limits, but it is costly for longer periods. If you can walk a short way into the city, there is free parking on the seafront to the west of the city centre, beyond Avinguda Argentina.
● In central Palma, freelance car

parking 'attendants' will often guard free spaces for motorists. If you see someone guiding you into a free space, he will expect a tip (€1 is sufficient). There is no danger in doing this, but be aware that many of these people are drug addicts using the money to fund their habit.
● Hotels, especially in Palma, will not necessarily have free car parking spaces for their guests. Ask about this when you book—it may be necessary to use a public car park or to pay for space in the hotel garage.

SECURITY
● Take common-sense security precautions as you would anywhere else. Never leave

anything on display inside the car; all valuables should either be taken away or locked out of sight in the boot.
● Never leave the keys in the ignition while parked at a petrol station or unloading luggage at a hotel.
● Hire cars can be particular targets for thieves, so it is best to remove any obvious signs.
● If you are involved in an accident that you suspect may be deliberate, drive on to the nearest well-lit petrol station before stopping.

WHAT TO DO IN AN ACCIDENT
Your car-hire company should give you an emergency contact telephone number for use in breakdowns and accidents. Make sure you inform your car-hire company as soon as possible. If it is your own car, contact your insurers immediately.
● Write down the name, address, registration number and insurance details of any other parties involved.
● If anybody is injured or if there is any dispute about the facts, call the police or emergency services on 112.
● If the car cannot be moved, and if you can safely do so, place a warning triangle on the road approximately 50m (164ft) to either side of your vehicle.

You pay a toll at the Palma end of the Palma–Sóller tunnel

MOTORCYCLES AND CYCLING

Car-free cycle routes are becoming common; try to wear a helmet

For some holidaymakers, hiring a car on this small island is unnecessary and they may find travelling on two wheels is sufficient for their itinerary. Mopeds are fine for short trips from resorts, while many prefer pedal power: cycling is a very popular activity on Mallorca.

SCOOTERS AND MOTORCYCLES

It's possible to hire anything from a 50cc scooter to a BMW or Harley Davidson motorcycle on Mallorca. Scooter rental firms proliferate in the seaside resorts, where they are popular with young Mallorcans and tourists alike. However, there are risks associated with riding scooters and avoidable accidents occur each year. It is mandatory to wear a helmet when riding a scooter or motorcycle and firms will typically include a helmet in the price of the rental. You'll need to show a valid driving licence to hire a scooter, which means that you have to have passed a driving test and be at least 17 years of age to hire a scooter. Insurance should also be included in the package and is essential. The price of hiring a small 50cc scooter starts from about €20 per day but you can expect to spend more hiring a motorbike. The island is popular with touring motorcyclists who

come for the Tramuntana's twisty mountain roads. You can bring your motorbike to Mallorca on the ferry services from northeast Spain (▷ 37), but this can be an expensive option. The alternative is to hire a motorcycle on the island. Several firms offer powerful touring motorcycles.

RIDING A SCOOTER SAFELY

● Helmets are mandatory.
● Use your lights at night.
● Watch out for car doors opening without warning.
● Make other road users aware of your intentions by using the indicators.
● Avoid riding along the inside of traffic when there is a right turn ahead.
● Don't drink alcohol before riding a scooter; you can be breathalysed.
● Don't carry a passenger unless the scooter is designed for two people.

CYCLING

Cycling is a popular activity on Mallorca and winter and spring see many cyclists on the roads. Traffic levels at this time of year are relatively low but it is still recommended to seek out quieter roads and avoid the fast main roads. Many of Mallorca's administrative districts have developed extensive networks of cycle lanes and created cycle

routes along scenic rural roads. Maps of these routes are available from local tourist information offices. The routes are usually clearly signposted and road quality is generally good, but watch out for potholes on some of the minor mountain roads. Palma itself has a number of cycle lanes but the best cycling is to be found outside the island's capital on the flat Pla I Llevant, around the coast and in the mountainous Serra de Tramuntana. Wherever you are based, there will be a cycle rental firm nearby. You might have to look a little harder to find specialist racing or mountain bikes (▷ 108). Each year cyclists are killed and injured in traffic accidents; despite local drivers' good awareness of cyclists, always ride cautiously.

CYCLING SAFELY

● Helmets are not mandatory but are strongly advised.
● Wear bright clothing and use lights at night.
● Don't cut corners on mountain descents.
● Watch out for car doors opening without warning.
● Make other road users aware of your movements.
● Avoid cycling along the inside of traffic when there is a right turn ahead.

Keep energy levels high when cycling long distances

TAXIS

Taxis are plentiful in Palma and all the main towns and resorts. Although they are a relatively expensive way of getting around, they are useful for short journeys and airport transfers. A tip of around 10 percent is expected but not compulsory.

IN PALMA

● Palma's taxis are either black or cream-coloured. You can hail one on the street whenever the green light is illuminated, pick one up at taxi ranks, or order a taxi by telephone (supplement payable).

● There are taxi ranks at the bus and train stations, on Avinguda d'Antoni Maura and Avinguda Jaume III.

● Fares are metered depending on the time of day. Between 6am and 9pm on weekdays, there is a minimum fare of €1.80 plus €0.80 per km, rising to €2.80 plus €0.80 per km for journeys outside the city limits.

Taxi! Day or night, it's not hard to find an official taxi in Palma

Fares are higher at night and at weekends and public holidays. There is a supplement of €1.65 for journeys to the airport or port.

● Wheelchairs and prams are carried free of charge.

OUTSIDE PALMA

● The livery of taxi companies varies around the island. Taxis can usually be hailed on the street, or hired at taxi ranks in town centres or outside the main hotels.

● Fares for local journeys are usually metered though it's wise to check in advance. There are supplements for late-night and weekend travel. A list of fares for longer journeys is usually displayed at taxi ranks. A taxi journey across the island from Alcúdia to Palma will cost around €50, but ask for a quote.

PALMA TAXIS	
Name	Telephone
Fono Taxi	971 728081
Radio Taxi	971 755440
Taxi Palma Radio	971 401414
Taxi Teléfono	971 743737

ISLAND TAXIS	
Town	Telephone
Alcúdia	971 549870
Pollença	971 866213
Santa Ponça	971 680970
Sóller	971 638484

VISITORS WITH A DISABILITY

Over the last few years, Mallorca has made great efforts to respond to the needs of disabled visitors, especially with regard to public transport. All new buildings must be accessible for wheelchair users and the majority of older buildings have been adapted, though attractions such as castles and caves can still prove difficult. Most hotels are happy to cater for disabled visitors, though it is important to discuss your particular needs and requirements in advance.

● All new buses are of the low-floor variety. All Palma's buses are wheelchair-accessible, though some older buses are still in use outside the capital.

● The Palma–Inca train line is fully accessible for disabled visitors.

● Most car-hire companies can provide specially adapted cars on request.

● Disabled parking bays are marked by a blue wheelchair symbol.

● Taxi drivers are generally helpful and they are required to carry wheelchairs free of charge. In Palma, you can order a taxi from Taxi Adaptat (tel 971 703529), which caters specifically for disabled passengers.

● The majority of beach resorts have level, traffic-free promenades which are suitable for wheelchair users. At Palma Nova, Magaluf, Illetes, Peguera and Santa Ponça, amphibious wheelchairs are available in summer for disabled swimmers.

INFORMATION

For holidaymakers from the UK, the Holiday Care Service (tel 0845 124 9971, www.holidaycare.org.uk) publishes a Mallorca fact sheet with advice for disabled travellers to the island.

This chapter is divided into the four regions of Mallorca (▷ 6). Places of interest are listed alphabetically in each region. At the front of each regional section that region's key sights are listed. For the location of all the sites described in each region turn to the Atlas (▷ 210–219).

The Sights

PALMA

Prepare to be surprised by Palma. The bay's beaches are heavily developed but this elegant capital has an enviable assortment of art galleries and museums, historic castles and palaces, secret courtyards and mansions, plus an eye-catching cathedral. The best way to enjoy Palma is to explore the compact city centre on foot.

MAJOR SIGHTS

Bath time: a tourist inspects the 10th-century Arab Baths

The cloistered courtyard of the Basílica de Sant Francesc

An opulent reception room at newly opened Can Marquès

BADIA DE PALMA

See pages 50–51

BANYS ÀRABS (ARAB BATHS)

☩ 211 D4 ✉ Carrer Can Serra, 7 ☎ 971 721549 ⏰ Daily from 9am; closes between 5 and 8pm depending on season 💵 Adult €1.50, child (under 10) free 🛗

Palma's 10th-century Arab bath-house is one of the few surviving examples of Islamic architecture in the city and probably formed part of a nobleman's palace in the city of Medina Mayurqa. The design, copied from the Romans, is identical to those found across the Arab world, with a series of chambers acting as changing rooms, and hot and cold baths. Best preserved is the *caldarium* (hot room), with a dome in the shape of a half-orange pierced by skylights and supported by 12 columns and horseshoe arches. Hot air was circulated beneath the floor from an underground fireplace and water channelled from a spring was splashed onto the stone to produce steam. The gardens, with their orange and palm trees and Arab-style pots, make a good place to relax.

BASÍLICA DE SANT FRANCESC

☩ 211 E4 ✉ Plaça de Sant Francesc ☎ 971 712965 ⏰ Mon–Sat 9.30–12.30, 3.30–6 💵 Adult €1, child free 🛗

This Franciscan church and convent dates from 1281, though the baroque façade was rebuilt in the 17th century after the original Gothic façade was struck by lightning. Outside the church is a statue of the Mallorcan missionary Junípero Serra (▷ 29) with a young Native American boy. You enter the complex through the convent on the right to reach a peaceful Gothic cloister of

orange and lemon trees, with an old well at the centre and tall cypresses standing guard. Take your time here—this is much the most impressive cloister in the city. The interior of the church is spoilt by the overblown baroque altarpiece topped by a statue of St. George on horseback.

Don't miss The tomb of the Mallorcan mystic Ramón Llull, completed in 1448, more than a century after his death, is found in a chapel behind the main altar.

CAN MARQUÈS

☩ 211 D4 ✉ Carrer Zanglada, 2A ☎ 971 716247 ⏰ Mon–Fri 10–6, Sat 10–2, Apr–Oct; Mon–Fri 10–3, rest of year 💵 Adult €6, child (under 12) free. Also included on €10 museums ticket 🎫 🛗 www.casasconhistoria.net

A visit to Can Marquès, the only seigneurial mansion in Palma open to the public, offers a rare glimpse into the lives of the Mallorcan aristocracy. It was built in the 14th century, though most of what you see is the creation of Don Martín Marquès, who, having made his fortune from coffee in Puerto Rico, returned to his native Palma in 1906. The Marquès family continued to live here until the death of Don Martín's daughter in 1969. The guided tour includes the two public rooms (used for entertaining guests), the private family rooms, the chapel, the kitchen and the servants' quarters.

Don't miss The *Modernista* staircase and wrought-iron candelabra are splendid.

CASA MUSEU J. TORRENTS LLADÓ

☩ 211 D4 ✉ Carrer de la Portella, 9 ☎ 971 729835 ⏰ Jun–Oct; Tue–Fri 10–6, Sat and holidays 10–2 💵 Adult €3, child (under 10) free. Also included on €10 museums ticket 🖼 €36 🎫 🛗 www.torrentsllado.com

The Catalan artist Joaquín Torrents Lladó (1946–93) settled in Mallorca in 1968, living at first in Valldemossa and later in Palma. Among his admirers was the English poet Robert Graves (▷ 67), who wrote: 'Most painters think they are painters, but Joaquín Torrents really is a painter'. After his death, Torrents' house and studio in Palma were turned into a museum, which opened in 2002. The permanent collection contains a wide spectrum of his work, from his early flirtation with abstract art to more conventional portraits, landscapes, still lifes, stage sets and graphic design. His studio on the first floor has been preserved much as he left it, with sketches of female nudes and an intimate portrait of his young son, born just two years before the artist's premature death.

CASA OLESA

☩ 211 D4 ✉ Carrer Morey, 9

The 16th-century house Casa Olesa has the best of all Palma's patios. Although it cannot be visited, the doors are usually left open and you can peer through the heavy iron gates. The house takes its name from the Olesa family, one of the noble Catalan dynasties that arrived in Mallorca at the time of the Christian conquest. They acquired it in the late 17th century and restored the patio in baroque style. Ionic columns on the ground floor support flattened arches, and a staircase leads to a gallery with a balustrade featuring the Olesa coat of arms. Note the paving stones set into the floor in a geometric pattern and the octagonal cistern. All the elements come together here in perfect architectural harmony. Keep an eye out as you stroll in the old town—many of the houses in nearby streets have similar patios.

Badia de Palma

A string of fishing villages turned pulsating resorts provide a non-stop diet of entertainment to millions of visitors each summer, making the bay of Palma the biggest holiday playground in Europe.

Sun seekers bask on the beach at Magaluf

A windmill at Santa Ponça, a quieter alternative to Magaluf

Street scene in S'Arenal and, right, the bay at Palma Nova

RATINGS	
Beaches	●●●●●
Good for kids	●●●●●
Historic interest	●●
Watersports	●●●●

TIP

● Parking in any of these resorts can be very difficult in summer so it is better to use the excellent network of local buses. The Palma city bus lines (Nos. 15, 17, 23) extend east to Platja de Palma and S'Arenal, while the Calvià area has its own network connecting Palma to Portals Nous, Palma Nova, Magaluf, Illetes, Santa Ponça and Andratx.

BASICS

➕ 217 C6
ℹ️ Tourist information offices at S'Arenal, Platja de Palma, Palma, Illetes, Palma Nova, Magaluf and Santa Ponça

SEEING BADIA DE PALMA

During the summer months, the stretch of coastline that runs for 25km (16 miles) around Palma Bay seems to be little more than an endless expanse of sand populated by sunburnt northern Europeans who rarely venture beyond their high-rise hotels or the resort bars serving bratwurst, burgers and chips. Generally, the east side of the bay around S'Arenal and Platja de Palma has been colonized by German visitors, while the west side around Palma Nova and Magaluf has long been the preserve of the British. But there is something for everyone here: quiet coves with a handful of sunbeds; beaches where locals outnumber visitors; glitzy marinas and gritty fishing districts, and in the middle of it all there is Palma itself. During the summer season the best way to get a feel for Palma Bay is to take a boat cruise (▷ 41).

HIGHLIGHTS

PORTITXOL AND CIUTAT JARDÍ
➕ 211 F5
Portitxol, a traditional fishermen's quarter to the east of Palma, has become trendy in recent years with the result that harbourside shops selling fishing tackle now rub shoulders with designer bars and hotels. You can get there by following the waterfront walk from Palma. The promenade curls around the small crescent beach of Es Portitxolet, passing the fishing district of Es Molinar on its way to Ciutat Jardí, whose lively beach is popular with local families in summer.

CASTELL DE SANT CARLES
➕ 217 C5 ✉ Carretera Dic de l'Oest ☎ 971 402145 ⏰ Mon–Fri 9–1, Sat 10–1 💶 Adult €3, child (under 18) free 🚌 1 🅿️ ♿ 🍴
Avinguda Gabriel Roca follows the broad sweep of Palma's seafront. Named after the engineer who supervised its building in the 1950s, it is more popularly known as Passeig Marítim (▷ 61). Both the path and the road come to an end at Porto Pí, the historic entrance to the port. The castle above Porto Pí was built by Felipe III in 1612; it is now a military museum. You can wander around the star-shaped fortress with its bastions, moats and sea views, and admire the collections of military uniforms, flags, lead soldiers and portraits of generals.

PUERTO PORTALS

➕ 216 C5 www.puerto-portals.com

This marina has been a magnet for celebrities since opening in 1986. Members of the Spanish royal family have been spotted at the waterfront restaurants and bistros, while millionaires shop at the boutiques on the promenade. It's fun just to wander around here, admiring the sleek yachts. The harbour was built beside the scruffy resort of Portals Nous, and the beach to the east of the marina is popular with locals.

PALMA NOVA

➕ 216 C5 ⓘ Passeig de la Mar, 13 ☎ 971 682365 ⓒ Mon–Fri 9–6, Sat–Sun 9–2

One of Mallorca's earliest holiday resorts, 'New Palma' is often unfairly linked with its neighbour Magaluf. While Magaluf remains a raucous nightlife capital, Palma Nova is quieter and better suited to families with young children. Two beaches, divided by a headland, shelve gently into the sea around a broad sandy bay backed by a promenade with restaurants and bars. Touristy it certainly is, but tacky it isn't.

PORTALS VELLS

➕ 216 B6

Beyond Magaluf you get a glimpse of how Palma Bay used to look. South of the town, a lane winds through pine woods to the west of the bay. Narrow roads lead down to Platja El Mago, a sheltered cove that contains Mallorca's first official nudist beach, and Portals Vells, a lovely beach hiding beneath the cliffs. From Portals Vells a path leads around the cliffs to Cove de la Mare de Déu. The road from Magaluf fizzles out before you reach the lighthouse at Cap de Cala Figuera.

BACKGROUND

Until the 1950s, the coastline around Palma was undeveloped. All that changed in a generation as hotels mushroomed around the bay and the population doubled. At first, tourism grew out of control, and parts of the bay have been scarred for ever, but in recent years there has been an effort to turn the tide. The biggest surprise is not that mass tourism has taken over the Badia de Palma, but that so much of its original beauty survives.

MORE TO SEE

PLATJA DE PALMA

➕ 217 D5 ⓘ Plaça Meravelles ☎ 971 264532 ⓒ Mon–Sat 9.30–1.30, 4–6.30

This long, nondescript beach with a palm-lined promenade and views across Palma Bay is a few minutes from the airport. The resort has swallowed up the neighbouring villages of Can Pastilla and S'Arenal. Mallorca's best waterpark, Aquacity (daily 10–6, May–Oct, ▷ 120), is here.

ILLETES

➕ 217 C5 ⓘ Carretera Andratx, 33 (summer only) ☎ 971 405444 ⓒ Mon–Fri 9–3

On weekend afternoons the people of Palma flock to this lovely, low-rise resort. Two beaches look out over two rocky islets, one of them crowned by a watchtower.

SANTA PONÇA

➕ 216 B6 ⓘ Via Puig de Galatzó ☎ 971 691712 ⓒ Mon–Fri 9–6, Sat–Sun 9–1.30

Strictly speaking, Santa Ponça, 6km (4 miles) west of Magaluf, is not in the Bay of Palma but it is linked to the resorts. Jaume I landed here 700 years ago for the Catalan invasion (▷ 26) and a stone cross above the harbour, erected in 1929, marks the spot he launched the invasion.

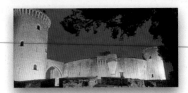

Castell de Bellver
●

This supreme example of Catalan Gothic military architecture combines museums of city history and classical sculpture with panoramic views over Palma Bay.

Bellver Castle stands guard over the Bay of Palma

You can't beat the view of the cathedral from Bellver Castle

The royal family lived on the first floor with the soldiers based below

RATINGS
Good for kids	◐ ◐ ◐
Historic interest	◐ ◐ ◐ ◐
Photo stops	◐ ◐ ◐ ◐
Value for money	◐ ◐ ◐ ◐

TIPS
● The easiest way of getting to the castle is on the City Sightseeing bus, so try to combine the two in one day.
● Entry is free on Sundays, though the museum and classical sculpture collection are both closed.
● Classical music concerts are held in the courtyard on summer evenings—check the local press or ask at tourist offices for details.

BASICS
✚ 217 C5
✉ Bosc de Bellver
☎ 971 730657
◉ Mon–Sat 8am–8.30pm, Apr–Sep; 8–7.15, rest of year
❓ The castle is open on Sun and public holidays, though the museums are closed. Open 10–7, Apr–Jun and Sep; 10–2, 4–9, Jul–Aug; 10–5, rest of year
💶 Adult €1.80, child (under 12) €0.90; free on Sun
🚌 City Sightseeing bus or Nos. 3 and 6 to Plaça Gomila
🅿 Large free car park
♿ Off the walkway around the moat

SEEING CASTELL DE BELLVER
Bellver Castle stands among pine woods overlooking Palma Bay, dominating the skyline as you look across the water from the cathedral. Because it is some distance from the centre of town, it can be quite difficult to get to unless you have your own car. A road leads up to the castle from Avinguda Joan Miró, but the only public transport is the City Sightseeing bus (▷ 38). Alternatively, you can take a bus to Plaça Gomila and walk up to the castle, a steep 20-minute climb through woods. The name of the castle means 'lovely view', and many visitors come up here just for the vistas from the terrace. For the best views of all walk around the moat then climb onto the rooftop: all of Palma is visible.

HIGHLIGHTS

THE CASTLE
Having a good look at the castle building before you go in by walking around the perimeter of the moat. Uniquely among Spanish castles, Bellver Castle is circular, with three semicircular buttresses and the round Torre de Homenaje watchtower connected to the main castle by a drawbridge. Once inside, all the rooms lead off Patio de Armas, a central courtyard and parade ground with a well for collecting rainwater. Note the differing architectural styles of the two storeys: the ground floor, designed for the soldiers, has semicircular arches with a flat roof, while the royal family's upper gallery has Gothic arches and rib vaulting. The upper floor also contains the chapel, dedicated to St. Mark, as well as the throne room and the kitchens, still blackened by woodsmoke. From here steps lead up to the roof terrace and its views of the courtyard. Step inside the towers and you may be able to make out the inscription 'Vive Napoleon', carved by French prisoners of war.

THE DESPUIG COLLECTION
Cardinal Antoni Despuig (1745–1813), born in Mallorca, went on to become Archbishop of Valencia and Seville and a Minister of State at the Vatican. During his time in Italy he amassed a large collection of antiques—mostly classical Roman sculpture—that he displayed in the garden of his estate at Raixa near Palma. In 1922 Palma City Council

acquired part of the collection and it is now displayed in three rooms on the upper floor. The first room looks at the Cardinal's life; the other two rooms contain marble busts, statues and fragments of sculpture.

CITY HISTORY MUSEUM

A set of rooms on the ground floor houses Palma's municipal history museum. The displays start with archaeological finds from prehistoric caves around Palma, including Son Oms, destroyed during the expansion of Son Sant Joan airport. There are exhibits on Roman and Islamic Palma and the Catalan conquest, as well as Palma's courtyards and *Modernista* architecture. Although not as comprehensive as the Museu de Mallorca (▷ 60), it does provide a quick overview.

BACKGROUND

Bellver Castle was begun in 1300 on the orders of Jaume II and completed some 10 years later. The original architect, Pere Salvà, also built the Palau de l'Almudaina in Palma. Although the castle was designed as a royal residence, it has hardly ever been used as such and served as a prison for almost 600 years. The first prisoner was the uncrowned Jaume IV, after his father, Jaume III, was defeated at the battle of Llucmajor in 1349, bringing to an end the short-lived kingdom of Mallorca. Many years later the castle became a military prison housing Napoleonic officers and the liberal general Luis de Lacy, who was executed here by firing squad in 1817. Another famous prisoner was Gaspar Melchor de Jovellanos, Treasury Minister to Carlos IV, a captive for six years in a single room. In more recent times the castle was used to house Republican prisoners during the Spanish Civil War.

Circular Bellver is an unusual shape for a Spanish castle

CASTLE GUIDE

GROUND FLOOR
City History Museum
Room 1: Introduction
Room 2: Prehistory
Room 3: Roman Palma
Room 4: Medina Mayurqa
Room 5: The Catalan Conquest (13th–15th centuries)
Room 6: Expansion (16th–19th centuries)
Room 7: Modernist architecture and the 20th century
Room 8: Tourism

FIRST FLOOR
Capilla de San Marcos (St. Mark's Chapel)
Sala de Jovellanos (Jovellanos Room)
Salón del Trono (Throne Room)
Sala de las Reinas de Mallorca (Queens' Room)
Cocina (Kitchen)
Colección Despuig (Despuig Collection)

La Seu (Catedral)

Towering above the waterfront and the old sea walls, this spectacular symbol of the city holds a treasury of Mallorcan art and architecture spanning more than 700 years.

The Immaculate Conception statue overlooks the Portal Major

Detailed religious carvings adorn the cathedral's façade

The Last Supper and, right, the cathedral and its reflection

SEEING THE CATHEDRAL

It is hard to imagine a church with a more spectacular setting than that of Palma Cathedral, commonly known as La Seu (the bishop's seat). Originally built on a cliff overlooking the harbour, the cathedral still stands out from its surroundings—despite the construction of a highway that separates it from the sea. For the best views of the cathedral, walk around to the seaward side or drop down to Parc de la Mar (▷ 61), where the pinnacles, gargoyles and flying buttresses are reflected in an artificial lake. Although nothing inside the cathedral matches this first impression from outside, it is worth paying the fee to look around. The entrance is on the north side, in Plaça de l'Almoina, facing the Palau de l'Almudaina. Unless you are attending a service, you must enter through the ticket office inside the old almshouse, Casa de l'Almoina. From here you pass through the museum to emerge in a side aisle beneath the main organ. After seeing the cathedral you can return to the museum before leaving.

HIGHLIGHTS

PORTAL DEL MIRADOR

Built between 1385 and 1430, this delicately carved doorway facing the sea was originally known as the Door of the Apostles, but its present name reflects its position as a vantage point. Five statues—St. James, St. John the Baptist, St. Peter, St. Paul and St. Andrew—stand to either side of a double doorway, separated by a sculpted Virgin and Child. There should have been statues of all the Apostles, as the empty niches indicate. The tympanum, above the portal, features a scene of the Last Supper presided over by God; around this archivolts depict Old Testament prophets and angels blowing trumpets. A gable with the head of Christ at its centre surmounts the entire doorway.

THE NAVE

Although the side chapels lining the aisles are filled with intricate details and religious art, it is the nave's overall impression of light and space that commands attention. Light streams in through stained-glass windows, and the rose window above the chancel is more than

Light pours over the nave from the enormous rose window

MORE TO SEE

CAPELLA DE LA TRINITAT

Trinity Chapel, dating from 1327, is one of the oldest parts of the cathedral. Situated behind the high altar, it is notable for its fine alabaster tombs of the Mallorcan kings Jaume II and Jaume III, which were placed here when the chapel was restored in 1946. The tombs, by the Catalan sculptor Frederic Marès, are rich in detail; note the weeping lions supporting the royal sarcophagi. The chapel is normally closed to visitors but opens approximately once a month for guided tours—ask at the tourist office for details.

MUSEU DIOCESÀ

✚ 211 E4 ✉ Carrer d'en Calders, 2
☎ 971 213100 🕐 Mon–Fri 10–1, 4–7
💶 Adult €2, child (under 10) free

The Diocesan Museum is in a wing of the bishop's palace, but a restoration programme means that it will be temporarily housed in a seminary in the Jewish quarter until at least 2005. The most emblematic item is a 15th-century painting of St. George slaying a dragon against a background of medieval Palma. The chronicles of the time say that St. George appeared on his white charger during the entry of the Catalan army into Palma in 1229.

12m (39ft) in diameter, making it one of the largest in the world. In it you can make out the shape of the Star of David. The window consists of more than 1,200 individual stained-glass panels—the glass has had to be replaced a number of times, most recently following damage caused during the Spanish Civil War. At the request of the bishop, Catalan architect Antoni Gaudí made a number of modifications to the cathedral between 1904 and 1914. Among his revolutionary changes were the opening up of windows that had previously been blocked off from view, and ringing the columns of the nave with wrought-iron electric candelabra in the shape of crowns. He was also responsible for moving the choirstalls from their position in the centre of the nave in order to open up the view of the altar, and for the restoration of the original 14th-century Gothic altarpiece, which now hangs in the southern aisle over the interior of the Portal del Mirador.

THE BALDACHINO

Gaudí's most controversial addition was this altar canopy, designed in the shape of an octagonal crown and thought to represent the crown of thorns placed over Jesus's head. It is decorated with vine leaves and ears of corn, clear symbols of the bread and wine used at the Eucharist. A candelabra, suspended from the ceiling by a series of ropes and pulleys, holds 35 brass lamps to illuminate the altar. The materials used, which include cardboard, cork, wood and silk brocade, were not intended to be permanent—this was in fact a provisional model for a project that was never finished, but has become an irremovable fixture. Behind the altar, look out for the 14th-century marble bishop's throne. When Gaudí began work on the cathedral this had been hidden from view, but he returned it to its rightful place in the centre of the chancel and surrounded it with his own ceramic designs featuring plant motifs and diocesan coats of arms.

CAPELLA DE SANT PERE

Miquel Barceló's (▷ 15) first major public work in Mallorca was the remodelling of the 14th-century chapel to the right of the main altar. To begin with, the entire chapel was covered with a second skin of terracotta, which was produced in a ceramic workshop in Italy and decorated with images of the parable of the loaves and fishes. Stained-glass windows 12m (39ft) high reflect the changing light onto the terracotta walls. Barceló was also responsible for the altar, the candelabra and the sculpture of the crucified Christ. The project, begun in

2002, was scheduled for completion by 2003, but was subject to delays, partly caused by the contentious nature of Barceló's work. The cathedral authorities objected to the original sculpture because it was thought to be too sexual. At the time of writing the chapel is not open but it is expected to be completed by 2005.

MUSEUM

Three rooms close to the cathedral entrance house its museum. The first room that you come to is the Vermells sacristy, at the foot of the belltower. Here the centrepiece is a great 16th-century processional monstrance (an ornament used for displaying the consecrated body of Christ) encrusted with silver and precious stones. Here too is the Book of Silver, a reliquary once believed to have been a portable altar carried by Jaume I during his conquest of the island. The most interesting exhibit, however, is the pair of 14th-century rimmonim, used in synagogues to keep the pages of the Jewish scriptures in place. They came from a synagogue in Sicily and are thought to be the oldest of their kind in the world. Leaving this room to the left, you come to the Gothic chapter house. Here are Gothic altarpieces and the lavish tomb of Bishop Gil Sánchez Muñoz (1360–1447), a former bishop of Mallorca who assumed the title of Clement VIII, an antipope set up in opposition to the pope during the schism in the Roman Catholic Church. The final room in the museum is the baroque chapter house, an oval chapel with an extravagant domed ceiling. The collections here are equally ornate, and include ivory crucifixes, silver candelabra and a 16th-century relic of the True Cross.

BACKGROUND

In 1229, according to tradition, a great storm arose at sea as Jaume I sailed towards Mallorca to begin the Catalan conquest of the island. The King vowed that if he landed safely he would build a magnificent church in honour of the Virgin Mary. On New Year's Day, 1230, the day after the invasion, he laid the foundation stone on the site of Palma's main mosque. There is no evidence that this story is true—what is known is that his son, Jaume II, ordered the building of the cathedral in around 1306 and that work continued until the completion of the main façade in 1601. The material used was limestone, quarried from Santanyí. An earthquake in 1851 meant the façade had to be rebuilt, and the cathedral continues to adapt to this day—as seen in the early 20th-century changes by Gaudí and the new chapel by Miquel Barceló.

Religious statues surround the Portal Major

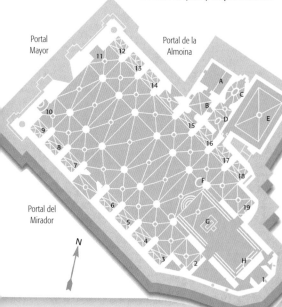

Light fantastic: the floodlit cathedral glows in the dark

Key to floor plan:
A Almshouse
B Belltower
C New Chapter House
D Old Chapter House
E Cloister
F Pulpit
G High Altar
H Bishop's Throne

Key to Chapels:
1 Trinitat
2 Sant Pere
3 Sant Antoni de Padua
4 Mare de Déu de la Corona
5 Sant Martí
6 Sant Bernat
7 Mare de Déu de la Grada
8 Sagrat Cor de Jesus
9 Sant Benet
10 Baptisteri
11 Animes
12 Immaculada Concepció
13 Sant Sebastià
14 Sant Josep
15 Todos los Santos
16 Pietat (with organ above)
17 Sant Crist
18 Sant Jeroni
19 Corpus Christi

Portal Mayor

Portal de la Almoina

Portal del Mirador

N

A detail of The Poetess, *one of Joan Miró's (below)* Constellations *series of gouaches painted 1940–41*

RATINGS	
Architecture	●●●
Artistic interest	●●●●
Good for kids	●●●●
Specialist shopping	●●●

TIPS

- Entry is free on 18 May (international museum day), 24 June (Joan Miró's saint's day) and 19 December (the museum's anniversary).
- A 50-minute video on Joan Miró, *The Light of Mallorca,* is shown hourly in the auditorium. It is usually shown in English at noon and 3pm.

BASICS

217 C5

Carrer Joan de Saridakis, 29, Cala Major

971 701420

Tue–Sat 10–7, Sun 10–3, 15 May–15 Sep; Tue–Sat 10–6, Sun 10–3, rest of year

Adult €4.80, child (16–18) €2.50 child (under 16) free

Camera/video fee €5 (no flash)

€11.75

6

www.a-palma.es/fpjmiro

A detailed site with visitor information in Catalan, Spanish, English and German, and a brief biography of Miró.

FUNDACIÓ JOAN MIRÓ

Paintings and sculptures by one of the 20th century's greatest artists are displayed in a stunning modern setting.

The Catalan artist Joan Miró (1893–1983) was heavily influenced by Mallorca and he moved permanently to the island in 1956. As a child, he spent his summer holidays here with his Mallorcan mother and he often spoke of the inspiration that he drew from the Mediterranean light and the changing colours of the sea and sky. In 1981 Miró donated his studio to Palma City Council; following his death, his widow donated the remainder of the land and commissioned the architect Rafael Moneo to design a museum to house Miró's work.

THE PAINTINGS

The permanent collection contains more than 130 paintings and numerous sketches, but only a small number are on display at any one time. They are shown in the Sala Estrella, the central exhibition space. Inevitably, there is a strong focus on the later period of Miró's life and the work produced in Mallorca during the 1960s and 1970s. These paintings demonstrate Miró's love of simple forms; there are similarities with the naïve peasant tradition seen in *siurells* (▷ 21).

THE SCULPTURES

During his time in Mallorca Miró became interested in sculpture and several works are displayed in the grounds. *Personnage Gothique* (1974), outside the main entrance to the museum, is characteristic of his style. The large bronze figure has a head shaped like a bird, a torso like a television and legs cast from a donkey's yoke. Look out too for *Femme et Oiseau* (*Woman and Bird*, 1962), in the Sala Estrella, and *Femme* (1981), in the gardens behind the museum.

THE STUDIO

Miró's studio was designed by a friend of his, Catalan architect Josep Lluís Sert. It has been left virtually untouched since Miró's death and you can almost feel his presence; the unfinished canvases seem to be awaiting his return. Behind the studio is Son Boter, Miró's 17th-century farmhouse. Some of the walls are decorated with graffiti and sketches for his paintings and sculptures.

First of a kind: the Modernist Gran Hotel in Plaça de Weyler

La Llotja, Palma's 15th-century stock exchange

Sitting pretty at the Museu d'Art Espanyol Contemporani

FUNDACIÓ LA CAIXA (GRAN HOTEL)

➕ 211 D3 ✉ Plaça de Weyler, 3
☎ 971 178500 🕐 Tue–Sat 10–9, Sun 10–2 🎫 Free 🚇 🚹 💻 🍴
www.fundacio.lacaixa.es

The grand building that houses the headquarters of La Caixa cultural foundation is interesting for two reasons. One, it was designed in 1903 as Palma's first luxury hotel, the Gran Hotel, at a time when the city was just waking up to the possibility of a future in tourism, and two, it was the first significant example of *Modernisme* in Palma: see pages 137–139 for further buildings.

Leading Catalan Modernist architect Lluís Domènech i Montaner (1850–1923), who is best known for his Palau de la Música Catalana in Barcelona, designed the Gran Hotel. The façade of the five-storey building displays typical Modernist features such as multicoloured ceramics and extravagant floral motifs on the balconies, arches and bay windows.

The ground floor, previously occupied by the hotel's reception rooms, now houses a bookshop and trendy café, while the upper floors are used as exhibition space. It is always worth checking to see what is on as the exhibitions are rarely disappointing and frequently fascinating.

A large gallery on the first floor showcases the paintings of Hermen Anglada Camarasa (1871–1959), founder of the so-called Pollença school of artists. Only two of the works are permanently on display, and both reveal his fascination with gypsy themes. *Valencia* (1910) is a monumental canvas depicting Valencian gypsy dancers wreathed in flowers, while *El Tango de la Corona* (1910) is of Argentinian tango dancers in similar style.

LA LLOTJA

➕ 210 B4 ✉ Plaça de La Llotja
🕐 Tue–Sat 11–2, 5–9, Sun 11–2
🎫 Free

This 15th-century mercantile trading exchange marks the high point of Gothic civil architecture in Palma. Designed by Guillem Sagrera, who also worked on the cathedral, it combines elements of both military and ecclesiastical styles. The turrets and battlements resemble a castle, while the gargoyles, the windows with their pointed arches, and the angel over the door could all have come from a church. Today, the spiralling columns and rib vaulting of the interior make a striking setting for the art exhibitions held here. The area around La Llotja, where the city's tapas bars and clubs are concentrated, is particularly lively at night.

LA SEU

See Catedral, pages 54–57

MUSEU D'ART ESPANYOL CONTEMPORANI

➕ 211 E2 ✉ Carrer de Sant Miquel, 11
☎ 971 713515 🕐 Mon–Fri 10–6.30, Sat 10.30–2 🎫 Free 🚇 €18 🚇 🚹
www.march.es/palma

An 18th-century mansion close to Plaça Major now houses an overview of 20th-century Spanish art, with 70 works by 52 different artists. The house was rebuilt in the early 20th century for the Mallorcan banker Joan March, who also owned Palau March (▷ 64). From the covered patio, with its elaborate skylight and mosaic floor, a grand marble staircase leads to the galleries. Room 1 contains the biggest names, including an early portrait by Picasso (*Tête de Femme*, 1907) and works by Joan Miró (*Le Perroquet*, 1937), Salvador Dalí (*Composition*, 1946) and Juan Gris (*Carafe et Bol*, 1916).

Room 2 is devoted to the Dau Al Set group of abstract artists from Barcelona, such as Antoni Tàpies, whose large-scale canvases can also be seen in Room 4. Among the other artists whose work appears in the museum are the sculptor Eduardo Chillida (1924–2002) and the painter Eduardo Arroyo (born 1937). **Don't miss** Miquel Barceló's canvases, in room 13, explore the themes of water and space. Look too for his *Large Pot with Skulls* (2000). This is a recurring image in Barceló's work, which has been influenced by his trips to Mali, West Africa (▷ 15).

MUSEU ES BALUARD

➕ 210 B3 ✉ Plaça Porta de Santa Catalina ☎ 971 908200 🕐 Daily 10am–midnight, Jun–Sep; Tue–Sun 10–8, rest of year 🎫 Adult €6, child (under 12) free; reduced price of €4.50 on Tue; free entry on 20 Jan, 1 Mar, 18 May, 12 Sep 📖 Catalogue €50
🎧 Audiotour included 🚇 🚹 💻 🍴
www.esbaluard.org

This stunning museum, which opened in 2004 inside the 16th-century bastion of Sant Pere, imaginatively combines historic military architecture with modern art. If you do not want to go into the museum, you can still visit the terrace, which is open to the city as a new semi-public space. Sculptures are scattered around the ramparts, and there are seats where you can take in the view of the castle and the cathedral. The museum is based on the modern art collection of newspaper magnate Pere Serra. Displays vary, but they are likely to include works by Joan Miró and Miquel Barceló. A highlight is the walk around the Passeig de Ronda, on top of the walls.
Don't miss The *Aljub* (cistern) in the basement supplied water to ships arriving in Palma. It is now a space for art installations.

THE SIGHTS

Above and bottom left, Museu de Mallorca has an extensive collection of medieval art as well as Islamic and Roman treasures

Religious figurines are exhibited on the first floor

MUSEU DE MALLORCA

Mallorca's top museum contains artistic and archaeological treasures encompassing 2,500 years of history.

The Museum of Mallorca is housed in the 17th-century palace of the count of Aiamans. Although the collections serve as a useful introduction to the various stages of Mallorcan history, the museum's main draw is its stunning exhibits—especially those in the prehistory section.

TALAIOTIC TREASURES

The tour of the museum is arranged chronologically, beginning in the basement. Here there are archaeological finds from the Talaiotic and pre-Talaiotic periods, when the people of Mallorca lived in caves and built stone towers (*talaiots*) like those at Capocorb Vell (▷ 97). Also on display is a complete skeleton of *Myotragus balearicus* (▷ 24), which was wiped out soon after the arrival of the first human beings on the island. A dimly lit room contains the highlight of the museum, a collection of small bronze statues of warriors. The figures, dating from the fourth century BC, are naked apart from their helmets. Each one follows a similar form, with the warrior in aggressive posture, his right arm raised as if holding a sword and his left arm around a shield. Nobody knows exactly when or how these statues arrived in Mallorca but they were almost certainly worshipped in an early religious ritual.

ROMANS AND MOORS

Exhibits from Roman and Islamic times are displayed on the ground floor. A mosaic pavement from a Christian basilica near Campos represents the Roman era. In the Islamic section, the Almohad Treasure is a remarkable cache of coins and jewellery. It was hidden in a clay pot and buried in a cave by a Muslim family during the Catalan invasion of Mallorca in 1229. The gold coins, minted in Morocco at the end of the 12th century, have Arabic inscriptions. Among the items of jewellery is a pair of beautiful gold earrings with delicate filigree work depicting birds of prey and verses from the Koran.

GOTHIC TO MODERNIST

The two upper floors cover Gothic, Renaissance and baroque religious art, together with Modernist furniture and 20th-century paintings.

RATINGS

Good for kids	● ●
Historic interest	● ● ● ●
Value for money	● ● ● ●

TIP

● If time is short, skip the upper floors and concentrate on the prehistory and Islamic galleries.

BASICS

✚ 211 D4
✉ Carrer de la Portella, 5
☎ 971 717540
🕐 Tue–Sat 10–7, Sun 10–2
💶 Adult €2.40, child (under 18) free; free on Sat and Sun
🏢 🏃

Parc de la Mar was created to reflect the cathedral in its lake

Born to shop: designer boutiques line shady Es Born

Enjoy live music and other street entertainment in Plaça Major

PALAU DE L'ALMUDAINA

See pages 62–63

PALAU MARCH

See page 64

PARC DE LA MAR

🚇 210 C5 ❓ Summer Nights programme of free concerts and films at Ses Voltes (tel 971 724090) 🔲

This public space was created in the 1960s on land reclaimed from the sea during the construction of the dual carriageway linking Palma to its port. Before the building of the road the cathedral had been reflected in the sea so an artificial lagoon was built to restore this image. At the time, the park was criticized as a misguided attempt to cover up a disastrous mistake, but over the years it has become accepted— even loved—by the people of Palma. The mural on the south side of the park was created by local artist Lluís Castaldo from a Joan Miró painting. From this side of the lake the views of the Palau de l'Almudaina and the cathedral rising out of the Renaissance walls are stunning. On the north side, beneath the walkway along the ramparts, is Ses Voltes, an imaginative open-air theatre staging free concerts on summer evenings. Nearby, in the vaults of the old walls, is the Ses Voltes art gallery (Tue–Sat and Sun am). Both the theatre and gallery were built during the 1980s; since then Parc de la Mar has become a popular meeting place. There are plans to extend the park to the seafront by burying the road in an underground tunnel.

PASSEIG DES BORN

🚇 210 C3 🔲

Es Born has always played a significant role in Palma's life and today the short street, which connects the main shopping districts to the cathedral and the sea, acts as a focal point for visitors. The name is derived from its days as medieval arena for jousting contests. Originally, this was a narrow creek and the promenade you see today was created in 1613 after the river was diverted in an attempt to prevent floods. The stone sphinxes at either end, and the fountains at the north end, were added in 1833. Es Born has become Palma's promenade *par excellence*, not only a place for strolling but also for concerts, demonstrations and fairs. Can Solleric (Tue–Sat 10–2, 5–9, Sun 10–1.30), at the north end, is a modern art gallery, bookshop and café housed in a baroque 18th-century mansion. It was built for a family of oil merchants from Alaró and now houses the city's main tourist office.

PASSEIG MARÍTIM

🚇 210 A3 🔲

Aside from Parc de la Mar, the building of the dual carriageway along Palma's seafront has had one positive effect—the creation of a waterside walk between the cathedral and the port. The footpath and cycle track extends 5km (3 miles) east to the harbour at Portitxol and west to Porto Pí, though the most popular stretch is just west of Avinguda d'Antoni Maura. It is easiest to begin this walk on the north side of the road, following the palm-lined Passeig de Sagrera past La Llotja (▷ 59) and the 17th-century Consolat del Mar. This former maritime tribunal, with a pair of cannons outside the door, is now the headquarters of the Balearic government. From here you can cross to the fishing port where an auction takes place each morning and fishermen can be seen mending their nets. Between the fishing harbour and the yacht club the path follows the coast as it curves around the bay, offering superb views of both the cathedral and Castell de Bellver (▷ 52–53) across the water. A good place to take in the views is El Pesquero, a boardwalk café beside the fishing port.

PLAÇA MAJOR

🚇 211 E3 🔲

This large, open plaza, at the centre of a shopping district, is one of the liveliest places in town. It is home to a changing cast of portrait painters, musicians, street vendors, mime artists and 'living statues', who spring to life when you drop a coin into their hat. The cafés around the square are mostly overpriced and of poor quality, but they nevertheless make good vantage points. The square, with a portico at ground level and four storeys of mustard-coloured, green-shuttered housing, was laid out in the 19th century on the site of the previous headquarters of the Spanish Inquisition. The Inquisition's infamous Casa Negra (Black House) was demolished, along with a neighbouring convent. This was the site of Palma's main fish and vegetable markets until 1951. Today, craft markets are held daily in summer and at weekends throughout the year.

A convincing 'living statue' in Plaça Major

Palau de l'Almudaina

Once a Roman, Arab and Christian power base, history echoes around this citadel's walls. Currently it serves as a royal palace, a national heritage museum and the military headquarters of the Balearic Islands.

Under the Gothic arches visitors admire a Flemish tapestry

A triptych glows golden in the Santa Ana chapel

Debauchery depicted in a 15th-century Flemish tapestry

RATINGS			
Architecture	●	●	●
Good for kids	●	●	
Historic interest	●	●	●
Photo stops	●	●	●

TIP

● The main entrance can only be reached by a flight of steps, so disabled visitors need to alert the staff or one of the soldiers on guard in order to gain access to a separate entrance to the right.

BASICS

✚ 210 C4
✉ Carrer del Palau Reial
☎ 971 214134
🕐 Mon–Fri 10–6.30, Sat 10–2, Apr–Oct; Mon–Fri 10–2, 4–6, Sat 10–2, rest of year
💶 Adult €3.20, child (5–16) €2.30; free for European Union citizens on Wed
📷 €7.20
🎧 Guided tours €4 including admission; audiotours €2 in English, French, German, Italian and Spanish
🏛 🏃

www.patrimonionacional.es
The official website of Spanish National Heritage, with information in Spanish and English on all the royal palaces, monasteries and convents.

SEEING PALAU DE L'ALMUDAINA

Like the cathedral, the palace is best seen from the seafront, from where it takes on a distinctly Moorish feel, a reminder of its earlier days as an Arab fortress. The entrance is on Carrer del Palau Reial, opposite the main façade of the cathedral. The palace is divided into two distinct parts, the Palau del Senyor Rei (King's Palace) and Palau de la Senyora Regina (Queen's Palace), together with common areas such as the chapel, Great Hall and royal baths. Only the King's Palace and some of the common areas are open to the public. The state rooms contain treasures such as Flemish tapestries, and it is worth taking the audiotour for a detailed description. The Palau de l'Almudaina is the official residence of King Juan Carlos whenever he is in Palma, which means that it is sometimes closed for royal functions. Although the palace is used for ceremonial occasions, the King prefers to stay at Marivent, his summer palace in Cala Major.

HIGHLIGHTS

PASEO DE RONDA

This narrow corridor (first discovered during restoration work in 1967) is where the tour of the palace begins. Note the black-and-white coffered ceiling, typifying Mudéjar architecture. The style, which combines both Moorish and Gothic elements, was first developed in Spain by Islamic craftsmen living under Christian occupation.

HALL OF KINGS

The Great Hall of the palace originally occupied two floors, but following the collapse of the roof in 1578 it was rebuilt on separate levels and the ground floor was divided into smaller chambers. One of these is now known as the Hall of Kings, after the modern portraits of the kings of Mallorca on the walls.

MIRADOR DEL MAR

This sea-facing terrace offers fine views over the port. From here you can see the Arc de la Drassana, a 10th-century Moorish archway that served as the entrance for vessels to the royal dockyards.

ARAB BATHS

Discovered during restoration, these baths date back to Roman times. With a cold room, a warm room and a hot room heated by an underground furnace, they are similar in style but much better preserved than the Banys Àrabs (▷ 49). The small size of the chambers suggests that they were designed as private baths for the king.

PATIO DE ARMAS

The palace's central courtyard is also known as the Patio de Honor (Courtyard of Honour). At the centre, hidden beneath four palm trees, a fountain gushes from a stone lion dating from Arab times. St. Anne's Chapel, built in 1310, dominates the west side of the courtyard. The doorway is a rare example of Romanesque art in Mallorca; mythological figures decorate the marble columns. From the courtyard there is a good view of the Torre del Angel, the central keep of the Arab fort.

THE KING'S STUDY

The Royal Staircase leads up to the state rooms on the first floor. After passing through anterooms you reach the King's Study, still used by King Juan Carlos. This was the room where Jaume I met secretly in 1229 to receive the surrender of the last Muslim *wali* of Palma. Next to the study is the Sala de Tinell (Throne Room), or Great Hall. The King holds receptions here during his annual summer visit to Palma.

BACKGROUND

There has been a castle on this strategic site above the harbour since the Romans built one here soon after their conquest of Mallorca, and the discovery of a megalithic settlement beneath the present palace suggests an even earlier history. The fort was destroyed by Vandal invaders who replaced it with one of their own in the fifth century. The Muslims converted it into an *alcázar* (fortress) and, following the Catalan conquest, it became a royal palace. It was Jaume II, the conqueror's son, who rebuilt it in the Gothic style you see today, employing the greatest architects and craftsmen. Since the collapse of the Mallorcan kingdom in 1349, the palace has only sporadically been used as a royal residence.

The palace's Moorish architecture contrasts with the cathedral in the background

MORE TO SEE

S'HORT DEL REI

Although no longer a part of the palace complex, the King's Garden is closely linked to the history of the Almudaina. At one time it was used as a kitchen garden, supplying oranges, lemons and grapes for the royal table. Wild beasts such as lions and bears, gifts to the king from visiting dignitaries, were also kept here. In the late 19th century the garden was sold for development and a hotel and theatre were built on this site, but in 1967 the land was returned to public use. Now, beneath the walls of the palace, alongside Avinguda d'Antoni Maura, is a peaceful area of fruit trees and tinkling fountains. Sculptures include a statue of a Balearic slinger and the egg-shaped *Monument* by Joan Miró. At the southern end of the gardens black swans can be seen swimming beneath the Arc de la Drassana.

PALMA PALAU DE L'ALMUDAINA **63**

Corberó's Orgue del Mar *sculpture appears to be rippling like water*

The view of the cathedral from Palau March's courtyard

RATINGS	
Artistic interest	●●●●●
Good for kids	●●●●
Photo stops	●●●●
Value for money	●●●●

TIP

● Cappuccino Palau March, in the same building but reached by the steps to the corner of Carrer del Conquistador, is a terrace café serving excellent sandwiches, salads and snacks.

BASICS

➕ 210 C4
✉ Carrer del Palau Reial, 18
☎ 971 711122
🕐 Mon–Fri 10–6.30, Sat 10–2, Apr–Oct; Mon–Fri 10–5, Sat 10–2, rest of year
💶 Adult €3.60, child (under 12) free
📖 Catalogue €50 (Spanish only)
🏛 🎫
☕ Cappuccino Palau March

www.fundbmarch.es
A limited site with information in English, Spanish and Catalan.

PALAU MARCH

Modern sculpture, traditional nativity scenes and extravagant murals come together in an enjoyably quirky museum.

The opening of the Palau March museum in 2003 caused a sensation in Palma, revealing previously unseen vistas of the cathedral. The house was built in the 1940s for the Mallorcan financier Joan March (1880–1962), who was popularly known as 'Franco's banker' and rose to become one of the world's richest men. The legitimacy of his fortune has often been questioned but he knew how to spend it. This museum reflects his eclectic tastes and those of his son Bartolomé March (1917–1988), another passionate art collector.

THE SCULPTURE TERRACE

It is difficult to imagine a more spectacular setting for this collection—an open courtyard in the shadow of the cathedral. In front of the main door, on a mosaic pavement, is a bronze torso by Auguste Rodin (1840–1917). Among the other artists whose work is on display are Henry Moore (1898–1986) and Barbara Hepworth (1903–75). But two large abstract works by contemporary Spanish sculptors steal the show. *Orgue del Mar (Mediterranean Organ)* by Xavier Corberó (born 1935) combines marble columns with a series of golden balls. *Línies al Vent (Lines to the Wind)* by Andreu Alfaro (born 1929) is a wavy steel sculpture set on a balcony directly beneath the cathedral.

EL BELÉN NAPOLITANO

The museum contains a collection of nativity scenes, with 2,000 figures made from wire, wood and clay. Beside the traditional figures of Jesus, the Holy Family, angels, shepherds and kings are innkeepers, gypsies, slaves, fishermen and musicians, all sculpted in great detail.

MUSIC ROOM

On the top floor you can see the original murals by Josep Maria Sert, completed in 1944. The highlight is the Music Room, decorated with exotic images of musicians and Carnival dancers, with billowing curtains and acrobats flying through the sky with balloons.

Don't miss The collection of 16th-century maps and navigational charts compiled by Mallorcan cartographers are richly illustrated.

SERRA DE TRAMUNTANA

Mallorca's mountain range shelters some of the island's most delightful villages and its most important religious site. But this region's biggest attraction is the rocky landscape itself, with cliffs plunging down to the Mediterranean and footpaths winding through woodland. The views are mesmerising all year round.

MAJOR SIGHTS

The harbour at Port d'Andratx attracts shoppers and sailors

The stairway to Alaró: local legends surround the well-defended mountain stronghold. Continue walking up to reach the chapel

THE SIGHTS

ANDRATX

✚ 216 B5 🚌 Buses from Palma to Port d'Andratx, Andratx and Camp de Mar

In common with other towns on the Mallorcan coast, Andratx was built inland from its port to protect it from pirate raids. These days visitors converge on the port, but Andratx retains a sleepy provincial feel, really only coming alive on market day. Two buildings dominate the town—the 13th-century church of Santa Maria and the 15th-century Castell Son Mas, now the town hall. Beyond the castle, in the village of Sa Coma, is the Centro Cultural Andratx (Tue–Sat 10–6, Sun 10–4), which puts on several exhibitions of contemporary art each year. There is a sculpture court and artists' studios, together with extensive gardens of orange, lemon and fig trees.

The biggest draw is Port d'Andratx, once a quiet fishing village but now a stylish harbourside town. There is not much to do but stroll along the promenade admiring the yachts and sit at the waterfront cafés watching the sunset. The nearest beach is across the hills at Camp de Mar.

BANYALBUFAR

✚ 212 B4 🚌 Occasional buses from Palma to Estellencs

The name of this village in Arabic means 'vineyard by the sea', and it has been known since Moorish times for its fertile soil. Arab settlers built the terraced hillsides sloping down towards the coast and the elaborate system of irrigation channels and cisterns. The village was once famous for wine, supplied to the crown of Aragón, but these days the main crop is tomatoes. West of the village, the Torre de Ses Animes is a 16th-century watchtower offering marvellous views along the coast.

CASTELL D'ALARÓ

Imaginations can run wild at this ruined castle and atmospheric chapel perching on a rocky peak.

✚ 213 E3 ✉ Puig d'Alaró
☎ 971 182112
🍴 Meals available at Es Verger (▷ 168) and at the hostel

RATINGS				
Good for food	●	●	●	
Historic interest	●	●	●	
Walkability	●	●	●	●	●

The ruined castle of Alaró seems almost to grow out of the landscape, so that from below it is hard to distinguish its walls from the rocky peak on which it stands. The Moorish fort that stood on this site was so well protected that its commander was able to defend it for two years after the Christian conquest. In 1285 this was the setting for the heroic resistance of the soldiers Cabrit and Brassa (▷ 27).

The road to the castle begins just outside Alaró, winding up through the terraces of olive trees to Es Verger. This farmhouse restaurant is popular with local families, who eat roast lamb here at weekends. The road continues beyond Es Verger but its condition worsens and it is far better to walk. Eventually you arrive at a clearing, Es Pouet, which is the farthest you can travel by car.

From here it is a short, steep walk to the castle. There is not much left to look at, though there are fine views across the plain framed by the ruined windows and arches. However, this is not the end of your walk. Keep going for a few more minutes and you will reach a small chapel and sanctuary, Nostra Senyora del Refugió, founded as a hermitage in 1622. This is one of the most atmospheric spots in Mallorca. Candles are lit in the chapel, alongside *ex votos* and notes of thanks to the Virgin for everything from recovery from illness to the birth of a child. There are majolica tiles on the walls, a pink-and-white stuccoed ceiling and an altar carved from a single slab of marble. You can clamber up onto the rocks behind the belltower for views across the sierra. From the terrace you can see as far as Palma, with Cabrera shimmering across the sea. If the walk hasn't taken your breath away, then the views certainly will. Spend the night in the simple hostel (▷ 179) to experience the true tranquility of this place.

Literary deity Robert Graves lived at Ca n'Alluny in this golden-stoned village from 1946 to 1985. Tiles, right, are dedicated to saints

DEIÀ

The adopted home of poet Robert Graves is a beautiful village huddling beneath the Teix Mountain.

There are many pretty villages in Mallorca, but, thanks to the English poet and novelist Robert Graves, none attracts quite the same attention as Deià. Author of such works as *Goodbye To All That*, and *I, Claudius*, he moved to Deià in 1929 with Laura Riding and returned in 1946 to spend the rest of his life in the village.

BOHEMIAN VILLAGE
The presence of Graves attracted a stream of writers, artists and muses to Deià throughout the 20th century—among the visitors to his home were Ava Gardner, Anthony Burgess, Kingsley Amis and Anaïs Nin. Although the village has become a retreat for wealthy visitors, with two luxury hotels and smart restaurants, the bohemian spirit lives on. About half of the residents are foreigners, many of them artists and ageing hippies. Graves himself would probably have deplored this trend—he was known in the village as Don Roberto and immersed himself in local life—but there is no doubt that he started it. Among the residents today is his son Tomás, a printer, author and musician.

TOMB WITH A VIEW
Climb Carrer d'es Puig to the parish church of Sant Joan Baptista at the top of the village. Beside the church is the small cemetery where Robert Graves is buried: it takes a while to find his tomb with its simple handwritten inscription: Robert Graves, Poeta, 1895–1985, EPD (En Paz Descanse, Rest In Peace). The names on the tombstones reveal the cosmopolitan nature of Deià, with a corner reserved for foreign writers and artists. There are fine views out to sea from here.

CA N'ALLUNY
In 2003, following the death of Graves's widow, Beryl, the government announced the establishment of a Robert Graves Foundation to buy Ca n'Alluny, his house and garden in Deià, and convert it into a museum. The house will be decorated with furniture and artefacts from the 1950s, including the original printing press with which Graves published his own poems. It is scheduled to open in 2005.

RATINGS
Good for food	● ● ●
Photo stops	● ● ●
Specialist shopping	● ● ●

TIP
● A 30-minute walk from the village leads down to Cala de Deià, a shingle cove with a small beach and a couple of fish restaurants that open in summer. You can also bring a car down here—take the main road out of Deià towards Sóller and turn left at the sign saying 'Depuradora'.

BASICS
✚ 212 C3

🚌 Buses from Palma, Valldemossa and Sóller

🅿 Pay-and-display

www.deia-mallorca.com
Official website of the town hall, with information on local sights and services in Catalan, Spanish and English.

www.deiamallorca.com
Website edited by Tomás Graves, with news and information from Deià in English, Catalan and Spanish.

Looking down La Granja's open-sided gallery; grounds outside contain shrubs, woods and wandering farm animals. Inset, a sundial

LA GRANJA

One of Mallorca's oldest agricultural estates is now a living museum of rural crafts and traditions.

The rows of tour buses in the car park attest to the popularity of this place, which is heavily promoted as an example of 'the other Mallorca'. Not everything that you see is authentic and it certainly feels more like a tourist attraction than a working farm, but nevertheless a visit to La Granja gives a genuine insight into traditional rural life.

THE FARM
The natural spring that spouts 10m (33ft) into the air here has been used for irrigation since Roman times. A Moorish farmhouse stood on the site and after the Catalan conquest the land was given to Count Nuno Sanç, a lieutenant of Jaume I. In 1239 he passed the farm to the Cistercian order, which founded its first convent here, but in 1447 it reverted to its role as a manorial estate. Today La Granja is a working farm with pigs, turkeys, chickens and goats, and displays of farm implements in the old farm buildings. The gardens contain a thousand-year-old yew tree and an 18th-century bathhouse, and there is also the option of a short walk (1.2km/0.7 mile) in the woods.

THE HOUSE
The tour of the house begins on the first floor, among drawing rooms and halls filled with family portraits. There is a theatre and a children's room filled with period toys. The ground floor rooms, where the servants worked, contain a wine press, an oil mill and workshops where you might see displays of embroidery, carpentry and basket-making. You may also be offered a tasting of *empanadas* (pasties) and *coca* (Mallorcan pizza) in the medieval kitchen. Finally, go down to the cellar, with its prison cells and gruesome torture chamber.

FOLK FIESTA
On Wednesday and Friday afternoons musicians in folk costume play bagpipes, flutes and drums, and women dance the *ball de pages*, a traditional matriarchal dance performed at village festivals. Blacksmiths and candlemakers work in the courtyard, and there are tastings of sausages, cheese, wine, liqueurs, fig cake and *bunyols* (▷ 163).

RATINGS

Good for food	● ● ●
Good for kids	● ● ● ●
Historic interest	● ● ●
Specialist shopping	● ● ●

TIPS
● Come on a Wednesday or Friday and you can save the cost of lunch by helping yourself to all the free samples of food. Otherwise, the restaurant serves traditional Mallorcan cuisine, with a good three-course lunch menu for €12.
● The shops in the courtyard sell pottery, perfume and other gifts, but they are rather pricey.

BASICS
✚ 212 C4
✉ 2km (1 mile) west of Esporles
☎ 971 610032
◉ Daily 10–7, Apr–Oct; 10–6, rest of year
🎫 Adult €9, child (4–14) €4.25; adult €11, child €5.30 on Wed and Fri pm
📖 €1.20
❓ Folk fiesta Wed and Fri 3.30–5
🏛 🚻 🛍 🍴

www.lagranja.net
Informative site in English, German and Spanish, with a good photo gallery and descriptions of the history, fauna, flora, crafts and folklore.

THE SIGHTS

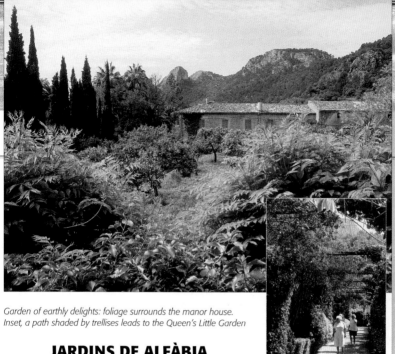

Garden of earthly delights: foliage surrounds the manor house. Inset, a path shaded by trellises leads to the Queen's Little Garden

JARDINS DE ALFÀBIA

Peaceful, landscaped gardens of water, fruit trees and ornamental plants reflect three centuries of Arab rule.

The gardens at Alfàbia, at the southern entrance to the Sóller tunnel, almost certainly date back to Moorish times. There is evidence of an Arab house since the 12th century; following the Catalan conquest, the estate belonged to Ben-Abet, a Muslim official who had converted to Christianity. The water is supplied by a mountain spring originating 60m (197ft) above the house in the foothills of the Serra d'Alfàbia.

FOUNTAINS AND CASCADES
An avenue of plane trees leads from the car park to the ticket office. The tour of the gardens begins to the left of the house, climbing a stairway lined with irrigation ditches to reach a fountain and a pair of stone lions (below). At the top of the stairway the façade gives on to the spray pergola, rebuilt in the 18th century and the most notable feature of the gardens. These days the water jets are controlled by an electric switch and you can turn them on and off as you please.

TO THE LAKE
From the spray pergola a covered walkway leads through an ornamental garden created for Isabel II when she visited the gardens in the 19th century; it is known as the Jardinet de la Reina (the Queen's Little Garden). A double stone staircase takes you down to the lake and the biggest area of the gardens, with palm trees, acacia, eucalyptus, bamboo, cedar, citrus trees, lily ponds and shady walks. You'll find plenty of hidden corners, and seats beside the lake.

INSIDE THE HOUSE
The way out of the gardens takes you through the house, a combination of Moorish, Gothic and Renaissance styles. The highlights are the library with its manuscripts and the 15th-century Flemish oak chair in the salon, carved with scenes of the lovers Tristan and Isolde.

Don't miss The coffered Mudéjar ceiling inside the porch, with the coats of arms of Arab families and Arabic inscriptions in praise of Allah, dates from the 13th century.

RATINGS	
Good for kids	● ● ●
Historic interest	● ● ●
Photo stops	● ● ● ●

TIPS

● The gardens make a good place to relax before or after the drive over the Coll de Sóller.
● Ses Porxeres, the restaurant beside the car park, serves excellent Mallorcan cuisine.

BASICS

✚ 212 D3
✉ Carretera de Sóller, 17km (11 miles)
☎ 971 613123
🕐 Mon–Sat 9.30–6.30, Apr–Oct; Mon–Fri 9.30–5.30, Sat 9.30–1, rest of year
💶 Adult €4.50, child (under 10) free
🅿 €2.50
♿ No wheelchair access
🅿 🚻 📷

Lluc Monastery

Mallorca's holiest and loftiest shrine attracts worshippers drawn by
an image of the Virgin and the legends with which it is associated; others
come for the uplifting mountain location.

*The view from the pilgrims' path.
Left, the basilica's baroque face*

*Pilgrims' progress: a plaque on
the path to Lluc's hilltop crucifix*

*Looking down at the rooftops of
Lluc and the basilica*

SEEING LLUC

Lluc Monastery stands in the heart of the Serra de Tramuntana
mountain range, surrounded by wooded hills, valleys and,
further to the northeast, steep sea cliffs. Although you could visit
the monastery in under an hour, it is best to allow half a day
here. Most people time their visit to take in a service and hear
the choirboys sing during morning mass. If you want to soak up
the atmosphere of the place, it is better to come late in the day
after most of the day-trippers have left, or do as many Mallorcan
pilgrims do and stay the night. The monastery is the focal point
of what has become a small village, with restaurants, shops and
banks. Other attractions include an interesting museum, a
botanical garden, an environmental exhibition centre and walks
in the nearby hills.

HIGHLIGHTS

THE BASILICA

The large Plaça dels Pelegrins (Pilgrim Square) leads to the
monastery complex, where an avenue of yew trees links a stone
cross at one end with a fountain at the other. To the right is Els
Porxets, a beautiful arcade built in the 16th century to provide pilgrim accommodation. Rooms are on the first floor along a wooden
balcony with stabling for animals underneath. To reach the basilica,
you have to enter the monastery through the main door and continue past the reception office and along the corridor to a courtyard.
Just beyond the courtyard, in a small room on the right, an exhibition describes the history and iconography of Lluc. At a second
courtyard look right to see the façade of the church, inscribed with
the words *Ave Maria*. Dating from 1622, the basilica was built in the
style of a Latin cross with a single nave and a central dome. A path
to the right of the altar leads around the back to a small chapel
where La Moreneta (The Little Dark One) is kept. This statue of
blackened sandstone depicts Mary, the Virgin of Lluc, cradling the
baby Jesus in her arms as he holds open the Book of Life with the
Greek letters alpha and omega on its pages. Her crown, encrusted
with precious stones including diamonds, rubies, emeralds, sapphires

RATINGS	
Historic interest	●●●○
Outdoor pursuits	●●●○
Photo stops	●●●○
Walkability	●●●○

TIPS

● Drive 4 (▷ 144–45) and
Walk 5 (▷ 146–47) both start
from here.
● It is usually possible to get a
room in the guest quarters,
which are basic but comfortable (▷ 179). Telephone in
advance or ask at reception.
● The best place to eat here is
Sa Fonda, which serves local
cuisine beneath the stone
arches and wooden beams of
the former monastic refectory.

*Dancing the Sardana at Lluc, a
traditional Catalan custom*

JARDÍ BOTÀNIC

🕐 Daily 10–1, 2–6 🎫 Free ♿

This botanical garden was laid out in 1956 and restored between 1993 and 2001 under the direction of Brother Macià Ripoll, with the support of former choirboys and friends of Lluc. On the short trail around the garden you can see around 200 native species of plants, together with fig, quince and walnut trees. One section is devoted to medicinal plants and herbs, and there are several small pools attracting aquatic plants and birds. The garden is reached through an archway in Plaça dels Pelegrins, between Els Porxets and the gift shop.

CA S'AMITGER

☎ 971 517070 🕐 Daily 9–4 🎫 Free ♿

Ca S'Amitager, a small building near the entrance to the car park, houses the Serra de Tramuntana information centre. Pick up leaflets here on local walks; a small museum describes the ecology and wildlife of the sierra. One room is devoted to the *ferreret*, the Mallorcan midwife toad (▷ 13), discovered as a fossil in a cave near Sóller in 1978 and subsequently found to be still living in Mallorca. The rehabilitation of the black vulture is illustrated in another room.

FONT CUBERTA

The 'covered fountain' is situated at the top of the car park, at the farthest distance from the monastery. You will often see a queue of people here waiting to collect water from a natural spring.

ONE PEOPLE?

The Catholic Church may have been closely associated with the Spanish government during the Franco dictatorship, but these days it has become a powerful force for Catalan nationalism. At the end of the Way of the Rosary, on the site of the original chapel, look for a ceramic plaque depicting a map of the historic Catalan-speaking regions, including the Balearic Islands, Andorra and Catalunya Nord (Roussillon in France). The caption reads *Un Poble, Una Llengua, Una Cultura* (One people, One language, One culture).

and pearls, was a gift from the people of Mallorca in 1884—which is why the coats of arms of every Mallorcan town are displayed on the walls. You can climb the staircase for a close-up look at the Virgin, though be aware that for many visitors this is a sacred ritual. During services the statue is swivelled round so that it can be seen in a niche above the high altar.

THE CHOIR

For many people the highlight of a visit to Lluc is the chance to hear the choirboys of the Escolania, who sing most days during mass at 11.15am and again during vespers at 7.30pm. The prior of Lluc founded the choir, popularly known as Els Blauets after its blue cassocks, in 1531. He stipulated that it should be 'composed of natives of Mallorca, of pure blood, sound in grammar and song'. Although the morning service has become something of a performance, frequently interrupted by the flashing of cameras, it should be remembered that this is primarily an act of worship. To listen to the music without the distractions, and to experience a greater sense of spirituality, attend an evening service.

MUSEU DE LLUC

🕐 Daily 10–1.30, 2.30–5.15 🎫 Adult €2, child (under 10) free

The museum occupies the upper floors of one wing of the main building. It begins with a gallery devoted to archaeology, which includes a sarcophagus from the nearby burial cave Sa Cometa des Morts, discovered by one of the monks (you pass this cave on Walk 5, ▷ 146–47). Also on display is fifth-century BC Greek pottery found on a shipwreck near Puerto Portals. The next room, featuring liturgical treasures and vestments, is largely missable, but it is worth going upstairs to see the varied art collection with paintings by Joan Miró and the Catalan artist Santiago Rusinyol. A long gallery of Mallorcan pottery leads to the highlight of the museum, the rooms dedicated to Josep Coll Bardolet (born 1912). This Catalan painter settled in Mallorca in 1940 and the museum contains a wide range of his work: bright, colourful, impressionist paintings of Mallorcan landscapes and seascapes, olive trees, festivals, folk dancers, and his travels in Venice, Rome and England.

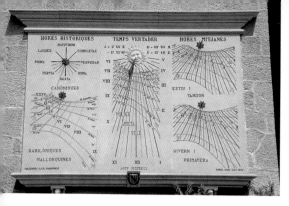

Sun worship: a sundial at Lluc, left, and, above, a monument

Left, the Virgin Mary with baby Jesus holding the Book of Life

Above, Bishop Campins in the courtyard of Lluc monastery, left

Walk this way: a granite station on the Way of the Rosary

THE WAY OF THE ROSARY

A pilgrim path, the Pujada dels Misteris (Way of the Rosary), begins beside a huge elm tree to the left of the monastery complex. Constructed in the early 20th century, the path is lined with granite monuments depicting the Stations of the Cross. It takes about 10 minutes to climb to the summit, with pauses along the way to enjoy panoramic views over the Albarca Valley, where lush farmland nestles in a fold beneath the sheer bulk of Puig Roig. The path leads up to a huge replica of a wooden cross brought from Jerusalem by Spanish pilgrims in 1910. Near here is a sculptural relief with a twisted, wrought-iron frame that bears the unmistakable stamp of the architect Antoni Gaudí. It was while Gaudí was working on his changes to Palma Cathedral (▷ 54–57) that his patron, Bishop Campins, commissioned him to work at Lluc.

BACKGROUND

The site of the monastery has been considered holy since pre-Christian times. Its name probably derives from the Latin word *lucus* (sacred forest), chosen by the Romans who found evidence of pagan worship here. However, following the Catalan conquest of Mallorca, when there was a need to establish a Christian iconography, a new legend grew up around Lluc. The story goes that a shepherd boy named Luke, newly converted to Christianity, discovered a statue of the Virgin in a cave, where it had remained hidden during the Moorish rule. He took it to the parish church in the village of Escorca but the next day it had disappeared, only to be found again in the cave. The third time this happened the priest took it as a message from God that the image was supposed to be worshipped in the cave; he ordered a chapel to be built on the spot. The first evidence of a shrine at Lluc dates from 1268; by the end of the 13th century it was attracting pilgrims from across the island and miracles were being attributed to the Virgin of Lluc. Eight centuries later Lluc continues to hold a special place in the Mallorcan psyche, both religious and secular (it is a popular honeymoon destination). A mass overnight pilgrimage to Lluc takes place in August (▷ 21).

BASICS

✚ 213 E2
☎ 971 871525
🕐 Daily 9am–8pm
🎫 Monastery free, entrance charge for museum (€2)

🅿 ♿ 🛏 📷 🍴

🚌 Buses from Palma via Inca; also from Port de Pollença and Port de Sóller (May–Oct)

www.lluc.net
Comprehensive site in Catalan maintained by the Missionaries of the Sacred Heart, with information on pilgrimages, Els Blauets and the history of Lluc. The site is currently under construction in other languages.

The cloisters connecting the church and the dormitories

Seek out rural solitude in the foothills around Orient

Enjoy waterfalls, caves and rivers in La Reserva

Hole in the wall: Na Foradada seen from Son Marroig

THE SIGHTS

MIRAMAR

🗺 212 C3 ✉ Carretera Valldemossa–Deià ☎ 971 616073 🕐 Tue–Sun 10–7, May–Oct; 10–5, rest of year 💰 Adult €3, child (under 12) free 🅿 🚻

Archduke Ludwig Salvator (▷ 30) bought Miramar (the first property he acquired in Mallorca) in 1872. Originally, the site had been occupied by a monastery and the school of languages founded by Jaume II in 1276—at the request of Ramón Llull—to teach Arabic to missionaries. The present house, built by Salvator, incorporates a small section of cloister and the original Gothic columns from the Santa Margalida convent in Palma. It is now a museum dedicated to the memories of both Llull and the Archduke. The gardens contain the pool where the Archduke would swim, benches arranged in the shape of a Byzantine cross, and a promenade with sea views. **Don't miss** A carved wooden sculpture of Ramón Llull is set inside a geometric cube, said to represent the cosmos. The sculpture was a gift from the hermits of Ermita de la Trinitat in 2003.

ORIENT

🗺 213 D3

This lovely village, one of the smallest in Mallorca, is the only settlement in the Vall d'Orient, a 'golden valley' of almond and olive groves. The most dramatic approach is from Alaró, where the table mountains of Puig de S'Alcadena and Puig d'Alaró loom on either side of the road to form a gateway. The village has a population of just 30, yet it manages to support two hotels and several restaurants used to weekend trippers from Palma. Some good walks start from here. The ascent to Castell d'Alaró (▷ 66), begins on a marked path 200m (656ft) beyond L'Hermitage Hotel.

LA RESERVA

🗺 212 B4 ✉ On the slopes of Puig de Galatzó, 3.5km (2 miles) from Puigpunyent ☎ 971 616622 🕐 Daily 10–7, Apr–Oct; 10–6, rest of year; last entrance two hours before closing 💰 Adult €9.90, child (3–10) €4.95 📖 Plant guide €1 🎢 Adventure trail €23.50 (minimum age 8) 🅿 🚻 🛍 www.lareservaaventur.com

This private nature reserve and outdoor activity centre opened in 1992 on the slopes of Puig de Galatzó, a mystical mountain believed to be the most magnetic in Europe. Revered across Mallorca, it is home to many legends, including that of El Comte Mal (The Wicked Count), a 17th-century nobleman whose ghost is said to haunt the valley. Bring strong shoes and warm outdoor clothing for the 3.7km (2-mile) walking trail. It follows marked paths through typical mountain scenery, with waterfalls, caves and streams. La Reserva calls itself a 'paradise of plants' and is worth buying a booklet and checking information panels to identify the various species of flora along the way. Mammals to look out for include Pyrenean brown bears, mouflon (wild sheep) and emus. The centre arranges activities ranging from horse-riding to rock climbing; there is also an adventure trail with rope bridges and zip slides. **Don't miss** Bird of prey flying displays take place daily at 2pm.

SA CALOBRA

🗺 213 E2 ⛴ Boat from Port de Sóller ☎ 971 633109 💰 Return €20

The small cove at Sa Calobra has been spoilt by thoughtless tourism development and these days the best part of a visit is the journey there. You have two choices—the boat trip from Port de Sóller (▷ 41) along the deserted north coast, or the

heart-stopping drive down from the C710. The road drops 800m (2,624ft) in just 12km (7 miles), with endless hairpin bends and one particularly dramatic switchback where it turns 270 degrees to pass under itself. Once at the coast, ignore the souvenir stands and overpriced restaurants and take the path through the rock tunnels to Torrent de Pareis. Here a small pebble beach lies at the entrance to a tall, narrow canyon that channels a fast-flowing torrent of water after rain.

SON MARROIG

🗺 212 C3 ✉ Carretera Valldemossa–Deià ☎ 971 639158 🕐 Mon–Sat 9.30–2, 3–7, Apr–Sep; 10–2, 3–5.30, rest of year 💰 Adult €3, child (under 10) free 🅿 🚻 🛍 🍴 Mirador de Na Foradada, closed Thu

Archduke Ludwig Salvator (▷ 30) owned most of the land between Valldemossa and Deià, but his favourite home was Son Marroig. He bought the house in 1877 and lived there for his last years in Mallorca—between 1908 and 1913. On his death, his secretary Antoni Vives inherited it, to whose family it still belongs. The house itself is rather gloomy but it does contain a good collection of memorabilia and books from the Archduke's library. There are also paintings by Antoni Ribes Prats, the son-in-law of Antoni Vives, who opened the house to the public in 1929. Most people soon make for the garden and its white marble rotunda, imported from Italy. Admire the views over Na Foradada, a jagged peninsula with a hole in the rock offering a window onto the sea. To walk to the peninsula you need to buy a ticket and ask for permission at the house. The 3km (2-mile) path begins at a green gate to the left of Son Marroig; when the path divides, keep right and follow the trail down to the sea.

Let sleeping dragons lie: endangered species have found sanctuary on Sa Dragonera. Inset, bathers in the warm, shallow waters

SA DRAGONERA

Rare species that have long disappeared from the mainland continue to thrive on this island wildlife refuge.

The islet of Dragonera, almost 4km (2.5 miles) long and 700m (2,296ft) wide, is a continuation of the Tramuntana range, separated from the rest of Mallorca by a narrow channel at Sant Elm. It takes its name from its shape, said to resemble a sleeping dragon. During the 16th century the island played host to the notorious Turkish corsair Barbarossa (Redbeard), who used it as a base for his attacks on Mallorca and Menorca. Today it is a protected nature reserve.

GETTING THERE
Boats depart from the small jetty at Sant Elm (for details, contact Cruceros Margarita, mobile tel 639 617545) and take 20 minutes to reach the island. You land at the harbour at Cala Lladó, where there is a visitor centre that issues maps and information on walking routes.

WHAT TO DO
There is a stark contrast between the two sides of Dragonera; vertical cliffs drop straight into the sea along the west coast, while narrow inlets and coves form a gentler coastline on the east side. Two paved routes are open to visitors: the road that runs the length of the island along the east coast, and the road that climbs west from Cala Lladó to the lighthouse at the summit of Puig de Na Pòpia (353m/1,158ft). Cap de Tramuntana, at the northern tip, offers dramatic views along the north coast of Mallorca—allow about an hour for the return hike from Cala Lladó. The walks from Cala Lladó to Cap des Llebeig on the southern cape and across the island take a little longer.

WHAT TO LOOK FOR
Sa Dragonera was designated a natural park in 1995 to protect Balearic wildlife. Among the native plants here are the dwarf fan palm and the cliff violet. Seabirds such as shearwaters and cormorants are frequently seen during the spring and autumn migrations, and the island is home to Europe's largest colony of Eleanora's falcons. Look out too for Balearic lizards, which have died out on the mainland but continue to flourish both here and on the island of Cabrera (▷ 95).

RATINGS				
Birdlife	●	●	●	● ●
Photo stops	●	●	●	●
Walkability	●	●	●	●

TIPS
● There are no facilities on Sa Dragonera, so take plenty of food and water, and check the time of your return trip.
● Cruises operate around Sa Dragonera from Sant Elm, Peguera, Port d'Andratx and Palma Nova in summer.

BASICS
✚ 216 A5
🛈 Parc Natural de Sa Dragonera, Sant Elm
☎ 971 180632
🚢 Boat trips from Sant Elm hourly from 10.15–1.15 daily, May–Sep; Mon–Sat, rest of year; last return 3pm
🎫 Return boat trip: adult €10, child (under 10) €7
👫

Sóller

●

**Set in an aromatic valley of orange groves
and surrounded by the highest peaks of the Tramuntana, Sóller's elegant
architecture, fountains and shady squares enchant visitors.**

*Watching the world go by from
a café in central Sóller*

*Fishing nets drying on the quay
in Port de Sóller*

*Sóller lies in a fragrant valley in
the Serra de Tramuntana*

RATINGS			
Good for food	●	●	● ●
Good for kids		●	● ●
Specialist shopping	●	●	● ●
Walkability		●	● ●

TIPS

● Negotiating your way around
the Sóller traffic can be difficult—instead, follow signs to
the car park on the edge of
town or leave your car outside
the botanical gardens and
walk in.

● Pick up a delicious local ice
cream from Sa Fàbrica de
Gelats, opposite the covered
market in Plaça del Mercat.

BASICS

✚ 212 D3

ℹ Plaça d'Espanya (in an old railway
wagon outside the station)

☎ 971 638008

🕐 Mon–Fri 10–2, 3–5, Sat 9–1, Mar–
Oct; Mon–Fri 9–3, Sat 9–1, Nov–Feb

🚌 Buses from Palma, Valldemossa and
Deià

🚂 From Palma

🚻 At station

www.sollernet.com
Private website in Catalan, Spanish and
English, with tourist information, public
transport timetables, maps of Sóller and
work by local artists.

SEEING SÓLLER

Sóller is one of Mallorca's most appealing towns, and getting
there is part of the fun. These days it is a lot easier thanks to a
new road tunnel, but there is nothing to beat arriving by train.
The 27km (17-mile) journey from Palma, in a vintage wooden
carriage that rattles down the mountainside, is a throwback to an
earlier age of travel (▷ 40). Once in Sóller, most people stroll
around the shops, visit the market and sit in the main square
admiring the Modernist architecture. If you want more stimula-
tion, though, there are good walks into the countryside through a
valley of orange trees and an enjoyable tram ride to the port.

HIGHLIGHTS

THE RAILWAY STATION

The first place that many people see on arrival in Sóller has a claim to
fame as the oldest railway station building in the world. The house,
Can Mayol, was built in 1606. Steps from the platform lead down to
the inner courtyard with a stone well once used for watering horses.

PLAÇA CONSTITUCIÓ

The central plaza, downhill from the station, is a delightful place to sit
with a glass of freshly squeezed orange juice from one of the cafés.
On the south side is the neo-Gothic church of Sant Bartomeu, with a
Modernist façade by Gaudí's pupil Joan Rubió. Rubió also designed
the Banco de Sóller next door, with its twisted iron window grilles, circular corner balcony, and a gargoyle of a lion. His house, Can Prunera,
with more decorative ironwork, can be seen at Carrer de Sa Lluna 90,
in an attractive shopping street off the northeast corner of the square.

JARDÍ BOTÀNIC

✉ Carretera Palma-Sóller, 30km (19 miles) ☎ 971 634014 🕐 Tue–Sat 10–6, Sun
10–2 🎟 Adult €3, child (under 12) free
www.jardibotanicdesoller.org

This botanical garden is divided into several zones planted with
Mediterranean flora. Zones 1 to 6 contain plants of the Balearics,
while other sections are devoted to the Canary Islands, Corsica,

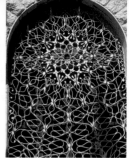

High security: Modernist window grilles at the Banco de Sóller

Above and left, taking the wood-panelled tram to Port de Sóller

ornamental and medicinal plants, and fruit trees. Attached to the garden, and included on the same ticket, is the Museu Balear de Ciències Naturals, a small museum of geology and botany. Among the exhibits is a skeleton of the extinct *Myotragus balearicus,* discovered by English palaeontologist Dorothea Bates in 1909 (▷ 24).

PORT DE SÓLLER
✚ 212 D3 🛈 Carrer Canonge Oliver, 10 ☎ 971 633042 ⏰ Mar–Oct
The tramline from Sóller to Port de Sóller opened in 1913 and trams still trundle down to the port, passing so close to the orange groves that you can almost reach out and pluck fruit from the trees. Port de Sóller is a low-key resort, busy with day-trippers but reverting to calm at night. It is the departure point for various boat trips (▷ 41). You can walk up to the lighthouse on the west side for superb sunset views, but much of the east side, used as a naval base, is off limits.

BINIARAIX AND FORNALUTX
From Plaça Constitució, walk along Carrer de Sa Lluna and you will reach the orchards and olive groves of the foothills of Puig Major. Keep straight ahead at a crossroads, follow signs across a bridge, and after 2km (1 mile) you will find the quiet hamlet of Biniaraix; 2km (1 mile) further is Fornalutx, often voted Spain's prettiest village. It is not a secret—there are several restaurants with terrace views where you can eat lunch before walking back—but the setting is undeniably beautiful.

BACKGROUND
Sóller, which lies in a valley of citrus trees in the middle of the Tramuntana range, is the only sizeable town along the north coast. It is famous for its oranges, and developed export markets in Barcelona and Marseilles. With the opening of the railway to Palma in 1912, and its subsequent electrification in 1929, the fruit merchants of Sóller were able to reach the markets of the capital. Even then, Sóller remained largely cut off from the rest of Mallorca, accessible only by road via the Coll de Sóller pass (▷ 144–45). The opening of the tunnel in 1997 made Sóller much more accessible and it is now a popular base for walkers.

MORE TO SEE

MUSEU DE SÓLLER
✉ Carrer de Sa Mar, 9 ☎ 971 634663 ⏰ Mon–Fri 11–4, Sat 11–1.30 💰 Donation expected
This is an old townhouse containing displays of pottery, costume, umbrellas, fans, musical instruments, and works by local artists.

CEMENTERI
✉ Carrer Can Fabiol ⏰ Daily 8–5 in winter, 8–8 in summer
The cemetery behind the station is one of the most impressive in Mallorca, with fine sculptural monuments from the 19th century reflecting the wealth of the merchants who made their fortune by exporting oranges.

MERCAT MUNICIPAL
✉ Plaça del Mercat ⏰ Mon–Sat 8–1
The covered market, just north of the main square, was inaugurated in 1952. It is busiest on Saturdays when a street market is also set up outside.

Valldemossa

**See the piano, hear the music, buy the book…
this small town in the mountains offers the full Chopin experience.
It's also the birthplace of Mallorca's only saint.**

Craft stalls line a square in Valldemossa's open-air market

Green for go: the belfry at Reial Cartoixa monastery

Explore the pretty lanes and alleys of Valldemossa

SEEING VALLDEMOSSA

Valldemossa, the highest town in Mallorca, is set in a green vale beneath the Puig d'es Teix. The best approach is from Palma—as you drive through the mountain pass Valldemossa appears ahead of you, its stone cottages and terraced fields nestling in the valley with the tiled green belfry of the monastery rising above the rooftops. Tourism has almost overwhelmed this small town of around 2,000 people and the Reial Cartoixa is second only to Palma Cathedral in the number of visitors it receives. This has come about because of a brief stay by the Polish composer and pianist Frédéric Chopin and his mistress, the French novelist George Sand, who rented rooms in the monastery during the winter of 1838. In recent years another celebrity couple, actors Michael Douglas and Catherine Zeta-Jones, have put the town back on the map. Any visit has to centre on the Reial Cartoixa, which contains Chopin's cell as well as the municipal museum.

HIGHLIGHTS

REIAL CARTOIXA

✉ Plaça Cartoixa ☎ 971 612106 🕐 Mon–Sat 9.30–6.30, Sun 10–1, Mar–Sept; Mon–Sat 9.30–5.30, Oct; Mon–Sat 9.30–4.30, rest of year 💶 Adult €7.50, child (under 10) free 📷 €9 🚻 In gardens 🏛

Having been given Valldemossa's royal palace in 1399, the Carthusian order founded the Royal Carthusian Monastery on the site. The community prospered and monks lived here until their expulsion in 1835. On its dissolution the monastery passed into private hands and was divided among a number of families. This joint ownership system survives today, with different owners responsible for separate areas, which is why you will find competing gift stalls in many rooms.

The tour of the monastery begins in the neoclassical-style church, built in the 18th century in the shape of a Latin cross. Note the frescoes by Manuel Bayeu, a brother-in-law of Spanish painter Francisco Goya, and the image of Santa Catalina Thomás, Valldemossa's saint, over the altarpiece. From the church, you enter the whitewashed cloisters. On your left is the old Carthusian pharmacy with its frescoed ceiling and shelves of ceramic and glass jars and painted wooden pill

RATINGS			
Good for food	●	●	●
Historic interest	●	●	● ●
Musical interest	●	●	● ●
Specialist shopping		●	● ●

TIPS

● Try to get here as early as possible to visit the Reial Cartoixa before the tour groups start to arrive.
● On the road from Palma to Valldemossa, stop off at the Lafiore glass factory at S'Esglaieta (▷ 124), where you can watch glass being blown.
● Follow the twisting road for 6km (4 miles) down to the coast at Port de Valldemossa, a seaside hamlet with a small gravel beach and a fish restaurant on the quay.

BASICS

➕ 212 C3
ℹ Avinguda de Palma, 7
☎ 971 612019
🕐 Mon–Fri 10–2, 3–6, Sat 10–1
🚌 Buses from Palma, Deià and Sóller
🅿 €2 per day
🚻 Public toilets in the gardens behind Reial Cartoixa

www.valldemossa.com
Information on the monastery and the town in Spanish and English.

Archduke Ludwig Salvator: A marble bust in Reial Cartoixa

boxes. A painting of the saints of medicine, Cosmas and Damien, hangs on one wall. The next rooms that you come to are labelled the Prior's Cell, though 'cell' is an inappropriate word to describe a suite of rooms which included a private chapel, library, bedroom, dining room and garden. Of particular interest here is the 15th-century ivory triptych in the library, where the prior would meet with the monks for half an hour each week; it was the only time they were allowed to speak. Look out too for the bedroom cabinet with its macabre display of hairshirts and whips used for penitential flagellation, and a skull that provided a constant reminder of mortality.

CHOPIN'S CELLS

The most interesting rooms in the Reial Cartoixa are those displaying mementoes of Chopin and Sand. Cell 2 contains the Mallorcan piano

The Mallorcan piano used reluctantly by Chopin

A tile depicting the patron saint of Mallorca, Catalina Thomás

Antique glass in the pharmacy in Valldemossa's monastery

Frederic Chopin's portrait in the Reial Cartoixa

on which Chopin composed Raindrop Prelude while waiting for his own piano to arrive from Paris. Also in this room is a lock of Chopin's hair and various original scores and manuscripts autographed by Chopin and Sand. Cell 4 was actually occupied by the couple. On the left is their bedroom, with Chopin's original Pleyel piano standing in front of a Polish flag. Glass cabinets contain correspondence and documents. There is a reproduction of Chopin's death mask and, outside in the garden, a replica of his tombstone in Paris. On a clear day the views from the terrace stretch all the way to the south coast.

MUSEU MUNICIPAL

The Municipal Museum is housed inside the Reial Cartoixa and entered on the same ticket. The first room contains the Guasp printing press (one of the oldest in Europe), built in 1622 and in use for more than 300 years. Also on this floor is an exhibition on the life of Archduke Ludwig Salvator (▷ 30), and the Serra de Tramuntana art gallery, featuring paintings inspired by the landscapes of northern Mallorca. You may recognize scenes such as *Vista de Valldemossa* (1974) by the Catalan artist Josep Coll Bardolet (born 1912), who has lived in Mallorca since 1940 and is now an 'adopted son' of Valldemossa. Among other familiar views are *Cartoixa de Valldemossa* (2001) by Bernat Reüll. The upper floor of the museum is devoted to 20th-century art, with several works by the Mallorcan artist Juli Ramis (1909–90). They trace his career from youthful portraits and self-portraits to an impressionist view of Port de Sóller (1929), a 'blue period' represented by *Dama Blava* (*Blue Woman*, 1940) and his 'abstract drippings' (1961). Also on display is a large collection of paintings and prints by Joan Miró, and a series of drawings by Pablo Picasso from his book *The Burial of the Count of Orgaz*.

PALAU DEL REI SANÇ

✉ Plaça Cartoixa 🏛 Included on Reial Cartoixa ticket 🎵 Piano concerts

The royal palace adjoining the monastery was built in the early 14th century by Jaume II for his asthmatic son Sancho (Sanç in Catalan), believing that the pure mountain air would be beneficial for his health. Of the original palace, only the defence tower and a stairway survive. The tour of the state rooms is largely uninspiring, and the

Painted lady: George Sand's portrait in the Reial Cartoixa

Left, the interior of the church and, above, the Reial Cartoixa

main reason for visiting is to hear the concerts of Chopin piano music, which take place hourly. On Monday and Thursday mornings these are replaced by folk dances performed by a local group, El Parado de Valldemossa. The palace is in the same square as the Reial Cartoixa; to get there from inside the monastery, take the doorway that leads out from the cloisters beside the Prior's Cell. Afterwards you can walk around the back of the palace to the original entrance on Carrer de Jovellanos, where a stairway leads to a wooden drawbridge. There are wonderful views from the adjoining terrace, Miranda des Lledoners.

COSTA NORD

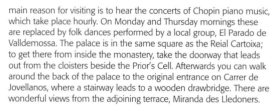

✉ Avinguda de Palma, 6 ☎ 971 612425 🕐 Tue–Sun 9–6, Mon 9–3, Apr–Oct 💶 Adult €7.50, child (5–12) €4.50 🏢 🚻 🛈 🍴
www.costanord.com

American actor Michael Douglas, who has a home near Valldemossa, founded this multimedia cultural centre in 2000. Although it has since been taken over by the Balearic government, it retains close links with Douglas. Visitors are first shown a film in which Douglas describes his passion for the landscapes and culture of the Tramuntana, and are then taken to a recreation of the *Nixe*, a yacht belonging to Archduke Ludwig Salvator, another wealthy foreigner who loved Valldemossa.

BACKGROUND

Despite its history as a royal residence, Valldemossa's fame rests on the visit by Chopin and Sand. They had come to Mallorca in the hope that the climate would alleviate Chopin's tuberculosis and to continue their affair away from the gossip of Paris. When they found rooms in the former monastery, they were both captivated by the setting—Chopin wrote that it was 'the loveliest spot on earth' and Sand wrote that 'whatever poet and painter might dream, Nature has created'. But the visit was a disaster. The people of Valldemossa were very conservative and objected to Sand, a liberated woman who wore trousers, smoked cigars, refused to attend church and lived with a man who was not her husband. Sand took her revenge in her book *Winter in Majorca*, describing the islanders as monkeys, savages and thieves.

MORE TO SEE

CASA NATAL BEATA

✉ Carrer Rectoría, 5
🕐 Daily 9–8.30

Mallorca's only saint, Santa Catalina Thomás (1531–74), was born in Valldemossa but spent most of her life in a convent in Palma, where she was renowned for her piety. Almost every house in Valldemossa has a ceramic plaque by the front door asking her for help. An easy walk through the cobbled streets of the town leads to her birthplace, now a shrine. From the Reial Cartoixa, head east along Carrer Uetam and fork right downhill to the parish church of Sant Bartomeu. The house is in the lane to the left of the church.

ERMITA DE LA TRINITAT

✉ Carretera Valldemossa–Deià
🕐 Daily 9.30–7 in summer, 9.30–6 in winter

A steep, narrow lane (signposted 'Ermita') leads off the Valldemossa–Deià road to this peaceful and beautiful hermitage, founded by Joan Mir in 1648. This is one of only two places in Mallorca where hermits live in silent contemplation. The other is Ermita de Betlem (▷ 86). A cool, whitewashed porch lined with ceramic tiles of saints leads to the patio, where an old well and a palm tree stand in front of the chapel. From the terrace there are views over the vegetable garden, tended by the hermits, and out to sea. Notices remind you to respect the silence. Outside, beneath the trees, barbecues and tables are set up for local families to enjoy weekend picnics.

THE NORTHEAST

The Northeast is perhaps Mallorca's most diverse region, with well-preserved Roman ruins, caves, a birdwatcher's paradise at Parc Natural de S'Albufera and summer holiday fun on the beaches of the bay of Alcúdia. Highlights also include Pollença, the genteel resort town which inspired British murder-mystery writer Agatha Christie.

Formentor
Pollença PM-220 Port de Pollença
C710 Alcúdia
Lluc C713
Coves de
Campanet
PM-213 C713 Parc Natural
Sa Pobla de S'Albufera
Inca C712
Artà C715
C713 C712
PM27 PM-324
Sineu PM-324 C715
Petra PM-332
Algaida C715 Manacor PM-402
C714
Felanitx
PM-512

MAJOR SIGHTS

Medieval Artà seen through the balustrade of the Santuari de Sant Salvador. Inset, vestiges of the Taláiotic era at Ses Païsses

ARTÀ

Two enormous monuments—the parish church and the castle-sanctuary at the summit—dominate this ancient town.

It is possible to drive all the way to the castle but a better alternative is to leave your car near the tourist office in the old railway station on the edge of town. From here you can walk along Artà's main street, Carrer del Ciutat, lined with cafés, restaurants and shops selling basketware—a local speciality. Keep going uphill, passing the town hall on Plaça d'Espanya, until you reach the parish church of Transfiguració del Senyor with its small museum (Mon–Sat 10–2, 3–5). From the church, a cypress tree-lined flight of steps leads to the castle walls.

CROWNING GLORY

The Santuari de Sant Salvador (daily 8.30–6 in winter, 8.30–8 in summer) is inside a walled enclosure, parts of which date from Moorish times. You can walk around the battlements and climb onto the tower for views over Artà's rooftops. The chapel dates from 1825, but the statue of the Virgin behind the altar is much older. Probably brought over by Catalan soldiers during the conquest of Mallorca, it was worshipped in a shrine on this spot. In 1820, the old chapel was used as a hospital during a plague epidemic and then burned down to prevent infection, with only the Virgin being saved. The paintings on the wall, by Salvador Torres, depict Jaume I receiving the surrender of the Muslim *wali* and Ramón Llull being stoned to death in Tunisia.

TALAIOTIC VILLAGE

Just outside Artà, signposted from the road to Capdepera, are the remains of Ses Païsses (Mon–Sat 9.30–12.45, 4–7.30, Apr–Oct; Mon–Sat 9.30–12.45, 4–5, rest of year; closed 20 Dec–2 Jan), a walled Talaiotic village occupied between the 12th and first centuries BC. The entire site, set in a holm oak wood, is still surrounded by a perimeter wall 374m (1,227ft) long, 3.5m (11.5ft) high and 3.6m (12ft) thick. The main entrance gate, with two huge vertical stones supporting a massive lintel, is particularly impressive. A well-marked path leads around the ruins, and you can climb onto the central circular *talaiot* to peer inside. The village was abandoned after the Roman occupation of Mallorca and its inhabitants moved to the foot of the hill, the site of modern Artà.

RATINGS		
Historic interest		● ● ●
Specialist shopping		● ● ●
Walkability		● ● ●

TIP

● The coastline north of Artà contains some of Mallorca's wildest and least-known beaches. From the petrol station on the eastern outskirts of Artà, on the road to Capdepera, follow signs for Cala Torta. A rough country lane leads down to the coast where you will find the horseshoe-shaped coves of Cala Torta and Cala Mitjana, and the narrow creek of Cala Estreta.

BASICS

🔲 215 J4
🛈 Estació del Tren, Avinguda Costa i Llobera
☎ 971 836981
🕐 Mon–Fri 10–2
🚌 Buses from Palma and Cala Rajada
❓ Market Tue

Alcúdia

Roman remains, medieval walls and a carefully preserved old quarter ensure
that Alcúdia is one of Mallorca's most historic and interesting towns.
Christmas is celebrated with spectacular arrangements of lights.

The Porta del Moll, gateway to
Alcúdia's old town

Behind ruins of Roman Pollentia,
the parish church of Sant Jaume

A dock in a bay: Port d'Alcúdia is
busy with sightseeing boats

RATINGS				
Historic interest	●	●	●	●
Photo stops	●	●	●	○
Specialist shopping	●	●	●	○
Walkability	●	●	●	○

TIPS

● Visit Alcúdia on a Tuesday or
Sunday morning when a large
street market takes place on
Passeig de la Mare de Déu de
la Victòria, beside Porta del
Moll.
● The vegetarian restaurant
Ca'n Simó (▷ 171) has a good
four-course lunch menu.

BASICS

🚏 214 G2
🏢 Edifici Ca Ses Monges, Carrer Major
☎ 971 897100
🕐 Mon–Fri 7.45–2.25
🚌 Buses from Palma, Pollença and
Port d'Alcúdia
❓ Market Tue and Sun

www.alcudia.net
The website of the town hall, with local
information and details of excursions in
Catalan, Spanish, English and German.

SEEING ALCÚDIA

Set on a peninsula between two sandy bays, Alcúdia is divided
into two distinct parts. To the south, by the harbour, is the resort
town of Port d'Alcúdia, often confusingly referred to as Alcúdia in
tour brochures. Of greater interest is the old town of Alcúdia, just
inland. Much of the town is still enclosed by its medieval walls,
begun in 1298 and recently restored. Outside the walls is the
Roman capital of Pollentia; excavations are still taking place but
the main areas can be visited. If you arrive by car there is a large
parking area just outside the walls, in front of the parish church,
and Roman Pollentia's remains can be seen across the road.

HIGHLIGHTS

ROMAN POLLENTIA

✉ Avinguda dels Prínceps d'Espanya ☎ 971 184211 🕐 Tue–Fri 10–3, Sat–Sun
10.30–1 💶 Adult €2, child (under 16) free; includes entry to Museu Monogràfic 🏛
The ruins of Pollentia are the only significant remains from the Roman
occupation of Mallorca; excavation started during the early 20th century. The visit begins in the La Portella district, where you can see the
remains of three houses. The first and best preserved is La Casa dels
Dos Tresors (House of Two Treasures), with rooms arranged around a
central atrium. Nearby is La Casa del Cap de Bronze, where a bronze
head of a girl, now on display in the museum, was first discovered. A
porticoed street, with some of the columns still standing, separated
the two houses. From here a path leads to the forum, Pollentia's main
square. Here are the remains of a temple to the gods Jupiter, Juno
and Minerva, together with shops, workshops and inns–Pollentia's
commercial zone between the first century BC and third century AD.

TEATRE ROMÀ

The Roman theatre, which dates from the first century, is reached by
taking a signed path from the south side of Avinguda dels Prínceps
d'Espanya. Another path runs behind the Roman forum, linking the
theatre to the Oratori de Santa Anna. Unlike the rest of the Roman
city, the theatre can be freely visited at any time. You can make out
the orchestra pit, the stage and seating tiers hewn out of rock. Once

thought to have been an amphitheatre for gladiatorial combats, it is now believed to have been used exclusively for plays. The council puts on musical and dramatic events in the theatre each summer.

MUSEU MONOGRÀFIC DE POLLENTIA
✉ Carrer Sant Jaume, 30 ☎ 971 547004 ⏰ Tue–Fri 10–4, Sat–Sun 10.30–1
🎫 Adult €2, child (under 16) free; includes entry to Roman Pollentia
Some of the finds recovered during excavation of Roman Pollentia are displayed here, including coins, jewellery, musical instruments and toys. Of particular note are the marble statue of an army officer, a bust of the emperor Augustus, and the Cap de Nina, a fine bronze head of a girl dating from the second century. The museum is housed in a 14th-century Gothic hospital beside the parish church of Sant Jaume.

THE OLD TOWN AND THE WALLS
Inside the medieval walls, Alcúdia is a delightful maze of narrow, traffic-free lanes and carefully restored Gothic and Renaissance mansions. A good example is Can Torró at Carrer d'en Serra 15 (Tue–Fri 10–1, 5–8, Sat–Sun 10–1), a 14th-century mansion that is now a public library and sculpture garden. The walls around Alcúdia were begun by Jaume II in 1298; to make a complete circuit, follow Camí de Ronda, a path that goes right around the town inside the walls. You will pass three gateways, including Porta de Mallorca, the original entrance to the town from Palma, and Porta del Moll, the historic entrance from the port. Carrer Major runs between the two, passing the 1929 town hall, with its Modernist clock tower, before reaching the main square.

BACKGROUND
Alcúdia takes its name from the Arabic *al-kudia* (the town on the hill). The Romans recognized the strategic importance of this site and established it as their capital after their conquest of Mallorca in 123BC. It was sacked by Vandals, rebuilt by Moors and fortified by Christian conquerors. After years of neglect, recent decades have seen the rebuilding of the medieval walls, the pedestrianization of the old town's streets and the restoration of several façades: Alcúdia is now a very pleasing town in which to stroll.

2,000 years ago Romans watched plays from these stone tiers

MORE TO SEE
ORATORI DE SANT ANNA
A footpath from the Roman theatre leads to this 13th-century chapel, seen opposite the cemetery beside the main road to Artà. Built by Diego Espanyol, it was one of the first churches on Mallorca after the Christian conquest. Above the doorway is a statue of the Virgin and Child known as the *Mare de Déu de Bona Nova* (Our Lady of Good News).

PORT D'ALCÚDIA
➕ 214 G2 ℹ Passeig Marítim ☎ 971 547257 ⏰ Mon–Sat 9.30–8
The original port town and fishing village is now a mega-resort stretching south from the port beside Mallorca's longest beach. The area down by the harbour still has an enjoyable nautical feel, with a wide, palm-lined promenade. East of here are the docks, where ferries depart for Menorca and Barcelona.

PENINSULA DE LA VICTÒRIA
This wild headland between Alcúdia and Pollença bays is the setting for some wonderful walks (▷ 150–51).

Take care walking around the walls of Castell de Capdepera

Inspect stalagmites and stalactites at the Coves d'Artà

See frescoes, a shrine, a spring and monks at Ermita de Betlem

CALA MILLOR

⊞ 219 J5 🛈 Parc de la Mar ☎ 971
585409 🕒 Mon–Fri 9–5 🚌 Buses
from Palma; also from Cala Rajada and
local resorts in summer

In contrast to much of the east
coast, which is made up of a succession of narrow creeks and
coves, Cala Millor has a long
sandy beach that stretches for
some 2km (1 mile). A promenade runs the length of the
beach, continuing north to Cala
Bona, a smaller-scale resort
based around a fishing and yacht
harbour. At the south end of the
beach a footpath leads up to
Punta de n'Amer, a wild headland and protected nature
reserve with dunes, pine woods
and rocky scrub. There is a 17th-
century watchtower at the
summit, and a café with views
along the coast. Cala Millor has
grown to become a busy resort
in summer but out of season it
has a much quieter feel. In summer you can take boat trips along
the coast—north to Cala Rajada
or south to Porto Cristo.

CALA RAJADA

⊞ 215 K3 🛈 Plaça dels Pins ☎ 971
563033 🕒 Mon–Fri 9.30–2, 3.30–6.30,
Sat 9.30–2 🚌 Buses from Palma via
Artà; also from Cala Millor in summer

A quiet fishing port on Mallorca's
eastern tip has developed into a
major resort popular with
German visitors who crowd out
its beaches in summer. A short
walk south from the harbour
leads to the town beach, Platja
de Son Moll, though there are
better choices to the north and
east, including the small cove of
Cala Gat and the broad curve of
Cala Agulla. A walk of about 2km
(1 mile) through pine woods
leads across a headland to the
lighthouse at Punta de
Capdepera, the most easterly
point on the island. If you feel

like a complete change of
scenery, fast ferries depart from
the harbour for Ciutadella in
Menorca (▷ 41).

CASTELL DE CAPDEPERA

⊞ 215 K3 ✉ Plaça del Sitjar, 5,
Capdepera ☎ 971 818746 🕒 Daily
10–8, Apr–Oct; 10–5, rest of year
🎟 Adult €2, child (under 13) free
🍴 €2 🚻 🚌 In Plaça de l'Orient

This 14th-century fortress, the
largest in Mallorca, completely
dominates the village over which
it stands. At one stage the castle
was the village, as all the inhabitants lived within its walls. It is
possible to bring a car up here,
but parking is extremely limited
and it is preferable to climb the
long flight of steps, which begins
near the village square, Plaça de
l'Orient. You can walk right
around the battlements and the
crenellated walls, though take
great care if you have children
with you as there are holes large
enough to fall through, and no
rails. Within the walls is the
Gothic chapel of Nostra Senyora
de la Esperança, with an image
of Our Lady of Hope over the
altar. According to legend, during
a siege of Capdepera, the villagers placed the statue on the
castle walls and the invaders
were driven away by fog.

COVES D'ARTÀ

⊞ 215 K4 ✉ Carretera de les Coves,
Canyamel ☎ 971 841093 🕒 Daily
10–7, Jul–Sep; 10–5, rest of year
🎟 Adult €8, child (7–12) €4 🍴 €1.50
🚌 Tours every 30 minutes ⓘ No dis-
abled access ⛴ Boat trips from Cala
Rajada in summer 🅿 🚻 In car park
📷
www.cuevasdearta.com

French geologist Édouard Martel
first explored the underground
grottoes at Cap Vermell in 1876,
though they had been known for
centuries as a haunt of pirates

and smugglers, and a hiding
place for Moors after the
Christian conquest. Like the other
cave systems at Campanet
(▷ 87) and Coves del Drac
(▷ 98–99), this is a fantasy land
of stalactites and stalagmites
forming outlandish shapes, complete with music, coloured
lighting and special effects. The
guides point out chambers with
names like Paradise, Purgatory
and Hell, and conjure up images
of elephants and organ pipes in
the stone. One of the stalagmites, known as the Queen of
Columns, is 22m (72ft) tall and
reaches just 50cm (19.5 in)
from the ceiling; at the present
rate of growth, it will take another
5,000 years to bridge the gap.

ERMITA DE BETLEM

⊞ 215 J3 ✉ 10km (6 miles) north of
Artà ☎ 971 589078 (often switched
off) 🕒 Daily 8.30–6 🎟 Free ⓘ Mass
at 10am Sun 🅿

A winding road from Artà, beginning behind the Santuari de Sant
Salvador, leads through a
wooded valley to this small hermitage founded in 1805. It is
one of only two in Mallorca
where monks still live according
to the rules laid down by the
Venerable Joan Mir in 1648 (the
other is Ermita de la Trinitat at
Valldemossa, ▷ 78–81). From
the car parking area a path lined
with cypress trees leads to the
chapel. Inside, an altarpiece by
Manuel Bayeu depicts the nativity of Christ. You can climb to the
belvedere behind the church for
views over Alcúdia Bay, or take
the path from the car park (signposted 'font') to arrive at a
spring, where there is a shrine to
the Virgin set inside a cave and a
fountain for collecting spring
water. The path continues down
to the coast at Colònia de Sant
Pere, a pleasantly low-key fishing
village and beach resort.

THE SIGHTS

Campanet's caves, less busy than others, are home to Henrotius jordai, *a species of blind beetle that has adapted to life underground*

COVES DE CAMPANET

These intruiging limestone caverns in the foothills of the Serra de Tramuntana might be smaller in scale than Mallorca's other cave systems but remain fascinating.

Most visitors to Mallorca take in one set of caves and it is a matter of personal preference which you choose. Although the cave system at Campanet is the smallest of those open to the public, it is every bit as impressive as the better-known Coves d'Artà (▷ 86) and Coves del Drac (▷ 98–99).

SUBTERRANEAN TREASURES
A local shepherd discovered the caves by chance in 1945 and three years later they were opened to visitors. The passage of underground water over thousands of years has eroded the limestone into curious shapes, and created extraordinary stalactites and stalagmites. In some places the two meet to make columns up to 5m (16ft) tall.

PALM TREES AND PASTA
The 40-minute guided tour takes you through three separate chambers. It begins in the Sala de la Palmera (Palm Tree Chamber), so called because of a large stalagmite said to resemble a palm trunk. With imagination, you will probably be able to discern many different shapes in the rocks, but the guides have their own ideas. They will show you Spaghetti Cave, with stalactites like thin strips of pasta, and the Chapel of the Virgin, where you can make out an image of the Madonna and Child set in stone.

STAR-CROSSED LOVERS
The next room is the Sala del Llac (Lake Chamber), where a pair of seated Buddhas overlooks an underground pool. The tour ends in the Sala Romàntica (Romantic Chamber), the largest chamber of all. Some 50m (164ft) underground, it takes its name from the figures of Romeo and Juliet said to be seen here. There are stalactites in the shape of a church organ and a cascade where the guides play tunes on the hollow columns. Afterwards, back in the real world, you can relax on the terrace with views over the countryside and the nearby oratory of Sant Miquel.

RATINGS				
Geological interest	●	●	●	●
Good for kids	●	●	●	
Value for money	●	●	●	

TIPS
● Photography is not allowed inside the caves.
● The last tour of the day starts 45 minutes before closing—6.15pm in summer and 5.15pm in winter.

BASICS
✚ 213 F3
✉ In the village of Campanet, signposted at Carretera Palma-Alcúdia, 39km (24 miles)
☎ 971 516130
🕐 Daily 10–7, Apr–Sep; 10–6, rest of year
💶 Adult €9, child (5–10) €4
📖 €1
🎫 Tours every 30 minutes
🅿 🚻 🛍

Some of Mallorca's most beautiful beaches are on Formentor.
Inset, the view of Cap de Formentor from Mirador des Colomer

FORMENTOR

A heart-racing drive takes in panoramic views, heavenly beaches and a peek at Mallorca's original luxury hotel.

Nervous drivers should not even think about tackling the 20km (12-mile) journey from Port de Pollença to Cap de Formentor, where the Serra de Tramuntana finally drops into the sea. Those that do, however, will be rewarded with some of Mallorca's most dramatic scenery.

POINTS OF VIEW
After ascending via a series of bends you arrive at a large car park at Mirador des Colomer. Climb the steps for views over Es Colomer, a rocky islet named 'the dovecote' because of the seabirds it attracts. Below you the cliffs drop 200m (656ft) into the sea, while to the left there are views of Cala Bóquer, a small cove beneath the jagged limestone ridge of Cavall Bernat. On the far side of the road a rough track leads up to Talaia d'Albercutx, a restored watchtower at a height of 375m (1,230ft). You can climb to the top for fabulous 360-degree views. The ruined buildings beneath the tower are former barracks, used to house the prisoners who built the Formentor road.

ON THE BEACH
The road levels out and travels through pine woods on its way to the cape. On the right is Formentor beach. Nowadays the beach is popular with day-trippers who arrive by boat from Port de Pollença, but it was previously the private beach of the Hotel Formentor, opened in 1929 by Argentinian entrepreneur Adan Diehl. This was once *the* place to stay in Mallorca; visiting celebrities have included Elizabeth Taylor, as well as royalty and politicians such as Winston Churchill. The hotel has lost its exclusivity but retains a certain old-fashioned appeal; although the beach is now public, in the summer the hotel employs a beach manager to prevent the masses from spoiling the guests' view.

TO THE LIGHTHOUSE
The road continues to twist and turn all the way to the lighthouse at the end of the cape. Just before the tunnel, look left for a glimpse of the isolated cove of Cala Figuera, only reached by boat or on foot. The lighthouse's café has views from the terrace to the island of Menorca.

RATINGS
Good for kids	● ● ● ○
Fauna and flora	● ● ● ○
Photo stops	● ● ● ●

TIPS
- The car park at the lighthouse gets very full and it is better to come early or late in the day.
- About 12km (7 miles) from Port de Pollença you will see a lone pine tree on the right. This is El Pi de Formentor, immortalized in poetry, painting and song. The path opposite leads to Cala Figuera.

BASICS
- 214 H1
- Carrer de les Monges, 9, Port de Pollença
- 971 865467
- Mon–Fri 8–3, 5–7, Sat 9–1
- From Palma and Pollença to Formentor beach in summer
- From Port de Pollença in summer
- At lighthouse
- At lighthouse; also on Formentor beach in summer

Primitive art is exhibited at Muro's Museu de Mallorca

MUSEU DE MALLORCA, MURO

✚ 214 G3 ✉ Carrer Major, 15, Muro
☎ 971 860647 🕓 Tue–Sat 10–3 (also Thu 5–8), Sun 10–2 💶 Adult €2.40, child (under 12) free 🛗

A 17th-century palace in Muro houses the ethnological section of the Museu de Mallorca (▷ 60). Most of building has been preserved, with rooms leading off the entrance hall and a courtyard. Rural history and crafts are the mainstay of the collection. Items displayed in a series of recon-structed rooms include a kitchen, bedrooms and a pharmacy. In the child's bedroom, look out for the model of a church with the priest in the pulpit, altar boys and a congregation of men and women seated separately. **Don't miss** Musicians, devils, animals, and men on horseback feature in the collection of *siurells* (▷ 21), made in Marratxí between 1955 and 1970.

SA POBLA

✚ 214 G3 🚌 Buses from Palma, Inca, Muro and Alcúdia 🚊 From Palma and Inca; 15-minute walk from the railway station ❓ Market Sun

Sa Pobla stands at the heart of Mallorca's richest agricultural area, on the flat farmland drained from the marshes around the S'Albufera reserve. The potato harvest attracts large numbers of migrant workers and Sa Pobla has the only mosque on Mallorca outside Palma. The one real attraction is Can Planes (Tue–Sat 10–2, 4–8, Sun 10–2), at Carrer Antoni Maura 6, north of the town centre. The ground floor features work by Mallorcan artists of the late 20th century. Upstairs is a delightful toy museum, with antique dolls' houses, rocking horses, toy cars and even a model bullring. Buses from Palma stop outside the museum.

A misty early morning at S'Albufera, when only the sound of frogs and the chatter of birds breaks the silence

PARC NATURAL DE S'ALBUFERA

The most important wetland reserve in the Balearic Islands attracts 200 species of migrant and resident birds, and an audience of birdwatchers.

✚ 214 G3 ✉ Carretera Alcúdia–Artà, 5km (3 miles) ☎ 971 892250 🕓 Daily 9–7, Apr–Sep; 9–5, rest of year 💶 Free 🅿 Outside reserve, opposite Hotel Parc Natural 🛗 www.mallorcaweb.net/salbufera

RATINGS				
Birdlife	●	●	●	●
Photo stops	●	●	●	
Walkability	●	●	●	●

Until the 18th century this area was a swamp, but much of it was drained for agriculture to create the fertile farmland that still exists around Sa Pobla today. The British-owned New Majorca Land Company built the network of canals in the 19th century, and the land was subsequently used for growing rice and harvesting reeds for paper manufacture. It was only in 1988, as the sprawling tourist develop-ment of Port d'Alcúdia began to spread south, that the Balearic government declared S'Albufera a natural park.

Cars are not allowed in the reserve, so park at the designated car park beside the Pont dels Anglesos bridge and walk the 1km (0.6 mile) to Sa Roca information centre, where you must reg-ister. Here you can pick up a map and a list of recent bird sightings, and look into the small museum, Can Bateman, with its audiovisual displays of birds. There are footpaths and bicycle paths around the reserve, but most visitors stick to a short circuit around Sa Roca, with bird-watching hides overlooking a lagoon. Among the species that breed here are osprey, kestrel, night heron, red-crested pochard and purple gallinule; summer visitors include purple heron and Eleanora's falcon; in winter flocks of wigeon, teal and grey heron can be seen.

Birds are the star attractions at S'Albufera

Pollença

The most appealing of all Mallorca's towns is
set in a narrow valley between two hills, with historic churches,
interesting museums and a pretty, café-lined square.

Fishing boats vie with cruisers
for space at Port de Pollença

A cockerel, symbol of Pollença,
at the foot of the steps of Calvari

Nightlife in Pollença: a café
beside the church in Plaça Major

RATINGS				
Cultural interest	●	●	●	○
Good for food	●	●	●	○
Specialist shopping	●	●	●	○
Walkability	●	●	●	○

TIP

● If you can, make it to
Pollença on the evening of
Good Friday when the statue
of Jesus is taken down from
the cross and carried down the
Calvary steps by hooded peni-
tents in a torchlit procession. El
Davallament, as it is known, is
one of the oldest religious festivities in Mallorca.

BASICS

✚ 214 F2
🈺 Carrer Guillem Cifre de Colonya
(next to Museu de Pollença)
☎ 971 535077
🕐 Mon–Fri 8–3, 5–7, Sat 9–1
🚌 Buses from Palma and Alcúdia
❓ Market Sun

SEEING POLLENÇA

Pollença, at the eastern end of the Tramuntana range, is an
attractive town of 17th- and 18th-century houses built in a maze
of narrow, medieval streets. Most of the action takes place
around the Plaça Major, the central square that springs into life
each Sunday as the setting for one of Mallorca's busiest markets.
The lanes around the square are perfect for strolling, with numerous art galleries, restaurants and speciality shops. Pollença was
built between two hills, each of which is topped with a sacred
site. A stairway from the town centre climbs to the Calvari chapel,
and a longer walk leads to the sanctuary on the summit of Puig
de Maria. Port de Pollença, 6km (4 miles) away, is an enjoyable,
old-style holiday resort with a fine beach set in a horseshoe bay.

HIGHLIGHTS

PLAÇA MAJOR

Plane trees surround Pollença's main square, which is built on two
levels. Dominating the northern side is the church of Nostra Senyora
dels Àngels, an 18th-century replacement of a church established in
1236 soon after the Catalan conquest of Mallorca. Alongside the
church, the Café Espanyol is a popular meeting place. Among the
bars lining the east side of the square is Club Pollença, housed in a
19th-century manor house on the corner of Carrer del Mercat. This
old-timers' café, known to everyone as El Club, hosts concerts and art
exhibitions, and is home to a number of active sports clubs. On
Sunday mornings the upper level of Plaça Major is taken over by a
colourful market that attracts visitors, locals and a large number of
British residents. Fresh produce and flowers are sold on the square,
while artists set up their stalls in the lanes behind the church.

EL CALVARI

To the right of the church, Carrer del Temple leads to Plaça de
l'Almoina, a small square where you will find La Font del Gall, a stone
fountain dating from 1827. It is topped with a cockerel, the heraldic
symbol of Pollença. From here, Carrer de Monti-Sion climbs to a for-

The way to Calvary: there are 365 steps up to the chapel

mer Jesuit convent, now used as the town hall. To the left of the building a flight of 365 steps, lined with cypress trees, leads to the Calvary chapel, built in 1799 and containing a 14th-century carving of the Mare de Déu del Peu de la Creu (Mother of God at the foot of the cross). After the Catalan conquest a gallows was built on this site and convicted criminals would climb the steps to their deaths. From the top of the steps there are fine views across the rooftops towards Puig de Maria, and a nearby belvedere offers views over Pollença Bay. The stairway has been extended into the town centre where it ends in an open square, Plaça Seglars.

MUSEU MARTÍ VICENÇ

✉ Carrer del Calvari, 10 ☎ 971 532867 🕐 Tue–Sat 10–1.30, 3.30–7, Sun 10–1.30
🎫 Free 🏛 ♿
www.martivicens.org
The artist Martí Vicenç (1926–95) specialized in the Mallorcan fabric

Pollença lies at the northern tip of the Serra de Tramuntana

MORE TO SEE

PONT ROMÀ (ROMAN BRIDGE)

Situated near the northern entrance to Pollença from the C710 to Lluc, the so-called Roman bridge spans the Torrent de Sant Jordi, a seasonal river. The bridge has been heavily restored and little of the original remains, but there is evidence that this may have been part of a system of bridges and aqueducts built to carry water from the mountains to the Roman capital at Pollentia.

CASA MUSEU DIONÍS BENNÀSSAR

✉ Carrer Roca, 14 ☎ 971 530997 🕐 Tue–Sun 11–1, Apr–Oct; occasionally open in winter and on summer evenings 💶 Adult €2, child (under 10) free

The 17th-century former home of the painter Dionís Bennàssar (1904–67) has been restored and furnished in period style and now houses an exhibition of his work.

known as *roba de llengües* (cloth of tongues), and his brightly coloured woven patterns continue to be produced at his workshop, Galeries Vicenç, on the roundabout at the junction of the Port de Pollença road. After his death his widow, Antònia Capllonch, opened a museum in his memory in their townhouse near the foot of the Calvari steps. As well as examples of his textiles, the museum includes his paintings and wooden sculptures, together with an ethnological display of old looms, spindles and kitchen equipment. The gift shop sells an interesting range of contemporary Mallorcan crafts.

MUSEU DE POLLENÇA

✉ Carrer Guillem Cifre de Colonya ☎ 971 531166 🕐 Tue–Sat 10–1, 5.30–8.30, Sun 10–1, Jul–Sep; Tue–Sun 11–1, rest of year 💶 Adult €1.50, child (under 12) free 🚹 In cloisters

Pollença's municipal museum is housed in the former Dominican convent, built between 1588 and 1616. Most of the displays are situated on the first floor. The eclectic collection includes modern art (the winners of the Salón Estival de Pintura, an annual competition held in Pollença since 1962), archaeology, and a Buddhist mandala, a meditative pattern created out of coloured sand by Tibetan monks and presented by the Dalai Lama. Two rooms are devoted to Atilio Boveri (1885–1949), an Argentinian painter who spent four years in Pollença and produced a number of local landscapes. Afterwards you can look into the baroque cloisters of the convent, the venue for Pollença's international summer music festival (see Background).

PUIG DE MARIA

➕ 214 G2 ☎ 971 184132 🍴 🏨 🚹

From the outskirts of Pollença, a twisting road leads in about 2km (1 mile) to the summit of 'Mary's mountain' (333m/1,092ft). Although you can take a car most of the way, it is not advisable as the road is in poor condition and there are several sharp bends, plus very limited parking space at the top. In any case, you will have to walk the final section on a medieval, stone-flagged mule path. The first sanctuary here was founded in 1348; it was abandoned three centuries later but hermits returned in 1917 and stayed until 1988. The present church dates from the 14th century, as does the nearby defence tower. Although monks no longer live here the place retains its spiritual atmosphere and you can look around the old monastery buildings, including the refectory with its arched Gothic ceiling. If you are inspired, you can stay the night in the simple hostel and wake to a view of Pollença Bay.

Top of the hill: Calvary chapel is worth the climb

PORT DE POLLENÇA

214 G1 Carrer de les Monges, 9 971 865467 Mon–Fri 8–3, 5–7, Sat 9–1 Buses from Palma and Pollença Market Wed

Like other towns around the Mallorcan coast, Pollença was built back from its harbour to protect it from piracy and invasion. Until the 20th century Port de Pollença was no more than a fishing village with a handful of summer cottages and a daily stagecoach to Pollença, but all that changed in the 1920s when it became one of Mallorca's earliest beach resorts. Today, the charm of that period remains, with old-style villas along the seafront and few high-rise hotels. South of the harbour a wide beach runs around the bay, dramatically situated between the Formentor and Victòria peninsulas. To the north, the wide promenade of Passeig Anglada Camarasa, named after the local painter whose work can be seen in the Fundació La Caixa (▷ 59) in Palma, leads to the Pine Walk, a romantic seafront path where pine trees lean into the water across tiny beaches and small jetties. Port de Pollença is justifiably popular and at times it is a little too crowded, but it is hard to beat for an old-fashioned, bucket-and-spade holiday.

Water flows under the Pont Romà only in the wetter seasons

Follow Port de Pollença's promenade along the seafront

You can see across the bay to Alcúdia from Port de Pollença

BACKGROUND

When Jaume I conquered Mallorca in the 13th century he distributed land among his followers, awarding Pollença to the Order of the Knights Templar. These military monks, known for their autocratic rule, established their temple on the site of the parish church and erected gallows on the summit of El Calvari. They called the town Pollença, a Catalan version of its Arab name that in turn derives from the old Roman capital of Pollentia at Alcúdia (▷ 84–85), with which it is sometimes confused. Pollença was attacked in 1550 by the Turkish pirate Dragut, a battle re-enacted each year on 2 August by the inhabitants of the town in a festival known as Moros i Cristians (Moors and Christians).

During the 20th century Pollença established a reputation as an artists' colony, based around Hermen Anglada Camarasa (1871–1959), the founder of the Pollença school, who lived on the seafront at Port de Pollença. Another artist drawn to Pollença was the British violinist Philip Newman (1904–66), who founded the Pollença Festival in 1962. This international music festival (▷ 134), supported by the Spanish royal family, continues to attract performers of the calibre of Montserrat Caballé and the London Symphony Orchestra; concerts are held each July and August. Pollença and its port are home to a large British community, with an active English-speaking Residents Association and regular Church of England services. Despite this, the town has maintained a balance between the demands of tourism and the need to preserve its Mallorcan character.

MORE TO SEE

CALA DE SANT VICENÇ

214 G1 Plaça Sant Vicenç (Jun–Sep only) 971 533264 Mon–Fri 10.15–2, 3–6 Buses from Pollença

When the people of Pollença head to the beach, they choose Cala de Sant Vicenç, where four small coves huddle together beneath the limestone ridge of Cavall Bernat. Although the setting has been somewhat spoilt by the appearance of a few ugly hotels close to the beach, this is still a beautiful spot. For the best views of Cavall Bernat, walk to the edge of the headland.

CALA BÓQUER

214 G1

An easy walk of 3km (2 miles) from Port de Pollença leads through a wild valley to this peaceful cove beneath the ridge of Cavall Bernat. The path begins on Avinguda Bocchoris, just behind the promenade, and climbs past the fortified Bóquer farmhouse before continuing down to the sea. In spring, several species of wild flowers and migrating birds can be seen along the way.

THE SOUTH

Dominated by the fertile Pla I Llevant and the manufacturing centres of Inca, Manacor and Algaida, it is tempting to overlook the South. But don't: The area has some great beaches, a vibrant viniculture centred in Binissalem and Felanitx, and perhaps Mallorca's most amazing attraction, the cave networks of the east coast.

MAJOR SIGHTS

Binissalem's church peeks above almond trees. Left, a statue in Plaça de l'Església

Cabrera welcomes tourists not prisoners these days

BINISSALEM

➕ 213 E4 🚹 Town hall, Carrer Concepció, 7 ☎ 971 511043 🚉 From Palma and Inca ❓ Market Fri www.ajbinissalem.net

This small town on the plain is best known for its wine and you will see the island's largest producer, Vinos Ferrer, as you drive past Binissalem on the old road from Palma to Inca (tours Mon–Fri 11am and 4.30pm, Sat 11am, €6, book in advance, tel 971 511050). There are also a couple of smaller bodegas in town—Vins Nadal (Carrer Ramón Llull 2, tel 971 511058), who make the excellent Albaflor range, and Vins Ripoll (Carrer Pere Estruch 25, tel 971 511028), where you can buy wine straight from the barrel. The best time to be here is in the final week of September, when wine flows freely during the annual harvest festival (▷ 134).

Rather surprisingly, Mallorca's best-preserved ensemble of 17th- and 18th-century manor houses is to be found in the streets around the church square, Plaça de l'Església. There are particularly good examples in Passeig des Born, an attractive cobbled lane behind the church.

Can Sabater (Carrer de Bonaire 25, Mon–Sat 10–2, also Tue and Thu 4–8) was the home of the writer Llorenç Villalonga (1897–1980), who wrote novels—including *Bearn (The Dolls' Room)*—about the moral decline of the Mallorcan nobility. The house is now preserved as a museum, with Villalonga's original desk and library on display upstairs.

CABRERA

➕ 216 B8 🚹 Excursions A Cabrera, Colònia de Sant Jordi ☎ 971 649034 🕐 Daily departures at 9.30, Apr–Oct 💶 Mon–Fri €28, Sat €32, Sun €34 child (3–10) half price 🍴 🚢 On boat www.excursionsacabrera.com

In 1991, after many years of military occupation, the island of Cabrera, 10km (6 miles) south of Mallorca, was declared a national park. Among the species protected here is the Balearic lizard (including endemic sub-species not found elsewhere), and now 80 percent of the world population lives on the island. Ospreys, peregrines and Eleanora's falcons build their nests on the cliffs; there are colonies of Balearic shearwaters and Audouin's gulls; and dolphins can sometimes be seen in the coastal waters.

The easiest way of visiting Cabrera is to take one of the excursion boats that leave Colònia de Sant Jordi each morning in summer (reservation essential). On arrival, you can pick up leaflets in various languages from the small information office on the harbour, or take the short walk from the quayside to the beach at S'Espalmador, where you can swim or snorkel in crystal-clear waters.

You are not allowed to wander freely on Cabrera, but the park rangers offer two guided walks. The first walk, leaving at 11.30am daily, takes you up to the castle overlooking the harbour. Built in 1410, it became most famous as a prison for French soldiers defeated in the Battle of Bailén in 1809 (▷ 29). Unable to escape, and without regular supplies, the prisoners survived on a diet of lizards and rats. You can still see graffiti etched into the castle walls by some of the prisoners. On the second walk, departing at

1pm, you will see a monument to the French soldiers who died on Cabrera; it was placed here some 30 years later by a French prince. Nearby is Can Feliu, an old wine cellar now housing a small museum on the history of the island.

On the way back to Mallorca the boats usually stop off in Sa Cova Blava (Blue Grotto), where you can swim inside a natural cave with a depth of 40m (131ft).

CA'N GORDIOLA

➕ 218 E5 ✉ Carretera Palma-Manacor, 19km (12 miles) ☎ 971 665046 🕐 Mon–Sat 9–8, Sun 9–1.30, Apr–Oct; Mon–Sat 9–7, Sun 9–1.30, rest of year 💶 Free 🏛 €6.60 🅿 🍴 🛍 🚢 www.gordiola.com

The Gordiola family has been making glass in Mallorca since 1719 and this mock castle on the Palma to Manacor road near Algaida is the best place to see the glassmaking craftsmen in action. In the workshop, which resembles a medieval church, you can watch the workers blowing glass and fashioning it with tongs before placing it in ovens reaching temperatures of over 1,000°C (1,832°F). From the courtyard beyond, steps lead up to the museum where there is an extraordinary collection of glass objects dating back to Egyptian and Roman times, together with more recent examples from Venice, China and elsewhere. Look into the library to see family portraits of the Gordiolas dating from the 18th century to the present day. If you want to take home a souvenir, the extensive gift shop stocks a wide range of Gordiola glass. **Don't miss** The bronze sculpture by Llorenç Roselló in the courtyard depicts a *foner* (Balearic slinger, ▷ 25).

THE SIGHTS

Cala Mondragó is an unspoilt natural park with several small coves to explore. Inset, a rock arch at Es Pontas near Cala Santanyí

RATINGS	
Good for kids	● ● ○
Photo stops	● ● ● ○
Walkability	● ● ○

TIPS
- Cales de Mallorca, north of Cala d'Or, means 'coves of Mallorca', but it is actually an uninspiring holiday resort set around a shopping centre.
- An attractive cove closer to Palma is Cala Pi, south of Llucmajor, where steps lead down to a small beach framed by cliffs on the edge of a wooded gorge. A clifftop path from here leads to Cap Blanc, with fine views of Cabrera (▷ 95) out to sea.
- Santanyí, the main town of the southeast, is a charming place built from the mellow local sandstone that was used in the construction of Palma Cathedral. One of the original town gates has survived, together with sections of the medieval walls. Cafés and bars line the pedestrianized main square, Plaça Major, in front of the church.

THE CALAS

Explore the *calas* (coves) in the southeast corner of Mallorca, where creeks lead to sandy beaches beneath pine-clad cliffs.

Unlike the built-up coastlines of the Bay of Palma and the northeast, the southeast has few long beaches and few major holiday resorts. Instead, from Cala d'Or to Colònia de Sant Jordi, and especially around Santanyí, unspoilt beaches and creeks punctuate the shoreline.

CALA D'OR
✚ 219 H7 🛈 Avinguda Perico Pomar 10 ☎ 971 657463 🕐 Mon–Fri 8.30–2, Sat 9–1 🚌 Buses from Palma via Santanyí
Cala d'Or ('golden cove') is the most southerly resort on the east coast. There are actually several rocky coves here, together with one decent-sized beach, Cala Gran. The whitewashed, flat-roofed houses around the harbour were designed in Ibizan style, and the harbour itself is now a glitzy marina. In summer a miniature road train connects the various parts of the resort as well as the fishing village of Porto Petro, whose harbour is now mostly filled with pleasure boats.

CALA FIGUERA
✚ 219 H8
Sheltering at the end of a long, narrow inlet, Cala Figuera is the archetypal Mediterranean fishing village; white-painted, green-shuttered cottages line the waterfront, and fishermen sit on the slipways mending their nets. Although this is a working port, fish restaurants above the harbour do good business from the crowds of day-trippers. A path leads to the cliffs for views over the harbour. The nearest beaches are found to the south and west, at Cala Santanyí and Cala Llombards.

CALA MONDRAGÓ
✚ 219 H7 🛈 Parc Natural de Mondragó, 5km (3 miles) east of Santanyí ☎ 971 181022 🕐 Daily 9–4 🅿 🍴
A clifftop path links the twin beaches at Cala Mondragó. There are hotels and restaurants beside the northern beach but development has been restricted since the area became a natural park in 1990. The information centre by the car park issues maps of walking routes through dunes, marshland, pine woods, and wild olive groves.

You can ride the waves at Colònia de Sant Jordi's beaches

COLÒNIA DE SANT JORDI

🔲 218 F8 🔳 Carrer Doctor Barraquer, 5 ☎ 971 656073 🚌 Buses from Palma

Beyond the Bay of Palma, this small-scale fishing port and holiday town is the only sizeable settlement along the south coast and the departure point for trips to Cabrera (▷ 95). From the harbour a promenade leads to the main beach, Platja d'es Port; from here you can walk east to a second beach, Es Dolç, which has views of Cabrera. The path continues to Cap de Ses Salines, Mallorca's southernmost point, passing remote beaches. The main draw, however, is Es Trenc, a 3km (2-mile) stretch of fine sand to the west of Colònia de Sant Jordi. Although well known—the beach is popular with nudists and families—it is one of the least developed beaches in Mallorca. To get there, take the road from Colònia de Sant Jordi to Campos and turn left following the signs. You'll pass through the Salines de Llevant, where mountains of rock salt among the marshes make an impressive sight. The road ends at a car park behind Es Trenc (fee payable in summer).

COSTITX

🔲 213 F4

This small village is surrounded by countryside typical of Es Pla (The Plain); explore it on Drive 8 (▷ 152–53). In the village itself, Casa de la Fauna Ibero-Balear (Tue–Fri 9–1.30, also 2nd and 4th Sat and Sun of each month; closed Aug) is a natural history museum in the Casal de Cultura. It is based on the work of a taxidermist who has collected birds, butterflies, mammals, fish, and reptiles representing more than 90 percent of Mallorca's fauna. On a hill above Costitx is Mallorca's astronomical observatory and planetarium (▷ 131).

You'll have to use your imagination to re-live village life at Capocorb Vell in 1000BC

CAPOCORB VELL

An abandoned village near the south coast gives clues to the Mallorcan lifestyle some 3,000 years ago.

🔲 217 E7 ✉ Carretera Llucmajor–Cap Blanc, km23 ☎ 971 180155 🕐 Fri–Wed 10–5 💰 Adult €2 📖 Can be borrowed 🅿 📷 👥 Across road—ask for key at the bar

RATINGS			
Good for kids	●	●	●
Historic interest	●	●	●
Walkability	●	●	●	●

Along with Ses Païsses at Artà (▷ 83), the ruins of Capocorb Vell, 12km (7 miles) south of Llucmajor, are the most significant remains of Mallorca's Talaiotic era (▷ 25). The village was built around 1000BC and inhabited until Roman times. Like other Talaiotic settlements, it was surrounded by walls and dominated by *talaiots*—conical or pyramid-shaped structures that acted both as burial chambers and defensive fortresses. At Capocorb Vell you can see the remains of five *talaiots* (three conical and two pyramidal), as well as 28 dwellings and livestock pens arranged along a prehistoric street. An account of archaeological findings is available at the café, but you will need to use your imagination if you are to conjure up an image of Talaiotic life among the crumbling stone passageways and lanes. The most interesting feature is the large square *talaiot* on the left as you enter the village. You can climb to the top to see the upper room, whose central pillar consists of huge blocks of stone piled one on top of the other. A hole in the floor gives way to a narrow spiral staircase, which leads to an underground chamber roofed with wild olive trunks. This room was almost certainly used for some sort of ritual, religious or funerary function.

Look for Talaiotic megaliths around Capocorb Vell

Coves del Drac and dels Hams

The Fairies' Theatre, Diana's Bath and the Enchanted City: the fantastic natural scenery in these magical underworlds surpasses the work of any architect. Music and lighting enhance Mallorca's most visited attraction.

Cave man: a sightseer gazes at stalactites in the Coves del Drac

Weird and wonderful: the caves were illuminated in 1935

Buïgas worked without payment for 15 months on the lighting

TIPS

● Photography is not allowed inside the caves.
● The paths can be slippery when wet, so wear sensible shoes.
● If the thought of crowds puts you off, consider going on the last tour of the day after most of the tour groups have left.

BASICS

✚ 219 J5
✉ 1km (0.6 mile) south of Porto Cristo overlooking Cala Murta
☎ 971 820753
◷ Tours at 10, 11, 12, 2, 3, 4, 5 daily, Apr–Oct; 10.45, 12, 2, 3.30, rest of year
💷 Adult €8.50, child (under 7) free
📖 €1.50
♿ Disabled WC but no wheelchair access to caves
🅿 ⊞ 🎫 ☐
www.cuevasdeldrac.com

SEEING COVES DEL DRAC

The Coves del Drac (Dragon Caves) are high on the must-see list of every traveller to Mallorca. Although the number of visitors means it can be difficult to appreciate their splendour while surrounded by hundreds of others, a visit to these caves is still a special experience. The hour-long tour begins with a walk along 700m (2,295ft) of underground paths, with stalactites and stalagmites all around you. Once inside the caves there is no easy way out, so think twice about going in if you are claustrophobic or have young children who may get scared. The climax is a magical concert on Lake Martel, Europe's largest underground lake.

HIGHLIGHTS

THE ROCK FORMATIONS

There are hundreds of caves like this throughout Mallorca, but few have been discovered. All have been formed through the gradual filtration of water into the limestone, creating a subterranean landscape in which the imagination runs riot. Many of the rock formations have been given names (The Ruined Castle, Snow-Covered Mountain, Fairies' Theatre, The Pagoda, Small Beach), and if you look carefully you can usually make these images out, but it is just as much fun to make up your own. The guides point out Diana's Bath, where thousands of crystal-white stalactites hang from the roof of the cave, like an intricately carved ivory triptych suspended over a pool. Facing this is the Enchanted City, a forest of stalagmites and pillars. Alongside the path are pools of clear water up to 5m (16.5ft) deep, whose dramatic reflections only increase the sense of walking through a fantasy world.

THE ILLUMINATIONS

Carles Buïgas (1898–1979), an engineer famous for his illuminated fountains for the 1929 World Fair in Barcelona, designed the electric lighting inside the caves in 1935. He returned to the caves in 1950 to update his work, increasing the power supply to 100,000 watts and adding 630m (2,066ft) of cable. In some ways the lighting detracts from the caves' natural beauty, but most people think this is a work of genius, reaching its climax in the artificial sunrise over Lake Martel.

THE CONCERT

The walk ends at an underground amphitheatre beside Lake Martel. An illuminated boat appears out of the darkness and you hear the strains of classical music. On another boat, a quartet is playing *Alborada (Dawn Song)* by Caballero. The musicians continue to play as the boats are rowed across the lake, their lights reflecting thousands of stalactites in the clear water. First held on 9 February 1531 the concert has changed little since, with music by Chopin, Handel, Schubert, and Offenbach's *La Barcarola (The Gondolier's Song)* as a finale.

THE LAKE

After the concert you can cross the lake by boat or walk over the foot-bridge to your right. If you have time to queue, it is worth taking the boat. French speleologist Édouard Martel discovered the lake while studying these caves in 1896 under the sponsorship of Archduke Ludwig Salvator (▷ 30). After paddling across the lake in a canoe, he recorded in his journal that it was 177m (581ft) long, 30m (98ft) wide and up to 9m (29.5ft) deep, with coral-like islands growing out of the lake to meet stalactites from the ceiling, forming columns 'whose beauty had not been touched by any light before ours'.

BACKGROUND

The first written record of the Coves del Drac dates from 1338, when Mallorca's governor wrote to the mayor of Manacor asking him not to impede a group of explorers who wished to search the caves. Talaiotic, Roman and Arab pottery has been found in the caves, suggesting that they may have been inhabited in pre-historic times. Following the Catalan conquest, treasure-hunters explored the caves, hoping that fleeing Moors had hidden gold there. By this time they were known as the Dragon Caves, possibly after the mythological dragon that appears in Mallorcan folklore as a guardian of treasure. First mapped in 1880, it was not until 1896, with the discovery of Lake Martel, that their full extent was revealed. In 1922 they were bought by lawyer Joan Servera Camps and developed for tourism. The installation of lighting turned the natural phenomenon into a busy tourist attraction.

Jaume Vadell conducted the orchestra at Lake Martel for 47 years and 30,000 concerts

MORE TO SEE

COVES DELS HAMS

✚ 219 J5 ✉ Carretera Porto Cristo–Manacor ☎ 971 820988 ◷ Daily 10–5.30, Apr–Oct; 11–4.30, rest of year 🎫 Adult €9.80, child (under 12) free
🅿 ♿ 🎁 🚻

www.cuevas-hams.com

If you want to avoid the crowds, these caverns on the edge of Porto Cristo make a good alternative. Pedro Caldentey, whose son provided the illumination, discovered them in 1905. The name of the caves means 'fish hooks'— and you can see why in the chamber known as Dream of an Angel, where thousands of fish-hook stalactites hang from the ceiling. The largest cave is known as Lost Paradise. Although there is no theatre here, the guided tour does include a brief concert on the Sea of Venice, and there is an underground lake filled with sea water.

The banqueting hall at 18th-century Els Calderers

You can't miss the church of Sant Miquel in Felanitx

A craftsman cuts out a jacket at a leather factory in Inca

ELS CALDERERS

✚ 218 G5 ✉ Signposted from Carretera Palma–Manacor, 37km (23 miles) ☎ 971 526069 🕐 Daily 10–6, Apr–Oct; 10–5, rest of year 💶 Adult €7, child (3–12) €3.50 🅿 ♿ 🍴 🛍 www.todoesp.es/els-calderers

This ivy-covered manor house on the edge of Sant Joan has been restored as an example of 18th-century aristocratic Mallorcan life. The first records of Els Calderers go back to 1285, when the manor belonged to the Calderers family, but the present building dates from 1750. You enter via a small staircase flanked by stone lions. The ground-floor rooms are arranged around a courtyard, beginning with the reception rooms, a private chapel and a wine cellar to the right. The master's sitting room, with armchairs in front of the fire, is where the owner of the estate would make conversation with his gentleman friends; the ladies, by contrast, were expected to indulge in music and sewing in the mistress's room. On the first floor are the bedrooms and servants' quarters, along with a large pillared granary where produce from the farm is still kept. The shop sells wine and jam, and offers tastings of *sobrasada* sausage.

Don't miss Stroll around the gardens where there are indigenous farm animals, chicken coops, stables, orange and carob trees, and shady picnic areas.

FELANITX

✚ 219 H6 🚌 Buses from Palma
❓ Market Sun

Felanitx, the main town of southeast Mallorca, is easily overlooked but fully rewards a short visit—particularly on a Sunday morning when local pottery is displayed on the church steps during the lively weekly market. The 17th-century church of Sant Miquel, reached by a monumental baroque stairway, dominates the town. Felanitx's coat of arms is carved on the tympanum above the door, and farther up, beneath the rose window, is a sculptural relief of St. Michael trampling the Devil underfoot. Devils are also in evidence at the town's big festival, held on or around 28 August, when children dressed as hobby-horses are chased through the streets by *dimonis* (devils) and *capgrossos* (bigheads) to the accompaniment of bagpipes and flutes. Just outside Felanitx is the Santuari de Sant Salvador (▷ 102).

INCA

✚ 213 F3 🚋 From Palma
❓ Market Thu

Many people visit the leather factories on the outskirts of Inca (▷ 131), but few people make it to the centre of Mallorca's third-largest town. If you arrive by train, walk down Avinguda Bisbe Llompart, opposite the station, and continue to the town hall on Plaça d'Espanya. On your right is Café Mercantil, which opened in 1936 as a meeting place for merchants and shoemakers during Inca's first period of industrial and economic expansion. At one stage it had a ballroom, a string quartet and piano concerts, and it is still a good place to sink into a leather armchair and read the papers over a coffee. Near here are several good pastry shops, including Ca'n Delante at Carrer Major 27. The main street, Carrer Major, continues to the 18th-century parish church of Santa Maria La Mayor, with its distinctive separate belltower from an earlier church. On Thursday mornings Mallorca's biggest weekly market takes place in the streets around the church.

MANACOR

✚ 219 H5 🚋 From Palma and Inca
❓ Market Mon

Mallorca's second-largest town—at first sight an ugly, sprawling place of ring roads, traffic jams and industrial estates—is known for its artificial pearl factories (▷ 132). The best known of these, Majórica, clearly signposted as you enter the town from Palma, offers intriguing tours of the production process (Mon–Fri 9–7, Sat–Sun 10–1).

The town centre is based around the parish church of Nostra Senyora dels Dolors (Our Lady of the Sorrows), whose minaret-like tower is a reminder that it was built on the site of a mosque.

About 1km (0.6 mile) out of town on the road to Cales de Mallorca is Torre dels Enagistes, a 14th-century fortified tower now housing a small archaeological museum (Mon–Fri 10–2).

Faking it: strings of artificial pearls are made in Manacor

Born in this basic house in Petra, Junípero Serra, right, founded the missions which grew into some of America's biggest cities

PETRA

The shrine to one of the greatest Mallorcans of all time is in this quiet, rural town, which is blessed with good restaurants.

Apart from a few modern cafés on the shady main square, Petra is much the same sleepy little village in which Junípero Serra (▷ 29) grew up in the 18th century. A statue of Serra stands on Plaça Junípero Serra and a plaque on the parish church pays tribute to this 'explorer, missionary, hero, civilizer born in the light of Spain'.

THE HOUSE AND MUSEUM
Junípero Serra was born in 1713 in a small house on Carrer Barracar Alt. To visit the house and the neighbouring museum, go to the caretaker's house around the corner at Carrer Barracar Baix 2. He will let you in and ask for a small donation. The house, with its arched doorway and whitewashed walls, is a typical rural 18th-century home. In 1932 it was bought by the Rotary Club of Mallorca and given to the city of San Francisco, who returned it to Petra in 1981.

THE CONVENT
A street of baked-earth houses, clad with bougainvillea, runs from the museum to the San Bernardino convent, where Serra went to school. Along here majolica panels depict the missions founded by Serra, including San Diego and San Francisco. Ring the bell to be let into the convent (daily 10–12.30, 4–5.30). Here, a series of tableaux tells Serra's life story—working on the farm in Petra, preaching at Ermita de Bonany, his first mission at San Diego, and his first baptism of a Native American, whom he named Bernardino after this convent.

ERMITA DE BONANY
➕ 218 G5
Serra preached his last sermon in Mallorca at this hilltop hermitage 4km (2.5 miles) from Petra, reached by a snaking lane. With an old well on the patio and palm trees all around, this could be one of his missions in California. It takes its name from the *bon any* (good year) of 1609, when the villagers made a pilgrimage here during a drought: their prayers were answered by rain. The views from the terrace at sunset are magical. You can stay the night in one of the basic cells.

RATINGS
Good for kids	●●
Historic interest	●●●
Photo stops	●●●●

TIPS
● Follow the signs in the town centre to Es Celler (▷ 175), one of Mallorca's best traditional cellar restaurants.
● Signs also point the way to Bodegues Miquel Oliver, Carrer Font 26 (Mon–Fri 9–1, 2.30–6.30), which sells good local wines.

BASICS
➕ 214 G4
🚌 Buses from Palma
🚆 From Palma and Inca
❓ Market Wed

Shop for fruit, vegetables or livestoock at Sineu's market

SANTUARI DE SANT SALVADOR

✠ 219 H6 ✉ Puig de Sant Salvador, 5km (3 miles) southeast of Felanitx
☎ 971 827282 🅿 🍴 🖵

Founded in 1348 and rebuilt in the 17th century, the monastery is dramatically perched on the highest summit of the Serra de Llevant (509m/1,679ft). The road to the peak passes a cave chapel where a statue of the Virgin (now kept in the church) is said to have been discovered in the 15th century. The approach to the monastery is marked by two enormous monuments, a 14m-high (46ft) stone cross and a 35m-high (115ft) statue of Christ. The gatehouse's walls are hung with jerseys of seven-times world cycling champion Guillem Timoner, while a chapel to the left has mementoes left behind by pilgrims. From a terrace below the statue of Christ you can see the ruins of Castell de Santueri, a 14th-century castle on the site of an Arab fortress some 4km (2.5 miles) to the south; it is possible to walk to the castle from here.

SINEU

✠ 214 F4 🚂 From Palma and Inca
❓ Market Wed

With a royal heritage dating back to the 14th century, Sineu is one of Mallorca's oldest towns, yet its buzzy galleries and cafés give it a modern feel. On Wednesdays the only country market at which livestock is sold, comes to town. Arrive early to see farmers haggling over pigs, chickens and sheep before heading for the *cellar* restaurants to eat *frit de porcella* (▷ 162). Notice the winged lion of St. Mark, Sineu's patron saint, at the top of the steps of the church of Santa Maria. The old railway station houses the S'Estació art gallery (Mon–Fri 9.30–2.30, 4–7).

Closer to heaven: Ramón Llull's monastery on Puig de Randa

SANTUARI DE CURA

High up on the summit of Puig de Randa, hermit Ramon Llull is remembered at Mallorca's first monastery.

✠ 218 F5 ✉ Puig de Randa, 9km (6 miles) south of Algaida ☎ 971 120260 🕐 Daily 10–6 🎫 Free
🛐 Mass Sat 7.30pm, Sun noon 🅿 🏛 🍴 🖵 Closed Mon
🍴 Closed Mon
www.mallorcaweb.net/santdecura

RATINGS	
Good for kids	●●
Historic interest	●●●
Photo stops	●●●●

Puig de Randa rises 543m (1,781ft) out of the plain above the pretty village of Randa. The table mountain has been a place of pilgrimage ever since Ramón Llull (▷ 27) founded Mallorca's first hermitage on the summit in 1275, following the Catalan's conversion from a dissolute, agnostic life to devout Catholicism. On the lower slopes of the mountain are two other sanctuaries, Nostra Senyora de Gràcia (clinging precariously to the cliff face) and Ermita de Sant Honorat.

Passing through a 17th-century doorway, you enter Santuari de Cura, on the site of Llull's original hermitage. Nothing remains from that time and most of the monastery was rebuilt in the 20th century after the arrival of Franciscan monks, who have been living here since 1913. The chapel on the right mostly dates from the 17th century; a crib is kept here throughout the year, according to Franciscan tradition, and there is a small statue of the Virgin carved out of Santanyí stone.

The Sala Gramàtica (Mon–Sat 10–1, 4–6, Sun 4–6), the former grammar school hall, is one of the oldest parts of the complex. It now houses a museum devoted to Ramón Llull, with copies of his manuscripts and various religious paintings. Outside there are peaceful gardens but most people head straight for the belvederes, which offer some of the best views in Mallorca.

To the west you can see Palma and occasionally Ibiza beyond; to the south there are dreamy views of Cabrera. From the viewpoint behind the monastery you can see almost the whole island, from the Serra de Tramuntana, Cap de Formentor and the bay of Pollença to the hills around Artà in the east. Look carefully and you can spy various towns and villages, such as Inca and Petra.

THE SIGHTS

This chapter gives information on things to do in Mallorca, other than sightseeing. Mallorca's best shops, arts venues, nightlife, activities and events are listed region by region.

What to Do

SHOPPING

Whether it's an early-morning visit to the local bakery for freshly baked pastries or a search for shoes on Palma's Avinguda Jaime III, shopping in Mallorca tends to be an enjoyable experience. Although there are chain stores and supermarkets everywhere, catering to the thousands of visitors, it pays to seek out the independent local shops and boutiques. Here you'll find some interesting specialities, enjoy a more personalized service and, more importantly, get an insight into the pace of Mallorcan life.

🎁 Shopping
🎭 Entertainment
🍸 Nightlife
⚽ Sports
✚ Activities
♥ Health and Beauty
👶 For Children

Bring your credit card: Palma is a great place for window shopping

LEATHER
Spain has a reputation for well-made, competitively priced leather goods, including bags, footwear and clothing, and much of it once came from Mallorca. Footwear, notably Camper shoes, is still made on the island, but not to the same extent. Inca is regarded as the island's leather capital, with numerous factory outlets, but you can buy leather goods all over the island at similar prices; Palma is just as good a place to browse. Hip footwear from Camper is also ubiquitous, and there are several Camper-only shops, such as the brand's factory outlet in Inca. The Sóller-based cobbler Ben

Calçat (▷ 123) is one of the few craftsmen still making traditional Mallorcan sandals, which make interesting reminders of your holiday.

PEARLS
One of Mallorca's few surviving traditional industries, the manufacture of artificial pearls, centres on Manacor and is dominated by Orquidea and Majorica (▷ 132). You can see jewellery being crafted in the factories but not the actual process of making the pearls. Manmade pearls are more durable than the real thing, but don't expect them to be cheap—a small item, such as a pair of earrings, will cost at least €20.

FOOD AND DRINK
A few of the Mallorcan specialities detailed on page 162 travel well enough to make the trip home. Bottles of good Mallorcan wine (▷ 163) from Binissalem or the Mallorcan aperitif *herbes* are the obvious examples. Expect to spend about €10 on a respectable wine in the wine shops of Palma. In the *bodegas* of Binissalem and the Pla I Llevant, the two key areas of viniculture, you can try before you buy. Some foods also make good souvenirs: the spicy sausage *sobrasada*, for example, or jars of preserved fruits. If you do intend to take food home with you, check your country's customs regulations.

SOUVENIRS
You'll find all the usual things in the souvenir shops in the resorts: towels, T-shirts and the like. But the most authentically Mallorcan souvenir is the *siurell,* a small clay whistle typically painted white with dabs of red and green. They've been made in Mallorca since Arabs occupied the island in the 10th century. A variety of shapes, such as a figure of a man riding a horse or playing a guitar, are produced.

CERAMICS
Marratxí, in central Mallorca, is the heart of Mallorca's pottery industry. It is here that the cheap and cheerful *siurells* are produced, but other ceramics are also made in the area's factories, including crockery, tiles and garden ornaments. These

WHAT TO DO

are sold in numerous outlets across the island, ranging from unmissable roadside emporiums to designer boutiques in towns such as Artà. An annual craft fair, Baleart, is held in Palma in December (▷ 133).

GLASS

Algaida's Gordiola glassworks (▷ 130) and the Lafiore factory shop near Valldemossa are the best sources of Mallorca's famous glassware. Their collections are huge, from pots and vases to ornaments and tableware. Quality is high and you can watch the glassblowers at work at both places. Designs range from the traditional to the avant-garde, so there is something for all tastes.

Colourful glassware is a Mallorcan speciality

OLIVE WOOD

It's hard to equate the relatively small olive tree plantations in Mallorca with the enormous quantity of olive wood products sold in the island. Plates, bowls, utensils and carvings—all are piled high and sold reasonably cheaply across Mallorca. The biggest shops are on the outskirts of Manacor. Olive wood makes for a durable, good-looking souvenir, but there are varying degrees of finishing quality. It's worth paying a little more for products that display some form of craftmanship, rather than the rougher, mass-produced items. Olive wood requires special care.

WHERE TO SHOP

Palma offers the most diverse shopping opportunities in Mallorca. Indeed, its assortment of shops rivals other major Spanish cities such as Barcelona and Madrid. Designer boutiques, antiques shops, souvenir shops and tempting delicatessens: Palma has them all in a relatively compact area. The capital's principal shopping areas border Avinguda Jaime III and extend throughout the pedestrianized zones just east of the city centre. Other Mallorcan towns may offer a less glossy shopping experience, but a brief exploration often yields some rewarding results: the Finca Gourmet delicatessen in Sóller, or the art galleries of Artà for example. Only in the biggest resorts is there a degree of mundanity.

MARKETS

Business starts early in the morning at Mallorca's weekly markets and most deals are are concluded in time for lunch. If you're self-catering they're a good way of buying fresh, local produce.
Monday: Caimari, Calvià, Manacor, Montuïri
Tuesday: Alcúdia, Artà, Campanet, Llubi, Porreres
Wednesday: Andratx, Capdepera, Llucmajor, Petra, Port de Pollença, Santanyí, Selva, Sineu
Thursday: Campos, Deià, Inca, Sant Llorenç
Friday: Algaida, Binissalem, Can Picafort, Son Servera
Saturday: Bunyola, Cala Rajada, Lloseta, Palma, Sóller
Sunday: Alcúdia, Felanitx, Muro, Pollença, Sa Pobla, Valldemossa

DEPARTMENT AND CHAIN STORES

Spain's leading department store, El Corte Inglés, can be found in Palma, along with other top Spanish chain stores: Zara for clothing and Camper for shoes. Outside the city cen-

tre large supermarkets, such as Decachlon, sell everything from bicycles to cheese. These, and the department stores, tend to open all day, every day.

SHOPPING MALLS AND FACTORY OUTLETS

Shopping malls have yet to colonize Mallorca—the only major out-of-town mall is the modern Festival Park complex north of Palma. So-called factory outlets are more common, selling leather in Inca and pearls in Manacor, among other items. They are not necessarily a guarantee of the lowest prices and not all the goods sold are manufactured in Mallorca, but they are accessible and can offer good value.

Bargain hunting for leatherwear in a factory outlet in Inca

HOURS AND PAYMENT

Typical opening hours are 10–1pm and 4.30–8pm, Monday to Friday, but many of the larger stores in the busier shopping areas (such as central Palma) forego the mid-afternoon siesta and open from 10 to 7pm. Many shops only open for the morning on Saturdays and most remain closed on Sundays. For all-night chemists see page 198.

Generally, all larger shops accept credit cards but it is wise to have euros available when shopping in smaller stores. Most smaller shops and boutiques, not to mention market traders, prefer to be paid in cash.

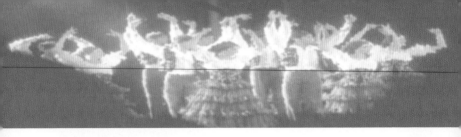

ENTERTAINMENT

Mallorca's two stylish new auditoriums, Sa Màniga in Cala Millor and Auditori d'Alcúdia, demonstrate the fact that the island is serious about widening its cultural horizons. Both venues, together with Palma's large auditorium, offer a varied menu of live music, theatre, ballet and opera, plus children's activities, films and workshops. It's all far from the stereotype clubbing scene—although it's not hard to find that too, particularly in Palma.

WHAT TO DO

CINEMA
Cinema is not a significant part of Mallorca's cultural life. Excellent modern screens at the Festival Park complex (▷ 131) show the latest blockbusters, and Mallorca's three main auditoriums often screen films (usually arthouse fare and Spanish films), but don't

Classical music festivals can be found across Mallorca

expect there to be a cinema in every town.

LIVE MUSIC
For all Mallorca's reputation as a clubbing mecca, there's enough live music to satisfy the most demanding and eclectic ears. The island's three auditoriums stage operas and classical concerts by visiting orchestras and groups throughout the year. Palma's own Balearic Symphony Orchestra (www.simfonica-de-balears.com) performs an annual season in the city and tours the island. The biggest dates in the classical calendar are the series of performances during the annual festival

Noches Mediterraneas at Costa Nord (▷ 81). But folk music is the traditional sound of Mallorca. Costa Nord, Son Marroig and La Granja periodically hold folk-music concerts and you may hear local musicians in village bars.

After-dinner shows are not a Mallorcan tradition, but they have caught on in recent years. Most resorts offer some sort of entertainment but the most famous shows are the Pirates spectacle and the cabaret of Son Amar, which run during the summer months. Prices often include meals, but may still be relatively high. Troupes of acrobats and magicians are not for everyone, and those who prefer jazz or the blues will find a pair of good venues in Palma. Live music performances in bars and clubs generally start late; at Bluesville in Palma acts arrive at midnight.

THEATRE
Several of the theatres in Mallorca have interesting programmes throughout the year. Artà theatre is noted for contemporary drama, while Palma's theatres offer a wide range of drama productions, with the Teatre Principal veering towards more traditional material.

Mallorca's theatres and arts centres also organize a large number of activities for children, particularly during the summer when demand for plays dwindles. Smoking is not allowed in the auditoriums, but most venues have bars that permit smoking.

WHAT'S ON
Major cultural events, such as Palma's ballet season and Castell Bellver's music festival (▷ 133), are listed in *Where To Go,* a quarterly booklet produced by the Balearic Isles' tourist board. You can pick one up from any tourist information office. Also check the English language *Majorca Daily Bulletin* newspaper (www.majorcadailybulletin.es), the website of the Balearic Isles' tourist board (www.visitbalears.com) and the website of Palma's city council (www.a-palma.es), all of which have detailed

Live music is staged in bars, clubs, theatres and cabarets

calendars of events. Rock, blues and jazz events, and much more, are advertized in the free *Youthing Guia de Mallorca* magazine, available from bars, cafés and venues.

TICKETS
For visitors to Mallorca, buying tickets directly from the venue's box office is the simplest plan. Credit cards are widely accepted, although a booking fee may be added. Prices vary considerably according to the show and other factors. The upper price limit is generally €50, with most theatre and concert tickets being considerably cheaper.

NIGHTLIFE

Mallorca's nightlife is most notorious for the raucous all-night hedonism of resorts such as S'Arenal and Magaluf. In reality it is generally more sophisticated than that, with lots to interest visitors of all ages during the summer months.

WHERE

Palma is home to a thriving (and imported) *tapas* bar culture centred in La Llotja. After grazing at a few haunts, people often move on to a bar for drinks or one of Palma's celebrated nightclubs. Thanks to the compact city centre, the geography of a night out is simple and most of the time you can walk from one area to another. As well as the concentration of *tapas* bars in La

Party people: Palma is the clubbing capital of Mallorca

Llotja, Santa Catalina to the west is an up-and-coming neighbourhood of bars, clubs and restaurants. Palma's biggest clubs are on the Passeig Marítim to the south of La Llotja and Santa Catalina.

On the western side of Palma's bay, Magaluf, home to one of Europe's biggest nightclubs, has a well-deserved reputation for a beer-fuelled nightlife for the under 30s. In Mallorca it is matched only by S'Arenal on the opposite side of the bay. S'Arenal is as German as Magaluf is British.

Nightlife in the heights of the Serra de Tramuntana and the central plains is quiet, consisting mainly of village bars.

There's more going on in the coastal towns, such as Port de Sóller and Port d'Alcudia, and things pick up in the resorts of the Cala d'Or and Cala Millor along the east coast.

We've recommended specific bars in Palma and well-established bars elsewhere, but in the main resorts bars change name and ownership with such frequency that recommendations would be meaningless—the best tactic is to try a few venues before settling on a favourite. In the resorts, bars often have a similar ambience; most have a television on and a selection of imported and Spanish beers. Many run drinks promotions during the busiest (and most competitive) months to lure customers inside.

WHEN

In Mallorca nightlife really means nightlife. A typical night out won't begin earlier than 9pm, starting with a visit to a *tapas* bar or restaurant. Serious bar-hopping begins at 11pm. Nightclubs open their doors by 12am, but clubbers won't start arriving until 1am and the party will peak at 3–4am. Doors close at 5–6am but some clubbers see in the new day with a *xocolata* (hot chocolate) and a pastry at a café before heading to bed. Most resort bars open from April to October, with only bars and clubs in Palma remaining open during the winter.

WHAT'S ON

Most clubs advertize specific events with flyers and posters. Sometimes presenting a flyer on entry will gain clubbers a reduced entry fee or a free drink. Events with famous acts

may be listed in the *Majorca Daily Bulletin* newspaper (www.majorcadailybulletin.es), on the website of the Balearic Isles' tourist board (www.visit-balears.com) or on the website of Palma's city council (www.a-palma.es).

Entry to bars and *tapas* bars is typically free, but nightclubs usually charge for entry, which can cost as much as €10–€20 at weekends. Many places offer special discounts, from free drinks to free admittance for women—these vary according to the night of the week, or the time of evening. Bars with live music may make a small

Many gay bars and clubs have a late-night cabaret show

additional charge. Spain's minimum legal drinking age is 16, but most nightclubs are for over-18s only.

GAY MALLORCA

The centre of Palma's gay and lesbian scene is Plaça Gomila to the west of the city centre, below Bellver castle. There are several gay bars and clubs on Avinguda Joan Miró, the oldest of which is the Black Cat. Ben Amics, the Gay and Lesbian Association of the Balearics, provides an information service on Thursdays (6–9) for locals and visitors: tel 971 715670 or visit www.benamics. com. Outside Palma, a few gay beaches are well established.

SPORTS AND ACTIVITIES

One of Mallorca's greatest strengths is the choice of outdoor activities available to visitors. Many people make the trip to Mallorca to pursue specific interests—golf, cycling and sailing—throughout the year. Resorts offer a number of activities to holidaymakers, from tennis and beach volleyball to water-skiing. Spectator sports are rather more limited. Mallorca has a Primera Liga football team with a stadium north of Palma and two racecourses. Several glitzy yachting events are held during the summer and the Tour of Mallorca is a winter cycling event.

BEACHES

There are more than 80 beaches along the Mallorcan coastline. They vary considerably; many are jam-packed with tourists during the summer and intensively developed but it is still possible to find relatively quiet and secluded beaches even in busy areas, such as Cala Mondragó (▷ 96) or Cala D'Or. Many of the busier beaches offer a number of activities—anything from volleyball contests to paragliding behind a motorboat or water

Two wheels good: use quiet lanes to see the countryside by bicycle

skiing. During the summer, when they are rigorously maintained, Mallorca's beaches have a reputation for cleanliness. Indeed, 51 beaches and 8 marinas were awarded Blue Flags (www.blueflag.org) for water quality, safety and eco-friendliness in 2004.

Note that the following beaches are nudist: Dique del Oeste and Cala Portals Vells in the southwest; S'Agulló in the northeast; Punta de n'Amer in the east; and Es Trenc, Cala Blava, El Bosque and Es Carnatge in the south and southeast.

BULLFIGHTING

Bullfighting is not followed as avidly in Mallorca as it is on the mainland, but there are several bullrings on the island. The format of the fights remains the same: after a horseback procession (*corrida*) into the ring, the bull is softened up by picadores before the matador moves to the centre of the stage. Palma's bullring (▷ 119) is the island's principal arena, but you'll also find a Plaça de Toros in Alcúdia, Felanitx, Inca and Muro.

CYCLING

Cycling, with golf and sailing, is one of Mallorca's three most popular sports. Every winter and spring thousands of keen cyclists arrive on the island for pre-season training. The island's long cycling history, starts with the first winter Tour of Mallorca in 1913, an annual five-day event taking place in February. Cyclists come to Mallorca for the diversity of terrain. In the morning you can inch up the long mountain roads of the Serra de Tramuntana and in the afternoon you can speed through the flat landscape of Es Pla.

Through a Balearic Islands' government scheme (▷ 194), 37 hotels are committed to

welcoming cyclists and their bicycles. They must each have an information area with route maps, a maintenance area and access to physiotherapists and masseurs. Bicycles are offered for hire, although most guests bring their own. The local government has also extended a network of cycle routes across the island. The signposted routes take riders past sites of interest on quiet roads or cycle paths. With Mallorcan villages less than 10km (6 miles) apart, there is always a place to stop for refreshments. A local tourist information office will provide route maps of bicycle rides in the region.

To hire a bicycle ask in a tourist information office for a

Get in the swing: Mallorca is a top destination for golfers

local hire firm. Some of the larger operators, who can supply bicycles of several styles across the island, are included in the listings, but most towns and many of the hotels have bicycles available for hire. Serious riders fly out their own bicycles to Mallorca. Ensure the bicycle is properly boxed or bagged for transit and note that some airlines will charge a fee for carrying it. Palma airport is very experienced and well-organized in dealing with oversized luggage.
Federación de Ciclisme de les Illes Balears, Francesc Fiol I Juan, 2, 07010 Palma
Tel 971 757628
www.webfcib.org

FISHING
Mallorca is not renowned for its fishing and although towns such as Port de Sóller and even Palma remain active ports, few people visit Mallorca specifically to go fishing. However, day trips can be organized in the ports; for local operators ask in a tourist information office.
Federación Balear de Pesca y Casting, Avinguda Joan Miró, 327, 07015 Palma
Tel 971 702088

FOOTBALL
Mallorca's football team (▷ 22) is one of the best in Spain; the team plays at the Son Moix stadium (▷ 118) to the north of Palma. It's the only option for watching first-class football on the island. The Spanish football season runs between September and the end of May. Tickets are generally available on the day for all but the biggest matches.

GOLF
There are 20 golf courses on the island—a remarkably high number for such a small place, and more are being developed. Most are of average difficulty, but the chief attraction is the variety: there are courses in the mountains, courses by the beach, courses in the city and courses on the plains. Another advantage is the mild climate—golfers, like cyclists, avoid the scorching summer months and arrive chiefly during spring and autumn. The courses themselves are invariably attractive, often with pine, almond and olive tree woodland, white-sand bunkers and water hazards. Clubs accredited by the Balearic Islands' government have a minimum of 25 buggies and trolleys and ensure players start with a gap of at least eight minutes between each group. Such clubs also have practice areas and P.G.A.-qualified instructors.
Federación Balear de Golf,

Avinguda Jaume III, 17, 07012 Palma
Tel 971 722753
www.fbgolf.com

HANG-GLIDING
Areas suitable for hang-gliding include Alcúdia, Artà, Bunyola, Inca, Pollença, Petra and Sa Calobra. It is recommended that pilots contact the Club de Vuelo Libre Mallorca for advice before setting off.
Club de Vuelo Libre Mallorca, Tel 655 766443; 871 950 859
www.cvlmallorca.com

HIKING
Year on year, through autumn, winter and spring, Mallorca has attracted ever-increasing numbers of hikers. They come to

Step by step: well-maintained footpaths lace the mountains

explore the Serra de Tramuntana and the beautiful trails that thread through the mountains and gorges. The government-funded Dry Stone Route project (Ruta de Pedra Sec) will see six renovated lodges offer overnight accommodation to walkers. There are currently two lodges (▷ 122). Specialist tour operators, such as Inntravel (▷ 158) in the UK, offer walking holidays.

Even if you're interested only in going for a day walk it pays to be prepared. Remember that the Serra de Tramuntana can be difficult mountain terrain. Always wear supportive footwear and carry a waterproof jacket and some food

and water. The tourist information offices in Pollença (tel 971 535077) and Sóller (tel 971 638008) can offer advice on safe and accessible routes.

HORSE RIDING

Horse riding is a very popular activity in Mallorca. Several riding schools and ranches, such as Son Menut (▷ 131) in Felanitx, exist to take visitors on hacks or provide tuition in disciplines such as jumping and dressage and are happy to look after inexperienced riders. The centres provide all necessary equipment and sometimes food and accommodation for multi-day rides.

You can also watch horse racing at Mallorca's two race

Saddle up for horse-riding excursions and lessons

courses; the most common events are trotting races.
Federación Balear de Hípica, Avinguda Dalias, 3B, 07193 Palmanyola
Tel 971 617730
www.fhib.org

KAYAKING

Sea-kayaking is a relaxing way of exploring some of Mallorca's hidden bays and in calm conditions is easily mastered. Several yacht clubs around the island offer kayaks for hire, with or without a guide or tuition.
Federación Balear de Piragüismo, Avinguda Joan Miró, 327, 07015 Palma
Tel 971 702019

ROCK CLIMBING

Mallorca's varied crags and cliffs attract rock climbers from across Europe. The local climbing scene is undeveloped, but a little research before departure will reveal hotspots, such as Fraguel near Bunyola. Other good areas include Alaró, Caimari, Valldemossa, Santanyí and some sea cliffs. Climbing is possible all year round, but March, April, October and November are the most suitable months.
Federación Balear de Montañismo, Carrer Francesc Sitjar, 1, 07010 Palma
Tel 971 291347

SAILING AND WINDSURFIING

Yacht charter is an increasingly widespread way of holidaying and many sailors use Mallorca as a base. Palma, after all, is the yachting capital of the Mediterranean. You can charter a yacht or motorboat with or without a skipper. Prices vary according to the boat, the season and several other factors. Alternatively, there are more than 40 marinas and 30 sailing clubs and many have operators who take visitors on day-long sailing trips, an excellent way to get a taste of yachting and see the island from another perspective. The Asociación Provincial de Empresarios de Actividades Marítimas de Baleares (www.apeam.com) is the trade association for larger yacht charter firms, with listings of many that operate from Mallorca.

Sailing is the island's most prestigious sport with events such as the Copa del Rey regatta attracting royal participants and some of the world's top sailors. But there's more to sailing here than money and mega-yachts. Many of the resorts, such as Port de Pollença, have dinghies and small catamarans on the beach available for hire and the sheltered bays are perfect for

learning the basics.
Windsurfing is also widely available at the larger sailing clubs, although the wind is not strong or consistent enough to attract expert windsurfers. The best stretch of coast is around Sa Ràpita on the south coast.
Federación Balear de Vela, Avinguda Joan Miró, 327, 07015 Palma
Tel 971 402412
www.federacionbalearvela.com

SCUBA DIVING

With water temperatures ranging from 10°C (50°F) in the winter to 25°C (77°F) in the summer, Mallorca is a justifiably popular destination for scuba divers. It's great for beginners too, because condi-

Cast away: sailors flock to Mallorca's Mediterranean coast

tions are generally forgiving and visibility good. Most of the coastal resorts have a scuba dive outfit (locations covered in the listings include Port de Sóller, Port de Pollença, Port d'Alcudia and Son Servera). Equipment and tuition by qualified instructors is usually available but note that dive insurance is compulsory in Spain. It may be covered by membership of an association such as BSAC (British Sub Aqua Club). Due to the competition between the dive outfits standards are generally high, with experienced guides and well-maintained equipment. Divers can expect to see several varieties of fish,

including conger, but there is not the profusion of fish you find at reefs. For experienced divers several operators offer wreck diving, night diving and cave diving. If you have diving certification, don't forget to bring it with you.

Snorkelling is a simple alternative to scuba diving, requiring just a mask, snorkel and perhaps fins. Mallorca's warm, shallow waters are perfect for snorkelling but don't forget to apply a high-factor waterproof sunscreen regularly.
Federación Balear de Actividades Subacuáticas, Polideportivo Son Moix, Camí La Vileta, 40, 07011 Palma
Tel 971 288242

HEALTH AND BEAUTY

Until recently, Mallorca was not an obvious choice for a pampering break. But the spa trend has reached the island and with the rise of European budget airlines flying to Palma, it is now possible to check into a chic spa for a couple of days of self-indulgent health and beauty treatments. Many of the top hotels offer some sort of spa experience, from just a jacuzzi and steam room to a full-on battery of treatments and gym equipment.

Unsurprisingly, the rise in the number of spas mirrors the number of new golf courses on the island; most of the major golf resorts have a spa for golf widows to enjoy while their partners are out on the course. Some of the luxury hotels with spas are listed below; most will have day

will find a municipal sports centre in most medium-sized towns. There are also a number of smart private health and fitness centres, such as Nord Esport in Pollença, which are listed in the regional sections.

Palma is the best place to get a stylish haircut, with several chains of Spanish hair

Scuba divers can explore underwater caves with trained guides

Relax with beauty treatments at Mallorca's collection of new spas

SWIMMING
There are 30 public swimming pools on the island. Most are in municipal sports centres. Note that a small number are outdoor pools and some of those may not be heated.
Federación Balear de Natación, Piscinas Son Hugo, Carrer Teniente Oyaga, 07004 Palma
Tel 971 764624
www.fbnatacion.com

TENNIS
Most towns have tennis courts, usually as part of the sports centre and available for a fee.
Federación Balear de Tenis, Avinguda Alemanya, 11, 07003 Palma
Tel 971 720956

passes available to visitors. Good-value deals, including accommodation and spa short breaks, are likely to be available in the low season (from October to April) and will be advertized on the hotels' websites.

So far there are few dedicated spas outside the hotels but as Mallorca moves upmarket you can be sure that more will appear. Thalassotherapy is tipped to be an increasingly popular treatment, with several spas, such as Altira Spa at the Mardavall hotel, already offering Mediterranean seawater and seaweed therapies.

Few people go to Mallorca and head straight into a gym but those that are so inclined

salons in the Mallorcan capital. But most resorts will have hair and beauty salons.

SPA HOTELS
Arabella Son Vida, Palma
Tel 971 787100 (▷ 180)
Balneari Sant Joan de sa Font Santa, Campos
Tel 971 655016
Hotel Dorint, Camp de Mar
Tel 971 136565
Illa D'Or, Port de Pollença
Tel 971 865100 (▷ 190)
La Residencia, Deià
Tel 971 639011 (▷ 185)
Hotel Mardavall, Son Caliu
Tel 971 629400 (▷ 182)
Marriot Son Antem, Llucmajor
Tel 971 129100 (▷ 192)
Gran Hotel Sóller, Sóller
Tel 971 638686 (▷ 187)

FOR CHILDREN

Mallorca has plenty for children and parents to appreciate. Many of the beaches are gently shelving, with shallows for children to play in. And during the summer high season the beaches are regularly cleaned. Resorts usually have a programme of supervised activities and areas, including swimming pools, for children of all ages. Check with your travel agent or the hotel before booking if you want specific services such as a nursery or babysitting.

Water slides and theme parks are favourites with children of all ages

Most interests are catered for. Sporty children (and their parents) will enjoy the island's outstanding mini-golf courses and the go-karting tracks in Magaluf and Arenal. A group of water parks—Aquapark, Aquacity, Hidropark—and the Western Park theme park offer high-octane excitement with water slides and rides, and will be packed with families in July and August.

Animals are central to several attractions: there are performing dolphins at Marineland (▷ 120), llamas and boar at Jumaica (▷ 130), wild animals at Auto-Safari (▷ 127) and fish at Mallorca's aquarium (▷ 129). You'll see more fish on the Nemo submarine trip (▷ 120), but this is a particularly expensive excursion.

Most children's attractions are found in the Bay of Palma and in a few of the resorts along the coast. Aquapark, Aquacity (one of the world's largest water parks),

Marineland and Western Park are on the Bay of Palma. A smaller water park can be found in Port d'Alcúdia (▷ 126) and several wildlife parks are on the east coast.

There's much less for children in the central plains and the Serra de Tramuntana, but many children will enjoy the shows at La Granja (▷ 123) in the mountains. The light shows in the caves on the east coast (Coves del Drac and Coves dels Hams) are always popular.

Economical alternatives to the theme parks' rides include taking the rickety train from Palma to Sóller, or seeing Palma from a horse-drawn carriage, which you can meet at the top of Costa de la Seu, beside the cathedral and Palau de l'Almudaina. In the summer, make a note of the children's shows that many resorts and attractions stage, such as the afternoon performances at Pirates (▷ 116).

WATCH OUT FOR

Wherever you go, children always get a warm welcome, but although Mallorca is an exceptionally child-friendly destination, there are certain things to watch out for. The most dangerous hazard is the strong summer sun. Apply a high-factor sunblock regularly to youngsters, especially after swimming: it's wise to follow the example of the Mallorcans and stay out of the sun during the middle of the day.

Families staying in high-rise hotels should check that any balcony railings are secure. When hiring a car, specify the number of child seats you require when booking.

Note that some of the rides in the theme parks and water parks may have age or height restrictions, although there are rides available in each park for all ages and sizes. Most parks are closed out of season, as are many children's attractions.

Prices are the final peril for families. The principal theme and water parks are some of Mallorca's most expensive attractions and most do not offer a discounted family ticket. This means that a family of two adults and two children should expect to spend up to €60 on tickets alone.

Be careful on mini-motorbikes

FESTIVALS AND EVENTS

During the Mallorcan summer you'll find a celebration somewhere on the island nearly every weekend. Filling up most of the calendar are religious festivals, an integral part of life in the Balearics. Every town and village has its own saint and these patron saints are honoured in fiestas with music, dancing, feasting and often fancy dress. Some, such as Sant Bartomeu, have a specific theme—devils in this case. Religious times of the year, such as Lent and Easter, are taken especially seriously on Catholic Mallorca, with elaborate processions and ceremonies. The highlight of the calendar is Semana Santa (Holy Week), with special events taking places all over the island. Note that festivals often mean that the host town's services shut down for the day: shops close and transport services are reduced. Whatever your interests, a tourist information office (▷ 204) will be able to suggest local events.

MUSIC AND CULTURE

Summer also brings a crop of music and cultural festivals, timed to coincide with the arrival of the bulk of the island's visitors. Classical music is well represented, with several headline events such as the Festival de Pollença. But folk, world and pop music all take their own place centre-stage during the summer.

In autumn a series of thanksgiving harvest festivals, celebrating anything from melons in Vilafranca de Bonany to wine in Binissalem, is a reminder of Mallorca's agrarian roots. These festivals take over towns and villages for a day or more and are a great opportunity to try local produce.

Another vestige of rural Mallorca can be witnessed in winter: *matances*. These are neighbourhood parties based around the slaughter and preparation of the family pig for future eating. The slaughterman (*matancer*) turns up on the designated morning and despatches the animal.

Family members then roll up their shirt sleeves and turn the pig into sausages, hams, lard and choice cuts of meat. The day ends with a well-deserved party and a pile of preserved pork. As fewer families own livestock and the younger generation moves into cities, the tradition is gradually dying out, but it's an effective way of preparing food for the larder.

SPORT

As well as cultural events, such as bullfights, there are a number of annual sporting highlights during the year. Top of the list are the glitzy Palma-based yachting regattas that attract royalty, celebrities and huge numbers of wealthy sailors. Although the races don't make for the most accessible spectator sport, you can see the yachts when they are moored in Palma's marinas.

Football, and the prospects of the Real Mallorca team, is keenly followed by islanders, who look forward to visits from Spain's top teams at the Son

WHAT TO DO

Watching the matadors at Muro's unique bullring

Moix stadium (▷ 118).

Cycling fans can catch professional teams racing in the five-day Tour of Mallorca every February. You won't see the biggest names in the sport in action, but it's still an exciting spectacle, which, like the sailing, you can watch for free.

FAIRS AND MARKETS

If you're more interested in souvenir hunting, visit one of Mallorca's craft fairs and markets. These are held at regular intervals during the year and include Baleart, Fira del Fang and Dijous Bo. Additionally, most Mallorcan towns have a weekly market selling food and handicrafts (▷ 105).

Whole towns are decorated with garlands and streamers for festivals

PALMA

Any time of the year is a great time to explore Palma. The compact capital's shops rival those of Barcelona or Madrid, with designer showrooms, department stores and idiosyncratic boutiques. Shopping is concentrated in the pedestrianized lanes in the heart of the city. To the south, for refuelling, there's an all-night tapas bar scene in La Llotja, and nightspots line the seafront. The headline sport is sailing, with several marinas inside the city limits.

⊕ SHOPPING

BOSSA
Plaza Cort, 3, 07001 Palma
Tel 971 213565
One of the upmarket designer-wear shops on Plaza Cort, Bossa eschews the mainstream and specializes in innovative jewellery designers from Spain and the rest of Europe. As well as jewellery the shop sells perfumes. Designers include Raquel Moreno, who is very successful in Spain (earrings from €90). Perfumes include hard-to-find Miller Harris by London-based perfumer Lyn Harris—Bossa is the only Spanish shop to carry the range. Oils from €26, perfumes from €45.
🕓 Mon–Fri 10–8, Sat 10–3

LA CASA DEL MAPA
Sant Domingo, 11, 07001 Palma
Tel 971 225945
All kinds of maps, from reproductions of historic maps of Mallorca to up-to-the-minute walkers' maps, are sold at this useful little shop, under an archway between Plaça Rosari and Carrer Jaume II. The shop also sells walking guides, postcards and stationery.
🕓 Mon–Fri 10–1.30, 5–7.30, Sat 10–1

COLMADO SANTO DOMINGO
Carrer Santo Domingo, 1, 07001 Palma
Tel 971 714887
This shop sells Mallorcan speciality foods, mainly *sobrasadas*, to tourists. Prices and quality are typical for Palma, but it is an entertaining place to visit, as you fight your way through a forest of sausages hanging from the ceiling. It also sells fig loaves, wines, fruit and vegetables.
🕓 Mon–Sat 10–8

EL CORTE INGLÉS
Avinguda Jaime III, 15, 07012 Palma
Tel 971 770177
www.elcorteingles.es
A Spanish institution, the El Corte Inglés department stores (there are two in Palma) offer a high-quality selection of all the goods you'll find up and down Avinguda Jaime III: designer clothes ranges, handmade shoes, electronics, sports equipment, household items and a section selling gourmet food, including excellent examples of Mallorcan specialities. If you don't have the time or inclination to explore Palma's shops, this is the best place to come for a quick retail fix. Prices are average but they'll wrap gifts for you.
🕓 Mon–Sat 9.30–9.30

Plaça Major is a good place to stop for refreshment during shopping trips in the neighbouring streets

ECLÉCTICA
Carrer Victoria, 4, 07001 Palma
Tel 971 718028
On a good street for hunting antiques, curios and objets d'art, Ecléctica is the best place to start. The stock is generally good quality and always interesting and original. Items for home decoration, from art deco lamps to ornaments, mingle with larger pieces of furniture.
🕙 Mon–Fri 10–2, 5.30–8

FORN D'ES TEATRE
Plaça Weyler, 9, 07001 Palma
Tel 971 715254
Forn d'Es Teatre is as notable for its mouthwatering pastries and pies as it is for its fabulous art deco façade. It's a famously good place to buy traditional *ensaïmadas*.
🕙 Mon–Sat 8–8, Sun 9–2

FRASQUET
Carrer Brossa, 19, 07001 Palma
Tel 971 721354
Those with a sweet tooth will find themselves ignoring the elaborate gold-lacquered decoration of this chocolate shop on the corner of Carrer Orfila and Can Danus, and homing in on Frasquet's amazing array of sweets and chocolates. As well as traditional sweets such as *torrons*, balls of almond paste coated in toasted pinenuts, the chocolatier is famous for producing Mallorca's finest chocolate.
🕙 Mon–Fri 9.30–2, 4.45–8, Sat 9.30–2

LIBRERIA RIPOLL
Carrer San Miguel, 12, 07002 Palma
Tel 971 711191
www.libreriaripoll.com
This is an excellent place to buy arty, out-of-the-ordinary postcards, antique maps and aged prints of Mallorcan scenes, fauna, flora and landscapes. You can also find rare books here, although they are mostly in Spanish. It's a quirky stop on an otherwise mainstream shopping street.
🕙 Mon–Fri 10–1.30, 4.30–8, Sat 10–2

LOEWE
Avinguda Jaume III, 1, 07012 Palma
Tel 971 715275
www.loewe.com
Loewe is a mainstay of Spain's fashion scene; the luxury Spanish fashion house was founded in 1846 and is now part of the Louis Vuitton group, with stores throughout the world. The Palma store sells beautiful leather goods and accessories for men and women, such as handbags, luggage, belts and purses. Styling is classic but contemporary and the workmanship is typically excellent.
🕙 Mon–Fri 9.30–8, Sat 9.30–2

The best-looking bakery in Palma sells excellent ensaïmadas

MAJORICA
Plaça des Mercat, 9, 07001 Palma
Tel 971 722919
Majorica is one of the two main producers of Mallorca's famous manmade pearls. Branches throughout the island sell pearl jewellery, from earrings to strings of coloured necklaces. Prices start from about €20 for a pair of earrings. This is one of two central Palma shops; the other is at Avinguda Jaume III, 11.
🕙 Mon–Sat 10–8

PICAROL
Carrer Forn del Racó, 1, 07001 Palma
Tel 971 711196
Sandals are one of the few traditional products still made in Mallorca and this small shop has a bright selection, plus other shoes. It is particularly strong on children's sizes. Carrer Forn del Racó is a narrow sidestreet close to Carrer Jaume II.
🕙 Mon–Sat 10.30–8.30

PILUCA OSABA
Passeig des Born, 20, 07012 Palma
Tel 971 720351
Upmarket and expensive boutiques line the shady Passeig des Born. This one specializes in importing beautiful Asian clothing, accessories and jewellery. The overall effect is high fashion rather than ethnic pastiche; the buyer-designer Piluca Osaba clearly has an eye on the season's catwalk shows. Prices are high, with scarves from €80 and kaftans from €280.
🕙 Mon–Fri 10–8, Sat 10–2

VIDRIERÍAS DE GORDIOLA
Carrer Victoria, 2, 07001 Palma
Tel 971 711541
The best place in Palma to buy Algaida's famous glassware, Vidrierías de Gordiola stocks glasses, candlesticks, vases and ornaments in coloured, handblown glass. Prices are slightly more expensive than buying direct from the factory in Algaida.
🕙 Mon–Fri 10–1.30, 5–8, Sat 10–1.30

VINOTECA BONS VINS
Carrer Sant Feliu, 7, 07012 Palma
Tel 971 727185
For an outstanding selection of wines, especially Mallorcan and Spanish vintages, head for this shop on the northern side of La Llotja. The staff are very knowledgeable and helpful and there are regular tastings, including evening get-togethers to help make up your mind. Bottles start from €7 to €8, but expect to spend upwards of €12 for the really good wines.
🕙 Mon–Sat 10.30–2, 6–late (11–12pm)

WHAT TO DO

ZARA
Passeig des Born 25, 07012 Palma
Tel 971 719828
You'll find good-quality, well-cut clothing for men, women and children at affordable prices in this branch of the well-known Galician fashion chain on the Born. Styles are very fashionable, so purchases may look dated next year, but Zara is an excellent destination for bargain hunters.
 Mon–Sat 10–8.30 winter; Mon–Sat 10–9 summer

🎭 ENTERTAINMENT

AUDITORIUM DE PALMA
Passeig Marítim, 18, 07014 Palma
Tel 902 332211
www.auditorium-pm.org
The largest auditorium in Mallorca, with 1,700 seats, opened in 1969 and occupies a central position on Palma's seafront. The Mozart room hosts the principal shows, with ballet, theatre and classical concerts featuring in most programmes.
 €15–€80

LA CAIXA FOUNDATION
Plaça Weyler, 3, 07001 Palma
Tel 971 178500
A wide range of activities and events, including art exhibitions, are held at the centrally located La Caixa.
Tue–Sat 10–9, Sun 10–2

CASINO MALLORCA
Urbanización Sol de Mallorca, Carretera Andratx, 07181 Palma
Tel 971 130000
www.casinodemallorca.com
High-rollers will head to the casino for poker, roulette, black jack and slot machines. For entry to the casino you will need to dress smartly; don't forget some form of ID, such as a passport.
Casino: nightly 8–5am

PIRATES ADVENTURE
Avinguda Sa Porrassa, 12, 07182 Magaluf
Tel 971 130411
www.piratesadventure.com
Professional gymnasts perform songs and dances on board a mock pirate ship. An adult version of this popular show is staged in the evenings. Tickets are expensive, but the price includes dinner, sangria and soft drinks during the show. Expect audience participation.
Shows from 6–11, times vary. Matinee performance 3pm
 May, Jun, Sep, Oct, adult from €42, child €25; Jul, Aug, adult from €47, child €26.50

House music: you can find jazz and blues nights at several clubs in Palma

SA NOSTRA CULTURAL CENTRE
Carrer Concepció, 12, 07012 Palma
Tel 971 725210
Supported by the financial firm Sa Nostra, this cultural centre in the middle of Palma houses art galleries and organizes creative activities and workshops for visitors.
Mon–Fri 10.30–1.30, 5–9, Sat 10.30–1.30

TEATRE MUNICIPAL
Passeig Mallorca, 9, 07011 Palma
Tel 971 739148
www.a-palma.es/ teatre_pm/teatre_pm.htm
There's something for everyone, from contemporary

dance, drama and film to children's activities, at this theatre to the west of Palma's centre.
 €8–€40

TEATRE PRINCIPAL
Carrer de la Riera, 2, 07003 Palma
Tel 971 713346
www.teatreprincipal.com
This grand 19th-century theatre in the centre of Palma (on Plaça Weyler) stages theatrical productions all year round, as well as annual opera and ballet seasons.
€10–€40

🌙 NIGHTLIFE

ABACO
Carrer Sant Joan, 1, 07012 Palma
Tel 971 714939
If Abaco has a theme, it is probably all about fall-of-the-Roman-Empire decadence. Behind a heavy wooden door in La Llotja, the whole of this palatial townhouse has been converted to a surreal nightspot. Classical music plays quietly in the background, flower garlands cascade from marble stairways and the main courtyard is decorated with mountains of fresh fruit, art, candles, busts and mirrors. All the rooms are similarly fantastical; the kitchen has colossal copper pans and vegetable displays covering every surface; the garden has fountains and caged birds. You'll be snapped back to reality by the drink prices—cocktails cost from €13, champagne up to €140 per bottle—but it is definitely worth one drink to see everything.
Mon–Sun 8pm–1am (2.30am summer)

ART DÉCO
Plaça Vapor, 20, 07011 Palma
Tel 650 391915
This bar-club in Santa Catalina overlooks the Passeig Marítim. The playlist is mostly pop music from the 70s, 80s and 90s and attracts smartly

dressed professionals who are noticeably older than the clubbers on the promenade below.
🕐 Thu–Sat 12–late

BARCELONA JAZZ CLUB
Carrer dels Apuntadores, 5, 07012 Palma
Tel 655 673834
www.barcelonacafejazzclub.com
The live music at this excellent small venue ranges from Cuban to trad jazz. It's a cosy place with couches and low stools, black walls and a good sound system, but there is little room to stand or dance; a live music cover charge of €3 is added to the cost of the first drink. You'll find the club up a flight of stairs on La Llotja's main street. The bar staff are friendly but will expect you to listen to the music rather than shout over the top of it.
🕐 Sun–Thu 8.30pm–1am (acts 10pm, 11pm, 12am), Fri–Sat 8.30pm–3am (acts 11pm, 12am, 2am)

BCM
Avinguda S'Olivera, 07182 Magaluf
Tel 971 131546
www.bcm-planetdance.com
BCM, one of Europe's largest nightclubs, promises sensory overload. With capacity for 5,500 people, a 10,000-watt sound system and a 400,000-watt light show, you know if you'll love it or hate it. The mainly young, British crowd dances to house, garage and techno played by star DJs on the high-ceilinged upper floor; over-30s prefer the lower floor.
🕐 Nightly 10–late

BLACK CAT
Avinguda Joan Miró, 75, 07015 Palma
Tel 971 405259
This popular, well-established gay club is at the heart of Palma's gay scene, surrounded by other gay-friendly venues. Inside you'll find a mix of locals and tourists.
🕐 Nightly 12–5am (show 3.30am)

BLUESVILLE
Ma de Moro, 3, 07012 Palma

Musically literate youngsters and older hipsters arrive for live sounds at Bluesville after 12am. Blues and bluesy rock is the soundtrack and the standard of the live acts is generally high. Beers cost €3. It's down an easily missed side street in La Llotja.
🕐 Daily 10.30pm–4am, live performances from 12am

LA BODEGUITA DEL MEDIO
Carrer Vallseca, 16, 07012 Palma
Tel 971 717832
This La Llotja bar is one of a chain of Havana-themed bars (another is in Puerto Portals). Décor is a collection of Cuban memorabilia with lots of

Put on your dancing shoes: Palma has several enormous nightclubs

scrawled signatures from tourists. Many of the twenty to fortysomething customers will be drinking Cuban cocktails, such as *mojitos,* and there's Cuban music on the stereo.
🕐 Daily from 8pm. Closes Fri–Sat 3am, Sun 1am

CAFÉ D'ES CASAL SÓLLERIC
Es Born, 07012 Palma
Tel 971 726122
Next door to the Casal Sólleric art centre at the top of Es Born, this café has a modern, arty interior with film posters and flyers for events and a large curved bar; a few tables line the pavement outside. It stays open until 2am serving coffee

from €1.05, *ensaïmadas,* sandwiches, beer and cocktails.
🕐 Daily 7pm–2am

GARITO CAFÉ
Dársena de Can Barbarà, 07015 Palma
Tel 971 736912
www.garitocafe.com
Garito is one of the most fashionable bars in Palma. DJ Nacho Velasco plays jazzy deep house to pre-club drinkers at the end of the week, but you'll hear an eclectic selection of music, from drum 'n' bass to soul and funk, on other nights.
🕐 Daily 7pm–late

IB'S
Passeig Marítim, 32, 07014 Palma
Tel 971 733671
Ib's is another of the city's big nightclubs, but it doesn't have the views of its rivals, Pacha and Tito's, primarily because it is beneath the seafront promenade.
🕐 Thu–Sat 10pm–late

L@RED CYBERCAFÉ
Carrer Concepció, 5, 07012 Palma
Tel 971 711754
With a welcoming, late-night bar serving beer and coffee and music you can surf the net here while having a drink.
🕐 Mon–Fri 10–2, Sat 5–3, Sun 5–12
💻 €1.50 per hour

PACHA
Passeig Marítim, 42, 07015 Palma
Tel 971 455908
www.pachamallorca.com
Pacha is certainly Palma's most renowned nightclub, and for good reason—the music policy is adventurous, the clientele trendy (if youthful) and the setting fabulous: it overlooks the Bay of Palma from a low cliff on the Passeig Marítim. With an outdoor terrace, two dance floors and several bars, there's somewhere to go whether you want to chill out or dance.
🕐 Summer, nightly 10pm–late, closed Jan

RIU PALACE
Carrer Llaud, Las Maravillas, 07610 Playa de Palma
Tel 971 743474
www.riupalace.com
In the heart of the predomi-nantly German resort of Arenal, RIU Palace is as rau-cous as its British counterpart in Magaluf, with live acts, dancers and top DJs. Music is mainstream house and techno, but the Soul Suite plays R & B, funk and soul in the summer months. The club has a capacity of 2,000.
🕐 Nightly 10pm–late

TITO'S
Passeig Maritim, 33, 07014 Palma
Tel 971 730017
www.pachamallorca.com
Tito's heyday was when Ray Charles and Marlene Dietrich were on the guest list: today it's a popular option for a less sophisticated night out. There are six bars in which to escape the hen and stag parties, and exciting views across the Bay of Palma. Entry is via an exte-rior, glass-fronted lift. The clientele is marginally less youthful than that of Pacha, but not as mature as Art Déco's (▷ 116).
🕐 Summer, nightly 11pm–6am; win-ter, Thu–Sat 11pm–6am

SPORTS AND ACTVITIES

CITY SIGHTSEEING BUS TOUR
www.city-sightseeing.com
See Palma from the top of a double-decker bus (▷ 38). The tour lasts 80 minutes and takes in all Palma's major sights, including Castell de Bellver. There are 13 stops and you can jump on or off at any of them. You can book online.
🕐 May–Sep 10–8, Oct–Apr 10–7
💷 Adult €13, child (5–15) €6.50

CLUB DE VUELO LIBRE MALLORCA
No fixed address
Tel 655 766443
www.cvlmallorca.com

Mallorca's main hang-gliding club is a good source of infor-mation on flying locations and equipment hire.

CLUB NÁUTICO CALA GAMBA
Paseo Cala Gamba, 07007 Palma
Tel 971 262849
Cala Gamba's sailing school has Optimist dinghies for chil-dren. Kayaking is also possible.
🕐 All year

CLUB NÁUTICO EL ARENAL
Carrer Roses, 07600 S'Arenal
Tel 971 440142
www.cnarenal.com
Whether you want to master the basics of navigation or learn to use a trapeze, there's

Palma is the yachting capital of the Mediterranean

something for everyone at this large, German-biased club. Boats range from Optimists for children to 420s for adults. Summer sports include swim-ming and kayaking.
🕐 Courses Jul–Sep
💷 Non-members: adult €155, child (0–15) €125 per 10-day course

CLUB NÁUTICO EL PORTIXOL
Paseo Barceló I Mir, 2, 07006 Portixol
Tel 971 242424
El Portixol's sailing school has Optimist dinghies for children.
🕐 All year

CRUESA MALLORCA YACHT CHARTER
Office at Passeig Maritim, 16, 07014

Palma
Tel 971 282821
www.cruesa.com
The fleet of this upmarket, family-owned yacht charter firm is based next to the city's Reial Club Náutico de Palma. Take your pick from sleek yachts, motor boats or large catamarans.
💷 €800–€6,000 per week

CYCLING
Palma is not the best place for cycling; although there are cycle lanes along the seafront, the roads are busy with both pedestrians and vehicles. But if you do want to hire a bicycle, try the following Palma-based firms:
Belori Bike–Tel 971 490358
Embat Ciclos–Tel 971 492358
Mitjort–Tel 971 322306
Royal Rent–Tel 971 744115

ESCUELA NACIONAL DE VELA DE CALANOVA
Avinguda Joan Miró, 327, Cala Major, 07015 Palma
Tel 971 402512
The national sailing school offers courses in a variety of disciplines.

ESTADIO SON MOIX
Camí dels Reis, 07011 Palma
Tel 971 221221
www.rcdmallorca.es
Home to Real Mallorca (▷ 22), the Son Moix stadium, which opened in 1999, seats 23,000 football spectators and is a good place to see some of the top teams in Spain's *Primera Liga*. Tickets are more likely to be in short supply for the big matches, but should be gener-ally available. Matches are played on alternate Sunday afternoons.
🕐 Jun–Sep
💷 €19–€42
🚌 No. 8

GOLF DE PONIENTE
Carretera Cala Figuera, 07182 Magaluf
Tel 971 130148
www.ponientegolf.com
This 18-hole, par-72 course,

WHAT TO DO

just 1km (0.5 mile) from Magaluf, opened in 1978. The wide fairways and large greens can be deceptive, and the 10th hole is regarded as one of the best golf holes on Mallorca. There's no shortage of bunkers and lakes for wayward golf balls.

🖐 Green fee €70
🍴 🖥

HIPÓDROMO SON PARDO
Carretera Palma–Sóller, km3, 07009 Palma
Tel 971 763853
www.hipodromsonpardo.com
Trotting races (*carreras*) with horse and trap are the most popular form of horse-racing in the Balearic Islands and have been practised in Mallorca for 200 years. Son Pardo was Europe's first floodlit racecourse when it opened in 1995. Gambling on the races is considered essential.

🕐 Winter, Sun 4.30; summer, Fri 9pm

PLAÇA DE TOROS
Avinguda Gaspar Bennazar Arquitecte, 32, 07011 Palma
Tel 971 755245
Palma's bullring dates from 1929 and is the island's main venue for bullfights. You can choose to sit in the sun (*sol*) or the shade (*sombre*)—the recommended option.

🕐 Mar–Oct

PUERTO PORTALS MARINA
Puerto Portals, 07181 Portals Nous
Tel 971 171100
www.puertoportals.com
There are 670 moorings at one of Mallorca's flashiest marinas.

REAL GOLF DE BENDINAT
Urbanización Bendinat, Carrer Campoamor, 07015 Calvià
Tel 971 405200
A tricky 18-hole, par-71 course, thanks to tree-lined fairways, steep slopes and testing greens. It is located between Palma and Ses Illetes and close to Puerto Portals.

🖐 Green fee €65
🍴 🖥

REIAL CLUB NÁUTICO DE PALMA
Muelle de Sant Pere, 07012 Palma
Tel 971 726848
www.club-nautico-palma.com
Learn to sail at the sailing club patronized by Spanish royalty and which hosts the famous Copa del Rey event each summer. Courses range from beginner initiation to tuition for racing yachtsmen. Kayaking is also available.

🕐 Courses Jul–Sep
🖐 Non-members from €250 per 5-day course

SKI CLUB CALANOVA
Carrer Condor, 22, Son Ferrer, 07180 Santa Ponça
Tel 971 130965

Hold tight! Taking on the water slides at Aquacity in S'Arenal

This club offers water-skiing tuition at Santa Ponça and Magaluf and water-skiing by the hour.

🖐 1 hour approx €80

SON VIDA GOLF
Urbanización Son Vida, 07013 Palma
Tel 971 791210
Son Vida was opened in 1964 by Prince Rainier of Monaco, making it the oldest golf course in Mallorca. The 18-hole, par-71 course is frequented by guests at the two on-site luxury hotels (▷ 180) and the owners of some of Palma's most exclusive nearby properties. Make reservations one month in advance for spring and autumn. Son Vida's sister course, Son Muntaner, is reserved for guests of the Arabella Sheraton Golf Hotel Son Vida, the Castillo Hotel Son Vida and the Mardavall Hotel and Spa.

🖐 Green fee €70
🍴 🖥

⊙ HEALTH AND BEAUTY

AYURVEDA
Conquistador, 8, 07001 Palma
Tel 971 713631
This is one of a chain of stylish hairdressers and beauty salons with branches in Portals Nous (tel 971 676026) and Archduque Luis Salvador, 2 (tel 971 757554). Men's haircuts start at €12.60, women's at €24.50, manicures at €8 and pedicures at €15.

🕐 Mon–Sat 10–8

ILLES FITNESS CENTRE
Carrer Protectora, 5, 07012 Palma
Tel 971 718044
At this small, modern sports centre just off Jaime III (south side) you'll find gym equipment, a pool and squash courts. You can also join classes. A five-day pass costs €25, but you can pay by the day: €8 for the gym, €10 for the gym and the pool. Squash courts cost €7 until 6pm, then €14.

🕐 Mon–Fri 8–10.30, Sat 10–9

MÓNICA RAMOS BEAUTY SALON
Carrer Federico García Lorca, 8 (first floor), 07014 Palma
Tel 971 457278
Pamper youself at this health and beauty salon in central Palma. Facials are from €42, exfoliation from €45, manicures from €15 and massages from €20.

🕐 Mon–Fri 10–8.30

SALONES LLONGUERAS
This chain of upmarket hair salons founded by Luis Llongueras, Spain's most famous hair stylist, has two branches in Palma:

Passeig de Mallorca, 14, 07001 Palma
Tel 971 715137
www.llongueras.com
⏰ Mon–Fri 9.30–7, Sat 9.30–12.30

Carrer Tous I Maroto, 15, 07001 Palma
Tel 971 721862
www.llongueras.com
⏰ Mon–Fri 9.30–7, Sat 9.30–12.30

✪ FOR CHILDREN

AQUACITY
Carretera Palma–Arenal exit 13, km15,
07600 S'Arenal
Tel 971 440000
www.aspro-ocio.es
Europe's biggest waterpark has
an exciting assortment of
attractions including the twisty
waterslide Anaconda, Surf
Beach, with 1m-high (3ft)
waves, the Congo River cruise,
the Mini Park for children and
the Black Hole. New attractions are Tsunami, a 50kph
(30mph) waterslide and a
Polynesian-themed children's
area. There's also a small zoo,
a petting farm and, somewhat
incongruously, a museum of
antique typewriters.
⏰ May, Jun, Sep, Oct 10–5; Jul, Aug
10–6
💰 Adult €20, child (3–12) €14, under-
3s free
🚌 23 and shuttle bus from Plaça
Espana, Ca'n Pastilla, Playa de Palma
and El Arenal
🍴 ▢

AQUAPARK
Carretera Cala Figuera, 07182 Magaluf
Tel 971 130811
www.aspro-ocio.es
This large, long-established
waterpark in Magaluf has
waterslides, rides and pools,
including the Tornado, a tubu-
lar slide that funnels you into a
whirlpool. The children's area
includes a new attraction: the
Enchanted Castle.
⏰ May, Jun, Sep, Oct 10–5; Jul, Aug
10–6
💰 Adult €16.75, child (3–12) €11.75,
under-3s free
🚌 Catalina Marqués 2 and 10
🍴 ▢

GOLF FANTASIA
Carrer Tenis, 3, 07181 Palma Nova
Tel 971 135040
www.golf-fantasia.com
Perhaps the best mini-golf
complex on the island, Golf
Fantasia is a cleverly landscaped complex of three
18-hole courses set around
waterfalls, caves and tropical
gardens.
⏰ All year, Mon–Sun 10–12am
💰 From €6.80
🍴 ▢

KARTING ARENAL
Carretera Nueva de Palma–Llucmajor,
km8, 07600 S'Arenal
Tel 971 440452
Children can emulate Formula

*The performing dolphins at
Marineland are always popular
with children*

1 champion Michael
Schumacher at this large go-
karting course to the east of
Palma in Arenal.
⏰ May–Oct 10–sunset

KARTING MAGALUF
Carretera Sa Porrassa, 07182 Magaluf
Tel 971 131734
www.kartingcompeticion.com
Children can let off some
steam at this large go-karting
course to the west of Palma.
⏰ May–Oct 10–sunset, closed Mon

MARINELAND
Carrer Garcilaso de la Vega, 9, 07184
Costa d'en Blanes
Tel 971 675125
www.aspro-ocio.es

There's a penguin pool, a rep-
tile house, an aviary and
collections of fish and monkeys at this marine park, as
well as rides on pirate ships
and miniature trains for children. But the main attractions
are the performing dolphins
and sealions. Many people
don't approve of such shows,
but this park puts money into
conservation and educational
programmes. There are up to
four exhibitions daily.
⏰ Feb–Dec, Jul, Aug 9.30–6.45; other
months 9.30–5.15
💰 Adult €16.50, child (3–12) €11.25,
under-3s free
🍴 ▢

NEMO SUBMARINE
Carrer Galeon, 2, 07181 Magaluf
Tel 971 130244
www.nemosub.com
Prospective submariners meet
in Magaluf for the boat trip to
Isla del Sech, where they
board the Nemo mini-subma-
rine for a 50-minute dive to a
depth of 30m (90ft). Undersea
action visible from its 1m (3ft)-
wide portholes includes fish,
wrecks and a fish-feeding
show by scuba divers. Free
pick-ups are available from
most resorts. It is advisable to
book ahead by telephone in
the summer months.
⏰ Mar–Oct 9–8
💰 Adult €49, child €39

WESTERN PARK
Carretera Cala Figuera, 07182 Magaluf
Tel 971 131203
www.western-park.com
Opposite the larger Aquapark,
Western Park has Wild West-
themed attractions including
waterslides, plus a cowboy
family show and a bird of prey
exhibition. Western Park's version of a Wild West town has a
jail, a saloon, a theatre and
fast-food restaurants.
⏰ Jun–Sep daily 10–6, rest of year
10–5
💰 Adult €16.50, child (3–15) €11,
under-3s free
🚌 Palma 10
🍴 ▢

SERRA DE TRAMUNTANA

The Serra de Tramuntana, like Palma, is a year-round destination. The mountain range is especially popular with walkers and cyclists in spring and autumn. But it has no nightclubs: nightlife revolves around village bars of varying degrees of sophistication and entertainment options are limited. However, the best place to base yourself is Sóller, which is rapidly evolving into a multi-talented town, with chic bars and shops, and a range of adventure activities.

ANDRATX AND ENVIRONS

⊕ THE FASHION HOUSE
Avinguda Mateo Bosch, 4, 07157 Port d'Andratx
Tel 971 673642
Port d'Andratx is the realm of the astronomically expensive boutique, selling designer clothes, shoes and sunglasses. A good example is The Fashion House, home to Valentino, Moschino and Versace, among other Italian designers. If cashmere pullovers are not your taste, you can always watch others flexing their credit cards.
🕓 Mon–Sat 10–1, 3–8

✪ CLUB DE VELA PORT D'ANDRATX
Avinguda Gabriel Roca, 27, 07157 Port d'Andratx
Tel 971 671721
Sailing and kayaking is offered at this medium-sized marina.
🕓 All year

✪ GOLF DE ANDRATX
Carrer Cromlec, 1, 07160 Camp de Mar
Tel 971 236280
www.golfdeandratx.com
This par-72, 18-hole course is made difficult by more than 60 bunkers, seven lakes and long, narrow fairways. One half of the course is in a residential area but the other has natural surroundings. The green fee includes compulsory buggy hire.
🖐 Green fee €90
🍴 💻 🏊

✪ GOLF SANTA PONÇA I
Avinguda del Golf, 07180 Santa Ponça
Tel 971 690211
Perhaps the most well-known golf course on Mallorca; royalty, celebrities and golf legends have trodden Santa Ponça I's swards. The testing 18-hole, par-72 course has wide fairways and water hazards.
🖐 Green fee €68
🍴 💻 🏊

✪ RAD-INTERNATIONAL
Gran Via de la Cruz, 49–51, 07180 Santa Ponça
Tel 971 697692
www.rad-international.de
Racing bikes for serious cyclists are available from Santa Ponça, Camp de Mar and Peguera in the southwest of the island (mornings only). Most riders bring their own shoes and pedals but LOOK and Shimano systems are available.
🕓 Daily 9.30–11
🖐 From €75 per week

WHAT TO DO

Port d'Andratx is one of the wealthiest areas in Mallorca, with designer shops and yacht marinas

RUTA DE PEDRA EN SEC
The Dry Stone Route is an ongoing project to create a durable footpath along the length of the Serra de Tramuntana from Andratx to Pollença. The plan is to build eight or nine refuges on the route where walkers can spend the night: two have been completed to date. The dormitory-style accommodation offers about 30 bunk beds in each refuge; reservations are strongly recommended. For more information contact Pollença's tourist office (tel 971 535077).

REFUGI TOSSALS VERDS (NEAR CUBER RESERVOIR)
Tel 971 173700
www.conselldemallorca.net/tossals

REFUGI MULETA (NEAR PORT DE SÓLLER)
Tel 971 173700
www.conselldemallorca.net/muleta

SCUBA ACTIVA
Plaça Monsenyor, Carrer Sebastian Grau, 7, 07159 Sant Elm
Tel 971 239102
www.scuba-activa.com
This diving school offers multilingual scuba diving courses for children and adults off the coast of Sant Elm and organizes twice-daily dives around the island of Sa Dragonera. Equipment is available for hire.
🕐 Apr–Nov, daily dives at 9 then 2pm
💶 Single dive plus equipment from €25

BANYALBUFAR

CAFÉ ES TRAST
Comte de Sallent, 10, 07191 Banyalbufar
This lively café-bar on the main road through Banyalbufar serves reasonably priced *tapas*—€2.10 for one dish, €6.30 for three, €10.50 for five—and cold beer.
🕐 Daily 10.30–midnight

BUNYOLA

CLUB HIPIC DE SON MOLINA
Carretera Palma–Sóller, km12, 07193 Bunyola

Tel 971 613739
This horse-riding centre in the foothills of the Tramuntana has two large arenas and offers tuition in a range of disciplines, including jumping and dressage. It has expertise with handicapped riders.
🕐 Mon–Fri 9–8, closed Aug
💶 Group class €15 per person

GOLF SON TERMENS
Carretera de S'Esgleieta, km10, 07193 Bunyola
Tel 971 617862
www.golfsontermens.com
The most naturalistic course on Mallorca, Son Termens, which opened in 1998, uses the hilly landscape of the Serra de

Traditional folk music can be heard at La Granja's afternoon shows

Tramuntana to craft a tough 18-hole, par-70 course. The 18th hole finishes at the friendly clubhouse.
💶 Green fee €68

CAIMARI

OLI CAIMARI
Carretera Inca–Lluc, km6, 07314 Caimari
Tel 971 873577
www.aceites-olicaimari.com
Caimari is the hub of olive-oil production in Mallorca. Although Mallorca's best oils are not produced here, good quality oils are sold at this olive mill and you can see the olives being crushed at harvest

time. Other Mallorcan products are also available in the shop.
🕐 Mon–Fri 9.30–2, 3.30–7, Sat 10–2, 4–7, Sun 10–2
💶 €4 for 500ml bottle

DEIÀ

HERBORISTERÍA L'ARXIDUC
Carrer Arxiduc Lluis Salvador, 2, 07179 Deià
Tel 971 639434
As befits a village with such a bohemian background, the most interesting shop in Deià is a healthfood shop, selling organic foods, homeopathic and herbal remedies, natural cosmetics, books and clothes.
🕐 Mon–Sat 10–1, 5–7

CAFÉ SA FONDA
Carrer Arxiduc Lluis Salvador, 5, 07179 Deià
Tel 971 639306
With jazz on the stereo, a large, elevated terrace and views up to the church, Sa Fonda is a pleasant place for a drink. The old village inn, on the mountainous side of the main road, appears to be the last bastion of Deià's laidback residents. You might hear live music on summer evenings.
🕐 Daily 12–12, closed Feb

SON MARROIG
Carretera Valldemossa–Deià, 07179 Deià
Tel 971 639158
On summer nights at Archduke Ludwig Salvatore's old mansion you can watch concerts in the gardens. Son Marroig is also the venue for Deià's classical music festival (▷ 134).
🕐 Jun–Sep; times vary
🅿 🚻 🛒

SA FONT FRESCA
Carrer Arxiduc Lluis Salvador, 30, 07179 Deià
Tel 971 639441
This family house, on a sharp corner of the main road at the southern end of Deià, has been converted into a bar-café serving *tapas,* snacks and beer. Entertainment is limited to table football and a TV.
🕐 Daily 7–10

ESPORLES

🎭 LA GRANJA
2km (1 mile) west of Esporles
Tel 971 610032
www.lagranja.net
Folk music and dance shows take place at this rural museum (▷ 123) on Wednesday and Friday afternoons.
🕐 Folk fiesta Wed and Fri 3.30–5
💶 Adult €11, child €5.30 on Wed and Fri pm
🏛 🖥 🍴

LLOSETA

🏬 BESTARD MOUNTAIN BOOTS
Carrer Estación, 40–42, 07360 Lloseta
Tel 971 514044
www.bestard.com
Few products are more authentically Mallorcan than a pair of Bestard walking boots. The family firm was established in Lloseta in 1940 and today produces a high-quality range of technical footwear from multi-activity trainers to four-season mountain boots.
🕐 Mon–Fri 9.30–7

🎭 TEATRO DE LLOSETA
Carrer Pou Nou, 07360 Lloseta
Tel 971 514033 (Town Hall)
In a startling contrast to its rustic surroundings, Lloseta's new arts centre (it opened in December 2003) is an angular, marble and glass building. The venue hosts theatre, dance, concerts, book readings and festivals. There's seating for up to 350 people.
🕐 All year
💶 From €5
🖥 🍴

PALMANYOLA

🎭 SON AMAR
Carretera de Sóller, km10.8, 07193 Palmanyola
Tel 971 617533
www.sonamar.com
Although after-dinner shows are new to Mallorca, this glitzy cabaret, an acquired taste, has been entertaining diners since 1963 with singers, dancers and magicians in a large 17th-century manor house near

Bunyola. Ticket prices are determined by the menus; drinks cost extra. Most people arrive on an organized excursion from their hotel, but seats are available independently.
🕐 Apr–Oct, dinner 8pm, show 9pm
🍽 Menus €50– €75, child's menus from €30
🍴 🍷

PUIGPUNYENT

✪ RESERVA PUIG DE GALATZÓ
Puigpunyent
Tel 971 616622
www.lareservaaventur.com
This small nature reserve around Galatzó Mountain (▷ 74) offers a range of activities for groups, including

Several scuba operators offer learn-to-dive courses to sub-aqua beginners

archery, rock climbing, horse-riding, zip-wire rides and orienteering. Individuals come here for hiking and to see the small collection of animals.
🕐 Apr–Nov 10–7; Nov–Apr 10–6
💶 Adult €9.90, child (3–10) €4.95

SÓLLER

🏬 ADREÇ
Carrer Sa Lluna, 6, 07100 Sóller
Tel 971 630201
Browse racks of fashionable clothes and accessories at this boutique on Sóller's main shopping street. It's particularly strong on delicate, colourful scarves and neat handbags.
🕐 Mon–Fri 9.30–1.30, 4.30–8.30, Sat 9.30–2

🏬 BEN CALÇAT
Carrer Sa Lluna, 74, 07100 Sóller
Tel 971 632874
This narrow shop is one of the few places to buy handmade traditional Mallorcan shoes, and the only place to watch the skilled cobbler, Ben Calçat, at work. Boots in sizes 34–47 cost €80; dapper canvas and leather shoes, with tyre treads for soles, cost €29.45. The traditional but stylish sandals are a good purchase.
🕐 Mon–Fri 9–1, 4–8, Sat 9–1

🏬 CAN TONI REIA
Carrer Sa Lluna, 27, 07100 Sóller
Tel 971 630424
Principally selling kitchen equipment, this shop also offers ceramics, glass and gifts. The pottery is good value.
🕐 Mon–Fri 9–1.30, 4–8, Sat 9–1

🏬 EUGENIO
Jerónimo Estades, 11, 07100 Sóller
Tel 971 630984
Try this small shop for olive wood handicrafts, including kitchen kit such as salad bowls and salt cellars, from €8.
🕐 Mon–Fri 10.30–8, Sat 10.30–6

🏬 FINCA GOURMET
Carrer Sa Lluna, 16, 07100 Sóller
Tel 971 630253
www.fincagourmet.com
Seasonal Mallorcan specialities are sold at this delicatessen. Expect to find jars of preserved fruits and conserves in winter and fresh produce in summer. A fine selection of *sobrasadas,* Menorcan cheeses and sought-after Mallorcan wines is stocked all year. Gift ideas? Try orange blossom honey, jars of Sóller olives or sundried tomatoes. Packets of almondy *carquinyol* biscuits cost €3. Prices reflect the high quality.
🕐 Mon–Sat 10–8, Sun 11–3

☕ CAFÉ CENTRAL
Plaça Constitució, 07100 Sóller
Tel 971 630008
For mid-shopping refreshments, pull up a wicker chair outside this friendly café on

Sóller's main square. A slice of almond cake, the house speciality, costs €2.70, with coffees for €1.80. Inside there's a long bar with bench seating.

🕐 8–9.30 (11pm in summer); winter, closed Wed

☕ CAFÉ SÓLLER
Plaça Constitució, 13, 07100 Sóller
Tel 971 630010

Tasty *tapas* are dispensed from a counter at the rear of this well-regarded *tapas* bar in Sóller's main square. Mixed *tapas* costs from €6, with *pa amb olí*, spaghetti pesto and grilled prawns some of the dishes. Try the good spinach and lamb *tapas*. Beers are served from the long bar and there's often low-key dance music playing.

🕐 Mon–Fri 8–1am (11pm in winter), Sat 8–5

🚤 BARCOS AZULES
Passeig Es Través, 3, 07108 Port de Sóller
Tel 971 630170
www.barcosazules.com

Barcos Azules run boat trips on a large catamaran from Port de Sóller to a number of destinations including Sa Calobra, Cala Tuent, Cap de Formentor, Menorca and circumnavigations of Mallorca. During July and August paella is served on Sunday outings. Private boat charters are also available.

🎫 Return trips from €20, child (6–12) €10, under-6s free

🚶 MALLORCA MUNTANYA
07100 Sóller
Tel 649 470497 / 669 334910
www.mallorcamuntanya.com

Two professional mountain guides, Salvador Suau and David Casajuana, have teamed up with the Sóller Hotel Association to offer nine guided walks of varying difficulty around the Serra de Tramuntana. Accommodation can be arranged in mountain refuges, hotels, hostals, *agroturismos* and Lluc's monastery. Both guides speak English,

German, French and Spanish
🕐 Mon–Sat
🎫 €15–€35

🤿 OCTOPUS DIVING CENTRE
Carrer Cononge Oliver, 13, 07108 Port de Sóller
Tel 971 633133
www.octopus-mallorca.com

This PADI-approved diving centre has two boats taking divers to 30 dive sites along the rocky west coast. Staff are multilingual. The centre offers nitrox tanks, and specialist equipment—including underwater cameras—can be hired.

🕐 May–Oct
🎫 3 dives €80

Olive wood products make attractive souvenirs, but choose carefully

⛴ TRAMONTANA CRUCEROS
Carrer Marina, 16, 07108 Port de Sóller
Tel 971 633109
www.tramontanacruceros.com

Two cruise boats and a 350-seat catamaran operate trips along the north coast, with various stopping-off points.

🕐 Daily 10, 11, 12.45, 3 to Sa Calobra
🎫 Adult €20, child (6–12) €10

VALLDEMOSSA

🏛 CAPAMUNTA
Plaça Ramon Llull, 3, 07170 Valldemossa
Tel 971 612390

A constant stream of tourists means there are numerous shops selling Mallorcan handicrafts in Valldemossa. This is

one of the better examples, with prices starting from €4 for pretty jugs and a typical selection of pottery and olive wood.

🕐 Mon–Fri 10–8.30, Sat, Sun 11–8.30

🏛 LAFIORE
Carretera de Valldemossa, km11, 07193 S'Esgleieta
Tel 971 610140
www.lafiore.com

Watch glass-blowers create all sorts of glassware, from colourful contemporary designs to classic pieces at this factory shop 7km (4 miles) from Valldemossa. Without the middleman you can find prices that are a little lower here than for similar items elsewhere.

🕐 Mon–Sat 10–8

🏛 L'OR DE MALLORCA
Carrer Blanquerna, 10–12, 07170 Valldemossa
Tel 971 616114

This souvenir shop is a cut above the rest, selling distinctive gold jewellery and handicrafts such as good-quality Mallorcan glassware.

🕐 Winter, 10–5; summer, 10–8.30

🏛 MUZA AND CO.
Carrer Uetam, 8, 07170 Valldemossa
Tel 971 616334

If you can't find any authentic Mallorcan handicrafts you like, this shop imports handicrafts, including textiles, jewellery and ornaments, from Asia and North Africa.

🕐 Winter, 12–6; summer, 12–9

🎵 COSTA NORD
Avinguda de Palma, 6, 07170 Valldemossa
Tel 971 612425
www.costanord.com

Not only does the long-running Mediterranean Nights festival draw top flamenco, salsa and jazz acts to Costa Nord (▷ 81), but the centre's bar-nightclub, Valldemossa Nixe Club, offers live music every Friday night.

🕐 Apr–Oct, Fri 9–late
🎫 Adult €7.50, child (5–12) €4.50
🏧 🎪 💻 🍴

THE NORTHEAST

The Northeast has a little bit of everything: lots of interesting boutiques in Pollença, two cutting-edge auditoriums for culture vultures and an exhausting array of watersports in the bay of Pollença. Nightlife is a little more refined in Port de Pollença than in Port d'Alcúdia. If it all gets too much you can escape on one of several boat trips or to any one of five golf courses and numerous beaches and resorts, although Cala Millor is particularly raucous.

ALCÚDIA AND PORT D'ALCÚDIA

🚌 SA LLUNA
Carrer Crístòfol Colon, 11, 07400 Alcúdia
Tel 971 545214
www.salluna.com
Choose from an interesting range of household items at this attractive shop for amateur interior decorators. Kitchen kit is a strong point.
🕐 Mon–Fri 10–1, 5–8, Sat–Sun 10–1

🎭 AUDITORI D'ALCÚDIA
Plaça de la Porta de Mallorca, 3, 07400 Alcúdia
Tel 971 897185
www.alcudia.net
This contemporary, 496-seat auditorium hosts music, theatre and other events. There are booths in which you can listen to a simultaneous translation of what is being said onstage.
🕐 Box office: Mon–Sat 10–1, 6–9
💶 €4–€36
🚌 🎭

🍸 ES CANYAR
Carrer Mayor, 2, 07400 Alcúdia
Tel 971 547282
www.escanyar.com
There's a more fashionable crowd than you find in Port d'Alcúdia at this central bar in the old town. The bar manager has good taste in drinks with Bombay Sapphire gin and Havana Club rum. Trip hop and jazz dominate the stereo. The interior looks good, with a large marble bar, low lights and abstract art on the walls; the outdoor terrace opens in the summer. Food, including *tapas* and specialities such as lemon chicken with rice, is served throughout the day.
🕐 Tue–Sun 9–12 (summer 1am, weekends 3am)

🍸 LINEKER'S BAR
Zona Commercial Marisol, Carrer Pedro Y Mas Rues, 07410 Port d'Alcúdia
Tel 971 891837
www.linekers-bar.com
A favourite with English football fans, thanks to its extensive collection of Gary Lineker memorabilia. You need an interest in football to fully appreciate this bar, one of a chain in the Mediterranean.
🕐 11am–late

🍸 MENTA
Avinguda Argentina, 07410 Port d'Alcúdia
Tel 971 891972

WHAT TO DO

There are lots of walking routes in the north of the island, including Boquer Valley near Pollença

www.mentadisco.com
The largest club in the north of the island, Menta has two dance floors, seven bars and an indoor swimming pool. The 18 to 30 crowd dance to pop hits and house music.

🕐 Summer, nightly 11pm–6am; winter, Fri–Sat 11pm–6am

⊘ ALCUDIAMAR
Paseo Marítimo, 1, 07410 Port d'Alcúdia
Tel 971 546000
www.alcudiamar.es
Much more than just a marina, Alcudiamar runs the town's busy quay area in the port. Tourists throng the bars and restaurants in the summer: Diablito is a pizzeria with a take-away service, and Marblau is a café-bar with music. There are 730 moorings at the marina with nautical shops for sailors.

🕐 Mon–Sun 10am–late

🏌 GOLF ALCANADA
Carretera del Faro, 07410 Port d'Alcúdia
Tel 971 220966
This new 18-hole course, designed by Robert Trent Jones and opened in October 2003, borders Alcúdia's bay and has views of the tiny island of Alcanada and its lighthouse. Groves of olive, oak and pine trees add interest to the par-72 course, which is more suited to experienced players than beginners.

👐 Green fee €70
🍴 ▢

⊘ HAMBLE BALEARICS
Paseo Marítimo, 1, 07410 Port d'Alcúdia
Tel 971 547889
www.hamblebalearics.com
Hamble Balearics is a sailing club offering Royal Yachting Association-approved courses (RYA) and yacht charter. RYA courses range from five to seven days and include all accommodation, meals, mooring fees and sailing kit, but you can have day-by-day tuition in your own boat (€290 per day). Seven yachts are available for charter (from 5 to 8 berths)

with low-season prices starting from €1,025 per week or at a daily rate (one fifth of a week's price).

👐 Courses from €695 per week

⊘ OCÉANO SUB
Avinguda del Mas Pas 1, Puerto Deportivo Cocodrilo, 07410 Alcúdia
Tel 971 545517
www.oceanosub.com
Multilingual instructors at this dive outfit take people out for anything from one to ten dives, and run PADI courses. Night dives and cave dives are also possible. Most people dive from Océano Sub's boat around Pollença Bay and Cap de Formentor, but shore dives

Artà's modern theatre stages classic and contemporary productions

for beginners are also available. Prices include insurance and free pick-up from hotel. Equipment can be rented; prices specified include equipment rental.

👐 1 dive €45, 2 dives €75, 10 dives €325. Night dive €40. Courses: 2-day introduction €240

⊘ HIDROPARK
Avinguda Tucán, 07410 Port d'Alcúdia
Tel 971 891672
www.hidropark.com
This theme park on the north coast is smaller than those in Arenal and Magaluf but still has plenty of waterslides in the water park and three 18-hole mini-golf courses, adding up to

a massive 54-hole complex that will keep most children amused for several hours.

🕐 Apr–Oct 10–6
👐 Adult €15, child (5–11) €8, under-4s free
🍴 ▢

ARTÀ

⊕ KÖTTER AZULEJOS
Carrer Antonio Blanes, 14, 07570 Artà
Tel 971 829639
An interesting idea: this German-run shop sells tiles, large and small, with which you can make your own mosaic or something as simple as a nameplate. It's good fun for children and amateur interior designers alike.

🕐 Mon–Fri 10–1, 5–7, Sat 10–1
👐 €2–€8

🎭 ARTÀ THEATRE
Carrer de Ciutat, 07570 Artà
Tel 971 829700
www.teatrearta.com
This modern theatre in a quiet courtyard on Artà's main street puts on a wide range of productions from contemporary to classic drama. It's the best place in the northeast of the island to see theatre.

🕐 Daily 9–8, closed Aug
👐 €20–€60
▢ ♟

🍷 ES PASSEIG
Carrer Ciutat, 22, 07570 Artà
Tel 971 829275
While this busy *tapas* bar on Artà's main street has some outside tables, most of the action is around the small bar. You can start the day here (breakfast costs €4) or arrive in the evening for *tapas* and a drink. There's also a brief menu for children.

🕐 Daily 9am–12am

🏌 CAPDEPERA GOLF
Carretera Artà–Capdepera, km3.5, 07570 Artà
Tel 971 818500
One of the cluster of courses around Artà, this scenic par-72 course has 18 holes, six artificial holes and a varied

selection of fairways.

🏌 Green fee €48

🍴 🖥

CALA MILLOR

🎭 AUDITÒRIUM SA MÀNIGA

Carrer de Son Galta, 4, 07560 Cala
Millor
Tel 971 587371
www.samaniga.com

One of the three principal
auditoriums in Mallorca, Sa
Màniga has a 466-seat theatre
for theatre, music and comedy
performances. There are also
four booths in which you can
hear simultaneous translation.

🕐 Box office: Tue–Sat 11–1, 6–9

🏌 Adult €12–€20, child (under 16)
€5–€6

🖥 🎭

🍸 CHEERS

Carrer Son Corp, 20, 07560 Cala Millor
Tel 971 586079
www.cheersbarmallorca.com

This long-established bar (it
opened in 1988) in Cala Millor
is perennially popular and
offers food until 10.30pm,
entertainment for children and
adults, television screens for
sports events, Playstations for
children and internet access.

🕐 9am–late

🚢 CRUCEROS CREUERS

Carrer Baladres, edificio Rossello, 07560
Sa Coma
Tel 971 810600
www.cruceroscreuers.com

Boat trips on the glass-
bottomed *Sea Odyssey* catamaran depart from Cala
Rajada, Cala Millor, Cala Bona,
Sa Coma and Porto Cristo during the summer months.

🏌 Return trips from €12

🦁 AUTO–SAFARI

Carretera Porto Cristo–Son Servera, km
5, 07680 Cala Millor
Tel 971 810909

Mallorca's only zoo is a 44ha
(108-acre) safari park with
giraffes, zebras, tigers and
monkeys, among other ani-
mals. Children won't want to
miss the 'baby zoo' of young
animals. It's a 4km (2.5-mile)

drive through the park, or take
an expensive mini-train.

🕐 Apr–Sep 9–7; Oct–Mar 9–5

🏌 Adult €11, child €8

🚌 Shuttle bus from Cala Millor in
summer

🍴 🖥

CALA RAJADA

🎈 MALLORCA BALLOONS

Ca'n Melis, 22, 07590 Cala Rajada
Tel 971 818182
www.mallorcaballoons.com

One-hour or 30-minute hot-air
balloon trips are offered by
Mallorca Balloons. Departures,
from the east coast, are
weather dependent.

🏌 1 hour: adult €130, child (4–11)
€90

*Kötter Azulejos in Artà is a good
place to buy decorative tiles*

CAPDEPERA

⛳ CANYAMEL GOLF

Urbanización Canyamel, Avinguda D'Es
Cap Vermell, 07580 Capdepera
Tel 971 841313
www.canyamelgolf.com

Reckoned by some to be the
most difficult course on the
island, 18-hole, par-73
Canyamel has one of the best
settings, close to the northeast
coast. There are sea views on
the way out (on a clear day
you can see Menorca from the
fifth tee) and views of the hills
around Artà on the way back.
Watch out for the house in the
middle of the ninth fairway.

🏌 Green fee €55

🍴 🖥

MURO

🎭 PLAÇA DE TOROS

Junction of Cervantes, Cristòfol Serra,
Cardenal Oliver and Fornés streets,
07440 Muro

Muro's bullring, the most
notable bullring on the island,
is famous for being hand-
chiselled out of a stone quarry
in the small town. It dates from
1920 and seats 6,945 people.

🍸 BUDDHA BAR

Santa Ana, 2, 07440 Muro

This *tapas* bar, specializing in
fish, with selections for less
than €10, is as close as you'll
get to nightlife in sleepy Muro.

🕐 9–9, closed Tue

POLLENÇA AND PORT DE POLLENÇA

👕 AINA

Placa Vella, 1, 07460 Pollença
Tel 971 530686

Buy smart clothes and shoes
for children at this delightful
shop, plus high-chairs, cots
and teddy bears. Cardigans
cost from €30, shoes from
€110 and duffel coats €90.

🕐 Mon–Sat 9.30–1.30, 4.30–8, Sun
9.30–1.30

💍 L'ARGENTERIA

Antoni Maura, 11, 07460 Pollença
Tel 971 533132
www.largenteria.com

L'Argenteria glitters with beautiful designer jewellery in silver,
gold and steel by artists from
all over the world. Most pieces
are one-offs and you can also
commission your own designs.
Prices range from €20 to €700
for chunky amber necklaces.
The jeweller also sells silver
picture frames and jewellery
boxes.

🕐 Summer, 10–1.30, 5–10; winter,
4.30–8.30

🚲 BICICLETES MEAN SI TORN

Plaça ca les Munnares, 07460 Pollença
Tel 971 532560

The only bicycle shop in
Pollença sells a good range of
clothing and equipment for
casual and serious cyclists.
Guided road and mountain

bike excursions can be booked here.

🕐 Mon–Fri 9.30–1, 4.30–8, Sat 10–1

🏛 BORIS JAKOB
Carrer de Jesus, 31, 07460 Pollença
Tel 971 533313
At the foot of the Calvary flight of steps, jeweller Boris Jakob has a small showroom exhibiting his handmade silver jewellery. Erring on the chunky side, many of the items are dramatically beautiful, but prices reflect the high quality of the jewellery. Pieces include rings, earrings, necklaces, bracelets and brooches.

🕐 Mon–Fri 9.30–1, 4–8, Sat 10–1

🏛 CASA BESTARD FOTOGRAFIA
Carrer Costa I Llobera, 2, 07460 Pollença
Tel 971 530309
For camera film, processing and digital camera equipment, including memory cards, head to this useful shop in the centre of Pollença.

🕐 Mon–Fri 9–1.30, 4–8, Sun 9–1.30, closed Sat

🏛 GALERIA MAIOR
Placa Major, 4, 07460 Pollença
Tel 971 530095
Galeria Maior is reckoned, by locals, to be the best art gallery in north Mallorca. Displays are varied, with an emphasis on modern painting and sculpture.

🕐 Jun–Sep Tue–Sat 10.30–1.30, 5.30–9, Sun 11–1.30; Oct–May Tue–Sat 10.30–1.30, 5–8, Sun 11–1.30

🏛 POLLENTIA
Carrer Antonio Maura, 24, 07460 Pollença
Tel 971 531102
This interesting shop, opposite L'Argenteria, is packed with all sorts of items from reclaimed buildings, including antiques, fixtures and furnishings. It will courier heavier items—such as solid wooden doors—back to your home country. Prices start from €12 for prints.

🕐 Mon–Sat 10–1.30, 5–8, closed Sun and Thu afternoon

🍷 DUNA
Carrer Alcúdia, 1, 07460 Pollença
Tel 971 532800
With live music and no-frills décor, this cavernous first-floor bar is popular with Pollença's youth and close enough to the central squares to be convenient for a late-evening visit. There's often live music from local rock bands.

🕐 9pm–late, closed Mon

🍷 EL MOJITO
Plaça Miguel Capllonch, 07470 Port de Pollença
Tel 971 866283
As much a bar as a restaurant, El Mojito serves up beers, wines and cocktails to

Open all hours: Pollença has a bustling café scene in the summer

accompany *tapas* and paellas (from €9). It's in the main square of Port de Pollença, with live Spanish music Thu–Sat.

🕐 9am–12am

🍷 MULLIGAN'S
Carrer Atilio Boveri, 5, 07470 Port de Pollença
Tel 971 867559
For a pint of good Guinness, head for this Irish pub at the western end of town close to the R Bar. For entertainment there is a large-screen television for sports events, and live music at the weekends.

🕐 10.30am–4am

🍷 LA POSADA D'ARIANT
Antoní Maura, 40, 07460 Pollença
Tel 971 530053
This chic café-bar on a busy street bordering Pollença's main square is a good place to start a night out. *Pa amb olí* and *tapas* (chicken croquettes, squid and meatballs from €4.20) are served with drinks.

🕐 12–12

🍷 Bottle of wine from €7.75

🍷 R BAR AND CAFÉ
Carrer Economo Torres, 19, 07470 Port de Pollença
Tel 971 867251
With sofas, funky music and a relaxed atmosphere, you might be tempted to spend the whole evening at this cosy but trendy bar in a small street in the western side of Port de Pollença. There are several other good bars within stumbling distance, plus a fish-and-chip shop, the Codfather.

🕐 7pm–4am

✪ CHARTER TUDOR DAWN
Moll Vell, 07470 Port de Pollença
Tel 649 875151 / 616 775958
Tudor Dawn, a 15m (50ft) schooner, can be chartered, with skipper Simon, for day trips around Port de Pollença. The boat sets out from the quay and you sail it, under Simon's guidance, around the coastline for a picnic lunch. Buoyancy aids, snorkelling and fishing gear is provided. Additional activities, including water-skiing and jet-skiing, can be arranged.

🕐 Jul–Aug

🍷 Adult €80, child (under 16) €70 per day

✪ CLUB NÁUTICO PORT DE POLLENÇA
Moll Vell, 07470 Port de Pollença
Tel 971 864635
www.rcnpp.net
Earn your waterwings at this British-dominated club. Few places are better for learning to sail than the Bay of Pollença and children will soon be

taking out Optimists and Laser Picos. Windsurfing, canoeing and fishing trips are also available during the summer.

🕒 Courses Jul–Sep

💶 Non-members: adult €93, child (6–16) €65 per 5-day course

🟠 GOLF POLLENSA
Carretera Palma–Pollença, km49.3, 07460 Pollença
Tel 971 533216/533265
www.golfpollensa.com

There are only nine holes at this sandy par-35 course, but they form perhaps the most beautiful course on the island, which overlooks the Bay of Pollença and has the Serra de Tramuntana for a backdrop. The twisting fairways, stone walls and groves of olive and oak trees present a challenge to golfers of all abilities.

💶 Green fee €55

🔲 🖥 🏊

🟠 RANCHO GRANDE
Son Serra de Marina, 07459 Port de Pollença
Tel 971 854121
www.ranchograndemallorca.com

Lessons, guided rides and long-distance hacks can be organized at this equestrian centre near Port de Pollença.

🕒 Daily 9–1, 3–7

💶 2-hour ride with guide €36, full day €100, group lesson €13 per person, 2-day winter hack €200

🟠 RENT CIFRE
Carrer Llevant, 25, 07470 Port de Pollença
Tel 971 865068

Racing and men's and women's touring bikes are available from Rent Cifre, located on one of the roads leading back from Port de Pollença's seafront at the west side of the town. A hotel collection service is offered.

🕒 Mon–Sat 9–1, 3–8, Sun 9–1

💶 From €5 per day

🟠 SAIL AND SURF POLLENSA
Paseo Saralegui, 134, 07470 Port de Pollença
Tel 971 865346

www.sailsurf-pollensa.de

This sailing club and school has operated in Pollença Bay for 30 years. It has a variety of boats, as well as windsurfers, for hire and also offers tuition. The boats are lined up on the beach so you can look before committing yourself. Port de Pollença's sheltered bay offers excellent sailing conditions.

🕒 Mon–Sat 9–6

💶 Laser dinghy €25 for 2 hours, €55 per day. Hobie Cat €45 for 2 hours, €90 per day. Windsurfer €30 for 2 hours. Yachts from €100 per day

🟠 SCUBA MALLORCA
Carrer d'El Cano, 23, 07470 Port de Pollença

The bays of Pollença and Alcúdia are perfect for teaching first-time sailors the basics of sailing

Tel 971 868087
www.scubamallorca.com

This PADI-approved British-owned dive centre takes divers out to spots around Pollença Bay and Cap de Formentor. Scuba diving courses are offered and hotel pick-up can be arranged.

🕒 Mar–mid-Nov

💶 1 day, 2 tanks from €70

🟢 NORD ESPORT
Cecili Metelo, 6, 07460 Pollença
Tel 971 531145

Nord Esport is a smart health and fitness centre in Pollença offering spa treatments, massage and physiotherapy. Aerobics, pilates and capoeira

classes are held in the well-equipped gym.

🕒 Mon–Fri 8.30–10.15, Sat 9.30–1.30, closed Sat in summer

💶 Sessions start from €8 per hour

PORTO CRISTO

🟠 CLUB NÁUTICO PORTO CRISTO
Carrer Vèlla, 29, 07680 Porto Cristo
Tel 971 821253

The sailing school has Optimist dinghies for children.

🕒 All year

🟠 ACUÀRIUM DE MALLORCA
Carrer Vèlla, 07680 Porto Cristo
Tel 971 820971

Piranhas, moray and electric eels, and fish from coral reefs can be found at this small aquarium opposite the Coves del Drac. There are 115 tanks over two floors.

🕒 Apr–Oct daily 10.30–6; Nov–Mar daily 11–3

💶 Adult €5, child (4–8) €2.5, under-4s free

SON SERVERA

🟠 ALBATROS DIVING
Puerto de Cala Bona, 18, 07559 Son Servera
Tel 971 586807
www.albatros-diving.com

Albatros is a well-respected dive centre in Cala Bona boating divers to about 20 dive sites on the east coast. Staff are multilingual and equipment is well maintained. Nitrox tanks and PADI courses are available.

🕒 Apr–Nov

💶 From €30

🟠 PULA MALLORCA
Carretera Son Servera–Capdepera, km3, 07550 Son Servera
Tel 971 817034

Since opening in 1995 all 18 holes at Pula have been redesigned. The par-70 course, which has featured on the PGA European tour, is now one of the longest and most demanding in Mallorca.

💶 Green fee €84

🔲 🖥 🏊 🍽

THE SOUTH

Life on the plains of Mallorca is rather low-key. Cala d'Or's beaches attract holidaymakers but inland this is the island's quietest region, triangulated by the commercial hubs of Inca, Llucmajor and Manacor. Entertainment and nightlife options are very limited outside Cala d'Or but there are plenty of appealing activities: wine tasting in Binissalem, learning to ride at Son Menut near Felanitx and shopping at Festival Park and the factory outlets of Inca.

ALGAIDA

⊕ VIDRIERÍAS GORDIOLA
Carretera Palma–Manacor, km19, 07210 Algaida
Tel 971 665046
www.gordiola.com
The gift shop at Ca'n Gordiola (▷ 105) displays a colourful selection of the factory's hand-blown glass, from ornate bottles with glass stoppers and blood-red goblets to plain glass jugs and vases.
🕒 Mon–Sat 9–8, Sun 9–1.30, Apr–Oct; Mon–Sat 9–7, Sun 9–1.30, rest of year

BINISSALEM

⊕ JOSÉ L. FERRER
Conquistador, 103, 07350 Binissalem
Tel 971 511050
www.vinosferrer.com
José L. Ferrer is one of the founding fathers of Mallorcan wine production. His sizeable *bodega* is impossible to miss, on the right side of the C713 as you enter Binissalem from the south. It's a worthwhile stop, with a large shop, knowledgeable staff and guided tours at 11am and 6pm (11am and 4.30pm in winter; €6); try the substantial Franja Roja Crianza. See page 163 for more information about Mallorca's wines.
🕒 Mon–Fri 8–7, Sat 10–2

CALES DE MALLORCA

⊕ CALA MONDRAGÓ BAR-CAFETERÍA
Cala Mondragó, Santanyí
Tel 971 657820
Few undeveloped beaches remain on the east coast, but beautiful Cala Mondragó, protected by natural park status, is a definite find. The open-air beach bar services three white-sand coves, each surrounded by pine trees, rocky promontories and calm, turquoise inlets. Park in the public car park at the top of the hill.
🕒 Daily 10–9

Head to Binissalem for wine-tasting and many of Mallorca's best wineries

⊕ CLUB NÁUTICO PORTO COLOM
Carrer Pescadores, 23, 07670 Porto Colom
Tel 971 824658
www.cnportocolom.com
Porto Colom's sailing school operates during the summer, with dinghies available for young sailors. The marina has 252 berths for yachts, as well as lifting gear. And fishing expeditions are run from the club.
🕒 Apr–Oct

⊕ CLUB NÁUTICO PORTOPETRO
Esplanada del Puerto, 07691 Portopetro
Tel 971 657657
Sailing and kayaking is offered at this small sailing club.
🕒 Apr–Oct

⊕ MALLORQUIN BIKES
Avinguda Fernando Tarrago, 19, 07660 Cala d'Or
Tel 609 237637
www.mallorquin-bikes.de
Mountain bikes, racing bikes and tourers are available from Mallorquin Bikes' large shop in Cala d'Or. They also offer guided cycling tours of Mallorca for groups (from €35 per person for a four- to five-hour ride), tailored according to ability.
🕒 Mon–Sat 9–2, 4–8, Sun 9–2
🚲 From €10 per day, child €5, helmet €1

⊕ VALL D'OR GOLF
Carretera Cala d'Or–Porto Colom, km 7.7, 07669 S'Horta
Tel 971 837001
One of the easier courses in Mallorca, this 18-hole, par-71 opened in 1985 as a nine-hole course. Most greens are surrounded by pine trees but there are views out to Cala d'Or.
🚲 Green fee €69
🎫 💼 🏊

⊕ JUMAICA
Carretera Porto Cristo–Porto Colom, km4.5, 07680 Cales de Mallorca
Tel 971 833979
This children's zoo, with ponies, llamas, rabbits and a variety of exotic birds, has a tropical backdrop of a banana plantation. There is also a good restaurant in the grounds serving Mallorcan cuisine.
🕒 Apr–Oct daily 9–7; Nov–Mar daily 10–4
🚲 Adult €6, child (4–12) €3
🎫 💼

CAMPOS

⊕ ALINA ESPACIO
Carrer Santanyí, 12, 07630 Campos
Tel 971 651594
www.alinavida.com
Part boutique, part art gallery,

Alina Espacio brings a little of Palma's sophistication to this rural town. Best described as a 'lifestyle store', you'll find contempory furniture, designer household accessories, lighting, fashion and music inside the shopping area. In Alina Gallery owners Elma Choung and Harald Adler host art exhibitions.

🕐 Mon–Fri 9–1, 3.30–8, Sat 9.30–1

COSTITX

⭐ OBSERVATORIO ASTRONÓMICO MALLORCA

Camí de l'Observatori, 07144 Costitx
Tel 971 876019
www.oam.es
www.mallorcaplanetarium.com

One for astronomers: Mallorca's principal observatory was opened in May 1991 and now has nine telescopes and 11 cameras. Although a scientific institution, it offers courses and activities. A planetarium (added in 2003) projects remote images from space in real time. Visits are aimed at local schoolchildren but it may be possible to join a guided tour (tel 971 513344, or visit the website).

🕐 Mon–Fri 10–12, 4–8

FELANITX

⊕ CERÁMICAS MALLORCA

Carrer Sant Agustín, 50–58, 07200 Felanitx
Tel 971 580201

There's a colourful range of Mallorcan pottery at this display room in the industrial side of town. Most collections have been created by local artists and there are often some attractive designs. Expect to spend €10 to €30 for items such as plates, vases, cups and bowls.

🕐 Mon–Fri 9–1, 3.30–7.30, Sat 10.30–1

⭐ SON MENUT RIDING SCHOOL

3rd Volta, 3040, Camí de Son Negre, 07208 Felanitx
Tel 971 582920
www.sonmenut.com

This smart riding school, in countryside southeast of Felanitx, offers tuition (including Spanish dressage) and guided excursions on horseback of one hour to a full day. Riders can go as far as the coast or explore the surrounding farmland. Guides and instructors are multilingual. There's also tidy accommodation, a restaurant, and tennis courts and a swimming pool for guests.

🕐 All year
🎫 Group class €12.50 per person, guided trail rides €12.50 per hour or €84.50 per person for a full day
🚗 Follow signs from the junction on the PM-512 outside Felanitx

Manacor is the centre of artificial pearl production on the island

INCA

⊕ CAMPER FACTORY SHOP

Polígono Industrial Estate, 07300 Inca
Tel 971 888233
www.camper.com

Camper is perhaps the most famous Mallorcan brand of footwear. The shoes are certainly distinctive (for men's styles think bowling shoes made fashionable; for women, expect anything from chic sandals to knee-high boots) and this factory outlet sells a moderately-sized selection from current and previous ranges in most sizes. Prices are keener here than in Camper shops in the rest of Europe.

🕐 Mon–Sat 10–8.30

⊕ FESTIVAL PARK

Carretera Palma-Inca, km7, 07141 Marratxí
Tel 971 140925
www.festivalparks.com

Festival Park is a colossal, modern leisure centre complex. Shopping figures significantly, with factory outlets and plenty of clothes shops, but there are also bars, restaurants, a cinema, a bowling alley and a reptilarium, Green Planet (see below).

🕐 Mon–Sat 10–10, Fri–Sun 12–10

⊕ MUNPER CREACIONES

Carretera Palma-Alcúdia, km30, 07300 Inca
Tel 971 881000
www.munper.com

The centre of leather production in Mallorca, Inca has several factory shops selling leather shoes, bag, and clothing, but you're no more likely to find a bargain here than in Palma. Munper is one of the easiest shops to find (on the left heading north out of Inca).

🕐 Mon–Fri 9.30–7.30, Sat 9.30–7

❄ GREEN PLANET

Fesival Park, Carretera Palma-Inca, km7, 07141 Marratxí
Tel 971 605481
www.festivalparks.com

Europe's largest reptilarium is arranged over five zones, each representing a continent and housing, in total, 10,000 species. Amphibians and invertebrates join the snakes, lizards, tortoises and alligators.

🕐 Mon–Fri 10–8, Sat 12–10, Sun 12–9
🎫 Adult €10, child (4–12) €7, under-3s free
🍴 🅿

LLUCMAJOR

⊕ CAN ORDINAS

Vall, 128, 07620 Llucmajor
Tel 971 660580

The traditional Mallorcan bread knife is a vicious-looking, hook-bladed tool. This hardware shop still makes hand-made examples, as well as selling other useful articles.

🕐 Mon–Fri 9–1, 4–7, Sat 9–1

MARRIOT SON ANTEM
PM 602, km 3.4, 07620 Llucmajor
Tel 971 129200
There are two 18-hole courses at Marriot's Son Antem golf resort, both of par 72. The East course is better suited to beginners, with wide fairways and fast greens, while the newer West course is more of a challenge, with narrow fairways and elevated greens.
Green fee €64

MANACOR

MAJORICA
Avinguda Majorica, 48, 07500 Manacor
Tel 971 550200
www.majorica.com
Mallorca's largest producer of artificial pearls has a factory shop in Manacor. An hourly tour doesn't reveal the secret of how the artificial pearls are formed, but does show jewellery (which you can later buy) being made.
Mon–Fri 9–6, Sat–Sun 9.30–12.30

OLIV-ART
Carretera Palma–Manacor, km47, 07500 Manacor
Tel 971 847232
This warehouse-style shop on the main road out of Manacor sells every olive-wood product imaginable at good prices (bowls €11 to €22, salad servers €11, smaller items €3 to €5). Kitchen utensils are a good purchase—olive wood is attractive and durable but needs to be washed carefully. There's an outdoor children's play area with life-size, if rather tatty, dinosaurs.
Winter, daily 9–7 (Sat–Sun 6.30); summer, daily 9–8 (Sat 9–7.30, Sun 9.30–7.30)

PERE SEDA BODEGAS
Carrer Cid Campeador, 22, 07500 Manacor
Tel 971 550219
www.pereseda.com
Although Mallorca's most famous wines come from Binissalem, the central plains, the Pla I Llevant, have their own Denominación de Origen. Pla I Llevant wine production is based at Felanitx and Manacor; Pere Seda is one of the largest producers in the area, cultivating indigenous and foreign grape varieties. You can buy direct from the *bodega* or place an order via the internet.
Mon–Fri 10–7, Sat 10–2

HIPÓDROMO MANACOR
Carretera Palma–Artà, km50, 07500 Manacor
Tel 971 550023
Manacor has a small racecourse, where trotting remains the main attraction (see Son Pardo, ▷ 119).
Winter, Sat 4pm

Spot black vultures and other indigenous birds at Natura Park

MONTUÏRI

ORQUIDEA
Carretera Palma–Artà, km30, Montuïri
Tel 971 644144
www.perlasorquidea.com
This large factory shop sells artificial pearls; prices are similar to its main competitor, Majorica in Manacor. There's a brief guided tour.
Mon–Fri 10–7, Sat–Sun 9–1

SANTA EUGÈNIA

NATURA PARK
Carretera de Sineu, km15.5, 07412 Santa Eugènia
Tel 971 144078
With winged creatures from ugly marabou storks and black vultures to 500 varieties of butterfly, and lots of mammals and reptiles, there is a lot for children to see at Natura Park.
Daily 10–7

SA RÀPITA

CLUB NÁUTICO SA RÀPITA
Esplanada del Puerto, 07639 Campos
Tel 971 640001
www.cnrapita.es
Sa Ràpita's sailing school has Optimist dinghies for children. This stretch of water also offers the island's best windsurfing; equipment and tuition is available in the summer.
All year
Rental equipment from €30

SINEU

ANTIK
Carrer de Tavernes, 1, 07510 Sineu
Tel 971 855142
Bargain hunters can browse the art deco antiques and curios at this interesting little shop: they'll find ornaments, lamps, jewellery, clothing and quirky furniture.
10–1, 5–8, closed Sat pm, Sun

S'INDIC
Plaça Es Fossar, 14, 07510 Sineu
Tel 971 520191
This café-bar is adjacent to the marketplace, Sineu's centre of activity with bars, cafés and restaurants. It stays open until the last person leaves at night and it's a good place for a coffee after the town's market (▷ 105) on Wednesday mornings.
9am–late

SA MOLA
Carretera Santa Margalida, 1, 07510 Sineu
Tel 971 855273
If you're in Sineu at a weekend, you might find live music at this dimly lit Irish pub-café-disco close to the train station. It's open for long hours and serves Guinness. There are several more bars beside the train station.
Mon 8–3pm, Tue–Thu 8–12am, Fri–Sat 8–6am

WHAT TO DO

THE ISLAND'S FESTIVALS

PALMA

CABALGATA DE LOS REYES (PROCESSION OF THE THREE KINGS)
5 January
Palma
A family-friendly event in which the Three Kings arrive by boat and lead a procession through Palma to hand out presents to good children.

SANT ANTONI ABAT
16–17 January
Palma, Artà and Sa Pobla
Known as the Blessing of the Animals, this is a procession of pets and farm animals that takes place in three locations: Palma, Artà and Sa Pobla.

SANT SEBASTIÀ
19 January
Palma and Costitx
On the night before the Saint's Day, bonfires and barbecues are held in Palma's squares and in Costitx.

SA RÚA
Weekend before Lent
Palma and rest of island
Bonfires, processions and fancy dress constitute this carnival held on the last weekend before Lent.

SEMANA SANTA (HOLY WEEK)
Easter
Palma and rest of island
Easter is taken very seriously in Mallorca. The week begins with the blessing of palm and olive branches at churches across the island followed by daily processions in Palma (the biggest is on Maundy Thursday) and other towns and villages. A figure of Christ is lowered from his cross in Pollença on Good Friday evening and carried down the town's Calvary steps; a similar ritual takes place in Felanitx.

PRINCESS SOFIA TROPHY
April
Palma

www.trofeoprincesasofia.org
This long-standing dinghy sailing regatta opens the summer's sailing season and attracts around 600 boats from 50 nations. Classes represented include Olympic class dinghies.

TEMPORADA DE BALLET DE MALLORCA (MALLORCA BALLET SEASON)
June–February
Palma
Tel 971 402612
www.temporadadeballet.com
Mallorca's annual ballet season is held in Palma's auditorium (▷ 116).
€17–€45

King Jaume I on horseback in the Plaça d'Espanya in Palma

FESTIVAL DE MÚSICA CASTELL DE BELLVER
June
Palma
www.simfonica-de-balears.com
This annual music festival in Castell de Bellver is staged by the Balearic Symphony Orchestra, which also plays regularly during seasons at Palma's auditorium.

DOMINGO DEL ANGEL (ANGEL SUNDAY)
Sunday after Easter
Palma
Angel Sunday is celebrated in Palma with processions and feasts.

INTERNATIONAL BOAT SHOW
April–May
Palma
www.firesicongressos.com
The Mediterranean's yachting capital is the perfect venue for this annual boat show. Visitors can ogle the beautiful and seriously expensive boats lining Palma's port area.
Daily 10–8
€5

COPA DEL REY
August
Palma
www.copadelrey.com
The largest and most prestigious cruising regatta in the Mediterranean is the year's yachting highlight. Based at the Reial Club Náutico in Palma, the event, founded in 1982, attracts royal patronage and hundreds of amazing yachts.

FESTA DE L'ESTENDARD
31 December
Palma
The anniversary of the Christian conquest of the city by King Jaume I in 1229 is commemorated every New Year's Eve. There's a tremendous procession from the town hall to the cathedral for a special Mass.

BALEART CRAFT FAIR
Mid-December
Palma
www.firesicongressos.com
This long-standing annual fair exhibits handicrafts from all the Balearic Islands.

SERRA DE TRAMUNTANA

TOUR OF MALLORCA
February
Serra de Tramuntana and rest of island
Professional cycling teams come to Mallorca for this preseason competition. The tour lasts five days and takes different routes around the island each year.

VINTAGE CAR RALLY
March
Serra de Tramuntana and rest of island

www.trofeo-baleares.de
Don't be surprised to be overtaken regularly by classic sports cars in early March—an annual vintage car rally attracts Porsches, Ferraris and other classic cars to the twisting roads of the Serra de Tramuntana.

MOROS I CHRISTIANS
8–10 May
Sóller
Local Sóller women helped vanquish a band of Turkish pirates in 1561 and the battle for Sóller is enthusiastically commemorated with this lively re-enactment.

DEIÀ INTERNATIONAL FESTIVAL
April–May, August–September
Deià
www.soundpost.org
This chamber music festival, with spring and summer programmes, has been held at Son Marroig since 1978 and boasts a lengthy roster of performers.

SÁ MOSTRA INTERNATIONAL FOLKLORE FESTIVAL
July–August
Sóller
www.samostra.org,
www.sollernet.com/samostra/mostraen.html
Now in its third decade, this festival brings music and dance from all over the world to Sóller.

FESTIVAL CHOPIN
August
Valldemossa
www.festivalchopin.com
Chopin's compositions dominate this festival—typically there are only a few works by other composers scheduled. It takes place every year in Valldemossa's chapel and also includes exhibitions and talks.

FESTIVAL BUNYOLA
October–November
Bunyola
www.festivalbunyola.org
Two months of concerts bring classical music to this small mountain town.

THE NORTHEAST

SEMANA SANTA (HOLY WEEK)
Easter
See Palma

FESTIVAL DE POLLENÇA
July–August
Pollença
www.festivalpollenca.org
This major classical music festival, founded by British violinist Philip Newman in 1962, is held in Pollença annually during July and August. The programme includes everything from solo musicians to orchestras.

Folk art favourites can be found at the Fira des Fang festival

THE SOUTH

FIRA DES FANG
March
Marratxí
This *siurell*-producing town holds an annual clay craft festival, with no shortage of the white, green and red figurines. Expect lots of whistling.

SEMANA SANTA (HOLY WEEK)
Easter
See Palma

SANT BARTOMEU
24 August
Montuïri
Good versus evil is the theme of one of Mallorca's most exciting festivals. Villagers dress up as women and devils and—accompanied by the sound of bagpipes, flutes and drums—perform a dance which dates back 400 years.

SANT AGUSTI
28 August
Felanitx
More make-believe dances, this time with children dressed as hobby-horses being chased by giants. See page 100 for details.

FESTA DES MELÓ
September
Vilafranca de Bonany
On the last Sunday of September the residents of this small village celebrate the end of the harvest with a melon festival.

FESTA DE VERMAR
September
Binissalem
Wine buffs shouldn't miss this annual festival of wine in Mallorca's top wine-producing area. There's no shortage of wines to taste.

FESTA D'ES BOTIFARRÓ
October
Sant Joan
Blood sausages are the object of the celebrations at this quirky autumnal festival, which revolves around singing, dancing and sausage consumption. Festivities start at midday with the lighting of bonfires to cook the sausages and continue late into the evening.

DIJOUS BO
November
Inca
The last of Inca's annual autumn fairs, Dijous Bo is the single largest market in Mallorca with everything from fruit, vegetables and livestock to leather goods and even cars for sale in a festive atmosphere. Fairground attractions keep children entertained.

WHAT TO DO

Out and About

This chapter describes five walks, four drives and one bicycle ride that explore all four regions of Mallorca The locations of the tours are marked on the map on page 136.

OUT AND ABOUT

1. Walk
Modernist Palma (▷ 137–39)
2. Walk
Palma's Jewish Quarter (▷ 140–41)
3. Drive
Western Tramuntana (▷ 142–43)
4. Drive
Eastern Tramuntana (▷ 144–45)
5. Walk
To Camel Rock (▷ 146–47)

6. Drive
Pollença and Alcúdia Bays (▷ 148–49)
7. Walk
The Victòria Peninsula (▷ 150–51)
8. Drive
Across the Plain (▷ 152–53)
9. Walk
Costitx–The Heart of Mallorca (▷ 154–55)
10. Bicycle Ride
Llucmajor to Cap Blanc (▷ 156–57)

KEY TO ROUTE MAPS IN THIS CHAPTER

★ Start point
━ Route
▬▬ Alternative route
▶ Route direction
❷ Walk start point on drive

❻ Featured sight along route
● Place of interest in Sights section
● Other place of interest
☼ Viewpoint
$\overset{621}{\blacktriangle}$ Height in metres

*Hot air: windmills, left, remain a common feature on the plains.
Above, local women talking together at La Granja*

MODERNIST PALMA

Modernist architecture and modern art—plus foodie and shopping treats—between the old town and Palma's most up-and-coming district.

Curvacious Can Corbella, above, catching the afternoon sunlight

Marvellous Modernism: looking up at Can Forteza Rey

THE WALK

Distance: 4km (2.5 miles)
Allow: 2 hours
Start/end at: Plaça de la Reina
Parking: Underground car park beneath Parc de la Mar

HOW TO GET THERE

Several bus services stop at Plaça de la Reina, including 6, 15, 17 and the City Sightseeing bus

The *Modernisme* artistic movement was a Catalan version of art nouveau that flourished in Barcelona around the turn of the 20th century. Modernist architects rejected classical forms in favour of wavy lines, undulating façades, and floral and geometric motifs, making widespread use of industrial materials such as ceramics, iron and stained glass. The best-known Modernist, Spanish architect Antoni Gaudí (1852–1926), worked on Palma's cathedral (▷ 54–57) and his influence can be seen across the city. This walk takes in some of the leading examples of Modernist architecture in Palma before ending in Santa Catalina, a buzzing district of restaurants and bars set around a market.

Start at the northern end of the S'Hort del Rei gardens and climb the steps towards the cathedral, emerging alongside Palau March (▷ 64). Turn left at the top of the steps, passing the Balearic Parliament building on your left to arrive at Plaça Cort in front of the Ajuntament (city hall). Turn left beside a huge old olive tree to enter the pedestrianized shopping district.

❶ On reaching the first street corner of the pedestrianized district, look up to your left at the façade of Can Corbella, one of the forerunners of Modernism in Palma. Note the Moorish-style horseshoe arches and stained-glass windows on the ground floor, the undulating wooden façade and the octagonal tower.

Turn right along Carrer Jaume II. The street ends at Plaça del Marquès del Palmer.

❷ On Plaça del Marquès del Palmer, step back to admire Palma's most distinctive Modernist building, Can Forteza Rey. Lluís Forteza Rey, a local jeweller and silversmith who met Gaudí while he was working on the cathedral, designed it in 1909. The upper half of the façade is covered

take the steps down to your left to arrive on Plaça de Weyler, where there are two more Modernist classics.

On your left is the Forn des Teatre, a bakery with a charming art nouveau shopfront. Open from 8am to 8pm, it is famous for its *ensaïmadas*. Across the street is the Gran Hotel, the first Modernist building in Palma, now home to Fundació La Caixa (▷ 59).

Continue a short way ahead to Plaça del Mercat on your left.

❸ Plaça del Mercat occupies the site of the city's oldest market place, which was used as a souk in Arab times. Nowadays it contains two of Palma's most traditional pastry and chocolate shops, Frasquet and Ca's Net, which face each other across the square. Also on the square is Can Casasayas, a pair of matching Modernist mansions—separated by a narrow lane—with balconies in the shape of carnival masks and the familiar curving façades.

Keep straight ahead along Carrer de la Unió, passing the top of Passeig des Born (▷ 61) to arrive among the arcades and boutiques of Avinguda Jaume III.

Two of a kind: Plaça del Mercat's twin Can Casasayas mansions

The famous frontage of the art-nouveau Forn des Teatre bakery

with *trencadís* (fragments of broken ceramic), which also distinguish Gaudí's work. Note the grotesque face set between a pair of winged dragons. The neighbouring building, Can Aguila, was built at the same time, as a department store, but is now a shoe shop. It is notable for the extensive use of iron and glass in its façade.

The archway in front of you leads into Plaça Major (▷ 61). Instead,

❹ The long, sloping avenue Avinguda Jaume III is Palma's principal shopping street. After passing the department store El Corte Inglés on your left, look out for Baró Santa Maria de Sepulcre on the opposite side of the road. If you feel like a break, stop at Ca'n Joan de S'Aigo, a smart coffee house with mirrors, chandeliers and red velvet sofas at Baró Santa Maria de Sepulcre, 5. The hot chocolate is a treat. (You'll

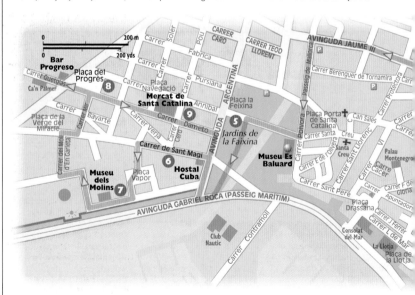

pass the sister establishment of the same name on Walk 2, ▷ 140–41.)

Continue to the top of Avinguda Jaume III, then turn left to walk along Passeig de Mallorca, a promenade following the line of the medieval walls. Ahead, in the old bastion of Sant Pere, is the Museu Es Baluard (▷ 59). Cross the bridge to reach Jardins de la Faixina.

5 The Jardins de la Faixina, a popular place for children to play, are filled with sculpture and monuments to Mallorcan heroes.

Cross at the traffic lights and walk a short way up Avinguda Argentina then turn left onto Carrer Sant Magí.

6 On the corner of Carrer Sant Magí is Hostal Cuba, a Modernist hotel of Moorish inspiration with a minaret-shaped tower. You are now entering the Santa Catalina district, built as a fishing village in the early 20th century. The mix of old-style neighbourhood shops with trendy modern restaurants and bars gives the area a cosmopolitan, villagey feel.

Continue along Carrer Sant Magí, passing the last working coalyard in Palma at No. 35 and Ferreteria

La Central at No. 37, an ironmonger's shop with a Modernist façade decorated with ornamental flower and vegetable motifs. Turn left into Plaça Vapor and walk to the viewpoint overlooking the harbour.

7 Several old windmills on the harbour have been restored and now house nightclubs, a cultural centre and the Museu dels Molins/Moli d'en Garleta (Tue, Thu and Sat 10–1).

Turn right to follow the sea walls before returning to Carrer Sant Magí along a narrow alley. Cross the road and follow Carrer Mir to the right of the church to arrive on Plaça del Progrès, at the heart of Santa Catalina.

8 On the left of Plaça del Progrès is Bar Progreso, dating from 1920, and almost opposite is Ca'n Palmer at Carrer Quetglas 5, with ceramic mosaics on the façade.

Turn right along Carrer Dameto to reach Mercat de Santa Catalina **9**, a thriving local market with delicatessen and wine stalls alongside traditional produce and fresh fish. After exploring the market, continue to the end of the street, then turn right on Avinguda Argentina and return to the centre of Palma's old town along the seafront.

There's a café on the ground floor of Fundació La Caixa

WHERE TO EAT

There are many restaurants and bars in the streets around Santa Catalina market, offering Mallorcan, Spanish, Basque, Italian and Japanese cuisine. For something different, try Afrikana (▷ 164). For a snack, try the cosy crêperie La Chaumière (tel 971 283752, closed on Mondays) on Carrer de la Pursiana. It's run by a friendly French couple who serve large crêpes with fillings.

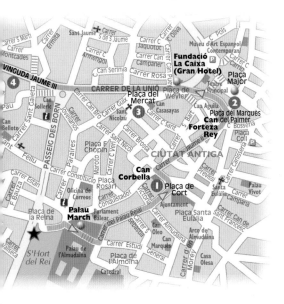

It's not expensive to stay the night in this Moorish hotel

PALMA'S JEWISH QUARTER

An easy walk through one of the lesser-known parts of the old town, exploring the dark, narrow backstreets of what was once a thriving Jewish neighbourhood.

THE WALK

Distance: 3.2km (2 miles)	
Allow: 2 hours	
Start/end at: Parc de la Mar	
Parking: Underground car park beneath Parc de la Mar	

HOW TO GET THERE

Buses stopping on Passeig des Born and Avinguda d'Antoni Maura (6, 15, 17) are just a short walk from Parc de la Mar

During the 14th century the district known as El Call was one of the most important Jewish quarters in Europe, an enclave of silk merchants, silversmiths, synagogues and scholars. The Jews of Palma were distinguished in many fields, including medicine, astronomy, navigation and cartography—in the 14th century a map of the known world was produced by father and son Abraham and Jafuda Cresques (▷ 28). An anti-Semitic riot in 1391 led to the decline of the Jewish quarter and the start of the forced conversion of Jews to Christianity. It is only since the 1970s that an active Jewish community has returned to Palma, though the former Jewish neighbourhood now has its own mosque—a sign of changing times.

Begin the walk on the south side of Parc de la Mar, facing the cathedral. Head east, walking beside the lake with good views of the cathedral to your left. Beyond the lake, climb to the road and continue across another small section of park with a playground beside the Renaissance walls. At the end of the park, look for a gap in the wall to enter the city through the 16th-century Porta de la Murada.

❶ Porta de la Murada is the gate to Sa Calatrava, one of Palma's most traditional areas and home to Palma's tanning industry in the 15th century.

Keep straight ahead, going gently uphill, and take the first turning left, Carrer de la Calatrava, to

enter a maze of narrow alleyways and streets. Turn right along Carrer de Can Salom and continue uphill onto Carrer d'en Calders. On the left, inside the old seminary, is the temporary home of the Museu Diocesà (▷ 56). The street ends in Plaça de Sant Jeroni.

❷ To the right of Plaça de Sant Jeroni are the church and convent of Sant Jeron, with the restored battlements and tower of the only surviving section of Arab walls beyond.

Fork left across the square and continue ahead along Carrer dels Botons. It was along here that the cartographer Jafuda Cresques was born. At the end of the street, cross the road and continue slightly to the right across Plaça del Pes de la Palla, formerly the city's straw market. Keep right along Carrer dels Socors to reach a small square, Plaça Llorenç Bisbal.

❸ On entering Plaça Llorenç Bisbal, note the pair of churches on your right. The first, the 15th-century Nostra Senyora dels Desamparats (Our Lady of the Abandoned), was founded by a group of converted Jews. It takes its name from its abandonment in the 17th century, when the Augustinian order built the

neighbouring church of Nostra Senyora dels Socors (Our Lady of the Help).

Turn left across the square and walk through an archway to enter Passeig per l'Artesania.

❹ Passeig per l'Artesania is a modern complex of craft workshops and shops where artists sell Mallorcan glassware, pottery, woodwork, leatherwork and recycled goods.

Cross Plaça de l'Artesania and turn right to reach Plaça Josep Maria Quadrado.

❺ As you enter Plaça Josep Maria Quadrado look up at the façade of Can Barceló, the four-storey apartment block on your left. The most notable feature of this Modernista (Catalan art nouveau, ▷ 137–39) building is the set of ceramic panels, produced in a local factory, depicting female artists, writers and musicians.

Keep right across the square and continue along a narrow alley to reach Carrer de la Samaritana, where there is a small mosque. Turn left here and then immediately right to reach Palma's most elegant coffee house, Ca'n Joan de S'Aigo. Founded in 1700, it is now famed for its almond ice cream. Retrace your steps to

Horse and carriage rides can take you down narrow, hidden lanes

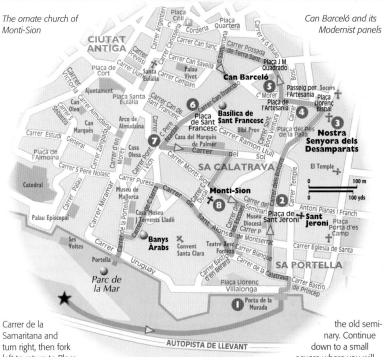

The ornate church of Monti-Sion

Can Barceló and its Modernist panels

Carrer de la Samaritana and turn right, then fork left to return to Plaça Josep Maria Quadrado. Turn right to reach Plaça de Sant Francesc ❻, dominated by the Basílica de Sant Francesc (▷ 49). Cross the square, keeping to the right, then turn right and immediately left along Carrer del Pere Nadal. Continue to the crossroads at the junctions of Carrer del Call, Carrer del Sol and Carrer de Monti-Sion.

❼ This crossroads was the main gate to the Jewish quarter. It was through here that a mob burst on 2 August 1391, killing 300 Jews and consigning this district to history.

The main streets of El Call lead off left from here. Take a sharp left along Carrer del Sol, passing the 14th-century palace of the count of La Cova. Farther along on the left is Can Marquès del Palmer, a 16th-century mansion with delicate, carved Renaissance windows. Turn right along a narrow alley, Carrer de la Criança, to emerge opposite the Jesuit church of Monti-Sion.

❽ The church of Monti-Sion was built on the site of an old synagogue. Note the elaborate portal of 1683, its columns decorated with motifs and statues of the Jesuit saints St. Ignatius and St. Francis Xavier.

Turn left along Carrer del Seminari and right along Carrer de les Escoles beside the walls of the old seminary. Continue down to a small square where you will see the Teatre Municipal Xesc Forteza, opened in 2003. Turn right and follow the lane around to reach Carrer de Sant Alonso, with two stone benches beneath a tree. Keep straight on along this street to a crossroads, and turn left along Carrer de Can Serra. Follow this street past the Banys Àrabs and around to the right, then turn left under an archway. Keep straight ahead through the Portella gate to return to Parc de la Mar, or turn right to walk along the top of the Renaissance walls.

WHERE TO EAT

La Taberna del Caracol
Great tapas at a backstreet bar near the end of the walk.
✉ Carrer de Sant Alonso, 2
☎ 971 714908
🕐 Mon–Sat 12.30–3.30, 7.30–11.30

WESTERN TRAMUNTANA

A circuit of western Mallorca, beginning with a coastal corniche before turning inland through vineyards and olive groves, passing mountain villages and watchtowers with dramatic sea views.

Harvest time in the fields and orchards of Puigpunyent

THE DRIVE

Distance: 62km (38 miles)

Allow: At least 2 hours

Start/end at: Andratx

HOW TO GET THERE

From Palma, take the PM1 motorway west and continue to Andratx on C719

Start in Andratx (▷ 66), taking the C710, which begins about halfway up the main street on the right as you approach Palma, and follow signs to Estellencs and Sóller. In about 400m (1,300ft) the road passes Castell Son Mas, a 15th-century fortress overlooking the town. Now restored, it houses the police station and town hall. At the next roundabout turn left, keeping on the C710. The road begins to climb, twisting and turning through pine woods. After 5km (3 miles) you will catch your first glimpse of the sea at the foot of the cliffs to your left. The road clings to the cliff top between the forested hills and the coast, passing through two tunnels on its way to Estellencs. Shortly before the second tunnel, pull in at the Mirador de Ricardo Roca to climb the steps to the lookout point for views over the north coast. There is a café here. The Mallorca Tourist Board (1905), whose first project was the construction of

the road between Andratx and Estellencs, built the mirador early in the 20th century.

❶ Estellencs is a pretty village of around 400 people, with stone houses, cobbled streets and a few restaurants, bars and hotels. A path leads down through orchards to a small cove with a shingle beach.

Continue on the C710 for another 7km (4 miles) until you see the circular watchtower of Torre de Ses Animes on your left.

❷ You can stop and climb up to the 16th-century Torre de Ses Animes, one of the oldest survivors of a line of coastal defences built along the north coast to deter pirates . Fires would be lit inside the tower to warn the villagers of danger. A ladder leads up to the roof, offering wonderful, windswept views as far as Sa Dragonera to the west. A short way along the road is a small parking area (signposted with a camera symbol) from which you can admire the terraces and stone walls of the fields outside Banyalbufar.

Continue to Banyalbufar **❸** (▷ 66) and drive along the main street. Beyond the village the road leaves the coast behind and starts to climb inland once again. When the C710 turns left to Sóller, keep straight ahead towards Palma and shortly afterwards turn right to La Granja **❹** (▷ 68). Leaving La Granja, turn right out of the car park on the narrow road to Puigpunyent. Stay on this road for 10km (6 miles) as it snakes through olive groves in the shadow of the Galatzó Mountain. Just after passing the Puigpunyent village sign, turn right (signposted Galilea and Palma) to bypass the narrowest streets and arrive at the centre of the village. Turn right again and continue past the church, with the option of a diversion to your right to visit La Reserva (▷ 74).

❺ Puigpunyent is a peaceful, rural village, but its proximity to Palma means it is attracting many foreigners buying second homes. The village's manor house, Son Net, is one of Mallorca's top hotels (▷ 186).

Stay on the C710 for another 4km (2.5 miles) to reach Galilea.

❻ It is worth parking your car outside the village of Galilea and walking up to the church square to admire the views, which stretch all the way from the Galatzó Mountain on one side to Palma Bay on the other.

From Galilea, the road winds slowly downhill towards the small village of Es Capdellà.

❼ A short diversion to the left of Es Capdellà leads to Calvià, the municipality that includes the beach resorts of Palma Nova, Magaluf and Santa Ponça. Once a poor rural village, Calvià mushroomed in the late 1990s and is now one of the richest towns in Spain. Despite this, it remains an unassuming place, with few signs of tourism. Glazed

OUT AND ABOUT

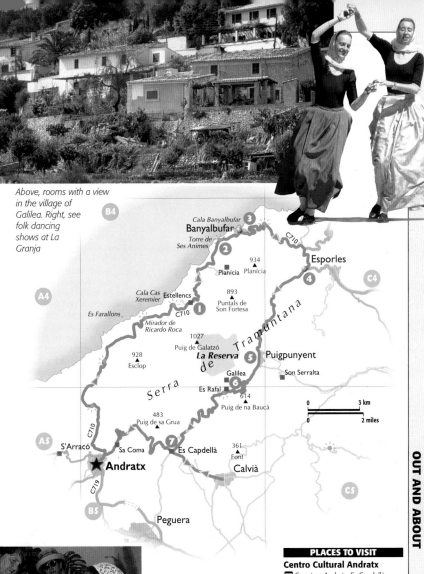

Above, rooms with a view in the village of Galilea. Right, see folk dancing shows at La Granja

Cala Banyalbufar **Banyalbufar** 3
Torre de Ses Animes 2
C710
934 ■ Planícia Planícia
Esporles
Planícia 4 C4
893 ■ Puntals de Son Fortesa
Cala Cas Xeremier Estellencs
1027 ▲ Puig de Galatzó
La Reserva 5 Puigpunyent
■ Son Serralta
928 ▲ Esclop
de
Galilea 6
Serra Es Rafal
614 ▲ Puig de na Bauçà
483 ▲ Puig de sa Grua
0 3 km
0 2 miles
S'Arracó 7 Es Capdellà
361 ▲ Font
Calvià
★ **Andratx**
Sa Coma
C719
B5
Peguera

B4
A4
A5
C710
C710
C5
Tramuntana

OUT AND ABOUT

Learn traditional Mallorcan needlework at La Granja

ceramic tiles in the church square tell the history of the town through a series of tableaux. Near here is the

13th-century church of Sant Joan Baptista, which was rebuilt in the 19th century.

Turn right in Es Capdellà and keep straight ahead at the crossroads to return to Andratx, passing carob and almond groves, with occasional glimpses of the sea. As the road levels out you pass the vineyards and bodega of Santa Catarina—one of the new generation of Mallorcan winemakers—which offers free tours and tastings. After passing the huge new cultural centre and art gallery on the outskirts of Andratx, you will see Castell Son Mas up ahead.

PLACES TO VISIT

Centro Cultural Andratx
✉ Carretera Andratx–Es Capdellà
☎ 971 137770
🕐 Tue–Sat 10–6, Sun 10–4
🎫 Adult €5, child (under 12) free
www.ccandratx.com

Bodega Santa Catarina
✉ Carretera Andratx–Es Capdellà
☎ 971 235413
🕐 Mon–Fri 9–5, Sun 12–2
🎫 Free
www.santa-catarina.com

WHERE TO EAT

There are great views from the terrace of Café Bellavista (tel 971 618004), in the centre of Banyalbufar. The two village bars in Galilea are both good for a snack, and lunch is served daily at La Granja (▷ 68).

EASTERN TRAMUNTANA

A drive into the mountains through spectacular gorges surrounded by craggy peaks. Confident drivers can take a helter-skelter journey over the Sóller Pass.

THE WALK

Distance: 98km (61 miles)
Allow: 3 hours
Start/end at: Lluc Monastery

HOW TO GET THERE

Lluc is on the C710 between Pollença and Sóller. It can also be reached via PM-213

Start at Lluc Monastery, taking the main road out of the car park. At the first junction, turn right (signposted Inca and Palma). After 1km (0.6 mile), turn left towards Inca, passing a petrol station on the left. The road drops steeply through a succession of bends with views across the plain to the Serra de Llevant. After 10km (6 miles) you enter Caimari.

❶ Known for its olives, the village of Caimari is home to the island's oldest olive-oil co-operative, Oli Caimari (▷ 122). You can visit the oil mill. The ethnological park, at the east side of the village, is an open-air museum of Mallorcan rural traditions, with a limekiln, a charcoal stove, a net for catching thrushes and a *casa de neu*, used for storing winter snow in the days before refrigeration. Access to the park is free at any time.

Turn right beside the olive groves on a minor road signposted to Mancor and continue between plantations of carob and olive trees. On reaching Mancor, turn left at the crossroads then left again on the main road towards Inca. After 1km (0.6 mile) turn right (signposted Biniamar and Lloseta). Pass through the hamlet of Biniamar and continue to Lloseta. Turn sharp right at a four-way junction to pass through the centre of the village.

❷ Lloseta is best known for its leather industry, in particular Bestard mountain boots (▷ 123). As recently as the 1960s there were 32 workshops in the village producing boots and shoes. Also of interest here is the 18th-century

palace of the Count of Aiamans, now a smart rural hotel, Cas Comte. You can reach it by climbing the steps beside the parish church.

Leave Lloseta, and after 1km (0.6 mile) turn right, following signs for Alaró. Stay on this road, the PM211, for the next 7km (4 miles) through the rural foothills of the sierra. Before you reach Alaró, turn right at a crossroads (signposted Castell d'Alaró and Orient). Look up as you drive along this short road and you will see a white farmhouse on the horizon, halfway up a mountain. This is Es Verger, the restaurant on the way to Castell d'Alaró (▷ 66). To visit the castle, turn left at the T-junction at the end of this road and follow the signs. You can take your car as far as Es Verger—after that it is easier to walk. If you do not want to visit the castle, turn right at the T-junction on the PM210 and continue for 8km (5 miles) as the road climbs to Orient. The twin plateaux of Puig d'Alaró and Puig de S'Alcadena face each

other across the road, guarding the entrance to the valley. Shortly after passing L'Hermitage hotel (▷ 186), you will see the village of Orient (▷ 74) nestling in the valley to your right.

❸ The tiny village of Orient has a population of around 30 people, but its bars and restaurants attract many visitors at weekends. It is worth parking your car and wandering up to the 17th-century church of Sant Jordi (St. George). If it is open, go inside to see the marble and gold altar and a wood crucifix.

Continue on the narrow, bendy PM210 for another 10km (6 miles) into Bunyola.

❹ Bunyola is a pleasing little town, previously the centre of production for Tunel, a herbal liqueur named after the nearby railway tunnel. In 1998, the company moved to Marratxí.

At the main square in Bunyola turn right and cross the railway line from Palma to Sóller. At the

Above, a view over Port de Sóller. Top, walking routes are signposted

Passing the gatekeepers: Puig de S'Alcadena and Puig d'Alaró

Wild flowers line Gorg Blau reservoir in the mountains

next round-
about turn right
onto the C711 to
Sóller. On reaching the
Jardins de Alfàbia (▷ 69)
you have a choice. The easier
option is to continue straight
ahead through the Sóller Tunnel
(toll payable). Alternatively, turn
left to head up the Coll de Sóller.

5 The 14 km (9-mile) route
over the Sóller Pass is one of
the scenic highlights of
Mallorca—although with 57
hairpin bends to negotiate, it is
not for nervous drivers. The
road climbs steeply towards
the pass (501m/155ft), where
there is a car park and a bar.
On a clear day the views from
the terrace stretch down to
Palma and far out to sea. Once
you are over the pass the
landscape changes, with huge
terraces of drystone walls and
views across the Sóller Valley.

The two routes are reunited at
the exit from the tunnel. Drive
straight ahead, bypassing Sóller
6 (▷ 76–77). After passing the
botanical gardens, turn right at
the third roundabout onto the
C710 (signposted Pollença and
Lluc). Stay on this road as it
climbs to the high sierra; the
views are superb the whole way.
After passing the road to
Fornalutx (▷ 77) on the right,
you arrive at Mirador de Ses
Barques on the left. You can
lunch at the terrace restaurant or
see the best views of Port de
Sóller from the belvedere. Soon
after this, the road reaches a
height of 1,000m (3,280ft), then
tunnels into the mountains to
emerge in a military zone before

carving its
way through a
deep gorge
between Mallorca's two
highest summits, Puig Major
(1,447m/4,688ft) and Puig de
Massanella (1,367m/4,429ft).
The Cúber and Gorg Blau reservoirs are popular birdwatching
spots. After a second tunnel you
pass the switchback road to Sa
Calobra (▷ 74) on your left. The
final stretch has spectacular
views, looking out to sea over the
sheer limestone walls and jagged
rocks of the Torrent de Pareis.
Stay on the C710 and follow the
signs to return to Lluc.

WHERE TO EAT

Restaurant Orient
Tuck in to generous portions of
rustic Mallorcan cuisine.
✉ On the main road through Orient
☎ 971 615153
🕐 Mon and Wed–Sat 1–4, 8–11, Sun
and Tue 1–6

TO CAMEL ROCK

A chance to explore the magnificent scenery of the Tramuntana Mountains, with the minimum of effort. The route starts at Lluc Monastery and takes in odd-shaped rocks, ancient burial caves and natural water springs.

The choirboys of Lluc sing at morning mass on most days

THE WALK

Distance: 3.2km (2 miles)

Allow: 2 hours

Start/end at: Lluc Monastery (▷ 212 E2)

Information: Serra de Tramuntana information centre, Ca S'Amitger, Lluc, tel 971 517070

HOW TO GET THERE

Lluc is on the C710 between Pollença and Sóller and it can also be reached on PM213 from Inca. Allow extra time for the journey here, especially in the summer, when the difficult roads are very busy.

Lluc Monastery (▷ 70–73) is a popular walking centre and the starting point for a number of serious hikes, including the ascents of Puig de Massanella and Puig Tomir. This easy walk, however, can be done by anybody equipped with a sturdy pair of shoes. You can pick up a map and descriptive leaflet at Ca S'Amitger, the environmental information centre in the car park. The walk is numbered 1 in a series entitled 'Getting to know the Serra de Tramuntana'.

Leave Lluc by taking the main road out of the car park, keeping to the pavement on the left-hand side. When you reach a concrete road on the left, turn off and pass through the gateposts. The way ahead, marked 'Camí Reservat', is a private access road to the monastery. Instead, turn right and climb through a gap in the wall (signposted Santuari de Lluc—Acampades), which brings you out by a dusty football pitch.

You may spot the choirboys of the Escolania here, having exchanged their blue cassocks for football kit.

Follow the path around the outside of the fence, then enter the football pitch through a gate. Leave through another gate in the far left-hand corner to arrive at a wooden footbridge.

This bridge crosses the Torrent de Lluc, a watercourse which is bone-dry for much of the year but fills rapidly with fast-flowing water after rain. After merging with the Torrent de Pareis the stream eventually flows into the sea at Sa Calobra (▷ 74).

Cross the bridge and clamber over the boulders to begin the climb up to a rocky ridge. This is a short but steep ascent through a shady grove of oak trees, following a path marked with red dots on the signposts. Wild goats can sometimes be seen here. After 150m (500ft) you come to an open area on your left where the ground has been artificially flattened.

This was the site of a *rotllo de sitja*, a round construction consisting of an earthen mound enclosed by a circle of stones. At one stage these were common features of the Mallorcan landscape, used by *carboners* (coalmen) to produce charcoal. Branches from oak trees were built up around the *sitja* into a conical shape, then burnt slowly to obtain the fuel.

Take the narrow path to your right opposite the *sitja* (signposted Es Camell).

This short diversion leads in about 50m (160ft) to the famous Camel Rock, an outcrop sculpted by wind and rain over thousands of years into the shape of a camel. Follow the path and descend the steps to arrive at a flat area, where there is a stone bench from which to contemplate this natural work of art.

Retrace your steps to return to the main path. Turn right and continue to climb until you arrive at a junction with a wooden waste bin in front of you.

It is worth taking another short detour here to enjoy the best views of the walk. Turn left and follow the wide path for around 100m (330ft) to reach the Mirador des Pixarells, where you will find more stone benches and a small sign forbidding camping and lighting fires. There are fine views across the sierra from here. Notice how the karstic limestone rock has been eroded into yet more fantastical shapes in various shades of russet and grey.

Return to the junction and keep straight ahead, passing a curious-looking pine tree whose distinctive shape has given rise to the nickname 'the witches' nest'.

OUT AND ABOUT

The famous Camel Rock: can you see the resemblance?

Just before the path descends, look for an opening in the ground to your left. This is Sa Cometa des Morts (Cave of the Dead), a prehistoric burial cave first discovered and explored by a monk from Lluc Monastery. A sarcophagus discovered in the cave is on display in the monastery's museum.

Stay on the path as it climbs gradually through the terraces where steep banks are divided by stone walls, then follows a zigzag course to reach a main road. Turn right here and walk beside the road for 200m (656ft). Take great care—the traffic can be fast here.

On your left you pass an access road to Binifaldó. This old stone farmhouse at the foot of Puig Tomir is now a forestry education centre. If the name is familiar, it is because Binifaldó is also Mallorca's leading brand of mineral water. The water comes from a nearby spring.

Turn right at a wooden gate, where the gatepost is marked with a red dot.

You are now on the old road from Pollença to Lluc, which has been in existence since at least the 13th century. At one time it was designated a *camino real* (royal path), and a toll was levied for maintenance of the route.

Stay on the path as it twists and turns, making a gradual descent towards Lluc. After passing a campsite, you arrive back at the football pitch from where you can retrace your steps to the monastery.

WHERE TO EAT

There are no facilities on this walk, so take plenty of water and a snack. You can stock up on provisions at a small shop near the entrance to the monastery. There are, however, several options at Lluc itself. Sa Fonda (tel 971 517022), in the old monks' refectory, offers traditional Mallorcan cuisine. Ca S'Amitger (tel 971 517046) and Sa Font Coberta (tel 971 517029) are restaurants situated at either end of the car park. For a lighter meal, you can pick up a pastry or a plate of *pa amb olí* at Café Sa Plaça in the main square.

A view across the valley of Lluc from the pilgrims' footpath

POLLENÇA AND ALCÚDIA BAYS

Enjoy farmland, moorland, marshes, dunes and coast on this tour of northeast Mallorca, perhaps combined with a walk in the S'Albufera nature reserve, a visit to a historic town, or an afternoon on the beach.

The Porta del Moll: one of Alcúdia's original defensive gates

THE DRIVE

Distance: 90km (56 miles)

Allow: 2 hours

Start/end at: Port de Pollença

Tourist information: Carrer de les Monges, 9, Port de Pollença, tel 971 865467

HOW TO GET THERE

Take PM220 from Pollença

Start on the seafront at Port de Pollença (▷ 93) and head south around the bay in the direction of Alcúdia.

❶ As you leave the harbour behind, the villas on the promenade gradually give way to the modern apartments and hotels of Llenaire. Beyond here, the beach gets narrower and less crowded. There are fine views across the Bay of Pollença, sheltered by the Formentor and Victòria peninsulas on either side. To your right is the S'Albufereta wetland reserve; to your left the fishing village of Barcarès, where many Mallorcans have weekend homes.

Turn left at the roundabout to enter Alcúdia **❷** (▷ 84–85). When you see the medieval walls and gateway ahead, keep to the right-hand lane. After rounding a bend, turn right at the

traffic lights in front of the church (signposted Can Picafort and Artà). You can see the remains of the Roman city of Pollentia on your left.

After passing the cemetery you reach a roundabout dominated by a large statue of a prancing horse. Take the second exit to the right, following signs for Artà. On your right you will see a football ground and the waterslides at Hidropark, clearly visible from the road. Keep straight ahead at the next roundabout to enter the sprawling resort area of Port d'Alcúdia. You are now on the C712 coast road, which leads around the Bay of Alcúdia, cutting the main hotel and shopping districts off from the beach. Despite driving parallel to the longest beach in Mallorca, you will get only occasional glimpses of the sea. The road crosses a bridge beside the entrance to the Parc Natural de S'Albufera (▷ 89).

❸ Parc Natural de S'Albufera is a rare and precious area of coastline with a variety of habitats, including marshland, pine woods and dunes. Sadly, from an ecological point of view, the boundary of the natural park does not extend as far as the shore and a number of large hotels have been built on the

seaward side of the road in a district known as Platja de Muro.

Keep straight ahead at the next roundabout to pass through the resort of Can Picafort.

❹ The main reason for stopping at Can Picafort, apart from the beach, is to visit the Son Real necropolis, which dates back to the 7th century. You can reach it by walking south along the beach and crossing the Son Bauló torrent. A short distance farther south a modern defence tower gives views over S'Illot des Porros (Leek Island), an offshore island with another prehistoric cemetery.

Leaving Can Picafort, the C712 continues uphill to a roundabout where you should keep straight ahead. You now leave the coast behind and the massif of Artà dominates the views. After swinging around two wide bends and passing a side road leading to Son Serra de Marina, a sign welcomes you to the Peninsula de Llevant nature reserve. Shortly afterwards, on seeing a Campsa petrol station ahead, turn right towards Petra. Stay on this road for the next 14km (9 miles) as it crosses moorland and woods. As you approach Petra (▷ 101), you will see the Ermita de Bonany ahead of you, perched on a hill. Turn right at the roundabout and stay on this road as it bypasses the Roman village of Santa Margalida.

❺ From Santa Margalida you can make a worthwhile diversion to Maria de la Salut, a small village chiefly notable for its unusual Byzantine-style domed church. Signs in the village point the way to Embotits Matas, the shop of an artisan sausage-maker. Here you can taste and buy products such as *sobrasada de porc negre*, a spicy sausage made with the meat of Mallorca's indigenous black pig.

OUT AND ABOUT

Sa Pobla is farming country, with irrigated fields and the windmills that once powered the water supply

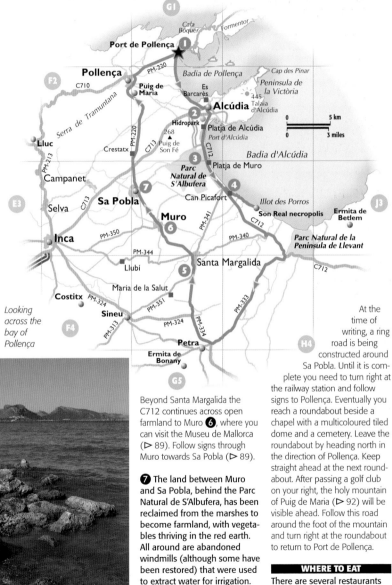

Looking across the bay of Pollença

Beyond Santa Margalida the C712 continues across open farmland to Muro **6**, where you can visit the Museu de Mallorca (▷ 89). Follow signs through Muro towards Sa Pobla (▷ 89).

7 The land between Muro and Sa Pobla, behind the Parc Natural de S'Albufera, has been reclaimed from the marshes to become farmland, with vegetables thriving in the red earth. All around are abandoned windmills (although some have been restored) that were used to extract water for irrigation. Modern evidence of Sa Pobla's agricultural importance is provided by the potato warehouse at the entrance to the town.

At the time of writing, a ring road is being constructed around Sa Pobla. Until it is complete you need to turn right at the railway station and follow signs to Pollença. Eventually you reach a roundabout beside a chapel with a multicoloured tiled dome and a cemetery. Leave the roundabout by heading north in the direction of Pollença. Keep straight ahead at the next roundabout. After passing a golf club on your right, the holy mountain of Puig de Maria (▷ 92) will be visible ahead. Follow this road around the foot of the mountain and turn right at the roundabout to return to Port de Pollença.

WHERE TO EAT

There are several restaurants along the seafront at Port de Pollença. One of the best is Stay (▷ 173, tel 971 864013), on the harbourside.

THE VICTÒRIA PENINSULA

Peaceful walking and magnificent coastal views can be enjoyed on a wild and lonely cape just a short distance from some of Mallorca's busiest beaches.

THE WALK

Distance: 13km (8 miles)

Total ascent: 480m (1,574ft)

Allow: 3–4 hours

Start/end at: Ermita de La Victòria (▷ 214 H2)

Tourist information centre: Carrer Major, Alcúdia, tel 971 897100

HOW TO GET THERE

Take the road out of Alcúdia towards Mal Pas. Continue to the yacht club at Bonaire. Turn right here and follow the coast road past a pair of small beaches.

When the road divides, keep right to climb to the hermitage

The long finger of the Victòria Peninsula pokes into the sea between the bays of Pollença and Alcúdia. Apart from the headland around Cap des Pinar, which is an official military zone, much of the rest of the peninsula has been designated a nature reserve and offers superb walks. Most of these walks (described in a series of leaflets available from the tourist office in Alcúdia) start from the Ermita de la Victòria, a 17th-century hermitage overlooking the sea; there is also a car park, a restaurant and public toilets.

Start the walk by taking the forest track that leads out of the car park, behind the hermitage. This is a steep climb but you are soon rewarded with fine views over Pollença Bay.

After about 750m (2,460ft), following a sharp right-hand turn, the path divides. The track on the left leads to Penya des Migdia, a rocky outcrop with the remains of an old watchtower and an abandoned cannon at the summit. You can climb to the top for views of the Formentor Peninsula and the pine forest from which Cap des Pinar takes its name. On a clear day you can see as far as the neighbouring island of Menorca.

The main path continues ahead, soon reaching a plateau with views out to sea on both sides.

Pollença is visible to your right, tucked between two hills. Beyond are the mountains of the Serra de Tramuntana.

At a junction with a wooden signpost, keep straight ahead, following the twisting path to the summit of Talaia d'Alcúdia (446m/1,463ft).

You are now at the highest point of the Victòria Peninsula. The ruined defence tower, of which only the base remains, dates from 1567. At one stage there were more than 30 of these watchtowers in Mallorca, strategically sited around the coast to guard the main entry points by sea. Across the bay

Platja des Coll Baix is just one of the bays along the peninsula's rugged coastline

The restored exterior of the Ermita de la Victòria

The altar inside the hermitage

to the north you can make out the Talaia d'Albercutx (▷ 88), watching over the Formentor Peninsula and the north coast.

Retrace your steps down the mountainside and turn right at the junction (signposted Platja des Coll Baix). The narrow path runs along a ridge on the slopes of Puig des Boc. After a while the path starts to descend, gently at first and then in a succession of sharp zigzags.

Keep an eye out over the cliff as you drop down towards the pass. At one point you have a dizzying vertical view over the idyllic cove of Coll Baix, whose sandy beach is framed by an unfeasibly turquoise sea.

Continue down this path to reach Collet des Coll Baix.

Here you will find a picnic area and a fountain supplying drinking water. A path to the left leads to the beach that you saw earlier from above. The descent is fairly straightforward, although it does involve some scrambling. This is a lovely spot, but swimming is not recommended because of the powerful currents.

To stay on the main route, turn right at the picnic area onto a forest track. Pass through a gate and into a car parking area. Follow this track through the woods for about 1km (0.6 mile), then take the path to the right (signposted Coll de Ses Fontanelles). The path is wide at first but soon narrows, crossing a dry riverbed several times before ascending steeply to a pass. Look carefully for the cairns that define the path. After reaching a ridge the

path starts to descend, with good views across the Bay of Pollença to Port de Pollença in the distance. Eventually you arrive at a small dam and the path widens into a track. Pass behind the houses of Bonaire and continue for 1km (0.6 mile) to a junction.

The path to your left leads to La Victòria campsite. Turn right here. Almost immediately, you come to a path to your left, signposted to Ermita de la Victòria. This is not the quickest way back—if you take this path you will drop down to a beach and have a long uphill walk to the hermitage. Instead, keep straight ahead and take the second path to your left. The path narrows, rising and falling before climbing steeply to the car park.

PLACES TO VISIT

The carved wooden statue of the Virgin above the altar in the hermitage (Tue 5–8, Wed–Sun 11–5) is venerated as La Mare de Déu de La Victòria (Our Lady of the Victory). A chapel has stood on

this site since the 13th century. According to legend, during a siege of Alcúdia one of the brothers held up the statue causing the rebel army to retreat. In 1644 Our Lady of the Victory became the patron saint of Alcúdia and 50 years later the hermitage was rebuilt in her honour. The people of Alcúdia still make the pilgrimage up here every year during the feast of La Mare de Déu de La Victòria on 2 July.

WHERE TO EAT

The Mirador de la Victòria restaurant (tel 971 547173, closed Mon) has one of the best settings in Mallorca, with sweeping sea views from the terrace. It serves classic Mallorcan cuisine. There is also a small café beside the church selling sandwiches, snacks and drinks.

WHERE TO STAY

If you want to stay the night, the top floor of the hermitage has been converted to a hostel offering simple rooms (tel 971 549912).

OUT AND ABOUT

A concrete bolt holds the summit of Talaia d'Alcúdia together

ACROSS THE PLAIN

Experience a completely different side to Mallorca on a drive across Es Pla, the agricultural heartland of the island with timeless villages and solid rural towns.

THE DRIVE

Distance: 99km (61 miles)	
Allow: At least 2 hours	
Start/end at: Algaida	

HOW TO GET THERE

Take C715 from Palma, heading east

For many people, the soul of Mallorca is to be found on the fertile plain known as Es Pla, an area of almond and apricot groves, sleepy villages and busy market towns. The population has declined as people have gone to work in Palma and on the coast, but many rural traditions live on. Farming has always been important here; as you drive across the plain you will see evidence of the area's agricultural history in the form of abandoned windmills, waterwheels and wells.

Begin in Algaida on the C715, the main road from Palma to Manacor, heading east from the Ca'n Gordiola glass factory (▷ 95). Very shortly you will see another mock castle, this one housing the Alorda factory shop, which produces leather goods. Turn left here and continue on the country road to Santa Eugènia, with dramatic views of the peaks of Alaró looming in the distance. After 6km (4 miles) you reach the Palma to Sineu road.

❶ A short detour left along this road leads to Natura Parc, where you can follow a walking trail to see farm animals and Mallorcan wildlife.

*Above, vineyards at Sencelles.
Below, the town's stone crucifix*

Turn left to stay on the main route and in 100m (330ft) turn right, following signs to Santa Eugènia.

❷ Santa Eugènia huddles beneath Puig de Santa Eugènia on the left and the windmills of Es Putxet on the right. An easy path leads up from the church square to a stone cross at the summit of Es Puig (246m/807ft). Despite its modest height, there are great views from the peak stretching across the low plain to the Tramuntana Mountains. Santa Eugènia contains the only Jewish cemetery in Mallorca.

Pass through the centre of the village and continue in the direction of the sierra. After 3km (2 miles) turn right towards Sencelles. The road travels through vineyards and passes the pretty hamlet of Biniali.

❸ Sencelles is a typical country village set in farmland growing vines, almonds and figs. It is known for its *xeremies*, a Mallorcan version of bagpipes that used to be played to summon farmers home from the fields.

Follow the signs for the centre of the village. When you reach the main square turn right beside the town hall and the parish church of Sant Pere. Turn right again on the outskirts of the village (signposted Costitx). Note the stone crucifix at the junction of the Costitx road. This is one of several built in the 18th century to define the village limits. Stay on this road for 4km (2.5 miles) to reach Costitx (▷ 97).

❹ Costitx is a good place for a break, with cafés around the two main squares. The Casal de Cultura, just off the main street, contains the Casa de la Fauna Ibero-Balear, a small natural history museum. Walk 9 (▷ 154) starts from here.

Keep straight ahead through the village. On reaching a junction turn right onto the main road to Sineu (▷ 102).

To visit Sineu, an old-fashioned market town with a strong sense of identity, turn right at the first signpost for it, passing the cemetery on your way to the town centre. Leave by following signs to Manacor. This will bring you back to the main road at Molí d'en Pau, an old windmill converted into a restaurant. If you do not wish to visit Sineu, stay on the main road and keep straight ahead at the roundabout by the windmill. Turn right at the next roundabout, signposted to Petra ❺ (▷ 101). When you see the village ahead of you, turn right to arrive near the church. You can park here to look around the village.

Continue around the church and follow signs for Felanitx through the centre of the village. On your way out of Petra, you pass the road up to Ermita de Bonany (▷ 101). Turn right at the next junction towards Felanitx. When you reach the C715 Palma to Manacor road keep straight ahead at the

OUT AND ABOUT

Parsley, sage, rosemary and thyme: herbs for sale at Sineu's market

The Molí d'en Pau restaurant is in a converted windmill

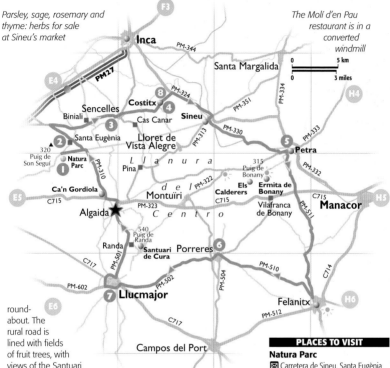

round-about. The rural road is lined with fields of fruit trees, with views of the Santuari de Sant Salvador (▷ 102) on a hill in front of you. Turn left at a junction, still following signs for Felanitx (▷ 100). Just before you reach the town take a sharp right turn (signposted Porreres) and continue for 12km (7 miles) across open fields to arrive in the centre of Porreres.

6 Porreres is notable for its 17th-century church, known as 'the cathedral of the plain' due to its size. The street leading from the church to the main square is named after Bishop Campins, a former Porreres priest who became bishop of Palma and was responsible for Antoni Gaudí's work on Palma Cathedral.

Leave Porreres following signs for Llucmajor. At the first roundabout keep straight ahead. A left turn leads to Santuari de Monti-Sion, an attractive 15th-century oratory with a five-sided cloister. Villagers built the road up to the sanctuary in a single day in 1954, and they still make the pilgrimage up here once a year for a communal picnic on the Sunday after Easter. Follow this road for 12km (7 miles) through open countryside, which gives way to pine woods. On reaching Llucmajor **7**, turn left towards Palma to drive around the ring road. At the far end of town turn right to Algaida on a section of dual carriageway. At the next roundabout turn left. Stay on this road as it undulates around Puig de Randa (▷ 102) before returning to Algaida.

PLACES TO VISIT

Natura Parc
✉ Carretera de Sineu, Santa Eugènia
☎ 971 144078
🕐 Daily 10–6, Apr–Oct; 10–5, rest of year
💶 Adult €7, child (3–12) €4.50

Casa de la Fauna Ibero-Balear
✉ Casal de Cultura, Costitx
☎ 971 876070
🕐 Tue–Fri 9–1.30; also 2nd and 4th Sat and Sun of each month; closed Aug
💶 Adult €3, child (under 6) free

WHERE TO EAT

Many restaurants on this route specialize in Mallorcan cuisine, including Molí d'en Pau (tel 971 855116, closed Mon) at Sineu and Es Celler (▷ 175) in Petra. Centro (tel 971 168372, closed Sat lunch, Sun evening), in Porreres, serves lunches, or wait until the end and eat at Algaida's Cal Dimoni (▷ 174).

COSTITX–THE HEART OF MALLORCA

Take an easy walk on paved roads through the wide, open countryside around Costitx, with panoramic views of the mountains across the plain.

Star gazing: the telescopes at the new planetarium in Costitx

OUT AND ABOUT

THE WALK

Distance: 6km (4 miles)	
Allow: 1.5–2 hours	
Start/end at: Plaça des Jardí, Costitx	
Parking: Plaça de la Mare de Déu, Costitx	

HOW TO GET THERE

Costitx is between PM324 and PM312, close to Sencelles (▷ 213 F4)

Costitx (▷ 97) is one of those places that has managed to survive the huge changes in Mallorca over the past 50 years. It is situated almost exactly in the centre of the island, on a quiet road between Sineu and Sencelles, which is overlooked by the majority of visitors. Fields of almond trees and cereal crops surround the cream-coloured cottages, and a bakery and a cluster of cafés are set around two neighbouring squares at the heart of the village. In prehistoric times Costitx was a significant centre of population, as evidenced by the remains of the Talaiotic culture discovered here. Following the Catalan conquest of Mallorca,

it became part of Sencelles, only gaining its independence in 1855. After a long period of decline Costitx is starting to recover; the population now stands at around 1,000 and a new cultural centre contains a museum, library and swimming pool. The astronomical observatory, opened in 1991, draws visitors and school children from across the island.

The walk starts in Plaça des Jardí, outside the parish church.

This was one of the first churches in Mallorca to be dedicated to the Virgin Mary. It was begun in 1696, though there were earlier churches on this site. The otherwise plain façade has a rose window and a statue of the Virgin in a niche above the door.

Leave the church behind you and walk straight ahead along Carrer Major, the main street of Costitx.

On your left you will pass S'Aljub, the village cistern. Originally built to provide drinking water for livestock, the granite and stone construction is a good example of Mallorcan rural architecture.

Continue to the end of this street on the way out of the village towards Sencelles.

A turn-off to the left leads to the Casal de Cultura, home to the natural history museum. To the right you will see an old windmill with an inscription above the doorway dated 1718. Also on the right, at a road junction, is a small shrine to Our Lady of Costitx, built in 1913. According to tradition, soon after the Catalan invasion of Mallorca a group of boys discovered a statue of the Virgin on this spot. Each year, on the Sunday after Easter, the Virgin is carried in procession from the church to the shrine and back.

Above, the parish church; below, the shrine to Our Lady in Costitx

Water works: the S'Aljub cistern

Leave the village and continue along the road to Sencelles. Most of this walk is on quiet country lanes, though there may be some traffic on this first section. After 1km (0.6 mile) take the left fork onto the small lane Camí des Horts (signposted Planetarium/Observatori).

The road to your left leads up to the observatory, which can be visited by prior arrangement (▷ 131).

Pass the observatory road and continue for 1km (0.6 mile) past a well until you reach a large house with a swimming pool in the garden. Turn left onto the surfaced road directly opposite this house. Stay on this road across open fields with good views of Puig de Randa ahead.

When you reach a crossroads, turn left along a rough track. This soon deteriorates further but remains wide enough for vehicles. Turn left at a T-junction onto a shady lane, which shortly becomes a paved road.

The road passes through the hamlet of Can Quiam, home to two of the most important *possessions* (agricultural estates) in Costitx.

Stay on this road past orchards

and citrus groves until you reach the access road to the observatory. Turn left here and right at the end of the road to climb the hill back into Costitx.

PLACES TO VISIT

Casa de la Fauna Ibero-Balear

✉ Casal de Cultura, Costitx
☎ 971 876070
🕐 Tue–Fri 9–1.30; also 2nd and 4th Sat and Sun of each month; closed Aug
💶 Adult €3, child (under 6) free

WHERE TO EAT

Bar Central (tel 971 513003), in Plaça de la Mare de Déu opposite the church, sells sandwiches and a lunchtime *menú del día* (closed Sun). There are other bars nearby, plus the Ca'n Font restaurant inside the Casal de Cultura.

OUT AND ABOUT

THE BULLS OF COSTITX

The estate of Son Corró, just outside Costitx, was the site of an important archaeological excavation in 1894 when a sanctuary from the post-Talaiotic era was discovered here. Among the finds were three bronze bulls' heads, together with their horns, probably dating from around the second century BC. These were especially interesting because they seemed to confirm the existence of bull worship in prehistoric Mallorca. The owner of the land put the bulls up for sale,

Are these bronze sculptures evidence of bull worship?

and they were bought by the National Archaeological Museum in Madrid, where they are now on display. Replicas can be seen on the wall of the courtyard in the

Casal de Cultura. Following a recent excavation, further bronze figures of a warrior and a Roman household god were discovered, suggesting that the sanctuary was still in use in Roman times. These are now on display at the Museu de Mallorca (▷ 60) in Palma. To visit the site, take the road out of Costitx to Sencelles and look for a sign to your right after about 1.5km (1 mile). Of the original horse-shoe-shaped building, all that remains are six stone columns and some sections of wall.

LLUCMAJOR TO CAP BLANC

This officially designated cycle route follows largely flat and little-used country lanes through orchards, taking in the breezy headland of Cap Blanc.

THE RIDE

Distance: 45km (28 miles)

Allow: 3–4 hours

Start/end at: junction of Camí de S'Aguila and the ring road (PM602) to the south of Llucmajor

HOW TO GET THERE

Take PM602 from Palma. From the roundabout at the western entrance to Llucmajor, follow signs to Santanyí. Camí de S'Aguila is the third road on the right

All along the watchtower: cyclists passing Sa Torre's lookout post

From the roundabout on PM602 at the western entrance to Llucmajor, follow signs to Santanyí. Camí de S'Aguila is the third road on the right. The bicycle route is signposted 'Ruta Cicloturistica de Llucmajor Camí des Cap Blanc'. Also look for the signpost to the police station, which is at the start point.

From the police station cycle south, away from Llucmajor. Follow the road for 1km (0.6 mile), until it forks. Take the right lane, signposted Camí de S'Aguila. Continue on this road as it winds through meadows and almond tree orchards. You'll soon start passing kilometre markers for the Camí de S'Aguila; the smoothly paved road will narrow after the 4km (2.5 mile) marker, but it should still be very quiet.

Continue along the Camí de S'Aguila, ignoring the right-hand turning for Camí de Sa Caseta after the 8km (5 mile) mark. The road, signposted Cap Blanc, bears left with a wall on the left side and a fence on the right. It

gets twistier. You'll arrive at a junction: the road bears left but take the right-hand turn (straight on), signposted Camí de Betlem. Taking the left-hand lane brings you to restaurant Cas Busso, where you can refuel with a snack and a cold drink. You can then retrace your path back to the junction and continue to Betlem. At the next junction turn right towards Cap Blanc. On your immediate left is Capocorb Vell (▷ 97).

❶ The village of Capocorb Vell, the most important Talaotic site in Mallorca, was inhabited until the arrival of the Romans. All that remains now are five defensive structures (*talaiots*) made from stone, and 28 dwellings along a prehistoric street, but look out for more megaliths in the

surrounding fields and orchards.

Follow the Carretera Militar (military road) to the right (not to Cala Pi).

As you reach the coast, there's a left turn and a short ride to the lighthouse on the rocky headland of Cap Blanc ❷ for views towards Cabrera Island (▷ 95). If you don't make a detour to the lighthouse, your first view of the sea will be as you round the right-hand bend, passing through a scrubby, wind-blasted landscape.

This main road heading north is straight so traffic will be travelling quickly, but it's wide enough for drivers to give cyclists a safe berth and the surface is very good. The road also starts to undulate for long but gradual inclines and downhill stretches. As you reach the built-up area of Badia Gran take a small road on the right signposted to Llucmajor and Sa Torre.

❸ You'll be able to see the church tower of Sa Torre for some time before you reach it. Sa Torre's second landmark is a derelict watchtower.

After passing Sa Torre, and the watchtower on your left, take a sharp right turn at the corner. You're now on the Camí de Sa

Cyclists can stop halfway at Cas Busso for an energy-restoring snack

OUT AND ABOUT

Head for heights: the cliffs of Cap Blanc with the lighthouse in the distance

You don't have to use a bicycle on this route; rollerbladers enjoy the quiet lanes too

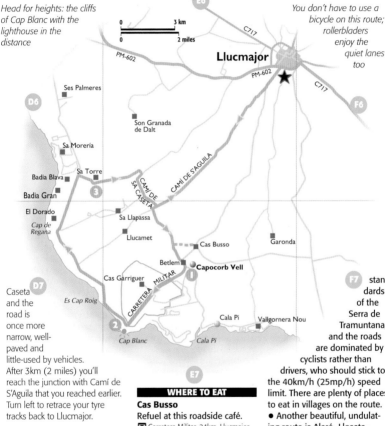

Caseta and the road is once more narrow, well-paved and little-used by vehicles. After 3km (2 miles) you'll reach the junction with Camí de S'Aguila that you reached earlier. Turn left to retrace your tyre tracks back to Llucmajor.

TIPS

● Cycling in summer's hottest temperatures can be a fool-hardy enterprise. The best seasons for cycling are spring and autumn; even then it is essential to avoid dehydration by drinking water regularly.
● Keen cyclists should bring their own pedals and shoes because it is possible to hire high-performance racing bikes on the island.
● Wearing a helmet is not required by law but is highly recommended; they can be hired easily.

WHERE TO EAT

Cas Busso
Refuel at this roadside café.
✉ Carretera Militar, 24km, Llucmajor
☎ 971 123002
🕐 Closed Tue
🍽 *Pa amb olí* from €2.50–€5
There's also a supermarket 200m (650ft) before the start point for stocking up on snacks and water for the ride.

OTHER BICYCLE RIDES

● The terrific Bunyola–Orient–Alaró–Santa Marí del Camí–Bunyola circuit is a favourite of fit cyclists; a section of it is covered in Drive 4 (▷ 144–145). There's some shade on most of the route, the hills are moderate by the vertiginous

stan-dards of the Serra de Tramuntana, and the roads are dominated by cyclists rather than drivers, who should stick to the 40km/h (25mp/h) speed limit. There are plenty of places to eat in villages on the route.
● Another beautiful, undulat-ing route is Alaró–Lloseta–Selva–Campanet but you'll need to arrange a lift back to the start if you don't want to make the return journey.
● For experienced cyclists, one of the most rewarding rides is the Pollença–Lluc–Selva–Campanet–Pollença circuit. Turn left at Lluc for a hair-raising run downhill to Selva where you take another left for Campanet and than make your way back to Pollença via the quiet lane (beyond the Coves de Campanet) that links the north side of Campanet to the PM220 road to Pollença.

WALKING IN MALLORCA

Mallorca offers a great variety of walking, from the high peaks of the Tramuntana to scenic coastal paths and quiet country lanes.

WHEN TO GO
The best months for walking are May, June, September and October, though winter can also be a pleasant time. The countryside of southern Mallorca is especially beautiful in February, when almond blossom covers the ground like a fresh fall of snow.

WHAT TO TAKE
- Walking boots or shoes
- Waterproof clothing
- Sunhat and suncream
- Insect repellent
- Water bottle
- Compass, torch and whistle in case of emergency

RIGHTS OF WAY
Many of the most popular walks in Mallorca cross private land and in recent years there has been a tendency for landowners to deny or limit access, even to traditional mule paths or pilgrim trails which may have been used for centuries. In part, this is because walking has become a victim of its own success, with growing numbers of hikers causing increasing problems of litter and erosion. It is not always clear whether you have a right of way, and signs indicating private property do not mean that you cannot walk. You can help future generations of walkers by observing a few simple rules (see below). Although signed footpaths in Mallorca are rare, the island government has recently laid out more than 250km (155 miles) of waymarked hiking routes where access is permitted. These include the Camí Vell de Lluc, an old pilgrim trail from Caimari to Lluc, and the Ruta de Pedra en Sec (Dry Stone Route), which crosses the sierra from Andratx to Pollença.

COUNTRY CODE
- Leave all gates as you find them.
- Do not disturb livestock.
- Do not drop litter.

- Do not pick wild flowers.

BOOKS
Landscapes of Mallorca by Valerie Crespi-Green (Sunflower Books, www.sunflowerbooks.co.uk): the first and the best walking guide to Mallorca, by an author who lives in Santa Eugènia. It includes maps and bus timetables to help you plan your walks. Updates are available on the website.

Walk! Mallorca (North and Mountains) and *Walk! Mallorca (West)* by Charles Davis (Discovery Walking Guides, www.walking.demon.co.uk): published in 2004, and accompanied by durable maps. The first book features walks around Alcúdia, Pollença and Sóller, while the second concentrates on Andratx and Palma Bay.

Walking in Mallorca by June Parker (Cicerone Press, www.cicerone.co.uk): first published in 1986, a comprehensive walking guide by a well-respected author who died in 1998. Includes background sections on flora, fauna, agriculture and rural industries, and also features two walks on Sa Dragonera.

Holiday Walks in Mallorca by Graham Beech (Sigma Press, www.sigmapress.co.uk): this book features town trails as well as mountain and countryside walks. Updates are available on the website.

MAPS
The most useful maps for walkers are the IGN 1:25000 series. These are available at La Casa del Mapa (▷ 114) in Palma, which also sells individual leaflets on some of Mallorca's most popular walks.

ACCOMMODATION
The island government maintains two refuges for walkers in the Serra de Tramuntana.

These offer dormitory beds, meals and showers in basic but comfortable accommodation. Bed linen is also available for hire or you can take your own sleeping bag. Refugi Tossals Verds (tel 971 182027), in the heart of the sierra, can only be reached on foot; Refugi Muleta (tel 971 634231) is situated beside the Cap Gros lighthouse above Port de Sóller. The refuges may be closed in winter or at weekends, so it is essential to book in advance. Another good option for walkers is to stay in one of Mallorca's monasteries, such as Lluc (▷ 70–73) or Castell d'Alaró (▷ 66).

GUIDED WALKS
The Palma tourist office organizes a number of guided walks. For details and bookings, tel 971 177715.

Mallorcan Walking Tours (mobile tel 609 700826; www.mallorcanwalkingtours.puertopollensa.com) offers a number of day walks of between 10km (6 miles) and 16km (10 miles) during spring (March–May) and autumn (September–November). These are ideal for holiday-makers who are already in Mallorca. If you want to plan your entire trip around walking, the company also has a one-week walking holiday based at Port de Sóller, and a week trekking across the Tramuntana from Valldemossa to Pollença.

WALKING ORGANIZATIONS
Tour operators such as Inntravel (tel 01653 617788, www.inntravel.co.uk) in Britain can organise walking holidays in the Serra de Tramuntana. The website for the Dry Stone Route (Consell de Mallorca) is currently only in Catalan but is fairly self-explanatory: www.conselldemallorca.net/fodesma/pedra. Click on 'senderisme' and 'refugis'. Translated versions of the website are forthcoming.

OUT AND ABOUT

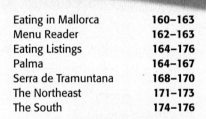

Eating

EATING IN MALLORCA

Mallorcan cuisine has its roots in rustic, peasant traditions. It is seasonal food designed to sustain farmers and fishermen, but scratch the surface and you'll find rich flavour combinations, deliciously fresh produce and truly interesting dishes. And don't imagine that the restaurant scene is unsophisticated either. It might be relaxed, but some of Spain's finest eateries can be found on the island.

Acclaimed chefs and adventurous diners have arrived on Mallorca, but traditional tastes remain popular

WHERE TO EAT

You can judge how seriously Mallorcans take their food by witnessing how many places serve it: bars, cafés, restaurants, pubs and *cellers* are everywhere. Choosing a favourite is a matter of trial and error. In general, avoiding anywhere that lists burgers and chips on a laminated menu and looking for places frequented by locals are sound tips for success. For good Mallorcan cuisine try exploring Gènova, on the western outskirts of Palma, where people from the capital go to eat out. You can also find excellent restaurants at out-of-town crossroads and roadsides. These places are where travellers have traditionally stopped to refuel; you can find one such concentration of Mallorcan restaurants just outside Algaida.

Another source of traditional Mallorcan food is a *celler,* an old wine cellar converted into a restaurant. These often have redundant wine vats in the dining room to prove the point. Towns in which you'll find good *cellers* include Petra and Sineu.

If you don't want a full meal, *tapas* bars (▷ 161) and cafés provide filling snacks. Cafés will often be open at all hours of the day, while *tapas* bars do most of their business in the evening. To blur the distinction, some cafés serve *tapas* dishes as well as sandwiches and pastries.

Because of numerous previous invasions and a regular stream of international visitors and settlers, Mallorca has perhaps a greater range of cuisines than you'd typically find on the Spanish mainland. French, Italian, Indian, Thai: Mallorca has them all, and in Palma you can even eat Argentinian, Ethiopian or Japanese food. In the resorts, however, the dominant cuisines are British and German, with lots of British-owned pubs and restaurants serving bratwurst and hamburgers.

Outside these areas, more Mallorcan restaurants, serving traditional dishes, have opened in recent years. See page 162 for a guide to Mallorcan specialities.

BREAKFAST

Breakfast is not the most important meal of the day for Mallorcans: They'll simply kick-start the morning with a strong, black *café solo* and a pastry. Most hotels, however, will offer a buffet breakfast for larger northern European appetites, with hams, cheese, breads, cereals and fruit.

LUNCH

Restaurants typically serve lunch from 1pm to 3pm or later. Mallorcans perfer to eat a late lunch but in tourist areas most restaurants will be open from 1pm. The *menú del día* is often an economical way of having lunch. For a set price you'll get three courses and maybe even a drink.

DINNER

If you arrive for dinner before 9pm, you're likely to be dining in an empty restaurant—Mallorcans don't go out to eat until late in the evening, typically from 9pm to midnight. While dressing for dinner is not strictly necessary, except perhaps in the smartest hotels, such as Scott's (▷ 174), Mallorcans manage to appear casually smart when they go out.

CHILDREN

Children are welcomed at the majority of

EATING

restaurants, but we have indicated in the listings those places where they are not.

VEGETARIAN FOOD
Seasonal vegetables play a large part in Mallorcan cooking and it is not difficult to find vegetarian dishes, including such tasty Mallorcan staples as *tumbet*.

DISABLED DINERS
Some restaurants, bars and cafés in Mallorca have limited access for wheelchair users. Many of the *tapas* bars in La Llotje, for example, are

(▷ 201) will be added to the bill—this tax is often applied in more expensive restaurants. Virtually all restaurants will take credit cards. We have indicated in the listings those restaurant that do not accept credit cards.

PRICES
The restaurant prices given are for the least expensive à la carte two-course lunch (L) and three-course dinner (D) per person and the least expensive bottle of wine. Where relevant, the price of the *menú del día* or the price of *tapas* has been included.

Dining alfresco is one of the great pleasures of Mallorca; sampling the superb wines is another

up or down flights of steps. Places that have an outdoor terrace are probably the most accessible. It's a good idea to check in advance whether there will be problems.

RESERVATIONS
Booking ahead is advised for restaurants in the middle to upper price range in the high season. Tables for dinner at the very best restaurants, such as Read's Hotel (▷ 169), may be booked up some time in advance, but lunch can be a less busy time. Popular local restaurants will often be full on Sunday lunchtimes.

DRESS CODE
In only a handful of exclusive restaurants, usually attached to expensive hotels, will you feel uncomfortable in casual clothing. While few restaurants ban customers from wearing T-shirts and shorts, most require that men wear something on top.

SMOKING
The majority of restaurants permit smoking. We have indicated in the listings those that do not permit it at all. Note that non-smoking areas are a novelty and restrictions may not be enforced.

MONEY
A 10 percent tip is customary. Restaurants will state on the menu whether a 7 percent tax

TAPAS IN MALLORCA
Tapas, snack-size portions of food once served free with a drink, are central to Spanish cuisine. But they're not a Mallorcan tradition; the idea was imported to meet tourists' expectations of eating out in Spain. It has caught on, however, and most towns in Mallorca will have a choice of places—bars, restaurants and cafés—serving *tapas*. Because it is not a local custom, you

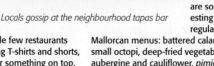

Locals gossip at the neighbourhood tapas bar

won't find the specially crafted dishes that you might find in Andalucía. Many Mallorcan *tapas* specialities are simply miniaturized versions of main dishes, such as meatballs or spicy sausages. But, as well as the basic choices such as olives and slices of ham, there are some more interesting variations that regularly appear on Mallorcan menus: battered calamari rings and small octopi, deep-fried vegetables such as aubergine and cauliflower, *pimientos de padrón* (deep-fried hot green peppers), ham croquettes and dates wrapped in bacon. You'll also find cured meats, pickled and marinated fish.

FIVE OF THE BEST TAPAS BARS IN PALMA
Bar Sa Volta (▷ 167)
La Bodeguilla (▷ 164)
La Bóveda (▷ 165)
La Cueva (▷ 166)
El Pilon (▷ 166)

Venturing into the world of authentic Mallorcan cooking can be a daunting experience if you don't know your *tumbet* from your *bunyols*. The menu reader (below) describes some of the Mallorcan specialities you're most likely to find on restaurant menus, from savoury dishes to local wines. The glossary of Spanish food (right) arms you with general words and phrases to help you decipher a menu. Each is given in Catalan, followed by the Castilian in brackets

Left, celler restaurants are lined by wine vats. Centre, roasting a suckling pig. Right, local cheeses

Pa amb olí
Bread, preferably crusty and brown, is rubbed with garlic and tomato then served with olive oil and sea salt; snacks don't get much better than this cheap Mallorcan favourite.

Tumbet
A ratatouille-like vegetable stew of onions, tomatoes and aubergines, or other vegetables such as courgettes and peppers, depending on the season.

Sobrasada
Large, cured sausages, the best being made from Mallorca's small, indigenous black pigs. Central to Mallorcan cuisine, they're flavoured with a combination of paprika, salt and spices and can be eaten in any number of ways, including raw as a pâté on toast or cooked with honey. Sausages flavoured with hot cayenne pepper will be strung with red string; those with white strings are flavoured with milder paprika. A *sobrasada* should have a rich red colour and feel soft to the touch; those made from the black pigs boast a black wrapper. *Botifarrós* are smaller Mallorcan sausages, which are strung together.

Cordero lechalî
Suckling lamb, commonly served in the form of *palatillas* (shoulders) and *piernas* (whole legs) gently roasted over rosemary sticks and garlic cloves until tender. A full-bodied Mallorcan red wine is the perfect accompaniment to this dish.

Sopas Mallorquínas
A robust winter dish made from stale bread and braised vegetables. It's a slightly misleading name because any liquid will have been absorbed by the bread.

Frit Mallorquín
Another unusual dish, often served in *tapas* bars on the island. Potatoes and vegetables are fried with chopped lamb or pork offal and flavoured with wild fennel and mint.

Arroz brut
'Dirty rice', a filling meal of meat, game, vegetables and rice, flavoured with *sobrasada*.

Trigueros
Wild asparagus, which grows all over the island, and is much sought after by locals, who scour the countryside for it.

Caracoles
Snails, mostly served in local restaurants with a garlicky mayonnaise called *aïoli*.

Lomo con col
Pork wrapped in cabbage leaves, often flavoured with *sobrasada*.

Seafood
Catches off Mallorca's shores include *cap roig* (scorpion fish), *mero* (grouper), *salmonetes* (red mullet) and *dorada* (sea bream) and all find their way to local markets and restaurants. Sóller is famous for big, red Mediterranean prawns. Have them grilled with garlic and parsley. *Longosta* (crayfish) are used in *calderetas* (fish soups and stews). A favourite Mallorcan dish is *pescado a la Mallorquina*, a fillet of fish topped with a light vinaigrette made from toasted pine nuts, sultanas, diced tomatoes and parsley. Don't leave the island without trying sea bass baked in rock salt, another delicious speciality.

Sweets
Ensaïmada
Mallorca's answer to the croissant—light, spiral-shaped pastries, dusted with sugar and

EATING

usually served with coffee or hot chocolate. Fillings can be savoury (such as so*brasada*) or sweet (such as pumpkin or apricots). Vegetarians beware: the texture is achieved by using lard. Poorly made *ensaïmadas* are not uncommon.

Bunyols
Potato fritters dipped in sugar and served with pumpkin or apricot jam.

Carne (Carne) Meat
ànec (pato) duck
anyell (cordero) lamb
bistec (bistec) steak
botifarra negra (butifarra negra) blood sausage
carn (carne) beef
conill (conejo) rabbit
fetge (hígado) liver
gall dindi (pavo) turkey
llengua (lengua) tongue

aubergine
bròquil (brécol) broccoli
carabassó (calabacín) courgette
ceba (cebolla) onion
cogombre (pepino) cucumber
col (berza) cabbage
enciam (lechuga) lettuce
espàrrecs (espárragos) asparagus
faves (habas) broad beans

Left, the digestif Herbes clears the head after a meal. Centre, almond sweets. Right, local pastries

Gato de almendra
A light almond sponge cake that you'll find in every bakery.

Drinks
Herbes
This aniseed-flavoured digestif comes in sweet or dry variations. The arresting flavour is created by 30 aromatic plants, including orange, camomile and mint.

Beer
Most beer (*cerveza*) will be from mainland Spain. If you want a draught beer ask for *una caña*.

Wines
Binissalem and Vi des Pla I Llevant wines are labelled as Protected Designations of Origin (PDO) and are the best wines on the island. Two Mallorcan grape varieties to look out for are Callet and Manto Negro. The most renowned vineyards are in Binissalem. Wine houses Anima Negra and Macia Batle produce some of Mallorca's best wines: 2001 was a good year, but there won't be many bottles remaining; 2002 was a very wet year, so vintages will be poor; but 2003 and 2004 are likely to be much better.

perdiu (perdiz) partridge
pernil dolç (jamón cocido) cooked ham
pernil (jamón serrano) cured ham
peus (pies) trotters
pollastre (pollo) chicken
porc (cerdo) pork
vedella (ternera) veal
salsitxa (salchicha) sausage
xoriço (chorizo) spicy sausage

Peix (Pescado) Fish
anxoves (anchoas) anchovies
bacallà (bacalao) salt cod
llenguado (lenguado) sole
lluç (merluza) hake
llobarro (mero) sea bass
moll (salmonete) red mullet
rap (rape) monkfish
salmó (salmón) salmon
truita (trucha) trout
tonyina (atún) tuna

Marisc (Mariscos) Seafood
anguila (anguila) eel
calamars (calamares) squid
cranc (cangrejo) crab
gambes (gambas) prawns (shrimps)
llagosta (langosta) lobster
musclos (mejillone) mussels
ostres (ostras) oysters
pop (pulpo) octopus

Vedures (Verduras) Vegetables
albergínia (berenjena)

mongetes tendres (judías verdes) green beans
pastanagues (zanahorias) carrots
patates (patatas) potatoes
pebrots (pimientos) peppers
pèsols (guisantes) peas
xampinyons (champiñones) mushrooms

Fruita (Fruta) Fruit
albercoc (albaricoque) apricot
cirera (cereza) cherry
gerd (frambuesa) raspberry
maduixa (fresa) strawberry
llimona (limón) lemon
poma (manzana) apple
préssec (melocotón) peach
meló (melón) melon
taronja (naranja) orange
pera (pera) pear
pinya (piña) pineapple
plàtan (platano) banana
raïm (uva) grape

Cooking methods
al forn (al horno) baked, roasted
a la brasa (a la brasa) flame-grilled
a la planxa (a la plancha) grilled
cru (crudo) raw
escumat (poché) poached
farcit (relleno) stuffed
fregit (frito) fried
rostit (asado) roast

EATING

EATING IN PALMA

Palma is a city that rewards a healthy appetite and a roving eye. One of the best Spanish cities for food lovers, an influx of foreign chefs in recent years has revitalised and modernised the restaurant scene. But local traditions are upheld with a fine line-up of Mallorcan specialists and many of the top restaurants depend on, and celebrate, high-quality local produce. The richest hunting grounds are the narrow streets of La Llotja for tapas bars and the Santa Catalina neighbourhood to the west of the city centre for a multi-cultural range of eateries.

AFRIKANA

Carrer Dameto, 17, 07013 Palma
Tel 971 287007

If you just can't take any more *pa amb olí*, chef Zamam from Ethiopia turns out wonderful dishes from all corners of Africa and the Caribbean at this cosy restaurant near Santa Catalina market. Start with aniseed-flavoured flatbread with a selection of dips, followed by aromatic beef from Madagascar, Kenyan peanut and vegetable curry, chicken Senegalese style or king prawns with vanilla and rum. There are always plenty of vegetarian choices. Dessert might be banana and ginger tart and you can finish your meal with coffee brewed in a clay pot. The owners also make their own ginger beer, hibiscus wine and Ethiopian honey wine. For a real treat, splash out on the five-course Ethiopian banquet at around €16 per person. A small selection of African crafts is on sale.

🕐 Tue–Sat 12.30–4, 8–12, Mon 8pm–midnight
🍷 L from €8, D from €20. Honey wine €2

ARAMÍS

Carrer Montenegro, 1, 07012 Palma
Tel 971 725232

The entrance to this chic restaurant, in a small group of shops at the top end of the La Llotja area, is easy to miss. Once you're inside, you'll find a smart, minimalist interior with a high, arched ceiling, candlelit tables, soft music, a bar and faux-arty black-and-

PRICES

The restaurants below are listed alphabetically, excluding Il and Le, and cover a range of prices. The prices given here are for a two-course lunch (L) per person and a three-course dinner (D) per person, without drinks, unless stated. The wine price is the starting price for a bottle of wine.

white photographs on the wall. The cuisine is international Mediterranean, with an Italian slant. Since revising its prices downwards, Aramís is better value, with starters such as rocket and parsley soup going for €6.70 and main courses costing from €11.70 for pasta dishes, including spaghetti carbonara and pasta with salmon and lemon sauce. Fish dishes include roasted fillet of sea bass. Panna cotta with mango sauce makes a tempting dessert. As you'd expect from a restaurant that offers wine-tasting evenings, the wine list has been thoughtfully compiled, with Riojas from €17.50. Although there's a €13 three-course *menú del día*, Aramís is better suited to romantic evening meals than lunching.

🕐 Mon–Fri 1–3, 8–11, Sat 8–11. Closed Sun
🍷 L from €20, D from €25. Wine from €15.70

BAR BOSCH

Plaça Rei Joan Carles I, 6, 07012 Palma
Tel 971 721131

Bar Bosch is a famous café and meeting place in the centre of Palma. Grab a table in the square with a sandwich (they're called *llagostes* and they cost from €3.25 for ham and cheese), a beer or an espresso and watch the world go by. Large slices of cake are also available. Although service

is highly organized and carefully choreographed, you'll be lucky to get a table at lunchtime, but it calms down at 2.30pm. Note that you pay more to eat outside in the square.

🕐 Mon–Sat 7am–3am, Sun 8am–1.30pm
🍷 L from €5. Wine from €7

LA BODEGUILLA

Carrer Sant Jaume, 1–3, 07012 Palma
Tel 971 718274

'Traditional Spanish cuisine with a creative touch' is how this restaurant near the top of Passeig des Born describes itself. There are actually two parts to La Bodeguilla. One side is a wine bar, perfect for a pre-dinner aperitif, with plates of ham and cheese to nibble and a selection of over 200 wines. The main restaurant, which stays open throughout the day, features classics such as garlic soup, venison with mushrooms and goose liver in puff pastry, and roast suckling pig. A popular starter is the *pica-pica* of gourmet *tapas* to share at €21 per person. Portions are generous, and the

EATING

service is friendly but discreet. La Bodeguilla makes a good venue for a romantic meal.

🕐 Wine bar Mon–Sat 11.30am–11.30pm, restaurant Mon–Sat 1–11.30

🍴 L and D from €25. Wine from €16

BON LLOC

Carrer Sant Feliu, 7, 07012 Palma
Tel 971 718617

Vegetarian cookery has been slow to take off in Spain but Palma's original vegetarian restaurant proves that meat-free eating does not have to be dull. Low lights and soft music create a soothing atmosphere. Popular with local office workers, the four-course lunchtime menu offers exceptional value and might feature salad, cream of fennel or beetroot soup, followed by jacket potatoes in a rich herb sauce and strawberry sorbet for dessert. The menu changes daily and there are always two choices for each course. Water is included but alcoholic drinks are available. This is part of a small foodie enclave near Passeig des Born; the same building houses a smart restaurant, a wine and *tapas* bar and a funky breakfast café.

🕐 Mon–Sat 1–4

🍴 L from €11.10. Wine from €6

LA BÓVEDA

Carrer Boteria, 3, 07012 Palma
Tel 971 714863

This popular Palma institution near La Llotja has a deserved reputation for serving the best *tapas* in town, and at busy times you will often find queues outside the door. This is just what a *tapas* bar should look like, with a lovely old tiled counter and customers standing at wine barrels demolishing platefuls of ham, chorizo and *tortilla* (potato omelette). Standard *tapas* dishes range from €5 to €12 and include dates wrapped in

bacon, garlicky grilled prawns and red peppers stuffed with cod. There are also more complete meals such as steak in pepper sauce. For a one-plate snack, it's hard to beat the *pa amb olí* topped with thin slices of Iberian ham. If you want to eat out of doors, there is a second branch around the corner with tables on a sea-facing terrace (Taberna de la Bóveda, Passeig Sagrera 3, tel 971 714963).

🕐 Mon–Sat 1.30–4, 8.30–12.30

🍴 L and D from €10. Wine from €7.50

CA'N CARLOS

Carrer de S'Aigua, 5, 07012 Palma
Tel 971 713869

The traditional Mallorcan cooking served up at Ca'n Carlos is of above-average quality and includes some out-of-the-ordinary dishes. But if you don't like the sound of *sepias con sobrasada*—cuttle fish chunks in tomato sauce with raisins, pine nuts, brandy and *sobrasada*—there are mainstream favourites such as stuffed aubergine, baked cod and *frit mallorquín* on the menu. The restaurant has a fine reputation but some diners report that service can be slow. You'll find it in a side street off the north side of Avinguda Jaime III.

🕐 Mon–Sat 1–4, 8–11

🍴 L from €15, D from €20. Wine from €11.40

CA'N PEDRO

Carrer Rector Vives, 4 and 14, Gènova, 07015 Palma
Tel 971 402479

If you're looking for good-quality Mallorcan specialities and a cheerful atmosphere, try Ca'n Pedro. There are two branches of the restaurant in Gènova; the larger one is at the top of the hill in the centre of the village, but the two are only a short walk apart and both are popular with visitors. All the Mallorcan favourites are here: *arroz brut*, snails, piqillo peppers, suckling pig and almond cake. Portions are generous, although the mixed grill (€9) is better value than the suckling pig (€15). Ca'n Pedro is a good place for a large group or family meal.

🕐 Thu–Tue 1–12am

🍴 L from €16, D from €22. Wine from €8

CANDELA RESTAURANTE

Apuntadors, 14, 07012 Palma
www.candelapalma.com
Tel 971 724428

This restaurant, on the main street through La Llotja, is perfectly placed to pick up a lot of custom from people leaving the many neighbouring *tapas* bars. It's a handsome place, with a large, subtly lit interior and a stylish design. Candela's cuisine is modern Mediterranean: simple starters, such as chicken consommé, are a surprisingly costly €9–€10, while main courses,

such as fillet of perch with mushroom risotto and chicory, cost from €18.50. Desserts, such as semolina pudding with vanilla and strawberries, are more inventive than usual. The location and trendy ambience perhaps justify the slightly inflated prices. Service, from the youthful staff, is efficient.

🕐 May–Sep 8–12am, Oct–Apr 7.30–11.30pm

🍴 L from €29, D from €37. Wine from €12

LA CUCHARA

Passeig Mallorca, 18, 07012 Palma
Tel 971 710000

This restaurant, on the east side of Passeig Mallorca close to Avinguda Jaime III, serves rustic Mallorcan dishes with a Basque twist. Expect starters such as black pudding with red peppers and leek. Mains cost €12–€13 for grilled sea bass or lamb fillet with rosemary sauce. Dessert includes praline mousse. Portions are not large—you'll wish there was more of the *risotto al cava* with its prawns, cava and dill—but the cooking is fine and flavourful. Look out for a few tongue-twisting Basque dishes such as *txistorra* (spicy Basque sausage) and *esqueixada* (marinated cod with tomato and black olives). La Cuchara's interior draws on classic rustic elements: red-and-white table-cloths, wine racks lining the walls and a tiled floor. Extras—bread, olives and oil—cost €1.50. The wine list has some reasonable Riojas and Navarras.

🕐 Daily 1–4, 8–12
🍽 L from €17, D from €22. Wine from €9.50

LA CUEVA TAPAS BAR
Calle Apuntadores, 5, 07012 Palma
Tel 971 724422

Choosing between *tapas* bars in La Llotja is a Sisyphean task. But you should certainly try La Cueva if you like fish: the bar's specialities are *gambas al ajillo* and *gambas a la plancha*. You'll also find one of the tastiest treats in Palma here: a €5.50 plate of fried whitebait. It's a mountain of hot, crispy and very fresh fish; just douse them in lemon juice and devour. La Cueva's *pa amb olí*, with crunchy, crusted bread, is just as good. The *tapas* selection also includes moreish kebabs for €4.50, kidneys in sherry for €5 and battered squid rings for €7. The house red is a good buy at €7, with Mallorcan wines going for a pricey €24. Décor includes a magnificent bull's head, stuffed and mounted on the wall.

🕐 Mon–Sat 12–12
🍽 *Tapas* from €4.50 per person. Wine from €7

FÁBRICA 23
Carrer Fábrica, 23, 07012 Palma
Tel 971 453125

Young British chef Alexei Tarsey is making waves at this fashionable restaurant in the buzzing Santa Catalina district. At lunchtime, it is full of trendy office workers enjoying one of the best deals in town, while at night it attracts a cosmopolitan yachting crowd from the nearby port. The food is Mediterranean with diverse influences from Asia, but always uses fresh market ingredients. Starters might be salmon tempura with mango, ginger and coriander, sautéed foie gras with peach chutney, or grilled asparagus with rocket, watercress, Parmesan cheese and mustard. Mains might include duck confit with apple and rosemary, monkfish red curry with coconut milk, or a roast red-pepper tart. Desserts are all homemade, such as hot chocolate fondant with vanilla ice cream. The wine list includes several good Mallorcan labels.

🕐 Tue–Sat 1–3.30, 9–11.30. Closed 1 Aug–7 Sep
🍽 L from €18, D from €30. Wine from €10

FLOR DE LOTO
Carrer Vallseca, 7, 07012 Palma
Tel 686 512241

This arty, offbeat, intimate bistro near La Llotja serves vegetarian and fish dishes, with influences ranging from Italian to Thai. You could start with Greek salad or carrot and ginger soup, while main courses include tagliatelle with salmon, Indian or Thai coconut curry, or the fresh fish of the day, simply grilled and served with basmati rice. The house speciality is *burani*, a rich casserole of courgettes, potatoes and feta cheese. For dessert, try the chocolate mousse with mashed banana. *Tapas* are always available and you can order a selection of mixed seafood and vegetarian *tapas* for around €12. The walls are decorated with emblems of the *flor de loto* (lotus flower), reflecting the owner's Buddhist beliefs. A flamenco guitarist plays here at weekends.

🕐 Tue–Sun 8–12
🍽 D from €20. Wine from €8

PARLEMENT
Conquistador, 11, 07001 Palma
Tel 971 726026

Local politicians and journalists lunch at this grand old dining room close to the cathedral. It might seem an imposing place but the staff, in traditional black-and-white attire, are easygoing. Cooking is ostensibly modern Mallorcan but there's nothing too adventurous about main courses such as crab canelloni or entrecôte of beef. Paella for two, at €11, is a speciality. Starters include pasta and salmon salad, and dessert include sorbet.

🕐 Mon–Sat, breakfast 10–12; L 1–4, D 8–11
🍽 *Menú del día* €15, D from €30. Wine from €14

EL PILON
Carrer Cifre, 4, 07012 Palma
Tel 971 717590

This terrific *tapas* bar specializes in seafood and has an open kitchen so you can see the chefs at work. Its seafood selection, displayed on a counter, includes king prawns, battered squid and octopus. Individual *tapas* cost from €4.40 while themed selections cost from €12.80 for the vegetarian option (*tumbet, peppers de padron*, cauliflower, aubergine and battered artichoke) to €18.20 for wild Mallorcan mushrooms, prawns, mussels and small squid. Watching the waiters is like watching a veteran chat-show host work a guest; they're friendly, amusing and professional. The décor piques interest if not appetite—turtles, sharks and gourds hang from the ceiling, and there are two house piranhas in a wall-mounted aquarium.

🕐 Daily 9–4, 6–12
🍽 *Tapas* from €4.40 per person. Wine from €9.05

EATING

SA LLIMONA

Carrer Fábrica, 27A; also at Carrer Sant Magí, 80, 07012 Palma
Tel 971 736096/971 280023

This pair of restaurants in Santa Catalina raises *pa amb olí* to an art form. You choose from a wide range of toppings—ham, salami, cured duck breast, smoked salmon, anchovies, cheese—and then it is make-your-own-meal. The waiter will bring you a side dish of salad, consisting of grated carrot and cabbage, olives, capers, pickled samphire, plus garlic and a tomato to rub on your bread. A basket on the table contains salt and a jug of olive oil. Finally the bread arrives, and the rest is up to you. If you don't fancy do-it-yourself, there is a small menu of ready-made salads, but really the whole point here is the *pa amb olí*.

🕒 Daily 8pm–midnight
🍴 D from €10. Wine from €8

SA VOLTA

Calle Apuntadores, 5, 07012 Palma
Tel 971 718440

Sa Volta, a small, no-frills *tapas* bar on Palma's main *tapas* thoroughfare, seats about 20 people around four tables. The hams hanging from the ceiling get an extra smoking from the customers at the bar. It's a warm, basement room with an arched roof and plain wooden tables. The garlicky *pa amb olí* is good, as is the plate of slivers of Serrano ham. Other Mallorcan *tapas* staples—squid rings, sausage, grilled prawns—are on the menu. Wine is available by the glass for €6.

🕒 Daily 12–12, closed 1–15 Aug
🍴 *Tapas* from €4 per person. Wine from €12

S'EIXERIT

Carrer Vicari Joaquin Fuster, 73, 07012 Palma
Tel 971 273781

This popular restaurant in Cuitat Jardí has a terrace overlooking the sea and a walled garden at the back. Inside the converted townhouse, a series of cosy dining rooms, decorated with paintings and antiques, make an indoor alternative if the weather prevents al fresco dining. Locals come to S'Eixerit for the fresh seafood and the house speciality, paella. The *menú del*

día at €9 is good value and includes a glass of wine, but it means that lunchtimes can be busy. The tasty desserts are homemade or order a platter of the Menorcan cheese, specially imported by head chef Ruben Perez.

🕒 Daily 1.15–4, 8.15–11
🍴 L from €18, D from €26. Wine from €10

SES ALBERGÍNIES

Carrer Rector Vives, 2, Gènova, 07015 Palma
Tel 971 404779

Packed with good restaurants, the district of Gènova on the western side of Palma is where the city's residents go for a night out. Ses Albergínies is usually top of diners' shortlists, so it is wise to book ahead. The kitchen is run by a former colleague of Marc Fosh at Read's (▷ 169) and cuisine is light, modern Mediterranean. If you can't get a table here, head up the hill to Ca'n Pedro (▷ 165).

🕒 1–3.30, 8–11.30. Closed Mon
🍴 *Menú del día* (Tue–Fri) €12.50, D from €25. Wine from €11

LA TABERNA DEL CARACOL

Carrer Sant Alonso, 2, 07001 Palma
Tel 971 714908

The 'tavern of the snail', hidden away in the back streets behind the cathedral and the Arab Baths, is well worth seeking out for its first-class *tapas*

at sensible prices. The atmosphere is one of rustic chic, with Gothic stone arches, wooden beams, whitewashed walls and strings of garlic and dried chillies hanging from the ceiling. The simple things are the best here, and with most dishes costing around €5 you can order several to share, from *frito marinero* (fried seafood) to *pimientos de padrón* (deep-fried spicy green peppers), scrambled eggs with Jabugo ham and the eponymous snails which come dressed in garlic and olive oil. If you still have room afterwards, they also serve excellent homemade cakes and desserts.

🕒 Mon–Sat 12.30–3.30, 7.30–11.30
🍴 L from €10, D from €15. Wine from €7.50

TAST CAFÉ-RESTAURANTE

Carrer Union, 2B, 07001 Palma
Tel 971 729878

One of the few Spanish chain restaurants to make it to Mallorca, Tast is much better than other fast-food options. Essentially it's a modernized *tapas* bar, with plates colour-coded according to price: salads cost from €5.45. Most importantly, Tast is close to Plaça Major and the square's surrounding shops.

🕒 Daily 12.30–12
🍴 L and D from €7. Wine from €7.75

VECCHIO GIOVANNI

Carrer San Juan, 3, 07012 Palma
Tel 971 722879

Vecchio Giovanni is a welcoming Italian restaurant in a busy La Llotja street between Apuntadores and the seafront. It's a popular, bright place, catering mainly for tourists, so don't expect to be amazed by the food: red peppers stuffed with shrimp, stone bass and angler are smothered in tomato sauce. Mains are inexpensive with pasta or pizza costing €7–€9. Desserts include the Mallorcan staple, almond cake. There are lots of tables for two, but it's more family oriented than romantic. Diners might find the Dalíesque paintings on the walls interesting—or off-putting.

🕒 12–3.30, 7–11. Closed Mon
🍴 *Menú del día* €8.50, D from €15. Wine from €11.61

EATING IN THE SERRA DE TRAMUNTANA

Many of the restaurants in the Serra de Tramuntana are dedicated to filling the stomachs of hungry walkers, who come down off the mountains for hearty Mallorcan meals of roast meats and seasonal vegetables. But for memorable gastronomic experiences there is also a heady selection of expensive eateries, such as Read's, Bens d'Avall and Es Faro. You'll also find a high standard of cuisine in the restaurants of the region's hotels (▷ 184), while the restaurants of the tourist hotspots of Deià and Valldemossa cater to all budgets.

ALARÓ
ES VERGER
Camí del Castell, 07340 Alaró
Tel 971 182126

A twisting road from Alaró leads up to this famous restaurant 4km (2.5 miles) from the village, housed in a white-washed farmhouse halfway up the mountainside on the way to Castell d'Alaró. It is possible to take a car up here, but the road deteriorates as you climb, with numerous potholes over the final stretch and very few passing places if you are unlucky enough to meet another car coming down. On the whole it is far better to walk, taking in the fabulous views. There is really only one thing to order here—roast shoulder of lamb, slow-cooked in a wood-burning oven and served deliciously tender with roast potatoes and salad (€10). Other hearty Mallorcan specialities include *arroz brut* and roast suckling pig. You can eat outside on the terrace in summer but there is no waiter service, so you must order your meal inside. No credit cards.
🕒 Daily 9–9
🍴 L from €13, D from €16. Wine from €4.60

DEIÀ
JAUME RESTAURANT
Carrer Arxiduc Lluis Salvador, 22, 07179 Deià
Tel 971 639029
This longstanding restaurant, in a smart, quiet townhouse on the road through Deià, has updated its appearance but

the cuisine is still solidly Mallorcan. Book a terrace table (Jaume fills up from 1.30pm) for lunchtime sunshine and views over an orchard of lemon trees and the gorge leading to Cala Deià. Look out for *tumbet* and Mallorcan sausages among the starters. Main courses include grilled squid and John Dory; roast pork with *tumbet* is good value at €9.90, with a large, hot helping of red peppers, tomatoes and aubergines with slivers of potato. The ubiquitous almond cake is on the dessert menu, but three scoops of the punchy lemon sorbet with a raspberry coulis is a refreshing alternative. The nine-page wine list includes Mallorcan red wines from €15.30 for Macia Batle Crianza 2000 from Binissalem.
🕒 1–3, 7.30–12. Closed Mon
🍴 L from €20, D from €24. Wine from €8.20

FORNALUTX
CA N'ANTUNA
Carrer Arbona Colom, 8, 07109 Fornalutx
Tel 971 633068
The views of mountains and orange groves from the terrace of this simple restaurant make it a popular place to eat in this small Tramuntana village. Sensibly, the cooking sticks to familiar, seasonal Mallorcan dishes such as *frit mallorquín*, rabbit, and pork ingredients such as *sobrasada*. Sunday brings weekend walkers and Mallorcan families to the restaurant, when it is advisable to make a reservation.
🕒 12.30–4, 7.30–11. Closed Mon
🍴 L from €16, D €20. Wine from €6

ORIENT
DALT MUNTANYA
Carretera Bunyola–Orient, km10, 07349 Orient
Tel 971 148283
www.daltmuntanya.com
With a large terrace making for a good viewpoint along Orient's main street, the

restaurant at this modern hotel is a useful dinner option in this tiny village. If you can't get a table outside, you might find the dining room a little impersonal. The menu is ambitious

yet traditional, with the emphasis on local and Balearic produce. A typical starter is a fig salad with Menorcan cheese or a selection of pâtés from Sóller with local pickles. Mains, costing €12–€18, might feature sea bass in almond crust—a departure from the traditional salt crust—with tarragon-flavoured tomato *concasse*.
🕒 Daily 1–3.30, 7–10.30
🍴 L from €17, D from €21. Wine from €11
🛏 19 (double from €96)

MANDELA
Carrer Nueva, 1, 07349 Orient
Tel 971 615285
The Genevan couple who run this restaurant at the top of the hill offer an interesting brand of fusion cooking: French-Indian cuisine. So you'll encounter main courses such as salmon with saffron sauce, chicken with green pepper sauce or duck breast with Marsala sauce. You'll also find dishes (for example Moroccan spiced prawns) that don't fall into either camp. Round off the meal with spiced ice cream for €4.80.
🕒 Winter: 1–3 Tue–Sun, 8–10.30 Fri–Sat. Closed Mon. Summer: 8–10.30 Mon–Sat. Closed Sun
🍴 L from €20, D from €24

ORIENT

Carretera Bunyola–Alaró, 07349 Orient
Tel 971 615153

Despite the explosion of new-wave restaurants across Mallorca, it is good to know that there are still village bars serving traditional peasant food. Restaurant Orient is situated beside the road which passes through the village on its way from Bunyola to Alaró. Local families come up here at weekends for long, leisurely lunches, while walkers and cyclists top up their calorie counts with much-needed refreshment. The main dining room has a picture window looking out over the citrus groves, or you can eat on the roadside terrace in summer. The food is classic Mallorcan, such as *sopas Mallorquínas* (meat and vegetable broth), *arroz brut* (rice soup), snails with garlic mayonnaise and roast lamb, all served in huge portions. Make sure you arrive with a healthy appetite.

Mon and Wed–Sat 1–4, 8–11, Sun 1–7

L from €10, D from €14. Wine from €9.40

PORT DE SÓLLER

ES FARO

Cap Gros de Moleta, 07108 Port de Sóller
Tel 971 633752

If there was a competition for the best view from a restaurant in Mallorca, Es Faro's

widescreen panorama would be in the running for the top prize. The restaurant is adjacent to the Faro lighthouse at the top of the hill on the southern side of Port de Sóller. From up here you can gaze out to sea, across the Tramuntana Mountains or into the harbour town. Standards (and prices) are equally lofty. Given Es Faro's location, it's no surprise that seafood is a speciality so expect to spend €17–€18 on main courses such as gilt head bream stuffed with asparagus or prawns sautéed in balsamic vinegar with an underwhelming black risotto. There's a tendency to complicate dishes but the portions won't leave you hungry and, like the quiet classical music playing in the background, the service is unobtrusive. Although there is a small car park at the top of the hill, it's a good idea to walk up because the road's narrow switchbacks get congested.

Winter: 12.30–3.30, 7.30–10.30. Closed Tue. Summer: daily 12.30–3.30, 7.30–10.30

Menú del día €25, L from €30, D from €34. Wine from €11

LA LUA RESTAURANTE

Santa Catalina, 1, 07108 Port de Sóller
Tel 971 634745

There is a cluster of restaurants at the far (north) end of Port de Sóller's harbour and La Lua is the one for fans of fish. Seating is on two floors, with the top floor offering the best views of the port. Décor is smart, with paintings for sale hanging on the walls. The restaurant seems to attract the more mature, predominantly British customer. The seafood available depends on the market prices—dorada, prawns and sea bass are regular fixtures on the menu. No seafood is served on Sundays. Starters cost from €4.80, mains from €8.10 (for steak) and ice creams for dessert from €4.25. Service can be haphazard.

1–4, 7–11. Closed Mon.

L from €13, D from €18. Wine from €8.75

ES PASSEIG

Paseo de la Playa, 8, 07108 Port de Sóller
Tel 971 630217

At the southern end of Port de Sóller (turn left as you enter

the town), Es Passeig is a smart, popular fish restaurant on the promenade. Its dark-wood interior—and the prices—set it above other restaurants on Port de Sóller's seafront, but the menu lives up to the surroundings. Simple starters, such as goat's cheese salad with fruit, cost from €9, while main courses, such as cod fillet with chickpea purée, cost twice that. There is a children's menu, on request.

Daily 1–3.30, 7.30–10.30 (weekend 11)

Menú del día €26, D from €30. Wine from €11

SANTA MARIA DEL CAMÍ

READ'S HOTEL AND RESTAURANT

Carretera Santa Maria–Alaró, 07320 Santa Maria del Camí
Tel 971 140261
www.readshotel.com

Marc Fosh's restaurant at Read's is the number one destination on the island for anyone with an appetite for imaginative, skilled cooking. The British chef's style is a blend of traditional French cuisine, modern Mediterranean techniques and Asian minimalism. Heavy sauces are absent; instead, dishes are light, fresh and forcefully flavoured. Themes are explored in each dish: fillet of salt cod with caviar, gelatine of vodka and cold celeriac and lime soup looks to northern Europe, while cardamom-glazed pigeon breast on cous cous with fresh herbs looks south. Expect to spend €15–€20 for a starter, €25–€30 for a main course and about €10 for a dessert such as vanilla panna cotta with rhubarb sorbet. At these prices the seven-course tasting menu is good value at €75. The sommelier is ready to recommend bottles from the wine list for each course. Vivid wall murals brighten the cavernous dining room. For less formal dining, Marc Fosh has opened a bistro, Simply Fosh, next to the main dining room. With a similarly bold interior, it is a lot of fun and very popular (reservations essential). He offers three courses from €25, with crowd-pleasing classics such as chilli spare ribs, Thai curry and spicy chicken tagine with cous cous. In the summer diners can eat on the terrace. Marc Fosh also holds monthly cookery demonstrations (see the website for details).

🕐 Restaurant and bistro: daily 1–3, 8–10.30

🍴 Read's Restaurant: L from €50 and D from €70. Wine from €18. Bistro: L from €25, D from €32

SÓLLER

BENS D'AVALL

Carretera Sóller–Deià, 07100 Sóller
Tel 971 632381
www.bensdavall.com

One of the best restaurants on the island, Bens d'Avall is as celebrated for its location as its food. As you drive from Sóller to Deià, look out for a right turn on a sharp corner, which will take you down a steep hill to the restaurant. When you're almost at sea level, the restaurant will be on your left, with fantastic views along the rugged Tramuntana coast. There's no better accompaniment to chef Benet Vicens Mayol's accomplished cooking than watching a sunset from the terrace. The seasonal menu is dominated by seafood with starters such as carpaccio of Sóller prawns with herbs, lemon, olive oil and a salad of fresh pesto. For €23, Bens d'Avall's fish of the day (often John Dory or sea bass) is barbecued over holm oak with tapenade, olive oil and sweet lemons. The kitchen's enthusiastic attitude to

desserts is more French than Mallorcan, with creations such as Cuban chocolate *millefeuille* with citrus fruit and spices. A six-course tasting menu costs €58 and there are options for vegetarians, and children— although Bens d'Avall is probably best enjoyed without them. During the winter months Benet Vicens Mayol holds workshops and cookery courses at the restaurant (see the website for details).

🕐 Tue–Sun 1.30–3.30, 8–10.30. Closed Sun pm, Mon

🍴 L from €36, D from €45. Wine from €20

CA'N QUIXOS

Plaça Constitució, 16, 07100 Sóller
Tel 971 633608

This smart restaurant in a prime position on the corner of Sóller's main square has six solid wood tables, a tiled floor and warm, low lighting. Mains include rabbit 'land and sea' (with fish), and look out too for peppered cod, grilled squid and stone-cooked fillet of beef. There's also paella for two at €9.95. Roast rabbit with onion was well cooked but bizarrely served with crisps as well as tomatoes and peppercorns. Service can be less than attentive. Desserts cost from €3 for fruit or apple tart.

🕐 12–3.30, 7.30–12 (earlier in winter). Closed Tue

🍴 *Menú del día* €12, D from €30. Wine from €8

SA COVA RESTAURANT

Plaça Constitució, 7, 07100 Sóller
Tel 971 633222

Tucked away on a corner of the main square, Sa Cova delivers fine, traditional Mallorcan meals in a cosy, friendly dining room. A *menú del día* is available for €11 (*sopa de Mallorca*, spaghetti, *arroz brut*) or expect to spend €5.50 on salads and €7–€10 on main

courses such as loin of pork.

🕐 Daily 1–4, 7.30–11

🍴 *Menú del día* €11 (Mon–Fri), L from €13, D from €16. Wine from €7.20

CA'N MARIO

Carrer Uetam, 8, 07170 Valldemossa
Tel 971 612122

Truly a well-kept secret, Ca'n Mario serves traditional Mallorcan food at keen prices to locals: paellas, *arroz brut* and *llom amb col* cost about €8. However, because the restaurant is off Valldemossa's tourist trail, you will need to speak competent Spanish when booking (recommended at weekends). The restaurant is not signposted from street level; you need to go into the building and up one floor. The airy interior is simply furnished, with red chequered tablecloths and wooden furniture.

🕐 Mon–Thu, Sun 1.30–3.30, 8–10, Fri–Sat 1–10. Closed Dec

🍴 L and D from €14. Wine from €8

SES ESPIGUES BAR RESTAURANTE

Marqués de Vivot, 4, 07170 Valldemossa
Tel 971 612339

This well-presented restaurant catches the afternoon sun on one of Valldemossa's main pedestrian streets. There are nice touches such as fresh flowers on the table and service is efficient, as it has to be in such a busy spot. The menu is mixed but features lots of Mallorcan dishes; the cooking is filling rather than refined. Starters include smooth liver-pâté with olives and crusty bread. Lamb chops arrive with rice, sautéed potatoes, carrots and mushrooms. Ses Espigues makes a good place for a lunch break during a day trip to Valldemossa.

🕐 Daily 10–11

🍴 L from €16, D from €20. Wine from €8

EATING

EATING IN THE NORTHEAST

The dining highlights of this region are evenly distributed along the northern coast of Mallorca, from Cavall Bernat at Cala Sant Vicenç in the west to Ses Rotges in Cala Rajada in the east. Stuck in the middle are the numerous restaurants of Alcúdia and Pollença, where the stiff competition keeps prices keen. There are fewer places to visit inland. Note that many places will close during the winter months because few tourists venture to the coast in the low season. Conversely, these restaurants will be packed in the summer, when booking ahead may be wise.

ALCÚDIA

CA'N SIMÓ

Carrer d'en Serra, 22, 07400 Alcúdia
Tel 971 546273

The old town of Alcúdia has seen many changes in recent years, including the arrival of several chic hotels. Once upon a time, all the action was down by the port, but the old town is now a fashionable place to stay and dine. One of the hotels, Ca'n Simó, has opened its own vegetarian restaurant to cater for the new breed of traveller coming to Alcúdia. Instead of a wide-ranging menu, there is a fixed-price *menú del día* offering two choices for each of four courses. Lunch might be salad or fruit juice, soup, vegetarian pasta or moussaka followed by cheesecake or coconut flan. Dinner is slightly more elaborate. After years of being marginalized, vegetarians are becoming more mainstream and even meat-eaters will enjoy this place, with its stone walls, bright colours and funky modern art.

🕐 Tue–Sun 12–4, 8–11.30, Mar–Oct; Tue–Sun 12–4, Fri–Sat 8–11.30, Nov–Feb
🍴 L from €12, D from €18. Wine from €10

ES CONVENT

Carrer del Progrés, 6, 07400 Alcúdia
Tel 971 548716
www.esconvent.com

The restaurant at Es Convent is a persuasive reason to stay at this hotel, and attracts diners in its own right. The stone walls, tiled floors, spotlights, low background music and comfortable chairs are a good start. The seasonal menu changes every three months, but you might expect to find a starter from €6 (for codfish croquettes) or, more typically, foie gras with Serrano ham, salt, olive oil and parsley for €16.50. Fish mains start from €18 (rolled red mullet stuffed with Mallorcan soups and *sobrasada*). Wild grouse in its juice, with candied cock's comb and tomato marmalade is an unusual combination of textures. Desserts include standards such as sorbet or interesting alternatives such as red-fruit sauté with balsamic and aniseed custard. Service is exemplary, with knowledgeable and enthusiastic staff. A mere 130 wines make it onto the wine list and the restaurant manager and maître'd is proud of his cellar, which houses four of wine critic Jancis Robinson's eight favourite Spanish wines. Wines cost from €12 to €90. Sweet wines are available by the glass from €3.50 to accompany tasty *amuse-bouches*, such as the house mint mousse served with Hojaldre sticks, a Mallorcan speciality. Prices are on the high side.

🕐 12–3, 7–10.30. Closed Mon
🍴 L from €24, D from €30. Wine from €12
🛏 4 (double from €95)

SA PLAÇA

Plaça Constitució, 1, 07400 Alcúdia
Tel 971 546278

This elegant restaurant on the main square of Alcúdia is run by the same owners as Ca'n Simó, but offers a completely different menu of Mallorcan, Mediterranean and Italian cuisine, making full use of local ingredients. The starters might include *trempo*, a Mallorcan summer salad served with apple and almonds, or courgettes stuffed with cabbage, raisins, pine nuts, sausage and Mallorcan cheese. Main courses vary from salt cod Mallorcan-style to grilled steak topped with goat's cheese, almonds and honey. For dessert, try almond cake with almond ice cream or pears in Lambrusco wine. A meal here can work out a little on the expensive side but it is worth it for a special occasion, and if you don't want to splash out there is a good-value lunchtime menu, with three courses plus wine and coffee for €12.

🕐 Thu–Tue noon–midnight
🍴 *Menú del día* €15, L from €24, D from €38. Wine from €10

ARTÀ

CAFÉ PARISIEN

Carrer Ciutat, 18, 07570 Artà
Tel 971 835440

There are several café-bar-restaurants on Artà's main street, but this is the most attractive and welcoming. You'll find the square-shaped bar in a high-ceilinged, Z-shaped room. The wicker chairs are comfortable, the

EATING

music is inoffensively low and jazzy and the restaurant hosts regular art exhibitions. Large portions of pasta—*paperdelle a le genovesa*, penne al salmón—cost from €8 to €12. A salad starter costs €5. It's all prepared from fresh ingredients and professionally presented. Café Parisien also makes a good place for a break, serving coffee and pastries to shoppers and sightseers.

🕒 9am–12am. Closed Sun in winter
🍴 L from €13, D from €17. Wine from €10.50

CALA RAJADA
SES ROTGES
Carrer Rafael Blanes, 21, 07590 Cala Rajada
Tel 971 563108
www.sesrotges.com

One of the most successful restaurants on the island, Ses Rotges has been run by the French Tétard family since 1974. It's the top draw in the northeastern corner of the island. Chef Gérard Tétard creates seasonal menus with gutsy French overtones, using the fresh, local ingredients. The five-course gastronomic (tasting) menu costs €80. Dishes such as pan-fried scallops with fennel juice on julienne beans and a superb roast pigeon breast with pan-fried duck foie gras and white grape and spinach salad are punctuated by refreshing sorbets. A rack of lamb with herbs is timed perfectly and served with baby carrots, mangetout and a small blanched tomato.

What the dining room lacks in views it makes up for with quiet intimacy: flower arrangements break lines of vision between the well-spaced tables. Laurence Tétard oversees the front of house and the superlative service, with son Alex providing multilingual

assistance and an informed opinion on wine choices.
🕒 1–3.30, 7.30–11. Closed Nov–mid-Mar
🍷 *Menú del día* €39.50, D from €47. Wine from €17
🛏 24 (double from €117.50)
🚗 Driving into Cala Rajada, take the third street on the right and then the first street on the left. Ses Rotges is between the main road through Cala Rajada and the seafront

CALA SANT VICENÇ
CAVALL BERNAT
Carrer Maressers, 2, Cala Sant Vicenç, 07469 Pollença
Tel 971 530250
www.hotelcala.com

The menu at Cavall Bernat, the main trattoria at Hotel Cala Sant Vicenç, changes every three months to ensure that the ingredients remain seasonal. Whatever the dishes, head chef Dominique L'Honoré gives a modern twist to Mediterranean classics. A lobster salad starter arrives with asparagus and a grapefruit sorbet, while a Binissalem red wine sauce adds a Mallorcan touch to a main course of fillet of beef with seasonal mushrooms. Themed tasting menus, of six, seven or eight courses, cost about €60. The olive-themed selection includes goat's cheese marinated in Mallorca's finest olive oil, Dauro d'Aubocassa, and sautéed strawberries with thyme ice cream and olive oil. An excellent wine list is dominated by Spanish wines, but there is still space for worthy New World wines such as California's Russian River Valley chardonnay. Cavall Bernat is one of the island's finest hotel-restaurants, with a well-drilled team of waiters.
🕒 Apr–Sep daily 7.30–10.30; Feb–Mar, Oct–Nov, closed Sun. Closed Dec–Jan
🍴 L from €32, D from €43. Wine from €12.50

POLLENÇA
CLIVIA
Avingudu Pollentia, 9, 07460 Pollença
Tel 971 533635

Perhaps the most popular restaurant in Pollença, Clivia has built up a loyal clientele by serving simple but skilfully prepared meals in a smart 100-year-old townhouse in the town centre. Go for the fish dishes—seafood is fresh and available according to season. The house speciality is roasted sea bass and the seafood platter is also recommended. Mains cost from €12, while starters cost from €5.50 up to an extravagant €11 for *gambas al ajillo*. Although there are two dining rooms and a terrace, reservations are recommended. Clivia is less casual than the other exceptional restaurant in Pollença, La Fonda (see below).
🕒 1–3, 5–10. Closed Wed
🍴 L from €17.50, D from €22. Wine from €11.50

EU CENTRO
Carrer Temple, 3, 07460 Pollença
Tel 971 535082

This restaurant has a lot going for it: an excellent location in a quiet side street near the cathedral, an attractive interior design of bare stone walls and tasteful art, and, not least, keen prices. The cuisine is ostensibly Mallorcan, but tourist standards such as canelloni have made it onto the menu. Starters are priced from €5.50 and mains from €6.60, while the specials board offers seasonal dishes such as baked cod on potatoes with *aïoli*. Mallorcan favourites such as paella, *tumbet* and roast kid are not forgotten. Quality is about right for the prices: average. Meals are let down by the cost-cutting and the desserts, which are limited to a selection of pots of ice creams. A

EATING

children's menu makes it a better bet for families.

🕐 11–3.30, 7–11. Closed Wed (Thu in Aug)

🍽 Menú del día €6.70, L from €12, D from €15. Wine from €6

LA FONDA

Carrer Antoni Maura, 32, 07460 Pollença
Tel 971 534751

Tuck into large portions of seasonal Mallorcan cooking at this welcoming, rustic restaurant, which has a wood-beamed interior. You can find it on the left side of the Plaça Major, as you face the church, and it offers better value than some of the restaurants on the actual square. The staff are friendly and the place is popular with locals. Most Mallorcan favourites, from *tumbet* to roast pork, are available. A paella comes with rice dyed black with squid ink (€17 for two persons), while more elaborate dishes, such as gilt head bream stuffed with prawns, cost up to €16. The *menú del día* is a good choice at less than €10.

🕐 12–3.30, 7–11. Closed Mon

🍽 L from €20, D from €35. Wine from €9

L'ILLA CAFÉ

Plaça Major, 7, 07460 Pollença
Tel 971 531621

This handsome café on Pollença's main square has a wood-panelled floor, stone walls, brown leather and chrome furniture, and some rather curious lightboxes of pictures of American singer and song-writer Bob Dylan. It opens for breakfast at 8am, with good coffee for €1 and is a good, central venue for a daytime snack while sightseeing, serving *tapas* (€2.50–€6), sandwiches (from €2.50) and *pa amb olí* (from €4.75, with ham). A slice of apple cake

costs €2.90. If the weather is fine, get an outside table.

🕐 8am–9pm. Closed Tue

🍽 L from €12. D from €18

PORT D'ALCÚDIA
KHUN PHANIT'S

Avinguda de la Playa, 7, 07410 Port d'Alcúdia
Tel 971 548141

For those tiring of Mediterranean cuisine, there is an excellent alternative down one of the streets running back from Port d'Alcúdia's beach: an authentic Thai restaurant. It's good value, with starters costing about €4 for staples such as wontons, satay or spring rolls, and mains from €9 for meat dishes to €12 for fish. Thai green or red curries cost €8.90 and takeaways merit a 10 percent discount. Vegetarian and children's menus are available.

🕐 12.30–3.30, 6.30–11.30. Closed Mon

🍽 L from €12 and D from €15. Wine from €9.25

PORT DE POLLENÇA
BRISAS

Avinguda Anglada Camarasa, 27, 07470 Port de Pollença
Tel 971 867000

One of a long row of mid-range restaurants along Port de Pollença's seafront, Brisas is a bright and breezy place close to the marina. The restaurant specializes in paella, fish and Mallorcan dishes, but you'll also find the tourist staples of pasta and pizza on the menu, at a wallet-friendly €6.40. Expect to spend a little more on a main course such as mussels in white wine.

🕐 Daily 12–4, 7–11

🍽 L from €13, D from €17. Wine from €12

GRAN CAFÉ 1919

Passeig Marítim, 07470 Port de Pollença
Tel 971 867535

This café, located on the

promenade opposite the marina, is one of the few places open in Port de Pollença in winter. In summer, visitors soak up the sunshine around the many outside tables, watching the sailing activity across the road. The café, styled as Belle Epoque meets Modernism, serves sandwiches, salads, cakes and drinks, including beer, sangria and watery orange juice. Prompt service from the black-suited waiters make this a useful venue for a quick snack.

🕐 Daily 8–11

🍽 L from €12, D from €19. Wine from €7.75

STAY

Moll Nou, 07470 Port de Pollença
Tel 971 864013
www.stayrestaurant.com

Out on a jetty next to the marina and facing Port de Pollença's harbour front, Stay has a superb location with huge windows and a terrace from which to appreciate the view. The brightly lit restaurant, popular with British expats, specializes in fresh, seasonal seafood, although it is just as respected for meat dishes such as pork escalopes with apples and calvados. Starters range from a light shrimp soup with Riesling for €6.70 to Stay's seafood salad with balsamic vinegar at €17. Piscine main courses start from €16 for grilled dorado with white wine sauce to the extravagant Menorcan lobster *calderette* at €56. The high prices are justified by the restaurant's location and liveliness rather than the food, but it does offer a €28 set menu, including wine, water and coffee. Watch out for the absurdly small cutlery.

🕐 Daily 12–4, 7.30–10.30

🍽 Menú del día €28.50, L from €20, D from €25. Wine from €14

EATING IN THE SOUTH

For such a quiet region, the south of Mallorca holds a particularly strong suit of restaurants. Grouped around a crossroads near Algaida are some of the best traditional Mallorcan restaurants on the island, perfectly located for a pitstop. In the centre of the island, Petra has a couple of restaurants serving outstanding Mallorcan cuisine. And on the east coast, in Portocolom and the resort of Cala d'Or, you'll find some sophisticated dining options among the popular tourist restaurants.

ALGAIDA

CAL DIMONI

Carretera Manacor–Palma, km21, 07120 Algaida
Tel 971 665035

Located next to Es 4 Vents (see below), this restaurant calls itself 'the house of the devil'. Why? Because it specializes in flame-grilling meat and blood sausages. Prices are keen with salads costing €3.30, roast pork or kid €10.80 and ice cream €3. If you like barbeques, you'll enjoy Cal Dimoni.
🕐 Daily 12–12
🍴 *Menú del día* €12, L from €13, D from €15. Wine from €15

CA'N MATEU

Carretera Manacor–Palma, km21, 07120 Algaida
Tel 971 665036

Just around the corner from Cal Dimoni, you'll find Ca'n Mateu in a 400-year-old inn. The restaurant serves traditional Mallorcan meals, such as roast suckling pig, and is good value for money. It has a children's play area outside.
🕐 12.30–4, 7–12. Closed Tue
🍴 *Menú del día* €10.50, L from €15, D from €20. Wine from €11

ES 4 VENTS

Carretera Manacor–Palma, km21, 07120 Algaida
Tel 971 665173

The best of the cluster of restaurants at this crossroads outside Algaida is Es 4 Vents. It specializes in Mallorcan and Spanish cuisine but adds a layer of sophistication to the rustic classics. Starters, such as *frito de pescado* or *chipirones*, typically cost €9 or €10. *Esgarraet* is a large plate of smoked salmon and cod with *pa amb olí*. The strips of salmon and cod, alternating with ribbons of roasted red pepper, are fanned out on a chilled tomato pulp. It's a delicious combination: the fresh, tart tomatoes offsetting the rich, smoky flavour of the fish and the sweet red pepper. Main meals are just as tasty, with dishes such as chicken breasts stuffed with prawns and mushrooms, and roast pork costing a reasonable €10.20. Fish options include cod with prawns and clam sauce and prawn and avocado salad. As with many Mallorcan restaurants, desserts are not such a priority, but the hazelnut biscuit ice cream is worth trying. Es 4 Vents is popular with families from Palma and other nearby towns, who dress up in their best clothes for Sunday lunch. Despite the large dining room, it's wise to book ahead at weekends.
🕐 12–4, 7.30–12. Closed Thu
🍴 L from €20, D from €23. Wine from €9

BINISSALEM

SCOTT'S BISTRO

Carrer Pou Bo, 20, 07350 Binissalem
Tel 971 870076

With fresh flowers and candles on the tables, crisp linen tablecloths and a welcome glass of cava on arrival, this discreet and romantic bistro is a strong favourite with guests staying at owner George Scott's hotel (▷ 191) just a few streets away. The menu changes regularly according to what is in the market, but features a mix of Mediterranean and international cuisine. Starters might include sizzling garlic prawns or a terrine of duck, quail and chicken breast, while main courses at around €15 could be steak, roast lamb or fresh fish, with a vegetarian choice always available. The staff speak English, German, French and Spanish, and the early start for dinner is also designed to appeal to northern European tastes.
🕐 Mon–Sat 7pm–midnight
🍴 D from €25. Wine from €11

CALA D'OR

PORT PETIT

Avenida Cala Llonga, 07660 Cala d'Or
Tel 971 643039
www.portpetit.com

Chef Gerard Deymier has been creating modern Mediterranean dishes at this exclusive restaurant since 1988. His repertoire is based around fresh, seasonal food and typically includes fish dishes such as cod fillet with sautéed fennel, crisp Iberian ham and bouillabaisse.

The emphasis is on light and healthy, if slightly unadventurous, cooking. There are no surprises on the dessert menu either, with chocolate profiteroles and apple tart the most substantial options. The restaurant overlooks Cala d'Or's harbour, a well-to-do haven for yachties, which explains the high prices. But you do get to enjoy the views from the open-air terrace while eating.

🕐 7–12am. Closed Nov–Mar
🍴 D from €40, tasting menu €47.50. Wine from €18

CAMPOS
SES ROTES VELLES
Carretera Campos–Colònia de Sant Jordi, km8.7, 07630 Campos
Tel 971 656159
www.agroturismosesrotesvelles.net
Close to the quiet resort town of Colònia de Sant Jordi (4km/2.5 miles) and the expanses of Es Trenc beach (2km/1 mile), this hotel-restaurant has a solid repertoire of typical Mallorcan dishes. Starters begin at €5 for a salad, but you'll also find snails, stuffed mussels and salt cod croquettes, season permitting. There are few surprises on the main course menu—squid, rabbit, pork and prawns all feature—but the simple dishes are all satisfying. Desserts include sorbet, ice cream, cheesecake and almond cake. The complex of buildings may be modern but there are pretty gardens to enjoy; there is also a cactus garden in nearby Ses Salines. Colònia Sant Jordi is the departure point for trips to Cabrera island (▷ 95).

🕐 Daily 12–3, 7–11
🍴 L from €15, D from €20. Wine from €10
🛏 10 (double from €90, discount for children under 12 years)
🏊

CAN PASTILLA
CA'N ANDREU D'ES PILLAR
Avenida de Fra Joan Llabrés, 8, 07007 Can Pastilla
Tel 971 262493
It might not be in the most scenic location, just minutes from the airport, but Ca'n Andreu is a great fish restaurant. The day's seafood is on display so you can pick the freshest fish and it will be cooked to order. The red mullet *escabeche* is recommended by author Vicky Bennison (▷ 205).

🕐 1.30–4.30, 8.30–11.30. Closed Mon and Sun pm
🍴 L from €12.50, D from €15. Wine from €8

PUIG DE SANT MIQUEL
Carretera de Manacor, km31, 07230 Montuïri
Tel 971 646314

With wonderful views across the Pla, this restaurant is a fixture on the coach-tour circuit. But thanks to a large outdoor terrace there's enough space to accommodate most visitors, who come for roast kid and other Mallorcan specialities. Expect to spend from €5 for a starter and from €10 for a main course such as *llom amb col*. The restaurant can be found next to the hermitage at the top of a hill just off the main Manacor–Algaida road (on the north side).

🕐 Winter: closed Sun pm, Mon
🍴 *Menú del día* €18, D from €20. Wine from €10

PETRA
ES CELLER
Carrer de l'Hospital, 46, 07520 Petra
Tel 971 561056
This typical *celler* restaurant is a two-minute walk from Plaça Ramón Llull. Venture beyond the unprepossessing exterior, down a stairway, and you'll enter a large, arched cellar with wooden tables and chairs, a long bar, an open log-fired oven for grilling meat and an olive press. The rustic

Mallorcan cuisine is tasty and prices are low. Starters, such as *pa amb olí*, cost from €3.50. Seasonal mains might include

stuffed aubergines, chops, roast rabbit or roast kid. Don't miss out on almond cake for dessert for the full gamut of Mallorcan specialities. Local wines are available.

🕐 1–4, 7–12. Closed Mon
🍴 L from €10, D from €13. Wine from €8.50

SA PLAÇA
Plaça Ramón Llull, 4, 07520 Petra
Tel 971 561646

Lunch outside at this hotel-restaurant—in a secluded but busy square with palm trees and a fountain—is extremely enjoyable. Sa Plaça is a Mallorcan restaurant that has succeeded in bringing sophisticated, inventive dining to the island's sleepy interior, far away from the hotspots of the coast and mountains. The chef is passionate about fresh ingredients and offers modern Mediterranean cuisine a notch above what you would expect for the prices. A €7.50 salad arrives with orange segments, a frothy orange dressing and five fleshy prawns. Mains start from €10 and the house speciality, *langostinos con chocolate*, costs €16.83. At €10, the *menú del día* is a bargain.

🕐 Daily 12–11.30
🍴 *Menú del día* €10 (Mon, Wed–Fri), L from €20 and D from €44. Wine from €9.61
🛏 3 (double from €109)

PINA
ES MOLÍ DE PINA
Carrer Sant Plàcid, 3, 07210 Pina
Tel 971 125303
Some of places in which you're most likely to find the best Mallorcan cooking are small towns in the island's interior—towns like Pina. Es Molí de Pina is a windmill restaurant, with an excellent seasonal menu. If you visit in the winter you might catch a dish called

escaldums de matances, which is served after a *matances*—the slaughter and preparation of the family pig, a tradition that continues in rural areas of Mallorca. *Escaldums de matances* is a rich casserole of chicken, pork meatballs and whole heads of garlic. If you miss out on this seasonal treat, console yourself with the almond cake and homemade almond ice cream.

🕐 Wed–Sat 1–4, 8–11
🍴 *Menú del día* €8 (Wed–Fri), L from €17, D from €20

PORTOCOLOM
CELLER SA SÍNIA
Carrer Pescadores, 07670 Portocolom
Tel 971 824323

At this appropriately located fish restaurant the day's fresh seafood is displayed at the door so you can see what catches your eye. The restaurant looks out across the port, although you can't see much from inside. The menu is weighted towards fish dishes such as cod with *aïoli* or sea bass with fennel, but you'll find a few traditional Mallorcan dishes. Expect to pay about €8 for a starter and €14–€18 for a main course, which is better value than many other restaurants in Portocolom.

🕐 Closed Dec–Feb. Closed Mon
🍴 L from €22, D from €29. Wine from €8

COLÓN
Carrer Cristobal Colón, 7, 07670 Portocolom
Tel 971 824783
www.restaurante-colon.com
This large, smart restaurant is in the middle of a row of restaurants on the seafront at Portocolom, a pretty harbour on the east coast. There's a roadside terrace overlooking the port and a spacious, low-lit interior. Cuisine is modern Mediterranean with an

Austrian twist. Prices are high, with starters costing about €14, fish main courses €23 and dessert another €10.

🕐 Open all day from 12. Closed Wed
🍴 L from €40, D from €45. Wine from €17

SINEU
CA'N FONT
Sa Plaça, 18, 07510 Sineu
Tel 971 520313
www.canfont.com

On the main square in Sineu, Ca'n Font is a *celler* restaurant—with huge wine barrels lining the walls and an arched ceiling to prove it. The food served is traditional Mallorcan, with *frit mallorquín* costing €6 and *calamar a la plancha* (grilled squid) €11. The restaurant is very busy on market day (Wednesday), when you need to be assertive to get served.

🕐 Daily 11.30–4, 7.30–11
🍴 L and D from €15. Wine from €4
ℹ️ 7 (double from €48)

MOLÍ D'EN PAU
Carretera Santa Margalida, 25, 07570 Sineu
Tel 971 855116

Although it's not the only restaurant housed inside a converted windmill, it certainly makes Molí d'en Pau, just outside Sineu on the Llubi road, easier to find. The menu is dominated by traditional Mallorcan favourites, such as *llom de porc* and *calamar a la plancha* (grilled squid), but

you'll also find more unusual dishes, such as sautéed calves' brains. The food is excellent value, with a filling *arroz brut* the cheapest option. If the dark interior is a bit overwhelming (windmills were designed without many windows), you can sit outside on the terrace, which is set back from the main road and has thatched umbrellas, wooden tables, a well and an aviary.

🕐 12–4, 7.30–11. Closed Mon
🍴 L from €15, D from €20. Wine from €8

RANDA
ES RECÓ DE RANDA
Carrer Fuente, 21, 07629 Randa
Tel 971 660997

Randa is a small, quiet village 10km (6 miles) north of Llucmajor. It's dominated by the Puig de Randa, a hill which has three sanctuaries around it. The restaurant inside the hotel Es Recó de Randa produces highly regarded Mallorcan and Spanish cooking, with cod and pork featuring prominently. There are views from the restaurant over the Pla and a secluded terrace in the garden.

🕐 Daily 12.30–4, 7.30–11.30
🍴 *Menú del día* €22.50, D from €30. Wine from €11
ℹ️ 14 (double from €145)

SENCELLES
SA CUINA DE N'AINA
Carrer Rafel, 31, 07140 Sencelles
Tel 971 872992
This restaurant offers good Mallorcan cuisine in a pleasant rural environment. Chef Aina Carbonell, a winner of the Mallorquin Cookery Competition (for turkey with almonds), produces traditional, meaty favourites such as roast suckling pig and lamb from the wood-burning oven.

🕐 12.30–3.30, 8–11. Closed Tue
🍴 *Menú del día* €22, D from €25

EATING

Staying

STAYING IN MALLORCA

Mallorca has a huge selection of accommodation, meaning that you can be choosy about where to stay. Wherever you go, most sights and beaches will be within a short drive. Accommodation ranges from large resort hotels to rural farmhouses, but we've focused on the more interesting hotels. Some are notable for their location, others for their food, but if you can't find the right place, turn to our list of useful organizations.

You can rest your head in chic designer hotels, converted townhouses or secluded rural fincas

HOTELS

As of 2004, there were 283,436 hotel beds available on the island, the majority being in the beach resorts (see below). But, as Mallorca aims upmarket, an increasing proportion of these beds is in four- or five-star hotels. Facilities at most of the hotels we have selected include air-conditioning, which is essential during the hot summer months (July and August), as well as all the modern features you would expect: television, telephone, minibar—and sometimes tea- or coffee-making facilities, although this is rare in Spain. Many have swimming pools or even a spa centre, and some offer specialist sport facilities—particularly golf.

Most hotels include breakfast (usually a buffet) in the basic cost of accommodation; we have stated where the price is room only. Full-board and half-board options can save money, but don't miss out on sampling Mallorca's excellent restaurants.

In the high season (May to September) prices can be double those in winter months. Deals, such as four nights for the price of three, are common in the low season and good value for walkers and cyclists enjoying the mild winter weather.

Hostals are cheap hotels (mostly located in Palma) and are not connected to a youth hostel scheme. Even in the capital's cheaper establishments, expect to spend €60 to €75 on a double room. By spending €105 to €150 per night you can get a characterful room in a townhouse hotel, but prices escalate for the city's most luxurious hotels. A smattering of luxury hotels across Mallorca charge rates from €150 to €450 per night, but even these will offer deals to get customers in the quieter months. Bear in mind

that a significant proportion of hotels close in winter; the coastal resorts are more or less empty from November to April.

FINCAS AND AGROTURISMOS

A *finca* (▷ 13) is a rural property that has been converted to provide guest accommodation. Typically, *fincas* fall into three categories: *hoteles rurales,* which are larger, manor house-style hotels; *agroturismos*—often smaller, simpler farmhouses; and *turismo de interior*—smart hotels in towns and villages. Accommodation varies widely: some *agroturismos* offer just one or two self-catering apartments, others a dozen bedrooms. Prices too are variable, depending on location, season and facilities. *Agroturismos* offer some of the most enjoyable accommodation on the island and the cooking at many is outstanding, but bear in mind that in rural areas alternative choices for an evening meal will be limited, and may require driving into a town.

RESORTS

The large beach-resort hotels provide the cheapest accommodation on the island, but you'll get the best prices at these by booking rooms as part of a package holiday through a travel agent, rather than independently. Most resorts are block-booked by major tour operators during the summer and are closed during the winter. They typically operate on an all-inclusive basis, and provide bars, swimming pools and entertainment.

FULL AND HALF BOARD ACCOMMODATION

A particular strength of many Mallorcan *fincas* and hotels is the high standard of cuisine in the

STAYING

restaurant. This applies especially to the rural hotels and the upmarket establishments, which are worth visiting even if you're not a guest.

SELF-CATERING ACCOMMODATION

With many expats renting out their properties for the summer, there is a large stock of self-catering accommodation on the island. Note that prices can more than double in the high season. Firms such as the long-established Mallorca specialists Try Holidays (tel 0870 7544545, www.tryholidays.com) provide a wide choice of apartments and villas.

SMOKING

Almost all the hotels on Mallorca will have rooms for smokers. We have stated where smoking is banned completely by a hotel.

PRICES

Prices given are for a double room for one night in the off-peak season and include breakfast but not the 7 percent IVA tax (▷ 201), unless stated otherwise. Prices can double during the summer and will vary widely throughout the year; always check rates carefully. All the hotels listed accept credit cards unless stated otherwise.

Accommodation ranges from comfortable to luxurious, with many hotels offering superlative dining

MONASTERIES

For a completely different experience, you could try staying at one of the island's hilltop sanctuaries and hermitages. Few of these are working monasteries, but they still provide quiet places of refuge, with simple accommodation, a spiritual atmosphere and unforgettable views. These days, the majority of visitors are walkers rather than pilgrims, or people looking for somewhere

Hair shirt not required: staying overnight at Puig de Maria monastery is a treat

cheap and characterful to stay. The two biggest sanctuaries, at Lluc (▷ 70–73) and Santuari de Cura (▷ 102), are still home to active religious communities. They both offer comfortable accommodation; the pilgrim rooms at Lluc all have their own private showers and there are a number of restaurants on site.

More basic are those monasteries where you sleep in a former monk's cell, making up your own bed and sharing rudimentary shower facilities, such as at Ermita de Bonany (▷ 101), near Petra, Puig de Maria (▷ 92), near Pollença, and Santuari de Sant Salvador (▷ 83), near Felanitx. All are run by caretakers rather than monks, and, except in the case of Ermita de Bonany, evening meals are available. For the authentic

pilgrim experience head for Puig de Maria or the small sanctuary of Nostra Senyora del Refugió above Castell d'Alaró (▷ 66), as both can only be reached on foot. Nostra Senyora del Refugió offers the most basic accommodation of all, with bunk beds in a dormitory building and no showers—though the sunset views from the terrace and the excitement of watching your dinner being brought up the mountainside by mule more than make up for the lack of creature comforts. *A Stay in Mallorcan Monasteries,* by Nick and Jill Carter, is available from www.mallorcanmonasteries.co.uk.

Lluc
☎ 971 871525
🍽 €30

Santuari de Cura
☎ 971 120260 🍽 €42

Ermita de Bonany
☎ 971 561101 🍽 €10 per person

Puig de Maria
☎ 971 184132 🍽 €13–€18

Santuari de Sant Salvador
☎ 971 827282 🍽 €30

Nostra Senyora del Refugió
☎ 971 182112 🍽 €12

There is accommodation of all types in Palma. The only shortage is in rooms costing less than €70 per night, which reflects Palma's popularity as a city break destination. In recent years there has been an influx of upmarket, designer hotels typically priced at around €200 per night. But you'll find a warmer ambience at several of the city centre townhouse hotels, such as San Lorenzo, Dalt Murada and the original boutique hotel, Palacio Ca Sa Galesa. Palma has year-round appeal, although prices do drop slightly in the winter.

ARABELLA SHERATON GOLF HOTEL SON VIDA

Carrer de la Vinagrella–Urbanizacion Son Vida, 07013 Palma
Tel 971 787100
www.starwoodgolf.com

The Arabella Sheraton Golf Hotel is located to the west of Palma, beyond the Son Rapinya district and north of the restaurant-packed Gènova district. The key attraction is the 18-hole, 72-par Son Vida golf course, which has almost as many water hazards as

palm trees. Buggies and equipment are available for hire, but most golfers will bring their own kit. Bedrooms at the Spanish-styled building all have television, telephone, stereo, ISDN and laptop connection. Décor is better than the usual bland designs of the luxury hotel chains; rooms are colourful and cosy. Staff are also happy to organize reservations at other golf courses in Mallorca.

🌐 All year
🛏 Double from €311
🛎 93
🏊 Indoor 🚗 ♿

ARMADANS

Marqués de la Cenia, 34, 07014 Palma
Tel 971 221554
www.hotelarmadans.com

One block away from the seafront, the Armadans is marginally cheaper than the other high-rise hotels on the Passeig. It makes up for the lack of sea views by being moderately stylish, for a large hotel. All rooms have en-suite bath-

---

room, television, internet connection, safe and minibar. Breakfast is an expansive buffet in an enormous dining room. The Armadans' clientele tends to be business-orientated, but the hotel is conveniently located for sightseeing.

🌐 All year
🛏 Double from €80
🛎 74
🏊 🚗 ♿

BENDINAT

Andrés Ferrat Sobral, 1, 07181 Portals Nous
Tel 971 675725
www.hotelbendinat.es

In the wealthy enclave of Bendinat, 9km (6 miles) west of Palma, near Portals Nous, Hotel Bendinat offers guests traditional—if rather expensive—accommodation. The restaurant serves Mediterranean-Mallorcan cuisine and even the breakfast has a Mallorcan slant. Clifftop views from the terrace are superb. Bedrooms have television, telephone and central heating, and there are extensive gardens and a swimming

---

pool outside.

🌐 Mar–Oct
🛏 Double from €180
🛎 52
🏊 ♿

BON SOL

Paseo de Illetes, 30, 07181 Illetes
Tel 971 402111
www.hotelbonsol.es

Once a haunt of film idol Errol Flynn, this family-owned hotel 8km (5 miles) west of Palma offers a variety of large, individually decorated bedrooms. They're all luxuriously furnished and fitted with television, telephone, central heating and tea- and coffee-making facilities. Beyond the sleeping quarters the hotel offers tennis courts, a swimming pool, a squash court and a gym, and other outdoor activities. Inside, guests can use a Moorish-styled spa with massage rooms, a sauna and Turkish bath. But the highlight of the hotel is outside: secluded sub-tropical gardens with waterfalls and pools for swimming tumble all the way down to the shore.

🌐 Closed 15 Nov–15 Dec
🛏 Double from €160
🛎 92
🏊 🚗 ♿

BORN

Carrer Sant Jaume, 3, 07012 Palma
Tel 971 712942
www.hotelborn.com

Palma has a shortage of mid-range hotels and this is by far the best place to stay if you want character and a central

---

location at a reasonable price. It is housed in a converted 16th-century palace at the top of Passeig des Born, but unlike

other similar establishments it has not gone for the luxury end of the market. Rooms are simply furnished but comfortable, and they are set around a charming courtyard where breakfast is taken beneath the palm trees in summer. The Born is extremely popular, so it's worth booking well ahead.

🕙 All year
🛏 Double from €69
🍴 29
♿

CIUTAT JARDÍ

Illa de Malta, 14, 07007 Ciutat Jardí
Tel 971 260007
www.hciutatj.com

The hotel Ciutat Jardí is 4km (2.5 miles) east of Palma, five minutes from the airport and just a few steps from the beach. It has been managed by the same Mallorcan family since 1934. The building is a fine example of 1920s architecture and the best rooms are in the two domed wings—the largest, the Great Dome, has 12 windows for a panoramic view—while other rooms have generously sized terraces. All the bedrooms have telephone, television, central heating, a hydro-massage bath and internet connection. Access for disabled guests is much better than average.

🕙 Closed 22 Dec–20 Jan
🛏 Double from €140
🍴 20
🏊 Outdoor ♿

CIUTAT DE PALMA

Plaça Pont, 3, 07014 Palma
Tel 971 222300
www.ac-hotels.com

Part of the stylish AC chain, this business-oriented hotel opened in 2003, set just back from the port in the trendy Santa Catalina district. The bedrooms and public areas have a sleek, modern design, with black, grey and white predominating and a small breakfast patio at the centre. There is a free coffee bar, open from 11am to 7pm, where guests can help themselves to drinks and light snacks, and the minibars in the rooms are free. The best rates are available at weekends. Ask for a room overlooking the port. Parking is available.

🕙 All year
🛏 Double from €80 (breakfast €10)
🍴 85
♿

CONVENT DE LA MISSÍO

Carrer de la Missió, 7A, 07003 Palma
Tel 971 227347
www.conventdelamissio.com

Don't be surprised if you feel less stylish than the black-clad staff at this slick boutique hotel in central Palma. The spartan hotel, once part of a church, is

one of Palma's trendiest places to lay your head. There's a slightly overwrought restaurant, a bar, wine cellar, chapel and an art gallery in the old refectory. Bedrooms have television, telephone—and gorgeous marble bathrooms.

🕙 All year
🛏 Double from €200
🍴 14
♿

DALT MURADA

Carrer Almudaina, 6, 07001 Palma
Tel 971 425300
www.hoteldaltmurada.com

For a top hotel in Palma, Dalt Murada is unquestionably outstanding value. Entrance to the hotel, in a mansion in the old town, close behind the cathedral, is through a gate on a side street off Carrer Conquistador. Dalt Murada's rooms are grand, if appealingly frayed around the edges, with antiques, tapestries, high ceilings and fairytale beds, but the hotel retains a warm homeliness. Bedrooms have telephone, television, central heating and internet connection. Large en-suite bathrooms are a highlight, with enormous oval baths and stone floors.

🕙 All year
🛏 Double from €110
🍴 3 doubles and 5 suites
♿

HOSTAL BRONDO

Carrer C'an Brondo, 1, 07001 Palma
Tel 971 719043
www.hostalbrondo.net

Few guesthouses are as centrally located as this one: it's a narrow lane between the Passeig des Born and Carrer Unió. Prices are about right for such a location, but it's not such a bargain as the Hostal Cuba (▷ 182). Rooms are available with or without en-suite bathrooms. Those without bathrooms have use of a clean shared bathroom and all rooms have a basin. There's also a communal lounge with television and drinking water. The staff say that they recommend restaurants popular with the locals of Palma.

🕙 All year
🛏 Double from €45 (without bathroom, room only)
🍴 10

HOSTAL CUBA
Carrer Sant Magí, 1, 07013 Palma
Tel 971 738159

This Modernist-style *hostal*, which opened in 1904, is one of the best budget choices in Palma. The rooms, all with showers, are individually furnished with a hotchpotch of antique furniture. It's located on the corner of Sant Magí and the main Argentina road, between the twin hotbeds of bars and restaurants in Santa Catalina and La Llotja. Although a little rickety, the Cuba is good fun, but you have to pay more for air-conditioning and heating, and don't expect a television. The outer rooms have the better views, but more noise from the main road. The airport bus stops right outside.

🕐 All year
🛏 Double from €37 (€42 with heating and air-conditioning)
🚪 20

MARDAVALL
Passeig Calvia, 07181 Costa d'en Blanes
Tel 971 629400
www.mardavall-hotel.com

It's no use coming to the Mardavall to escape the workplace; bedrooms at the high-tech hotel are equipped with ISDN, fax and internet connections, and there's even an IT 'butler' to help with technical problems. Other features in the bedrooms are similarly extravagant: bathrooms are lined with marble, sheets are Egyptian cotton and duvets are down-filled. Hotel services include babysitting, limousine travel and a butler. There are several restaurants and bars: Es Fum serves gourmet meals in the evening, S'Aigua is a brasserie for lighter meals during the day and *tapas* are served in Es Vent. The AltiraSPA, with hammams set around a blue-tiled saltwater

pool, provides Ayurvedic and thalassotherapy treatments. Of course, the problem with such places is that you can easily forget which country you are staying in—combat this by at least getting out of the hotel for a round of golf at one of the courses nearby.

🕐 All year
🛏 Double from €497
🚪 133
🏊 📺 ♿

MARICEL
Carretera d'Andratx, 11, Cas Catalá, 07184 Calvia
Tel 971 707744
www.hospes.es

Swathed in leather and cased in acres of marble, the Maricel's modern minimalist interior attracts a wealthy but youthful crowd of jet-setters. The grand old building itself has been through a number of incarnations and was once a decadent nightclub. It has a wonderful views of the sea; views, which the infinity-edge swimming pool and the steps leading through the rocks and into the sea capitalize upon. Sandstone from Santanyí has been used to create arches and alcoves to hide away in. Catalan architect Xavier Claramunt designed the bedrooms to emphasise light and space, but he's found space for a television, DVD player, hi-fi and internet access in each room.

🕐 All year
🛏 Double from €288 (room only)
🚪 29
🏊 ♿

PALACIO CA SA GALESA
Carrer Miramar, 8, 07001 Palma
Tel 971 715400
www.palaciocasagalesa.com

This was the place that started the trend towards boutique hotels in Palma when it opened in 1996, and it

continues to set the standards for others to follow. The hotel occupies a 16th-century palace behind the cathedral, whose restoration has won an award from Palma city council. Each of the 12 rooms and suites, all named after composers, is individually decorated with antiques and modern art; in addition to all the facilities you would expect from a five-star hotel, the rooms have their own tea- and coffee-making equipment. Most impressive of all are the public areas. The great hall is decorated in a mixture of Mallorcan, French and British styles, with polished floors, elegant furniture and dark Puerto Rican wood. There is a library where a fire is lit every evening in winter, and guests are encouraged to help themselves to free sherry.

Afternoon tea is served in a replica of Monet's kitchen at Giverny; on warm days you can take it outside to a patio with a tinkling fountain. There is a small indoor pool in the basement. The owners have filled the hotel with their own private art collection, including works by Joan Miró and contemporary Spanish artists Eduardo Arroyo and Lorenzo Quinn. Parking is available for €13 per day.

🕐 All year
🛏 Double from €297 (breakfast €19)
🚪 5 doubles and 7 suites
🏊 ♿

PALAU SA FONT
Carrer del Apuntadors, 38, 07012 Palma
Tel 971 712277
www.palausafont.com

A 16th-century palace on the outside, Palau Sa Font is a hip confection of funky colours, modern furniture and distressed ironwork on the inside. Best of all, the youthful guests find it perfectly placed for bar crawls in La Llotja. All the rooms have telephone, television and central heating. Breakfast, like the décor, is slightly more imaginative than

the standard hotel buffet, with *tortilla,* Serrano ham and smoked salmon. Don't miss the exciting views across Palma from the tower.

🅖 All year
🅑 Double from €140
🅘 19
🅢

PORTIXOL

Carrer Sirena, 27, 07006 Portitxol
Tel 971 271800
www.portixol.com

Scandinavian cool meets retro-50s architecture at this Swedish-owned design hotel, situated right by the harbourside in the up-and-coming district of Portitxol. Following a major refit in the 1990s, the shell of the building has been retained, but the interior has been completely redesigned, with clean white lines and a strong minimalist feel. There is a large outdoor pool, and a restaurant that has developed a reputation for its first-class seafood and fish dishes—some of which, such as the sashimi, betray a clear Japanese influence. Many of the rooms look out over the harbour, and a pleasant half-hour walk along the promenade leads to the city centre, with views of the cathedral thoughout. Parking is available.

🅖 All year
🅑 Double from €210
🅘 24
🅢 🅥 🅢

PUNTA NEGRA

Carretera Palma–Andratx, 12km, 07181
Costa d'en Blanes
Tel 971 680762
www.h10.es

Punta Negra is an upmarket resort hotel—with all the impersonality that implies. But the essentials for a resort hotel are right: it's clean, everything works and the service is competent. Rooms are large and some have a balcony with views out to the bay. The four-star resort hotel is 2km (1 mile) from Portals Nous and a short drive from Puerto Portals. It has its own small beach, two outdoor and one indoor swimming pools, a sauna and a Turkish bath. There's a room with internet-connected computers and all bedrooms are fitted with telephone, television and central heating. Buffet breakfasts are served in the large dining hall in the main building.

🅖 All year
🅑 Double from €61.68
🅘 13 bungalows, 96 doubles, 28 suites
🅢 🅢

PURO

Carrer Montenegro, 12, 07012 Palma
Tel 971 425450
www.purohotel.com

With its self-conscious attempts to portray itself as the height of ethnic bohemian chic, Palma's newest design hotel, opened in 2004, perhaps tries a little too hard. Indian cotton throws, Thai teak furniture, Guinean parrot-feather lamps and tented double beds by the rooftop plunge pool, all set in a restored 14th-century mansion with plenty of hidden corners where you can relax on sofas

and cushions, combine to create a chilled-out, hippy feel. Other features are free music and movies in the bedrooms via an interactive sound system, and huge spa-like bathrooms with tall mirrors and big, black baths. All bedrooms also have an internet connection. The champagne bar on the ground floor has become a popular place to meet, and the Opio restaurant serves Asian-Mediterranean fusion food—how about grilled asparagus with tangerine vinaigrette followed by steak with wasabi and sea-urchin butter?

🅖 All year
🅑 Double from €175
🅘 26
🅢 🅢

SAN LORENZO

Carrer San Lorenzo, 14, 07012 Palma,
Tel 971 728200
www.hotelsanlorenzo.com

This townhouse hotel in a quiet street north of La Llotja in the centre of Palma has a friendly, lived-in ambience. The rooms are cosy rather than fashionable and each has television, telephone, minibar and safe. Both the suites are located away from the main building and are more romantic: they're large, private and have their own terraces. A small, well-tended swimming pool has a few sun loungers around the edge and there's an outdoor bar. Excellent breakfasts are a hallmark of the San Lorenzo. The menu offers bacon and eggs in various combinations, all cooked to order; fruit juice is freshly squeezed. Note that parking in this central area can be a problem—there's a car park nearby on the Passeig Mallorca.

🅖 All year
🅑 Double from €120 (breakfast €8)
🅘 4 doubles and 2 suites
🅢 🅢

STAYING

STAYING IN THE SERRA DE TRAMANTANA

From mountaintop eyries to family-run *fincas*, the Serra de Tramuntana has an attractive range of accommodation. One type that you'll be relieved not to find is the high-rise hotel. In terms of price, the sky's the limit for the region's luxury hotels, such as La Residencia. But you can find good deals in the smaller *fincas*, especially those that are not too close to Deià or Valldemossa. Like Palma, the Serra de Tramuntana is a year-round destination. Some establishments will close in January or February but most will cater to walkers and cyclists in spring and autumn.

BANYALBUFAR
MAR I VENT
Carrer Major, 49, 07191 Banyalbufar
Tel 971 618000
www.hotelmarivent.com

Now in the third generation of the Vives family, this old-style seaside hotel continues to attract a loyal following of mostly British families, many of whom return year after year and know each of the staff by name. The biggest attraction here is the setting, high above the sea, with panoramic vistas from the terraces, balconies and picture windows. All of the rooms have sea views. There is an outdoor pool with a separate children's area, and a tennis court for the use of guests. The disadvantage of staying in Banyalbufar, especially for families, is that there is only a small rocky beach. The food in the restaurant here can be disappointing, catering to the tastes of visitors of a generation ago.
- ☺ Feb-Nov
- 🛏 Double from €113
- ⓘ 29
- 🏊

BINIBONA
BINIBONA PARC NATURAL
Finca Binibona, Binibona, 07314 Caimari
Tel 971 873565
www.binibona.com
This is one of the best example of eco-tourism on the island; the owners of Binibona Parc Natural, the Vicens family, are striving to make this 11-room

hotel as ecologically friendly as possible. Energy comes from solar panels, water is recycled to irrigate the garden and natural fertilizers are used to grow the vegetables and fruit. Bedrooms share jacuzzis and terraces, but all have telephone, television, central heating and ISDN.
- ☺ All year
- 🛏 Double from €140
- ⓘ 9 suites and 2 doubles
- 🄂

CAN FURIÓS
Camí Vell Binibona, 11, Binibona, 07314 Caimari
Tel 971 515751
www.can-furios.com

This small, private *finca* is run by an English-Spanish couple who have converted the 16th-century property into a small luxury hotel where children are thought to detract from the peace and quiet. Not only are bedrooms fitted with telephone and television, but the suites also have a DVD player. There's a high-speed ADSL internet connection in the reception. Best of all, prices of drinks are the same from the minibar as from the main bar. Décor is flowery rather than minimalist. Cooked breakfasts cost an extra €4.
- ☺ Mid-Feb-mid-Dec
- 🛏 1 Apr-31 Oct double from €200; 14 Feb-31 Mar, 1 Nov-14 Dec double from €150 per room per night. 20 per cent reduction for single occupancy
- ⓘ 7
- 🄂 🄂
- 🚗 From Palma follow C173 motorway

to Inca. Bypass Inca and at the third roundabout turn left into Inca town, following signs to Lluc and Selva. When you reach Selva, take the right turning in the middle of the village and follow signs to Hotel Can Furiós

ES CASTELL
Binibona, 07314 Caimari
Tel 971 875154
www.fincaescastell.com
Paola Cassini and James Hiscock welcome guests to their rustic stone *finca*, set amid 300ha (750 acres) of pine and olive groves on a working sheep farm. The bedrooms are cosy and decorated in traditional Mallorcan style, while original features of the house include an 11th-century olive press and a chimney. There is a small pool in the gardens, and dreamy views from the terrace that stretch across the plain to the mountains and the sea. Guests can reserve a four-course dinner (€30), which will be freshly bought from the market and prepared by a Uruguayan chef, with an emphasis on Italian and Spanish cuisine. This is a delightful rural retreat in an unspoilt corner of Mallorca that is fast becoming a centre for *agrotourism*.
- ☺ All year
- 🛏 Double from €125
- ⓘ 12
- 🄂 🄂
- 🚗 Follow signs from Selva or Caimari

BUNYOLA
SA MÀNIGA
Carrer Afores, 07110 Bunyola
Tel 971 613428
www.fincasamaniga.com
Sa Màniga is a large *agroturismo* in the foothills of the Tramuntana just outside Bunyola, with four sunlit rooms, each with telephone, television, a minibar and central heating. A pool outside is ringed with sun loungers, but the hotel is a good choice for active guests with golf, horse-riding, cycling and hiking all

available. Bunyola, an otherwise unassuming town a half-hour drive from Palma, is an excellent base for exploring the central portion of the Serra de Tramuntana, and, thanks to its prosaic appearance, has escaped the worst of the daytrippers and retains a local pace of life. The Palma–Sóller train stops there, and there are good local restaurants.

🕐 All year
💶 €100
ℹ️ 4
🚗 🍴

DEIÀ
COSTA D'OR

Llucalcari, 07179 Deià
Tel 971 639025
www.hoposa.es

The Costa d'Or overlooks the rocky west coast of the Serra de Tramuntana, and the views from the hotel are some of the best on the island. Guests can walk to a private cove via a path through the hotel's own pine forest. The hotel also has a swimming pool and a tennis court. With no television, bedrooms are basic but comfortable. Since being refurbished in 2004 prices have gone up, but they are justified by the hotel's prime location, a short drive north from Deià.

🕐 May–Nov
💶 Double from €137
ℹ️ 40
🚗 🍴

ES MOLÍ

Carretera Valldemossa–Deià, 07179 Deià
Tel 971 639000
www.hotelesmoli.com

This hotel, large by the standards of the Serra de Tramuntana, has superb views all the way to the coast and its own private beach. Bedrooms have telephone, television and central heating; those with balconies overlooking the coast

are the most sought after. Outside you'll find a 30m (100ft)-long heated swimming pool, a tennis court and some pretty gardens. It definitely falls into the luxury category, especially given its location near the tourist hotspot of Deià, but décor is classic rather than modern.

🕐 Mid-Apr–Nov
💶 Double from €197
ℹ️ 87
🚗 🍴

LA RESIDENCIA

Finca Son Canals, 07179 Deià
Tel 971 639011
www.hotel-laresidencia.com

The grande dame of Mallorcan country hotels was bought by the Orient Express chain from British entrepreneur Sir Richard Branson in 2002, but it has retained its atmosphere of informal luxury and remains the hideaway of choice for fashion models and A-list celebrities. It is set in two restored 16th- and 17th-century manor houses with terraced gardens overlooking the village. The two largest suites, each with their own terrace and pool, cost upwards of €2,000 per night in high season. All rooms have teddy bears, rubber ducks in the bathroom and Molton Brown toiletries. Facilities include indoor and outdoor pools, sauna and gym, beauty treatments, Turkish baths, tennis courts, an art gallery and shuttle buses in summer to Llucalcari beach where the hotel has its own bar. There is gourmet dining in El Olivo restaurant, upmarket bistro food at Son Fony, poolside lunches in summer and afternoon tea on the terrace. To maintain the romantic atmosphere, mobile phones are strongly discouraged and children under 10 are only

allowed to stay between 1 July and 15 August.

🕐 Feb–Nov
💶 Double from €265
ℹ️ 4 singles, 32 doubles and 23 suites
🚗 🍴 🛏️

SA PEDRISSA

Carretera Valldemossa–Deià, km64.5, 07179 Deià
Tel 971 639111
www.sapedrissa.com

With just eight rooms in a 17th-century farmhouse once belonging to Archduke Ludwig Salvator, Sa Pedrissa is a good example of the trend towards *agrotourism* in Mallorca. Breakfast here is a treat, with eggs, honey and olive oil straight from the farm. On summer evenings dinner is served out of doors on a terrace with views out to sea, while on chilly nights you can eat inside by the old olive press. The rooms may have rustic décor but the fittings are modern. Some are set in their own garden of olive trees; room 8, known as the Tower Suite, is a penthouse on two floors of the old tower, with sea views from the terrace and an espresso machine.

🕐 All year
💶 Double from €114
ℹ️ 8
🚗 🍴
🚌 On the road to Valldemossa, just outside Deià

S'HOTEL D'ES PUIG

Es Puig, 4, 07179 Deià
Tel 971 639409
www.hoteldespuig.com

Mentioned, if not immortalized, in a short story by Robert Graves, 'the hotel on the hill' is a small, friendly place opposite La Residencia with eight bedrooms, four of them with terraces. Each has a bathroom, telephone, television and central heating. Prices reflect its location in Deià, but standards are high.

🕐 All year
💶 Double from €96
ℹ️ 8
🚗 🍴

FORNALUTX
CA'N REUS

Carrer de l'Alba, 26, 07109 Fornalutx
Tel 971 631174
www.canreus.com

A few steps away from the Petit Hotel (▷ 186), Ca'n Reus

is another stylishly renovated townhouse hotel in this small village. Décor is slightly more traditional and less minimalist than the Petit Hotel, but just as pleasing. Both make good bases for hikers exploring the southern and middle sections of the Tramuntana. Bedrooms at Ca'n Reus have hair dryers, safes and central heating. There's an 'honesty' bar for guests. Dogs are welcome, and there's a 50 percent discount for children aged 2 to 12 years.

🕐 All year
🛏 Double from €100
🛈 7
♿

CA'N VERDERA

Carrer de Toros, 1, 07109 Fornalutx
Tel 971 638203
www.canverdera.com

Quiet and effortlessly chic, this designer hotel is everything you'd expect for the price. Each of the centrally heated rooms is individually decorated; some even have whirlpool baths, but you have to pay €20 more for a garden view. They're all equipped with a CD player as well as telephone and television. The hotel can organize activities such as golf, cycling and tennis, but many guests will prefer to just explore the village and its gorgeous surroundings.

🕐 Closed Dec–Jan
🛏 Double from €160
🛈 11
♨ ♿

FORNALUTX PETIT HOTEL

Carrer de l'Alba, 22, 07109 Fornalutx
Tel 971 631997
www.fornalutxpetithotel.com

This small, attractive hotel looks out across Fornalutx's valley. Once a convent (and then a school), the hotel has been decorated in a modern, airy style, with lots of pale-coloured linens, tiled floors

and tasteful furnishings. The Sa Capelleta suite lifts the spirits, with a high ceiling, arched alcoves and a large bed in the middle of the room. It gets better outside: there's decking among the citrus groves, tables in the shade and deckchairs around a pool and a jacuzzi (free of charge for guests). Bedrooms have central heating for the winter months.

🕐 All year
🛏 From €110 per night
🛈 8
♨
🗺 Hotel is on a quiet, traffic-free street on the left as you enter Fornalutx from the C710

ORIENT
L'HERMITAGE

Carretera Alaró–Bunyola, 07349 Orient
Tel 971 180303
www.hermitage-hotel.com

Parts of this former convent date back 400 years, but it is now one of the most well known hotels on Mallorca. The restaurant in the old olive mill draws many daytrippers to this serene, low-lying part of the Serra de Tramuntana, but hotel guests have the advantage of exploring the rest of the hotel, including the herb garden which supplies chef Bartolomé Bisbal. The hotel excels at organizing activities, from tai chi to painting classes, for its guests and there are also tennis courts and a sauna available. Despite the sophistication of the hotel and the restaurant, the bedrooms are not as swanky as you might expect. Those in the main building offer an authentically ancient experience, with creaky doors and draughty windows. The remaining rooms are in a pair of modern buildings at the back of the hotel. All have telephone, television and central heating, but no air-conditioning.

🕐 Closed Nov–Feb
🛏 Double from €169
🛈 24
♨

PUIGPUNYENT
SON NET

Castillo de Son Net, 07194 Puigpunyent
Tel 971 147000
www.sonnet.es

Opened in 1998 in a 17th-century manor house looking over a peaceful village, Son

Net has become one of Mallorca's top luxury hotels. The suites here are ridiculously spacious, with huge living rooms, marble bathrooms, jacuzzis and walk-in showers; one of them even has its own garden and swimming pool.

The main pool is lined with private *cabañas* (cabins), which allow guests to relax discreetly. The hotel offers honeymoon packages and also organizes various programmes based around golf, beauty treatments and learning Spanish. Artworks by Marc Chagall, David Hockney and Andy Warhol are on display in the corridors and bars. The restaurant, L'Orangerie, serves modern Mediterranean cuisine, though there is a tendency to create unnecessarily fussy dishes, such as pigeon and foie gras in coffee sauce.

🕐 All year
🛏 Double from €199
🛈 16 doubles and 8 suites
♨ 🍽 ♿

SANTA MARIA DEL CAMÍ
READ'S HOTEL AND RESTAURANT

Carretera Santa Maria del Camí–Alaró,
07320 Santa Maria del Camí
Tel 971 140261
www.readshotel.com

There are 23 themed bedrooms at this exclusive Relais & Chateaux hotel, 20 minutes from Palma. Each is individually and vividly decorated: the

STAYING

furniture is antique, the beds are enormous and the toiletries are from Molton Brown. Read's is justifiably proud of its restaurant (▷ 169) with British chef Marc Fosh at the helm and it has now been joined by an affordable bistro. There's also a new fitness centre, but staff admit that it is infrequently used, with guests preferring to laze outside or swim in the hotel's pool. No children under 14 years old.

🅖 All year
🅗 From €210
🅘 23
▨ ▨ 🅢

SÓLLER
CA'N AI
Camí de Son Sales, 50, 07100 Sóller
Tel 971 632494
www.canai.com

Perhaps one of the most captivating hotels in the Serra de Tramuntana, Ca'n Ai is a converted manor house surrounded by orange and lemon groves in Sóller Valley. It's the outdoor areas that impress immediately—there are plenty of places in the spectacular gardens and terraces to find seclusion. You can also enjoy the views and the heady scent of the citrus groves from the suites, each of which has a private terrace. The bedrooms are also fitted with a telephone, minibar and central heating, but don't have televisions—a refreshingly bold decision. Breakfast, lunch and dinner are served in the informal dining room, in which there are several levels of seating, so once again it is easy to find privacy.

🅖 Closed Nov–Feb
🅗 Double from €207
🅘 11
▨ 🅢

CA'S XORC
Carretera Deià–Sóller, km56, 07100 Sóller
Tel 971 638280
www.casxorc.com
'Fantastic', 'fashionable', 'a real pain to get to'—all descriptions that apply equally to Ca's Xorc, a hip mountain-top retreat overlooking Sóller where Claudia Schiffer celebrated her 30th birthday. But it's worth struggling up the twisty, nar-

row drive to the converted olive mill. The breathtaking views are matched by the luxurious interior with its candles, stone-flagged floors and psychedelic art. Rooms are kitted out with a music system, ISDN connection and gold bath fittings; the hotel's décor has Moroccan touches throughout. Sa Tafona, the restaurant in what was the mill itself, offers an adventurous Mediterranean menu with dishes such as royal lobster with pineapple jam or oxtail ravioli with truffle vinaigrette. The five-course tasting menu costs €59. Outside there is a swimming pool, jacuzzi and several interesting, sculpture-filled gardens around the hillside. And if it matters at all, Miss Schiffer stayed in room number 8.

🅖 Closed 15 Nov–15 Feb
🅗 Double from €155
🅘 12
▨ 🅢

GRAN HOTEL SÓLLER
Carrer Romaguera, 18, 07100 Sóller
Tel 971 638686
www.granhotelsoller.com
Sóller's first tourist hotel, which opened in the late 19th century, reopened in 2004 after a major renovation as a five-star spa resort. Details of the original building have been retained, including some Modernist tiled floors. The suites, which have king-size beds and jacuzzis, look out

over the sunny front gardens, while the double rooms all have their own balconies overlooking the river behind the hotel. There is a small saltwater pool and solarium on the rooftop, with magnificent views over the town and the mountains beyond, and an indoor pool, spa and sauna in the basement. The Can Blau restaurant offers creative Mediterranean cuisine, with lighter meals at lunchtime. The hotel is a short walk from Sóller's main square—trams to Port de Sóller go right past the door. Parking is available.

🅖 All year
🅗 Double from €225
🅘 27 doubles, 6 singles and 5 suites
▨ ▨ 🅢

VALLDEMOSSA
VALLDEMOSSA HOTEL
Carretera Vieja de Valldemossa, 07170 Valldemossa
Tel 971 612626
www.valldemossahotel.com

This tasteful hotel opened in 2003 in a restored *finca,* with its own orchards and gardens overlooking the village of Valldemossa. The hotel offers traditional luxury with modern touches, such as the large selection of DVDs available for free loan and internet access in the rooms. The three double rooms have their own balconies, while the suites each have a private terrace. The restaurant emphasizes local produce but some dishes are overcomplicated, such as octopus noodles with violet potatoes, asparagus and chilli-and-lemon sorbet. In summer you can dine on the terrace. Now that a new lift is completed, access is improved for visitors with limited mobility.

🅖 All year
🅗 Double from €244
🅘 3 doubles and 7 suites
▨ 🅢

Accommodation in the family-friendly holiday town of Port de Pollença ranges from expansive resort hotels to expensive luxury hotels. Elsewhere in the Northeast you'll find rural manor house hotels, chic townhouse hotels and even a guesthouse in the middle of a golf course. Largely dependent on its coastline for visitors, many establishments in the Northeast close for some of the winter. But hotels to the west of the region, such as those in Pollença make good out-of-season bases for exploring the north end of the Serra de Tramuntana.

ALCÚDIA
CAN TEM
Carrer de l'Església, 14, 07400 Alcúdia
Tel 971 243537
www.hotelcantem.com

Behind the medieval walls, Alcúdia is an appealing town of Gothic and Renaissance mansions sheltering in narrow streets. In recent years several of these houses have become stylish townhouse hotels. Magdalena and Toni Reus have converted their family home, in a quiet lane off the main street, into just such a place, combining antique furniture with bright modern paintings. From the spacious entrance hall with its stone arch, a curving staircase leads upstairs to the bedrooms, which have televisions and central heating. The shady garden makes a peaceful spot to relax, or have breakfast on sunny mornings.
🅞 All year
🛏 Double from €77
🛌 4
🅢

ES CONVENT
Carrer del Progrés, 6, 07400 Alcúdia
Tel 971 548716
www.esconvent.com
One of the more exceptional hotels in the north of Mallorca, Es Convent is a convent conversion, which opened in 2000. The chic townhouse hotel, in a quiet street in Alcúdia's old town, has just three suites and one double room, all with en-suite bathroom, central heating, minibar, TV and safe, as well as writing desks. It adheres to the typical blueprint for Mallorca's boutique hotels, with stone paved floors, a mixture of raw stone walls and whitewashed panels, and elegant linen furnishings.

In the reception area downstairs, the high-beamed ceiling is upstaged by spectacular stone arches. Guests can look forward to breakfast too: the thick orange smoothy is a step up from the usual orange juice, and they can order bacon and eggs or a continental breakfast.
🅞 Closed Jan and Feb
🛏 Double from €95
🛌 3 doubles, 1 suite
🅢

POLLENTIA CLUB RESORT (PORT DE POLLENÇA)
Carretera Port de Pollença–Alcúdia, km2, 07400 Alcúdia
Tel 971 546996
www.clubpollentia.com

Set back from the main road between Port de Pollença and Alcúdia, Club Pollentia is an unobtrusive, low-rise resort. There are two classes of accommodation, the cheaper Maris rooms and the larger Village rooms. Both are clean and are organized in small clusters in the landscaped grounds, each with its own buffet restaurant. All bedrooms have a bathroom, telephone, television, fridge, fan, central heating and a safe—the Village rooms also have sunbeds. On-site activities are free for guests. Facilities include three swimming pools, jacuzzis, tennis courts, squash courts, minigolf, an archery range, bicycle hire, a scuba centre, a health and beauty centre with gym, saunas, and a children's club. The hotel is good value for families wanting resort-style accommodation. Note that car-less guests have to take the bus to Port de Pollença and you have to cross a road to get to the beach, which is better suited to watersports than sunbathing. The resort is a popular base for cyclists in the off-peak seasons.
🅞 Closed Nov–Feb
🛏 Maris rooms from €61, Village rooms from €81
🛌 292
🏊 🛁 🅢

ARTÀ
CA'N MORAGUES
Carrer Pou Nou, 12, 07570 Artà
Tel 971 829509
www.canmoragues.com
This elegant, 18th-century townhouse hotel in Artà's old town offers guests a heated pool, solarium and sauna. Bedroom design is a mix of stylish, modern furnishings and rustic Mallorcan touches such as bare stone walls and wooden furniture. All rooms have telephone, television and central heating. There's an attractive courtyard, complete with orange trees, in which to enjoy breakfast. Four golf courses are within a short drive of Artà.
🅞 Closed Jan
🛏 Double from €123
🛌 8
🏊 🅢

STAYING

SANT SALVADOR

Carrer Castellet, 7, 07570 Artà
Tel 971 829555
www.santsalvador.com

The hotel-restaurant Sant Salvador is in a grand old palace in the centre of Artà close to the Gothic church and the castle. The German owners have created a colourful, vibrant interior with warm lighting and a smattering of antiques. The bedrooms are individually furnished and all bedrooms have central heating, telephone, television and fridge. Health and beauty treatments can be arranged. Ca'n Epifanio, the restaurant, serves Asian-Mediterranean fusion cuisine; it is open for dinner all week except Tuesdays. There are four golf courses close to Artà and beaches are a short drive away. Pets are welcome.

🅰 All year
🅱 Double from €180
ⓘ 8
🔷🔶

CALA RAJADA
SES ROTGES

Rafael Blanes, 21, 07590 Cala Rajada
Tel 971 563108
www.sesrotges.com

Best known for its French restaurant (▷ 172), Ses Rotges' hotel accommodation is on the second and third floor of this handsome corner building. The French-owned hotel is in a quiet area of town, a brief walk from the seafront. Don't expect modern minimalism in the bedrooms; décor is on the chintzy side, but the rooms are a good size and have telephone, television and central heating. Dinner at Ses Rotges can be an extravagant experience, but there are plenty of cheaper options in Cala Rajada's main street, two blocks away. In summer the patio outside is prepared for moonlit dining. Excellent

breakfasts are cooked to order.
🅰 Closed Nov–Mar
🅱 Double from €110
ⓘ 24
🔷

CALA SANT VICENÇ
CALA SANT VICENÇ

Carrer Maressers, 2, 07469 Cala Sant Vicenç
Tel 971 530250
www.hotelcala.com

Trapped between the tail-end of the Tramuntana Mountains and the deep-blue Mediterranean, the Cala Sant Vicenç is in a perfect location at the northwest corner of the island. It's the original hotel in the Suau empire and in it the family has developed one of Mallorca's top restaurants, Cavall Bernat, which offers a finely crafted, seasonally adjusted, modern Mallorquin menu. There's also a less expensive grill for lunchtimes and a trattoria. Bedrooms are as pretty as the hotel's dusky-pink exterior, and have television, telephone, minibar and central heating. The Cala Sant Vicenç's grounds are spectacular, with landscaped gardens and a swimming pool, which is heated in winter.
🅰 Closed Dec and Jan
🅱 Double from €125
ⓘ 38
🔷🔶

CAMPANET
MONNABER NOU

Possessió de Monnaber Nou, 07310 Campanet
Tel 971 877176
www.monnaber.com

On the western edge of the northeast and bordering the Serra de Tramuntana, Campanet is a quiet base for touring the northern end of the mountains. Monnaber Nou is an imposing manor house just outside the village. In the grounds there are three

swimming pools (two outdoor, one heated indoor) and tennis courts. Inside guests can use a gym and jacuzzi or have a

massage. Rooms have telephone, television and central heating, but make sure you get a room facing out; those looking into the interior courtyard can be gloomy.
🅰 All year
🅱 Double from €80
ⓘ 25
🔷🔶

POLLENÇA
DES BRULL

Marquès Desbrull, 7, 07460 Pollença
Tel 971 535055
www.desbrull.com

This boutique hotel on the edge of Pollença's centre opened in August 2003. It's in a converted 18th-century building, but the design is very modern and chic. Rooms have television and attractively plain bathrooms. Décor is a combination of metal fittings, stone walls and dark wood furniture. There's a bar and restaurant downstairs.
🅰 All year
🅱 Double from €90
ⓘ 6
🔷

POSADA DE LLUC

Carrer Roser Vell, 11, 07460 Pollença
Tel 971 535220
www.posadalluc.com

The monastery at Lluc owned this small townhouse in

Pollença's medieval core from the 15th to the 19th century. It is now a stylish hotel, graced with antique furniture and a pleasant garden. Rooms are

cosy, and fitted with a telephone and television. Note that Pollença's summer music festival takes place close by.
🅚 Closed one week Jan
🛏 Double from €111
ⓘ 8
♨ ♿

SON BRULL
Carretera Palma–Pollença PM 220, km49.8, 07460 Pollença
Tel 971 535353
www.sonbrull.com
Not to be confused with Des Brull (▷ 189), Son Brull is another chic hotel, which opened in 2003. Part of the Suau family's empire (▷ 172), it is on the main Inca–Pollença road, just outside Pollença. The bedrooms are large, with the sort of tasteful, minimal furnishings you'd expect for €200–€300 per night. They have ensuite bathrooms, television and DVD, telephones and internet connections. The spacious bathrooms even have baths with hydro-massage jets and a hi-fi. Golfers will appreciate Son Brull's proximity to Pollença's golf club, and the challenging new Alcanada golf course just 15 minutes away by car. The hotel has a spa and views of olive grove-clad hills.
🅚 Closed Dec–Jan
🛏 Double from €214
ⓘ 23
♨ ♿

SON SANT JORDI
Carrer Sant Jordi, 29, 07460 Pollença
Tel 971 530309
www.sonsantjordi.com
The best feature of this smart townhouse hotel is the fantastic interior design. Old elements of the manor house have been incorporated into the modern, minimalist bedrooms, so you'll find ancient tiling next to stylish bathroom fittings. The lights are movement-sensitive, another smart feature and bedrooms have fridges. Thick white curtains do their best to block out the hotel's worst feature—the

whine from scooters whizzing up and down the street outside—but they don't entirely succeed. If noise bothers you, avoid room 2 at the front of the building and ask for a room at the back, where there is an exotic garden, a pool and a sauna. Breakfast is a buffet.
🅚 All year
🛏 Double from €54
ⓘ 8
♨ ♿

PORT DE POLLENÇA
ILLA D'OR
Passeig de Colón, 265, 07470 Port de Pollença
Tel 971 865100
www.hoposa.es

The Illa d'Or opened in 1929, when tourism in Mallorca was in its infancy, and has retained a great deal of its original charm. Part of the attraction is the setting, a short stroll from the centre of the resort at the end of the 'Pine Walk' from the harbour. The clientele here is overwhelmingly British and many visitors have been coming since they were children. The hotel has gradually upgraded its facilities and now

has a beauty centre with a sauna, jacuzzi and gym, indoor and outdoor pools and a tennis court, but it still has the feel of an old-style, family-run hotel. In summer, meals are served out of doors on a seafront terrace. The hotel has its own jetty and there are several small beaches nearby. For a traditional seaside holiday, you couldn't do much better.
🅚 Closed Nov–Feb
🛏 Double from €91
ⓘ 120
♨ ♿ ♿

SON SERVERA
EL ENCINAR
Cami des Rafal des Sants, 07550 Son Servera
Tel 971 183860
www.elencinardearta.com
On a hill 5km (3 miles) from Artà, this 18th-century country house has been restored to offer nine bedrooms, a lounge with an open fireplace, a bar, a library and a wine cellar. And in sunny weather guests can use the barbecue outside. The medium-size bedrooms have television and central heating. Décor is low-key, with plain furnishings and tiled floors. The hotel is ideally located for the east coast's beaches and four golf courses nearby.
🅚 All year
🛏 Double from €96
ⓘ 9
♿

PETIT HOTEL CASES DE PULA
Finca Pula, 07550 Son Servera
Tel 971 567492
www.pulagolf.com
This *agroturismo*, a converted estate built in 1581, is a favourite with golfers, who can walk straight onto the middle of Pula's 18-hole golf course. Bedrooms are stylishly rustic, with beamed ceilings and bare stone walls. They're fitted with telephone, television and central heating. The hotel is just 10 minutes from the bars and restaurants of Cala Millor and Cala Rajada, but it has its own bar and restaurant, as well as a chapel. If the weather is fine, you can enjoy the outdoor pool, or a round of golf.
🅚 All year
🛏 Double from €120
ⓘ 10
♨ ♿

STAYING

STAYING IN THE SOUTH

Although areas of the South are arguably the least-developed parts of Mallorca, holidaymakers will still find an enormous selection of accommodation. Away from the resorts and their modern hotels, the South has a fine collection of country house hotels. These rural hideaways, such as Raïms and Sa Bassa Rotja, may not be quite as expensive as comparable hotels elsewhere on the island. Much of the coast closes for the winter, as do many of the inland hotels, when there are few reasons (other than golf) to visit the area.

ALGAIDA

RAÏMS

Carrer Ribera, 24, 07120 Algaida
Tel 971 665157
www.finca-raims.com

This 17th-century manor house with its own private chapel is situated on the edge of the village, so it feels like both a townhouse in the country and a country house in the town.

There is one room in the house plus four apartments in the various outbuildings, each tastefully decorated and with its own private terrace. The owner of the house is a winemaker; Raïms means 'grapes', and each of the apartments is named after a different grape variety. The cellar, one of the oldest in Mallorca, is always open for guests to help themselves to wine. The apartments give onto the garden, a delightfully shady retreat with palm and orange trees and a swimming pool at the centre. Dinner is served twice a week, and there are three excellent restaurants within walking distance.

ⓒ Closed Dec–Jan
🛏 Double from €100
ⓘ 5
📶 ♿

BINISSALEM

SCOTT'S

Plaça de l'Església, 12, 07350 Binissalem
Tel 971 870100
www.scottshotel.com

No room service, no reception—just an ambition to be 'the best, most elegant, most comfortable not-quite-a-hotel

in the Mediterranean'. Scott's is owned by genial American crime writer George Scott and the place reflects his personality. Huge handmade beds, cotton percale sheets, goose-down pillows, country-house furnishings and a breakfast

buffet served until noon have combined to make this a popular romantic getaway and a bolthole for celebrities in need of rest. There is a small indoor pool, a help-yourself bar and a sunny terrace with views of the church. The hotel is situated on the main square of the village.

ⓒ All year
🛏 Double from €175
ⓘ 2 singles, 10 doubles and 6 suites
📶 ♿

CALA D'OR

HOTEL CALA D'OR

Avenida de Bélgica, 33, 07660 Cala d'Or
Tel 971 657249
www.hotelcalador.com

The Cala d'Or, which dates from 1932, is surrounded by pine trees and overlooks the bay of Cala d'Or; rooms on the eastern side of the hotel get a

splendid sea view. Cala d'Or, the resort, is towards the southern tip of the east coast and close to several pretty coves and sandy beaches, and a trip to the natural park at nearby Cala Mondragó—one of the best beaches in the area— is recommended. Bedrooms have telephone, television and central heating. The hotel's facilities include an outdoor swimming pool and a children's play area. The décor inside is understated.

ⓒ Closed Nov–Mar
🛏 Double from €92
ⓘ 95
📶 ♿

CA'S CONCOS

SA GALERA

Carretera Santanyí–Ca's Concos, 07208 Ca's Concos
Tel 971 842079
www.hotelsagalera.com

A short drive from the unremarkable village of Ca's Concos, Sa Galera offers guests complete rural seclusion. The converted 13th-century manor house has spacious rooms, each individually decorated in neutral linens. Watch out for the low doorways. Each bedroom has telephone, television and central heating. Outside there is an attractive patio, and, farther away from the

main house, a large swimming pool with sunbeds. The hotel has bicycles for hire, and there are some beautiful lanes leading out of Ca's Concos to explore. Some of Mallorca's best-known beaches, including

Cala Mondragó and Es Trenc, are nearby, with good restaurants at Portocolom, 16km (10 miles) away—although Sa Galera does offer an à la carte menu in the evenings.

- Closed mid-Nov–Mar
- Double from €128
- 16

CAMPOS
SANT BLAI
Carretera Campos–Colònia Sant Jordi, km2, 07630 Campos
Tel 971 650567
www.santblai.com

The special feature of this large, family-friendly *agroturismo* in the southeast of the island is its small astronomy observatory with both a refracting and a reflecting telescope, through which guests can marvel at the starry skies in this quiet region. But that's not its only advantage: there's a swimming pool, self-service bar, barbecue and activities such as pony riding. And it's not far from the beach at Es Trenc. The four bedrooms and one apartment are decorated with wooden furniture and have telephone, television and central heating. They used to be the farm's cowshed, timber shed, stable, barn and granary.

- All year
- Double from €192
- 5

LLUCMAJOR
MARRIOT SON ANTEM GOLF RESORT AND SPA
Carretera Llucmajor, km3.4, 07620 Llucmajor
Tel 971 129100
www.marriot.com/pmigs

Golfers can double their enjoyment at Son Antem; the resort has two top-class 18-hole, 72-par golf courses, both designed by Francisco López Segales. Beginners will prefer the East course, while the West course is championship standard. The resort itself is what you'd expect from the international chain: a very high level of comfort and service but a little short on character. Bedroom facilities include a work desk but no internet connection. For non-golfers, there are two swimming pools, a spa and health club and tennis courts. An enormous range of excursions and activities, from water-skiing to day trips to Valldemossa, can be arranged, and there is a playground for younger guests.

- All year
- Double from €199
- 150

MANACOR
SON AMOIXA VELL
Carretera Cales de Mallorca–Manacor, km3.4, 07500 Manacor
Tel 971 846292
www.sonamoixa.com

Son Amoixa Vell is particularly popular with German visitors. Lying between Porto Cristo and Manacor, this grand 16th-century country-house hotel is conveniently located for the east coast's two main attractions: caves and beaches. Bedrooms are fitted with modern comforts and are centrally heated. The dining room is relatively formal, but cosy, and there is also a bar, lounge and library. Tennis courts, a gym, sauna and a beauty salon were installed in 2004.

- All year
- Double from €170
- 14 doubles and 1 apartment

PETRA
SA PLAÇA
Plaça Ramón Llull, 4, 07520 Petra
Tel 971 561646

Staying at this tiny hotel in Petra's main square is a bit of a treat. Not only are the rooms comfortably furnished, but the restaurant downstairs (▷ 175) is a cut above the average hotel restaurant. The three bedrooms are fitted with telephone, television, a minibar and en-suite bathroom. Petra isn't the sort of place you'd remain in for long—it's a pleasant village but there's little to do—but Sa Plaça is the perfect base for a visit to Fray Junípero Serra's birthplace and the hilltop hermitage, Ermita de Bonany (▷ 101), where he preached his final sermon in Mallorca before leaving for the Americas.

- Closed Nov
- Double from €109
- 3

PINA
SON XOTANO
Carretera Pina–Sencelles, km1.5, 07220 Pina
Tel 971 872500
www.sonxotano.com

Deep in the agricultural heartland of Mallorca, where tourists rarely tread, this small *agroturismo* offers guests rural tranquillity, delicious Mediterranean cooking and the chance to learn to ride horses—the Son Xotano riding school has Andalucian and Hispanic-Arab horses and acres of woodland to explore. The country house has lounges and dining rooms with open fireplaces, an open-air swimming pool and a putting green. Bedrooms are equipped with telephone and television, and are decorated in a warm, rustic fashion. If horse-riding doesn't appeal, there are bicycles to hire.

- All year
- Double from €162
- 16

STAYING

PORRERES
SA BASSA ROTJA

Finca Son Orell–Camino Sa Pedrera,
07260 Porreres
Tel 971 168225
www.sabassarotja.com

One of the more opulent
country-manor conversions on
Mallorca, Sa Bassa Rotja boasts
two swimming pools (one
heated), two tennis courts, a
gym, a health farm and a children's play area. The owners
have retained the rustic character of the 13th-century
mansion, but bedrooms are
richly furnished and there is
even a pillow menu, to fine-
tune nocturnal comfort. One
suite has been specially
designed for disabled guests.
The hotel is west of Felanitx
and about 19km (12 miles)
from the closest beach.

🕒 All year
🛏 Double from €150
🛈 25
🚗 ▨ ⚙

PORTO CRISTO AND
ENVIRONS
SA VALL

Sa Vall, 205, Son Macia de Manacor,
07509 Son Macia
Tel 971 554279

Just 15 minutes by car from
the beach and 10km (6 miles)
inland from the family-friendly
resort of Porto Cristo and its
nearby caves, this charming
agroturismo lies in an expanse
of almond groves. The beauti-
fully restored 16th-century
farmhouse has three apartments and two double rooms.
Both apartments and rooms
have a terrace, television, minibar and central heating, and
are furnished with antique
Mallorcan furniture. The airy
rooms overlook an outdoor
swimming pool, surrounded by
almond trees that blossom in
February. The rural location
makes Sa Vall a good choice
for hikers and cyclists.

🕒 All year
🛏 Double from €75
🛈 1 apartment (4 person), 2 apartments (2 person), 2 doubles
🚗
🚘 From the Palma–Manacor road turn
off to the village of Selani and follow
signs to Sa Vall

SON MAS

Carretera Porto Cristo–Porto Colom,
07680 Porto Cristo
Tel 971 558755
www.sonmas.com

Close to the Coves del Drac
and the beaches of the east
coast, Son Mas is a luxurious
country hotel. Two swimming
pools (the indoor pool is
heated), a sauna and a jacuzzi
have been added to the renovated 17th-century property.
All the bedrooms are spacious,
with a terrace or a balcony, a
living area and antique furniture, as well as telephone,
television and internet connection. The hotel's setting, in
extensive grounds, is superb;
bicycles are provided so guests
can explore the orchards or
cycle to the beach 4km (2.5
miles) away. Breakfast is buf-
fet-style, with Mediterranean
cuisine served at dinner.

🕒 Closed Dec–Jan
🛏 Double from €224
🛈 16
🚗 ⚙

RANDA
ES RECÓ DE RANDA

Carrer Fuente, 21, 07629 Randa
Tel 971 660997
www.esrecoderanda.com

The Puig de Randa is one of
the few areas of high ground
on Mallorca's Pla de Llevant,
the fertile central plain. This
means that the views from this
stylish small hotel are the best
in the region. Es Recó de
Randa is renowned for its
restaurant (▷ 176), which
serves Mallorcan and international cuisine. And to burn off

the extra calories, the hotel has
an outdoor swimming pool
from which you can look out
across the countryside.
Bedrooms are fitted with telephone, television and central
heating, and thankfully you can
turn the piped music off.

🕒 All year
🛏 Double from €135.83
🛈 14
🚗 ⚙

SES SALINES
SA CARROTJA

Sa Carrotja, 7, 07640 Ses Salines
Tel 971 649053
www.sacarrotja.com

The friendly Mallorcan family
that run this small farmhouse
hotel has furnished its bedrooms with antique furniture
as well as the modern features
you'd expect to find: telephone, television and fridge.
Five of the six rooms have their
own terraces and there are
two more communal terraces.
The open-air swimming pool is
heated and the organic vegetable garden provides food
for meals. Bicycles are available for guests' use, and there
is plenty of countryside, including Ses Salines salt pans, to
explore in this southeastern
corner of the island. The hotel
is not suitable for children.

🕒 All year
🛏 Double from €90
🛈 6
🚗 ⚙

S'HORT DES TURÓ

Carretera Ses Salines–Colònia de Sant
Jordi, km2.5, 07640 Ses Salines
Tel 971 649055
www.hortdesturo.com

This small hotel, with five
apartments, is perched on the
southern tip of the island,
close to Colònia de Sant Jordi,
making it a good base for a
day trip to the island of
Cabrera. Each centrally heated
apartment sleeps two people
and is kitted out with household equipment including a
fridge, oven, dishwasher and
kettle; there's a shared wash-
ing machine. The apartments
have also been fitted with
ADSL internet connections. The
décor is plain and simple. Pets
are welcome.

🕒 All year
🛏 Double from €154
🛈 5
🚗 ⚙

HOTEL GROUPS

Name of hotel group	Description	Website	Phone number
AC-Hoteles	Slick, luxury hotel chain, with one modern hotel in Palma but more opening throughout Spain.	www.ac-hoteles.com	902 292295
Design Hotels	Design Hotels represents two design-oriented hotels on Mallorca, Puro Hotel and Hotel Maricel.	www.designhotels.com	00 800 37 46 83 57 (toll-free reservations)
Grupotel	This is the largest hotel chain on Mallorca, with 34 economical modern hotels, many with beach frontage.	www.grupotel.com	971 890335
H10	H10 has 37 establishments in 12 countries, including some of the major resorts in Spain, but just one in Mallorca.	www.h10.es	971 680762
Hipotel	Hipotel has 13 high-quality modern hotels on Mallorca, many affiliated to golf courses and close to beaches.	www.hipotels.com	971 587652
Mac Hotels	There are four Mac hotels on Mallorca, three of them built in the Spanish style of the 1960s.	www.mac-hotels.com	971 010930
Marriot	This luxury hotel brand has one world-class hotel on Mallorca with two golf courses.	www.marriot.com	971 129100
Protur Hotel	The 17 Protur hotels on Mallorca suit most budgets and include aparthotels.	www.protur-hotels.com	971 587520
Reis de Mallorca	This independent group represents 30 of Mallorca's top hotels, distinguished by their cuisine, architecture, individuality or level of service.	www.reisdemallorca.com	971 770737
Sheraton	Two luxury hotels are loosely united under the Arabella Sheraton brand, the Hotel Son Vida and the Mardavall Hotel.	www.starwood.com	971 799999
Sol Melia	This fast-growing chain, the third-largest in Europe, has five mid-range hotels in Mallorca.	www.solmelia.com	902 144444

STAYING

USEFUL ORGANISATIONS

Two independent organizations can be of great use in finding interesting accommodation on Mallorca: the Associacio Agroturisme Balear and Reis de Mallorca. The Associacio Agroturisme Balear (tel 971 721508, www.topfincas.com) represents more than 100 fincas and small hotels. The fincas in the association's brochure range from low-cost agroturismos to luxurious boutique hotels. Accommodation can be booked directly with the hotel.

The brochure from Reis de Mallorca (tel 971 770737, www.reisdemallorca.com) features most of Mallorca's best hotels. Again, accommodation can be booked directly with the hotel.

Mallorca's local tourist offices (▷ 204) can provide information about accommodation and check availability for you. The Balearic government has highlighted hotels specializing in a variety of interests, including golf, cycling and hiking. You can find the hotel listings at www.balears-leisure-experiences.com or at the main tourist information offices in Palma.

Planning

WEATHER

Mallorca's island climate is surprisingly variable. Islanders like to boast of 300 days of sunshine annually and summers are typically very hot and sunny, but spring, autumn and winter can bring spells of wind, rain and cold temperatures at short notice. The surrounding sea moderates Mallorca's climate so there are no dramatic seasonal extremes, but temperatures will be lower in the mountainous Serra de Tramuntana the higher you travel.

WHEN TO GO
● The summer months of June, July and August make up Mallorca's high season. Accommodation will be booked to capacity as holidaymakers fly in to enjoy average high temperatures of up to 30°C (86°F) by day and sea water that is almost as warm. During these months the sun shines for an average of 11 hours per day and beaches are tightly packed with people; the sea temperature goes as high as 26°C (79°F). For many it is too hot to do anything active, which is why many of the visitors who come to Mallorca for golf, cycling or other activities arrive in the cooler months of April, May, September and October.

● These shoulder months are perhaps the best time to see Mallorca. Attractions are open, prices slightly lower, queues shorter and there is space to move freely on the beaches and roads. Bring a waterproof jacket and warm clothing: you're as likely to experience a week of wet, overcast days as a sunny heatwave. Although rainfall varies from year to year, typically 40 percent of the island's annual rain will fall in the autumn (September–November), 25 percent in winter (December–February) and a further 25 percent in spring (March–May).

● Temperatures in the winter can reach as high as 15°C (59°F) but heavy snow may fall in the Serra de Tramuntana during some winters. Sea temperatures will remain relatively warm, at about 14°C (57°F). However, only doughty dog walkers will frequent the beaches during the winter and the island's resorts close for the season and don't reopen until April. Most of the urban attractions remain open—Christmas is a busy period for Palma—but many of the visitors to Mallorca during the winter are walkers.

WEATHER WARNINGS
Although the mountain regions of the Serra de Tramuntana are not especially high, because they are exposed on the west coast to weather fronts coming in off the Mediterranean they can experience unpredictable weather conditions. The west side of the range is often cloudy and foggy while the inland side is clear, and conditions can quickly change from warmth and good visibility to cold and windy weather with low visibility. For this reason, take a waterproof jacket and some food and drink when walking in the mountains.

In summer, temperatures sometimes reach 40°C (104°F); consequently the risk of heat stroke and dehydration also rises. During such extreme temperatures it is advisable not to do anything too energetic.

WEATHER REPORTS
Spain's Instituto Nacional de Meteorología posts basic daily weather forecasts on its website (www.inm.es), but the BBC (www.bbc.co.uk/weather) offers a five-day forecast for Palma in English. Detailed forecasts follow the regular Spanish news programmes on television.

WEATHER STATIONS

Pollença
2m
7ft

PALMA
7m
23ft

TEMPERATURE IN PALMA

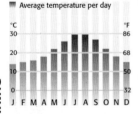

Average temperature per day

TEMPERATURE IN POLLENÇA

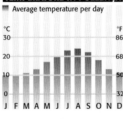

Average temperature per day

RAINFALL IN PALMA

Average rainfall

RAINFALL IN POLLENÇA

Average rainfall

TIMES ZONES
Mallorca is on CET (Central European Time), one hour ahead of GMT (Greenwich Mean Time).

CITY	TIME DIFFERENCE	TIME AT 12 NOON GMT
Amsterdam	0	noon
Berlin	0	noon
Brussels	0	noon
Chicago	-7	5am
Dublin	-1	11am
Johannesburg*	+1	1pm
London	-1	11am
Montréal	-6	6am
New York	-6	6am
Perth*	+7	7pm
Rome	0	noon
San Francisco	-9	3am
Sydney*	+9	9pm
Tokyo*	+8	8pm

Summer Time begins on the last Sunday in March and ends on the last Sunday in October. For starred cities, which do not have daylight saving, take off one hour during Summer Time.

PLANNING

PRACTICALITIES

- Outside the beach resorts, Mallorca retains many traditional values. Dress respectfully when visiting religious sites and avoid arriving at smart restaurants in beach wear.
- Although English and German are widely understood on the island, locals may speak up to another three languages: Spanish, Catalan and Mallorquín. Visitors making an effort to speak Catalan or even Mallorquín are genuinely appreciated by residents.

WHAT TO TAKE

- Outside the summer months (June–August) it is advisable to take a waterproof jacket, and from late autumn to spring some warm clothing is necessary; the evenings can be quite chilly.
- It's a good idea to bring your own equipment for specific activities, such as hiking boots or cycling kit, although most items can be purchased on the island.

PASSPORTS AND VISAS

- All visitors must have a valid passport (a national ID card can be used by EU nationals instead). You are required by Spanish law to keep one of these documents with you at all times, but in practice it is extremely rare to be stopped and asked. Turn to page 199 for tips on keeping your passport safe.
- EU visitors do not require a visa for entry. Visitors from the US, Canada, Japan, Australia and

New Zealand require a visa for stays exceeding 90 days.
- Always check with your consul about visa requirements and entry regulations as they are liable to change, often at short notice.

ELECTRICITY

- Mallorca's power supply is 220 volts. Plugs have two round pins and an adaptor is required.

LAUNDRY

- Your hotel's laundry service is the most convenient way to have your clothes cleaned. If your hotel does not offer a laundry, there are laundries (lavanderías) in Alcúdia, Palma, Pollença, Felanitx, Sóller and other large towns. Use the phone book to find the closest.
- Several dry cleaners (tintorerías) are located in Palma but they are not easily found outside the city.

PUBLIC LAVATORIES

- Public lavatories (lavabos) are free but are hard to find or non-existent outside Palma and the main towns and resorts.
- Use the washrooms in large department stores, museums, galleries, cafés, restaurants or bars, even if you end up having to buy something.

MEASUREMENTS

- Mallorca uses the metric system. Distances are measured in metres and kilometres, fuel is sold by the litre and food is weighed in grams and kilograms.

LOCAL CUSTOMS

- The typical greeting between friends is a kiss on both cheeks. Offer to shake hands when you meet people, even if it is not for the first time.

SMOKING

- Smoking is not permitted in public spaces such as museums, galleries, theatres and cinemas, but is common in bars and restaurants; only the smart establishments tend to have non-smoking sections.

CONVERSION CHART

FROM	TO	MULTIPLY BY
Inches	Centimetres	2.54
Centimetres	Inches	0.3937
Feet	Metres	0.3048
Metres	Feet	3.2810
Yards	Metres	0.9144
Metres	Yards	1.0940
Miles	Kilometres	1.6090
Kilometres	Miles	0.6214
Acres	Hectares	0.4047
Hectares	Acres	2.4710
Gallons	Litres	4.5460
Litres	Gallons	0.2200
Ounces	Grams	28.35
Grams	Ounces	0.0353
Pounds	Grams	453.6
Grams	Pounds	0.0022
Pounds	Kilograms	0.4536
Kilograms	Pounds	2.205
Tons	Tonnes	1.0160
Tonnes	Tons	0.9842

CLOTHING SIZES

Clothing sizes in Spain are in metric. Use the chart below to convert the size you use at home.

UK	Metric	USA	
36	46	36	
38	48	38	
40	50	40	
42	52	42	SUITS
44	54	44	
46	56	46	
48	58	48	
7	41	8	
7.5	42	8.5	
8.5	43	9.5	
9.5	44	10.5	SHOES
10.5	45	11.5	
11	46	12	
14.5	37	14.5	
15	38	15	
15.5	39/40	15.5	
16	41	16	SHIRTS
16.5	42	16.5	
17	43	17	
8	36	6	
10	38	8	
12	40	10	
14	42	12	DRESSES
16	44	14	
18	46	16	
20	46	18	
4.5	37.5	6	
5	38	6.5	
5.5	38.5	7	
6	39	7.5	SHOES
6.5	40	8	
7	41	8.5	

PLANNING

PRACTICALITIES 197

HEALTH

A neon green cross lights the way to a pharmacy

Spain's national health service works alongside the private sector, and its hospitals are generally of a high standard.

BEFORE YOU GO

● No inoculations are required, but it is a good idea to check when you last had a tetanus jab and, if more than 10 years ago, have a booster before you travel.

● Spain has a reciprocal agreement with other EU states entitling EU citizens to a certain amount of free health care, including hospital treatment. You must complete all the necessary paperwork before you travel. In the UK, pick up an E111 form at a main post office. In 2005 the E111 will be replaced by the European Health Insurance Card, which will act in the same way.

● EU citizens requiring treatment for a pre-existing condition while they are away should apply to their department of health for an E112 form.

● If you think you will need to renew a prescription while you are away, ensure you know the chemical name of the drug before you travel; it may be sold under another name in Mallorca.

● Taking out health insurance is strongly advised, despite the reciprocal health care. For non-EU visitors it is essential.

USEFUL NUMBERS
Emergencies
112
Ambulances
971 204111
Red Cross
971 295000
Balearic Institute of Health
971 175600

24-HOUR PHARMACIES
Avinguda Joan Miró, 188, Palma
971 402133
Carrer Balanguera, 3, Palma
971 458788
Pharmacies on duty
11888

IF YOU NEED TREATMENT

● In order to use an E111, you will need to confirm that the doctor you visit works within the Spanish Health Service. Make it clear that you want to be treated under this system.

● In some clinics there are separate surgery times for private patients and those treated under the health service. Again, make sure that you are treated at the appropriate surgery. If you are treated as a private patient or go to a private clinic you will not be entitled to your money back.

FINDING A DOCTOR

● A doctor (*médico*) can be found by asking at a pharmacy (*farmacia*), at your hotel, at a hospital or by looking in the phone book (*Páginas Amarillas*).

PHARMACIES

● Most towns in Mallorca have a pharmacy (*farmacia*), identified by a flashing green cross outside. Call 11888 for information about late-opening duty pharmacies.

● Staff normally provide good over-the-counter advice, often in English. For minor ailments it is worth consulting a pharmacist before finding a doctor.

● Drugs that are obtained on prescription in other countries may be available without one in Spain. Check with a pharmacist.

DENTISTS

● Dental treatment is not covered by the E111 agreement. For emergency treatment look under *Clínicas dentales* or *Dentistas* in the phone book.

OPTICIANS

● It is a good idea to pack a spare pair of glasses or contact lenses. Bringing your prescription means that an optician (*Opticos* in the phone book) can make another pair of glasses speedily.

HEALTH CONCERNS

● It is generally safe to drink tap water (unless marked *no potable*) but recurring water shortages in the summer mean that bottled water can be a more reliable option.

● The summer sun can be very powerful; prevent heatstroke and sunburn by avoiding the sun during the middle of the day, drinking water regularly and wearing a high-factor sunscreen.

HOSPITALS ON MALLORCA		
	Address	Telephone
Hospital de la Cruz Roja Española	Pons I Gallarça, 90, Palma	971 751445
Hospital General de Mallorca	Plaça de l'Hospital, 3, Palma	971 212100
Hospital Universitario Son Dureta	Andrea Doria, 55, Palma	971 175000
Hospital d'Alcúdia	Formentera, 5, Alcúdia	971 547373
Hospital Joan March	Carretera Palma–Sóller km12, Bunyola	971 212200
Fundación Hospital de Manacor	Carretera Manacor–Alcúdia, Manacor	971 847000
Hospital General de Muro	Carrer Veler, Urbanizacion Las Gaviotas, Muro	971 891900

SAFETY AND SECURITY

PERSONAL SAFETY
Crime rates in Mallorca are low and Palma is a relatively safe place when compared with other major Spanish cities. But pickpockets do operate in the city and in some of the larger resorts. Sensible precautions include:
● Never carrying more cash than you need.
● Keeping belongings close by in crowded areas.
● Being aware of ploys to distract your attentions by thieves working in pairs.
● Wearing bags slung diagonally across your chest rather than hanging from a shoulder. If you use a waist pack don't assume that it is safe since thieves will know that you're keeping valuables in it. Back pockets are also vulnerable to pickpockets.
● Sticking to brightly lit, main thoroughfares at night.
● Never leaving valuables on display in your car or unattended on the beach.
● Keeping valuables in the hotel safe.
● Taking a photocopy of your passport (kept separately) and noting the serial numbers of traveller's cheques in case of loss.

POLICE
There are several types of police force in Mallorca, each responsible for a different aspect of public order.
● Policía Municipal, the local police, are largely responsible for traffic and wear blue uniforms.
● Policía Nacional, wearing brown uniforms, keep law and order in urban areas.
● Policía Turistica: 100 multi-lingual tourist policemen started work in the resorts in 2004.
● Guardia Civil has a small presence in Mallorca, monitoring rural areas.
● Mallorcan police are generally approachable and, if asked, will give information and directions. But only the Policía Turistica are guaranteed to speak foreign languages. The Guardia Civil is a quasi-military department and perhaps the least forthcoming force.
● Report thefts to the police within 24 hours; you will need a police report if you intend to claim for the lost item through your insurance company.

INSURANCE
● As well as health insurance, it is advisable to have travel insurance (often part of the same policy). This will cover you in the event of the loss or theft of property.

LOST PROPERTY
● There are lost baggage facilities at Palma airport, representing eight airlines. If you lose something significant report its loss at a police station.
● If your passport is lost or stolen your consul can organize an emergency passport for returning to your home country.

A fee will be charged. A photocopy of your passport, or at least its serial number, will speed the process up. Consuls in Mallorca do not issue visas.

WHAT TO DO IF YOU ARE ARRESTED
● If you are arrested, for whatever reason, ask for your consul to be informed. Your consul can give you the contact details of local multilingual solicitors but they can't give you legal advice or pay any bills.
● The most common crimes involving visitors to Mallorca are driving offences. Drink-driving penalties are severe in Spain and can result in large fines or even imprisonment. If you are detained by the police always behave respectfully; your behaviour will have a bearing on how you are treated, even if you know a mistake has been made.

EMBASSIES AND CONSULATES IN PALMA

Country	Address		Telephone
France	Avinguda Argentina, 45, 07013 Palma		971 730301
Germany	Passeig des Born, 15, 07012 Palma		971 722997
Ireland	Carrer San Miguel, 68A, 07002 Palma		971 719244
United Kingdom	Plaça Major, 3, 07002 Palma	www.fco.gov.uk	971 712445
United States	Carrer Porto Pi, 9, 07012 Palma		971 403707

SPANISH EMBASSIES ABROAD

Country	Address	Telephone
Australia and New Zealand	15 Arkana Street, Yarralumla, ACT 2600, Canberra	06 273 3555
Canada	74 Stanley Avenue, Ottawa, Ontario K1M 1P4	613/747-2252
The Netherlands	Lange Voorhout 50, NL - 2514 EG The Hague	70/364 3814
Republic of Ireland	17a Merlyn Park, Ballsbridge, Dublin 4	(01) 269 1640
UK	20 Draycott Place, London SW3 2RZ	020 7235 5555
	visa information	0906 550 8970
	Suite 1a, Brook House, 70 Spring Gardens, Manchester, M2 2BQ	0161 236 1233
	63 North Castle Street, Edinburgh, EH2 3LJ	0131 220 1843
USA	150 East 58th Street, New York, NY 10155	212/355-4090
	5055 Wilshire Blvd., Suite 960, Los Angeles, CA 90036	323/938-0158

PLANNING

MONEY MATTERS

As a region of Spain, Mallorca has had the euro as its official currency since January 2002, when the peseta was replaced by euro notes and coins.

BEFORE YOU GO

● It is advisable to use a combination of cash, traveller's cheques and credit cards rather than relying on any one means of payment. Avoid carrying all your money in one place.

● Traveller's cheques are a relatively secure way of carrying money because you are insured if they are stolen. But keep a note of their numbers separate from the cheques themselves.

CHANGING MONEY

● You can change money at some hotels, bureaux de change and banks. Since the switch to the euro there are far fewer bureaux de change in Mallorca, with banks taking over much of their business.

● You can withdraw money from cashpoints (ATMs) using a credit or debit card, but confirm with

LOST/STOLEN CREDIT CARDS

Ring one of the following contact numbers in case of loss or theft:

American Express /cards
tel 902 375 637

American Express / traveller's cheques
tel 900 994 426

Diners Club
tel 902 401 112

MasterCard
tel 900 971 231

Visa
tel 900 991 124 / 91 519 21 00

Banks are the best place to change foreign currency

your card issuer before departure which Spanish banks will accept your card and what fee will be charged.

CASHPOINTS

● These are known as *telebanco* and are widespread throughout Mallorca. On-screen instructions are available in a choice of languages.

● If your card has the Maestro or Cirrus facilities you can pay for goods and services as well as withdraw cash.

● Your bank may charge you for

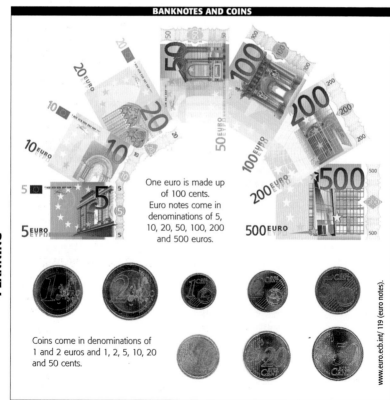

BANKNOTES AND COINS

One euro is made up of 100 cents.
Euro notes come in denominations of 5, 10, 20, 50, 100, 200 and 500 euros.

Coins come in denominations of 1 and 2 euros and 1, 2, 5, 10, 20 and 50 cents.

www.euro.ecb.int/ 119 (euro notes).

Goods you buy in the EU

These are in line with other EU countries. There is no limit on the amount of foreign currency or euros that you can bring into Spain. Tax-paid goods for personal use (such as video cameras) can be brought in from other EU countries without customs charges being incurred. Guidance levels for tax-paid goods bought in the EU are as follows:

- 3,200 cigarettes; or
- 400 cigarillos; or
- 200 cigars; or
- 1kg of smoking tobacco

- 110 litres of beer
- 10 litres of spirits
- 90 litres of wine
  (of which only 60 litres can be sparkling wine)
- 20 litres of fortified wine
  (such as port or sherry)

Visiting Spain from outside the EU

You are entitled to the allowances shown below only if you travel with the goods and do not plan to sell them.

- 200 cigarettes; or
- 100 cigarillos; or
- 50 cigars; or
- 250g of smoking tobacco

- 1 litre of spirits or strong liqueurs
- 2 litres of still table wine
- 2 litres of fortified wine, sparkling wine or other liqueurs
- 50g of perfume
- 250cc/ml of eau de toilette

Tipping is usually expected for services. As a general guide, the following applies:

Restaurants	5–10 per cent*
Bar service	change*
Cafés	5 per cent*
Tour guides	optional
Hairdressers	change–5 per cent
Taxis	3–5 per cent, more if carried luggage
Chambermaids	€1–€2
Porters	€1–€2
Toilet attendants	€1

Or more if you are impressed with the level of service

withdrawing money from another bank's cashpoint.

CREDIT CARDS

- Most restaurants, hotels and shops accept credit cards but some may need a minimum spend.
- Smaller shops and cafés prefer cash.

BANKS

- Spanish banks in Mallorca, including branches of La Caixa, Sa Nostra, Banesto and Santander Central Hispano, have foreign exchange desks (*cambio*) where you can change traveller's cheques or draw out money using a credit or debit card.

Remember to bring your passport for ID.
- Banking hours tend to be Monday to Friday 8.30–2 and Saturday 8.30–1.

WIRING MONEY

- In an emergency you can have money wired from your home country using international agents such as Western Union (tel 0800 833833, www. ukmoneytransfer.com), but this can be time-consuming and expensive.

TAXES

- Sales tax, at seven percent and known as IVA, is added to some goods sold in Mallorca, and even services such as hotel accommodation and meals in

restaurants. This tax is non-refundable.
- For all other goods and services 16 percent tax is added.
- Visitors from non-EU countries are entitled to a reimbursement of the 16 percent tax paid on purchases to the value of more than €90.15, which must have been spent in the same store.
- The store should provide an invoice itemizing all the goods, the price paid for them and the tax charged, as well as full address details of both the vendor and the purchaser. The goods must then be taken out of the EU within three months.
- When leaving Mallorca, take the goods and the invoices to the booth provided at Spanish customs, prior to checking in your baggage. This is where your claim will be processed.

Cashpoints accept most cards

10 EVERYDAY ITEMS AND HOW MUCH THEY COST		
Takeaway sandwich		€2.20–€3.20
Bottle of mineral water	(from a shop, half a litre)	€0.40–€0.80
Cup of coffee	(from a café, espresso)	€1–€1.85
Beer	(half a litre)	€1.85–€2.60
Glass of house wine		€1.85–€2.15
Spanish national newspaper		€1–€1.20
International newspaper		€1.50–€2.30
Litre of petrol	(98 unleaded)	€0.86
	(diesel)	€0.66
Metro ticket	(single)	€1.10
Camera film	(36 pictures)	€4–€5

PLANNING

COMMUNICATION

USING A COIN-OPERATED PHONE

1 Lift the receiver and listen for the dialling tone.

2 Insert the required coin or coins. The coin drops as soon as you insert it.

3 Dial or press the number.

4 If you want to cancel the call before it is answered, or if the call does not connect, press the coin release lever or hang up and take the coins from the coin return.

5 The call is answered.

In the age of the internet and the mobile phone it's easy to stay in touch with friends, family and even the workplace, and Mallorca presents very few technological problems to the traveller.

TELEPHONES

• All telephone numbers in Spain have a nine-digit number, which includes the area code. All area codes start with 9; the Balearic Islands' code is 971 and covers Mallorca, Menorca and Ibiza. You must include the area code even when making a local call. Areas can have two- or three-digit area codes.

• To call Spain from outside the country you will need to dial your country's international access code (usually 00 in Europe and 011 in North America) followed by Spain's country code, which is 34, then the area code and telephone number. To call the UK from Spain dial 00 44 then drop the first 0 from the area code.

• The Spanish phone book, *Páginas Amarillas* (Yellow Pages; www.paginasamarillas.es), contains the telephone numbers for the emergency services as well as Mallorca's telephone directory.

PUBLIC TELEPHONES

• Public telephone booths are blue and you won't have to go far to find one. Look for the *telefono* signs.

• They operate with both coins and phone cards (*tarjeta telefonica* or *credifone*), available from newsagents, post offices and other shops. Instructions are printed in English.

• Phones will accept 5, 10, 20 and 50 cent coins or phone cards of 6, 12 and 30 euros.

• The international operator number is 1008 for Europe, 1005 for the rest of the world. For national directory enquires dial 11818.

• Call charges are cheaper after 10pm on weekdays, after 2pm on Saturdays and throughout Sundays.

• Using the telephone in your

AREA CODES WITHIN SPAIN	
Madrid	91
Barcelona	93
Seville	95
Bilbao, Vizcaya	94
Valencia	96
Santander	942
Navarra	948
Granada	958

INTERNATIONAL DIALLING CODES	
Australia	00 61
Belgium	00 32
Canada	00 1
France	00 33
Germany	00 49
Greece	00 30
Ireland	00 353
Italy	00 39
Netherlands	00 31
New Zealand	00 64
Spain	00 34
Sweden	00 46
UK	00 44
USA	00 1

Check international call charges before using your mobile

hotel room is considerably more expensive than using a public phone outside, whatever time you call.

MOBILE TELEPHONES

• Check with your mobile phone operator before departure that you will be able to use your mobile phone in Mallorca. Most single, dual and tri-band phones will work abroad, but your contract with the operator may impose limitations.

• You will be charged a higher rate for calls made from your mobile phone when not in your home country and you will also be charged for receiving calls and picking up messages.

• For extended stays it might be worth buying a Spanish SIM card for your mobile phone, allowing

PLANNING

PUBLIC PHONE
INTERNATIONAL CALLS

CALL CHARGES FROM PUBLIC PAY PHONES (PER MINUTE)

	Peak rate	Reduced rate
Local	€0.06	€0.04
National	€0.10	€0.06
Western Europe	€0.18	€0.18
Eastern Europe	€0.40	€0.40
USA	€0.18	€0.18
North Africa	€0.40	€0.40
Australia	€0.96	€0.96
India	€0.96	€0.96
Japan	€0.96	€0.96
China	€0.96	€0.96

POSTAGE RATES FOR LETTERS UP TO 20G

Within Spain	€0.26
To Western Europe	€0.51
To Eastern Europe	€0.51
To America	€0.76
To Africa	€0.76
To Asia	€0.76
To Australia	€0.76

you to use a cheaper local telephone network.

THE INTERNET

● Internet cafés, where you can access web-based email accounts such as Hotmail, are gradually becoming more widespread in Mallorca. There are several in Palma and you are likely to find others in resort areas.

● Charges vary but should be less than €2 or €3 per hour.

USING A LAPTOP

● To use your laptop in Mallorca remember to bring a power converter to recharge it and a plug adaptor. A surge protector is also a good idea. To connect to the internet you may need a phone socket adaptor (available from www.teleadapt.com).

● If you use an international service provider, such as Compuserve or AOL, it is cheaper to dial up a local node rather than the dial-up number in your home country. Otherwise, sign up with a free local service provider.

● Dial tone frequencies vary from country to country so set your modem to ignore dial tones.

SENDING A LETTER

● Post boxes in Mallorca are

Email, below, is much quicker than the Spanish post, above

bright yellow and are widespread in towns and resorts.

● Stamps (*segells*) are widely available from tobacconists and newsagents, as well as post offices. Some hotels sell stamps and have a post box.

● The Spanish postal system is notoriously slow and unreliable; expect letters to take up to a week to arrive at an EU destination. Say a letter is *urgente* if you want to send it express, or send it as registered post (*certificado*) if it is important. Use the Postal Exprés system to send a parcel within Spain: it guarantees next-day delivery to main cities or within 48 hours to the rest of the country.

ADDRESSES

● The abbreviation s/n stands for *sin número* and signifies a building that has no street number. It may also, for example, be on a junction or street corner. This is predominantly used by businesses, shops and museums. The word for street, *carrer,* is often abbreviated to c/.

POST OFFICES

● Post offices are usually open Monday to Friday 9am–2pm but larger branches will open during the afternoon and on Saturday mornings.

● Palma's central post office is at Carrer de Consitució, 5.

INTERNET CAFÉS

L@Red Cybercafe
Carrer Concepció, 5, Palma
Tel 0171 711754

Café 1550
Avinguda de l'Argentina, 1,
Pollença
Tel 971 531330

Portality–Blue
Carrer Andratx, 32,
Portals Nous
Tel 971 677513

Highlander Bar
Carrer Mariscos, 12, Port d'Alcúdia
Tel 971 549831

PLANNING

TOURIST INFORMATION

Holidays in Mallorca can be researched through Spanish tourist offices worldwide. The official website of the country's tourist office (www.tourspain.es) is a good starting point. When you are in Mallorca, most towns have a source of tourist information, whether it is a kiosk or a staffed centre. These local tourist information offices will provide details on public transport, local events, places of interest and activities. Some may operate a last-minute accommodation booking service. The Mallorca Tourist Board, the world's first tourist board (▷ 31), is also a good source of advice and suggestions.

OPENING TIMES
● The early afternoon siesta persists in Mallorca, with many shops closing from 1 to 4.30pm and opening until 8pm on weekdays. The general rule is that the busier the area is with tourists, the more likely it is that places will stay open throughout the day.
● Banks, pharmacies and shops often close on Saturday afternoons.
● Opening times for individual attractions are given in The Sights section or in the listings. Most places are closed on Sundays and on public holidays.

MUSEUM PASS
Five museums in Palma's old town have joined forces to produce a combined entrance ticket, which is well worth buying if you plan to spend a few days in the city.
● The pass costs €10 and includes entry to the Cathedral Museum, Diocesan Museum, Can Marquès, Casa Museu J. Torrents Lladó and Museu de Mallorca.
● It is available at tourist offices in Palma or at any of the participating museums.

SPANISH TOURIST OFFICES

Great Britain
79 New Cavendish Street,
London W1W 6XB
Tel 020 7486 8077
www.spain.info

Germany
Kurfürstendamm, 63, 0707 Berlin
Tel +49 308 826 543

Italy
19, Vía del Mortaro, 00187 Rome
Tel +39 066 783 106
www.turismospagnolo.it

The Netherlands
8a, Laan Van Meerdervoor, 2517
The Hague
Tel +31 703 465 900
www.spaansverkeersbureau.nl

Mallorca Tourist Board
Fomento del Turismo de Mallorca,
Consitució, 1, 07001 Palma
Tel 971 725396
www.newsmallorca.com

PUBLIC HOLIDAYS

1 January (New Year's Day)	
6 January (Epiphany)	
Maundy Thursday (March/April)	
Easter Monday (March/April)	
1 May (Labour Day)	
15 August (Assumption of the Virgin)	
12 October (National Day)	
1 November (All Saints' Day)	
6 December (Constitution Day)	
8 December (Immaculate Conception)	
25 December (Christmas Day)	
26 December (St. Stephen's Day)	

TOURIST INFORMATION OFFICES IN MALLORCA

Palma
Plaça de la Reina, 2, 07012 Palma
Tel 971 712216

Aeropuerto, 07611 Palma
Tel 971 789556

Passeig des Born, 27, 07001 Palma
Tel 971 724090
www.a-palma.es

Port d'Alcúdia
Passeig Marítim, 07410 Alcúdia
Tel 971 547257

Cala d'Or
Perico Pomar, 10, 07660 Santanyí
Tel 971 657463

Cala Millor
Passeig Marítim, 07560 Son Servera
Tel 971 585864

Cala Rajada
Plaça dels Pins, 07590 Capdepera
Tel 971 563033

Cala Sant Vicenç
Plaça Cala Sant Vicenç, 07469 Pollença
Tel 971 533264

Colònia Sant Jordi
Carrer Doctor Barraquer, 5, 07638 Ses Salines
Tel 971 656073

Magaluf
Pare Vaquer Ramis, 1, 07182 Calvia
Tel 971 131126

Manacor
Plaça Ramón Llul, 07500 Manacor
Tel 971 847241

Palma Nova
Passeig de la Mar, 13, 07181 Calvia
Tel 971 682365

Pollença
Sant Domingo, 2, 07460 Pollença
Tel 971 535077

Port de Pollença
Monges, 9, 07470 Pollença
Tel 971 865467

Port de Sóller
Canonge Oliver, 10, 07108 Sóller
Tel 971 633042

S'Arenal
Plaça Reina M. Cristina, 07600 Llucmajor
Tel 971 440414

Sóller
Plaça Espanya, 07100 Sóller
Tel 971 638008

Valldemossa
07170 Valldemossa
Tel 971 612019

PLANNING

BOOKS, MAPS AND MEDIA

BOOKS

Vicky Bennison: *The Taste of a Place: Mallorca* (2003)
If you want to learn more about Mallorcan food, wine and restaurants, *The Taste of a Place: Mallorca* (£12.99, Chakula Press) is a well-informed gastronomic guidebook with restaurant reviews, recipes and accessible explanations of Mallorcan cuisine. Updated restaurant reviews are featured on www.thetasteofaplace.com.

Valerie Crespí-Green:
Landscapes of Mallorca (1984)
Landscapes of Mallorca lives up to its billing as the original and best walking guide to Mallorca. Written by a long-term resident, it describes 10 car tours, 60 walks of varying distances and degrees of difficulty and no fewer than 27 picnic locations.

Robert Graves (1895–1985):
Collected Poems (1975); *The White Goddess: A historical grammar of poetic myth* (1948)
Robert Graves is responsible for the most prominent body of written work to come from a resident of Mallorca. His first visit to the island was with his first wife, Laura Riding, an American poet and critic, before World War II. In 1946, after the war, he settled permanently on the island with his second wife, Beryl Hodge, remaining a resident of Deià until his death in 1985.
   Poetry, for Graves, took precedence over everything, but he also wrote literary criticism, successful novels such as *I, Claudius* (1934) and a resonant autobiography, *Goodbye to All That* (1929). The most recent edition of his Collected Poems draws on more than 20 volumes of poetry. His best poems tend to be love poems; unsurprising from a man who explained his belief that a powerful, female Muse inspired real poetry in *The White Goddess*.
   His son, William Graves, has written an account of 40 years of living in Deià called *Wild Olives*.

Agatha Christie (1890–1976):
Problem at Pollença Bay
The doyenne of murder-mystery writers stayed at the Illa D'Or hotel in Port de Pollença between 1931 and 1934. Agatha

Most newsagents will sell foreign newspapers and magazines

Christie was sufficiently inspired to write this short story and use it in a Parker Pyne story.

George Sand (1804–76): *A Winter in Majorca* (1841)
If your name was Amandine-Aurore Lucille Dupin, Baronne Dudevant, you too might be tempted to change it to George Sand, for simplicity's sake. George Sand made her reputation as a French novelist with an early series of romantic novels and later accounts of rural life in France. In between these two phases of her career she spent the winter of 1838 to 1839 in Valldemossa with her lover Frederick Chopin (1810–49). Her account of their Mallorcan sojourn has, oddly, been a foundation of Valldemossa's tourism industry ever since. It's odd because Sand and Valldemossa's locals patently loathed each other. When she wasn't characterizing the locals as monkeys, savages or thieves she was bemoaning the miserable weather and primitive living conditions. In one respect, selling the book so persistently is the islanders' final act of defiance.

MAPS
● This book has a map of central Palma (▷ 210–11) and an atlas of the island (▷ 212–19). The AA Island Map of Mallorca (sold separately) has a 1:75,000 scale and is marked with walking and cycling routes, attractions and other points of interest.

● In recent years the Balearic Government and local councils have planned walks and cycle rides in Mallorca and produced maps of the routes for tourists. These maps are usually available from local tourist offices free of charge. Look out, in particular, for the *Landscapes of Calviá* booklet by Valerie Crespí-Green and the *A Stroll Through History* series of walks through Palma, a project once financed by the eco-tax.

MEDIA
● The *Majorca Daily Bulletin* (www.majorcadailybulletin.es) is a daily English-language newspaper serving the Balearics' English-speaking communities. Other local papers include *Ultima Hora* and *Diario de Mallorca;* all include information about what's on locally.
● Most mainstream Spanish newspapers, including *El Pais* (www.elpais.es) and *El Mundo* (www.elmundo.es), are available on the island. Larger newsagents sell same-day editons of major national newspapers from Britain, Germany and other EU countries.

TELEVISION AND RADIO
● Most hotels have televisions with news channels in English, as well as the main Spanish television channels TVE1 and TVE2. TV3 is a Catalan channel.
● You can get the BBC World Service on 15485, 12095, 9410 and 6195 short wave, depending on the time of day, and 648kHz medium wave or 98.5FM.

PLANNING

WORDS AND PHRASES

Catalan is the dominant language on Mallorca and its pronunciation differs from Castilian (Spanish). It is more closed and less staccato than Castilian, but is likewise nearly always phonetic, with a few rules. When a word ends in a vowel, an n or an s, the stress is usually on the penultimate syllable; otherwise, it falls on the last syllable. If a word has an accent, this is where the stress falls.

Catalan

au	ow as in wow
c	ss or k (never th)
ç	ss
eu	ay-oo
g	g or j (never h)
gu	(sometimes) w
h	silent
j	j (never h)
ig	ch at the end of a word: *vaig* sounds like batch
ll	lli as in million
l.l	ll as in silly
ny	as in canyon
r/rr	heavily rolled
s	z or ss
tg/tj	dge as in lodge
tx	ch as in cheque
v	b (*vi*, wine, sounds like 'bee')
x	sh as in shake

Spanish

a	as in pat	ai, ay	as i in side
e	as in set	au	as ou in out
i	as e in be	ei, ey	as ey in they
o	as in hot	oi, oy	as oy in boy
u	as in flute		

Consonants as in English except:

c	before i and e as th
ch	as ch in church
d	at the end of a word becomes th
g	before i or e becomes ch as in loch
h	is silent
j	as ch in loch
ll	as lli in million
ñ	as ny in canyon
qu	is hard like a k
r	usually rolled
v	is a b
z	is a th

The words and phrases are given in Catalan, then the *Spanish*.

NUMBERS

1	u (un, una)/ *uno*	16	setze/ *dieciséis*
2	dos/ *dos*	17	disset/ *diecisiete*
3	tres/ *tres*	18	divuit/ *dieciocho*
4	quatre/ *cuatro*	19	dinou/ *diecinueve*
5	cinc/ *cinco*	20	vint/*veinte*
6	sis/ *seis*	21	vint-i-u/ *veintiuno*
7	set/ *siete*	30	trenta/ *treinta*
8	vuit/ *ocho*	40	quaranta/ *cuarenta*
9	nou/ *nueve*	50	cinquanta/ *cincuenta*
10	deu/ *diez*	60	seixanta/ *sesenta*
11	onze/ *once*	70	setanta/ *setenta*
12	dotze/ *doce*	80	vuitanta/ *ochenta*
13	tretze/ *trece*	90	noranta/ *noventa*
14	catorze/ *catorce*	100	cent/*cien*
15	quinze/ *quince*	200	dos-cents/ *doscientos*
		1,000	mil/*mil*
		million	milió/*millón*

USEFUL WORDS

yes/no	there	when	who	large	bad
sí/no	allà	quan	qui	gran	dolent
sí/no	*allí*	*cuándo*	*quién*	*grande*	*malo*
please	where	why	I'm sorry	small	open
si us plau	on	per què	Em sap greu	petit	obert
por favor	*dónde*	*por qué*	*Lo siento*	*pequeño*	*abierto*
thank you	here	how	excuse me	good	closed
gràcies	aquí	com	perdoni	bo	tancat
gracias	*aquí*	*cómo*	*perdone*	*bueno*	*cerrado*

When does the shop open/
close?
**A quina hora obre/tanca la
botiga?**
*¿A qué hora abre/cierra la
tienda?*

Could you help me, please?
**Que em pot atendre, si us
plau?**
¿Me atiende, por favor?

How much is this?
Quant costa això?
¿Cuánto cuesta esto?

I'm looking for…
Busco…
Busco…

I'm just looking
Només miro
Sólo estoy mirando

I'd like…
Voldria…
Quisiera…

I'll take this
M'enduc això
Me llevo esto

Do you have anything smaller/
larger?
**Té alguna cosa més petita/
gran?**
*¿Tiene algo más pequeño/
grande?*

Please can I have a receipt?
**Em dóna un rebut, si us
plau?**
¿Me da un recibo, por favor?

Do you accept credit cards?
Accepten targetes de crèdit?
¿Aceptan tarjetas de crédito?

Do you have a room?
Té una habitació?
¿Tiene una habitación?

I have a reservation for … nights
Tinc una reserva per a … nits
*Tengo una reserva para …
noches*

How much per night?
Quant és per nit?
¿Cuánto por noche?

Single room
Habitació individual
Habitación individual

Twin room
Habitació doble amb dos llits
*Habitación doble con dos
camas*

Double room
**Habitació doble amb llit de
matrmoni**
*Habitación doble con cama
de matrimonio*

With bath/shower/lavatory

Amb banyera/dutxa/vàter
Con bañera/ducha/váter

Is the room air-conditioned/
heated?
**Té aire condicionat/calefacció
l'habitacio?**
*¿Tiene aire acondicionado/
calefacción la habitación?*

non smoking
no fumeu
se prohibe fumar

Is breakfast/lunch/dinner
included in the price?
**S'inclou el desdejuni/el
dinar/el sopar en el preu?**
*¿Está el desayuno/la comi-
da/la cena incluido/-a en el
precio?*

I'll take this room
Em quedo l'habitació
Me quedo con la habitación

Please can I pay my bill?
El compte, si us plau?
La cuenta, por favor

I don't feel well
No em trobo bé
No me encuentro bien

Could you call a doctor?
Pot cridar un metge?
*¿Puede llamar a un
médico?*

Where is the hospital?
On hi ha l'hospital?
¿Dónde esta el hospital?

Call the fire brigade/police/
ambulance
**Truqui als bombers/la
policia/una ambulància**
*Llame a los bomberos/la
policía/una ambulancia*

I have had an accident
He tingut un accident
He tenido un accidente

I have been robbed
M'han robat
Me han robado

I have lost my passport/
wallet/purse/handbag
**He perdut el passaport/la
cartera/el moneder/la
bossa**
*He perdido el pasaporte/
la cartera/el monedero/el
bolso*

Is there a lost property
office?
**Que hi ha una oficina
d'objectes perduts?**
*¿Hay una oficina de obje-
tos perdidos?*

Where is the police station?
On hi ha la comissaria?
¿Dónde está la comisaría?

Help!
Auxili
Socorro

Stop thief!
Al lladre
Al ladrón

castle	church	museum	town	*aparcar*	*salida*
el castell	**l'església**	**el museu**	**la ciutat**		
el castillo	*la iglesia*	*el museo*	*la ciudad*	entrance	town hall
				entrada	**el ajunta-**
				entrada	**ment**
cathedral	lavatories	palace	no parking		*el ayun-*
la catedral	**els lavabos**	**el palau**	**prohibit**		*tamiento*
la catedral	*los aseos*	*el palacio*	**aparcar**	exit	
			prohibido	**sortida**	

What time does the restaurant open?
A quina hora obre el restaurant?
¿A qué hora abre el restaurante?

I'd like to reserve a table for … people at …
Voldria reservar una taula per a … persones per a les …
Quiero reservar una mesa para … personas para las…

A table for …, please
Una taula per a …, si us plau
Una mesa para … por favor

Is this table free?
Està lliure aquesta taula?
¿Está libre esta mesa?

Could we see the menu/wine list?
Podem veure la carta/carta de vins?
¿Podemos ver la carta/carta de vinos?

What do you recommend?
Què ens recomana?
¿Qué nos recomienda?

Is there a dish of the day?
Té un plat del dia?
¿Tiene un plato del día?

How much is this dish?
Què costa aquest plat?
¿Cuánto cuesta este plato?

I am a vegetarian
Sóc vegetarià
Soy vegetariano

I ordered …
He demanat …
Yo pedí …

Can I have the bill, please?
Em duu el compte, si us plau?
¿Me trae la cuenta, por favor?

The bill is not right
El compte no està bé
La cuenta no está bien

Where is the information desk?
On hi ha el taulell d'informació?
¿Dónde está el mostrador de información?

Is this the way to…?
Aquest és el camí per a anar a…?
¿Es éste el camino para ir a…?

Please take me to…
A…, si us plau
A…, por favor

Go straight on
Continuï de dret
Siga recto

Turn left
Tombi a l'esquerra
Tuerza a la izquierda

Turn right
Tombi a la dreta
Tuerza a la derecha

morning	*alora*	Thursday	*abril*
el matí		dijous	
la mañana	later	*jueves*	May
	més tard		maig
afternoon	*más tarde*	Friday	*mayo*
la tarda		divendres	
la tarde	spring	*viernes*	June
	primavera		juny
evening	*primavera*	Saturday	*junio*
el vespre		dissabte	
la tarde	summer	*sábado*	July
	estiu		juliol
day	*verano*	Sunday	*julio*
el dia		diumenge	
el día	autumn	*domingo*	August
	tardor		agost
night	*otoño*	week	*agosto*
la nit		la setmana	
la noche	winter	*la semana*	September
	hivern		setembre
today	*invierno*	January	*septiembre*
avui		gener	
hoy	Monday	*enero*	October
	dilluns		octubre
yesterday	*lunes*	February	*octubre*
ahir		febrer	
ayer	Tuesday	*febrero*	November
	dimarts		novembre
tomorrow	*martes*	March	*noviembre*
demà		març	
mañana	Wednesday	*marzo*	December
	dimecres		desembre
now	*miércoles*	April	*diciembre*
ara		abril	

What is the time?
Quina hora és?
¿Qué hora es?

I don't speak Catalan/Spanish
No parlo català/espanyol
No hablo catalán/español

Do you speak English?
Parla anglès?
¿Habla inglés?

I don't understand
No ho entenc
No entiendo

Please repeat that
Si us plau, repeteixi això
Por favor, repita eso

Please speak more slowly
Si us plau, parlimés a poc a poc
Por favor, hable más despacio

Good morning/afternoon
Bon dia/Bona tarda
Buenos días/Buenas tardes

Goodbye
Adéu-siau
Adiós

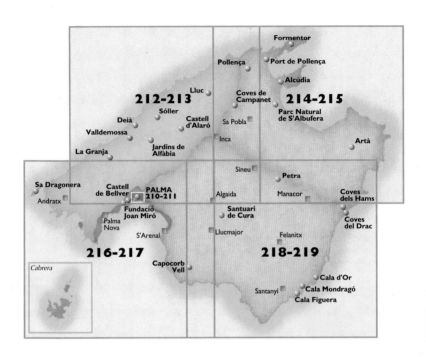

- Formentor
- Pollença
- Port de Pollença
- Alcúdia
- Lluc
- **212-213**
- Sóller
- Coves de Campanet
- Deià
- Castell d'Alaró
- Sa Pobla
- **214-215**
- Parc Natural de S'Albufera
- Valldemossa
- Inca
- La Granja
- Jardins de Alfàbia
- Artà
- Sineu
- Petra
- Sa Dragonera
- Castell de Bellver
- **PALMA 210-211**
- Algaida
- Manacor
- Coves dels Hams
- Andratx
- Fundació Joan Miró
- Santuari de Cura
- Palma Nova
- S'Arenal
- Llucmajor
- Coves del Drac
- **216-217**
- Felanitx
- **218-219**
- Cabrera
- Capocorb Vell
- Cala d'Or
- Santanyí
- Cala Mondragó
- Cala Figuera

	Motorway
	Motorway junction with and without number
	National road
	Regional road
	Railway
	Prohibited Zone
	Built-up area
■	Town / Village
	National park
●	Featured place of interest
✈	Airport
621 ▲	Height in metres
⌂—	Ferry route
⚘	Viewpoint

212-219
0   5 km
0   3 miles

216
0   4 km
0   2 miles

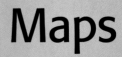

Maps

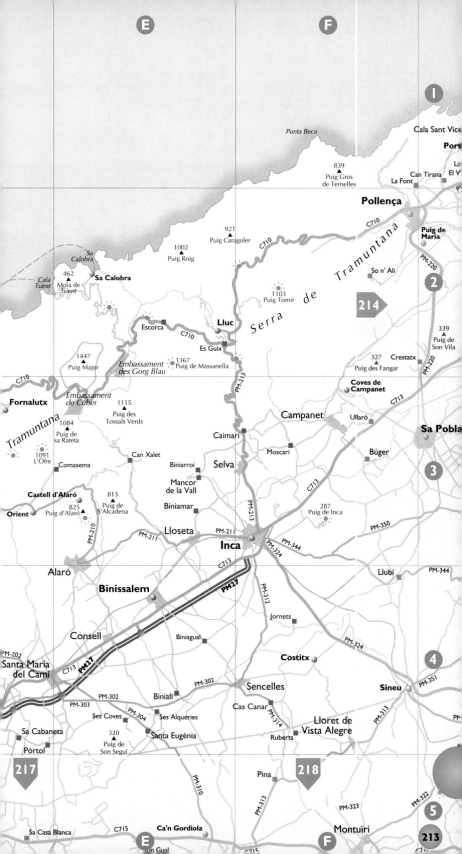

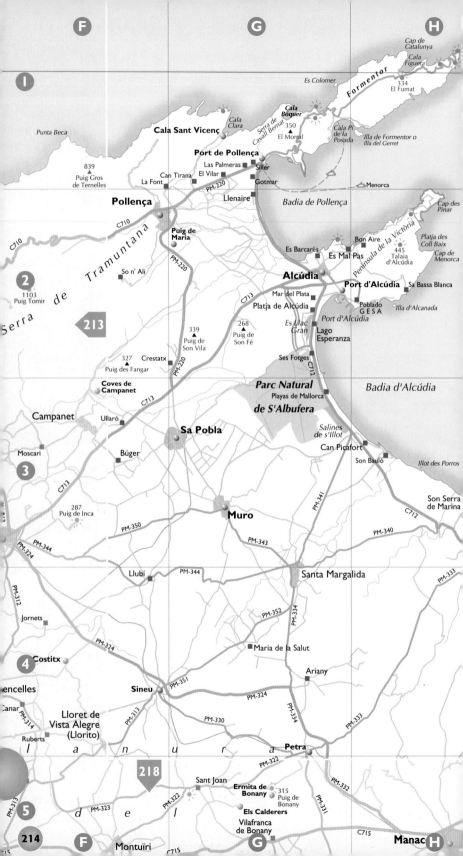

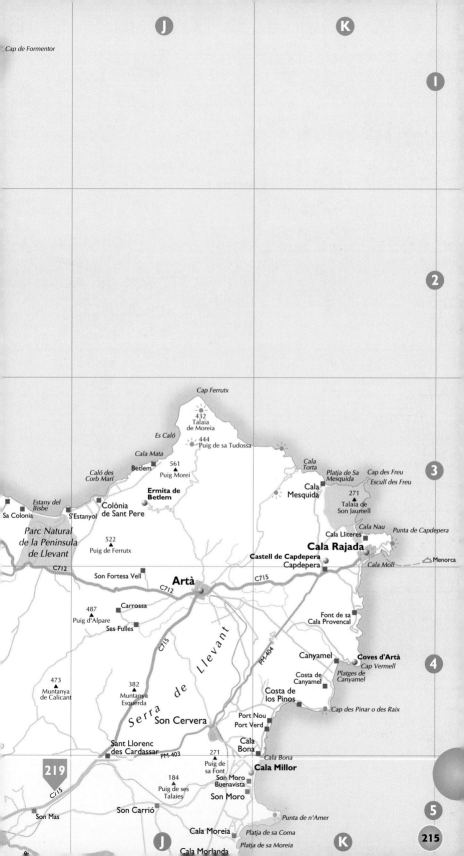

2

Cap de Formentor

Cap Ferrutx

432
Talaia
de Moreia

Es Caló

444
Puig de sa Tudossa

Cala Mata

Cala
Torta

Betlem

Cala
Mesquida

561
Puig Morei

Platja de Sa
Mesquida

Cap des Freu

Caló des
Corb Marí

Ermita de
Betlem

Escull des Freu

271

Estany del
Bisbe

Colònia
de Sant Pere

Cala
Mesquida

Talaia de
Son Jaumell

Sa Colonia

S'Estanyol

Cala Nau

Punta de Capdepera

Parc Natural
de la Península
de Llevant

522
Puig de Ferrutx

Cala Lliteres

Cala Rajada

Menorca

C712

Castell de Capdepera

Son Fortesa Vell

Capdepera

Cala Moll

Artà

C712

C715

487
Puig d'Alpare

Carrossa

Ses Fulles

Font de sa
Cala Provencal

C715

Llevant

PM-404

Canyamel

Coves d'Artà

Cap Vermell

473
Muntanya
de Calicant

382
Muntanya
Esquerda

de

Costa de
Canyamel

Platges de
Canyamel

Serra

Son Cervera

Costa de
los Pinos

Sant Llorenç
des Cardassar

PM-403

271
Puig de
sa Font

Port Nou

Port Verd

Cap des Pinar o des Raix

C715

184
Puig de ses
Talaies

Cala
Bona

Cala Bona

Son Moro
Buenavista

Cala Millor

Son Moro

Son Mas

Son Carrió

Punta de n'Amer

Cala Moreia

Platja de sa Coma

Cala Morlanda

Platja de sa Moreia

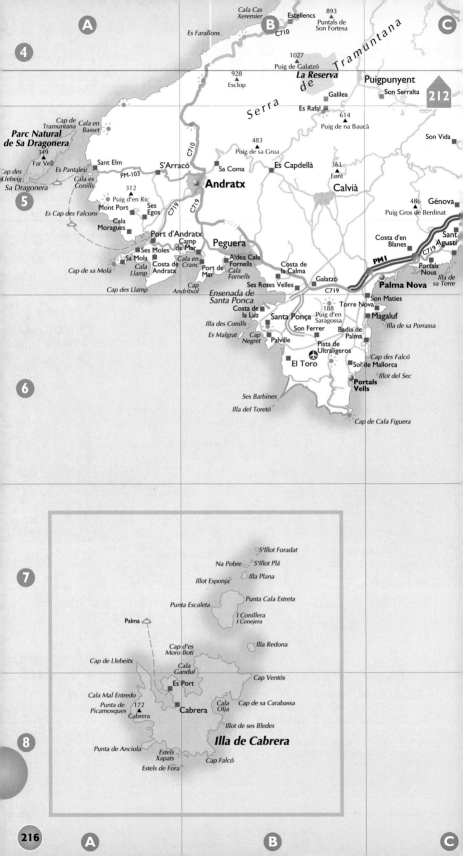

3

Parc Natural de Sa Dragonera

Cap de Tramuntana
Cala en Basset
349
Far Vell
Cap des Llebeig
Sa Dragonera
Es Cap des Falcons
Es Pantaleu
Cala es Conills
Sant Elm
PM-103
S'Arracó
312
Puig d'en Ric
Mont Port
Ses Egos
Cala Moragues
Port d'Andratx
Camp de Mar
Sa Mola
Ses Moles
Cala Llamp
Costa de Andratx
Cala en Cranc
Port de Mar
Cap de sa Molà
Cala
Cap Andritxol
Cap des Llamp

Cala Cas Xeremier
Es Farallons
Estellencs
C710
893
Puntals de Son Fortesa
1027
Puig de Galatzó
928
Esclop
La Reserva
Galilea
Es Rafal
614
Puig de na Baucà
483
Puig de sa Grua
Sa Coma
Es Capdellà
361
Font
Andratx
Calvià
Peguera
Aldea Cala Fornells
Cala Fornells
Costa de la Calma
Ses Rotes Velles
Galatzó
C719
Ensenada de Santa Ponça
Costa de la Luz
188
Puig d'en Saragossa
Torre Nova
Son Maties
Illa des Conills
Santa Ponça
Son Ferrer
Badia de Palma
Magaluf
Es Malgrat
Cap Negret
Palville
Illa de sa Porrassa
Pista de Ultraligeros
El Toro
Cap des Falcó
Sol de Mallorca
Illot del Sec
Portals Vells
Ses Barbines
Illa del Toretó
Cap de Cala Figuera

Serra de Tramuntana
Puigpunyent
Son Serralta
212
Son Vida
486
Génova
Puig Gros de Berdinat
Costa d'en Blanes
Sant Agustí
PMI
Portals Nous
Illa de sa Torre
Palma Nova

S'Illot Foradat
Na Pobre
S'Illot Plá
Illot Esponja
Illa Plana
Punta Escaleta
Punta Cala Estreta
I Conillera
I Conejera
Palma
Illa Redona
Cap d'es Moro Boti
Cala Ganduf
Cap de Llebeitx
Es Port
Cap Ventós
Cala Mal Entredo
Punta de Picamosques
172
Cabrera
Cabrera
Cala Olja
Cap de sa Carabassa
Illot de ses Bledes
Illa de Cabrera
Punta de Anciola
Estels Xapats
Cap Falcó
Estels de Fora

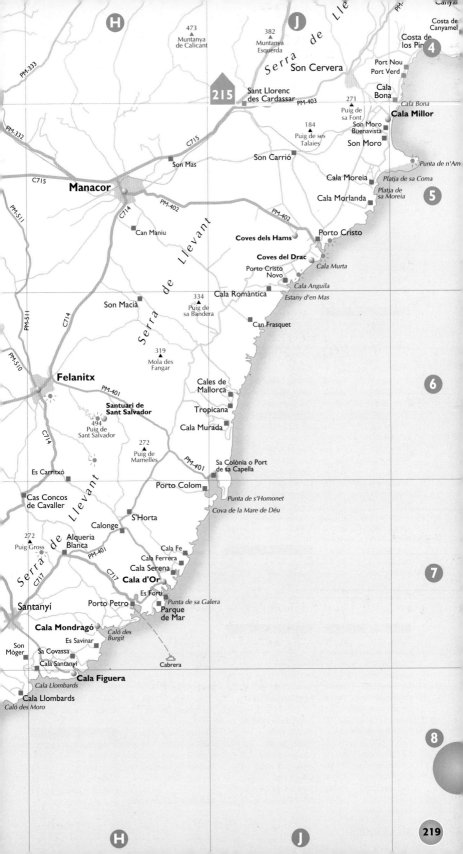

473
Muntanya
de Calicant

382
Muntanya
Esquerda

Serra de Lle

Canyal

Costa de
Canyamel

Costa de
los Pin

215

Son Cervera

Sant Llorenç
des Cardassar
PM-403

Port Nou
Port Verd

Cala
Bona

271
Puig de
sa Font

Son Moro
Buenavista

Cala Bona

Cala Millor

184
Puig de ses
Talaies

Son Moro

PM-333

PM-332

C715

PM-511

Son Mas

Manacor

C715

PM-402

Son Carrió

Cala Moreia

Cala Morlanda

Punta de n'Am

Platja de sa Coma

*Platja de
sa Moreia*

4

5

Serra de Llevant

Can Maniu

PM-402

Coves dels Hams

PM-402

Coves del Drac

Porto Cristo
Novo

Porto Cristo

Cala Murta

Son Macià

334
Puig de
sa Bandera

Cala Romàntica

Cala Anguila

Estany d'en Mas

Can Frasquet

6

319
Mola des
Fangar

Felanitx

PM-401

**Santuari de
Sant Salvador**

494
Puig de
Sant Salvador

272
Puig de
Mamelles

PM-401

Cales de
Mallorca

Tropicana

Cala Murada

Sa Colònia o Port
de sa Capella

Es Carritxó

Cas Concos
de Cavaller

PM-510

Serra de Llevant

Porto Colom

Punta de s'Homonet

Cova de la Mare de Déu

7

S'Horta

Calonge

272
Puig Gross

Alqueria
Blanca

PM-401

Cala Fe

Cala Ferrera

Cala Serena

Cala d'Or

Es Fortí

Punta de sa Galera

C714

C714

Serra de Llevant

C717

C717

Santanyí

Porto Petro

Es Savinar

Cala Mondragó

Porto Petro

Parque
de Mar

*Caló des
Burgit*

Son
Mòger

Sa Covassa

Cala Santanyí

Cabrera

Cala Figuera

Cala Llombards

Cala Llombards

Caló des Moro

8

PALMA STREET INDEX

MALLORCA ATLAS INDEX

ACKNOWLEDGMENTS

Abbreviations for the credits are as follows:

AA = AA World Travel Library, t (top), b (bottom), c (centre), l (left), r (right), bg (background)

UNDERSTANDING MALLORCA

5l AA/P Baker; 5c AA/K Paterson; 5r AA/J Cowham; 6l AA/P Baker; 6c AA/P Baker; 6r AA/C Sawyer; 6b AA/K Paterson; 7l AA/K Paterson; 7c AA/K Paterson; 7r AA/C Sawyer; 8tr Ca's Xorc; 8crt Read's Hotel; 8crb AA/K Paterson; 8bl AA/K Paterson; 8br AA/J Cowham; 9tl The Joan Miro Foundation; 9tr Museu Es Baluard; 9clt AA/K Paterson; 9clb AA/K Paterson; 9bl Photodisc; 9br Digital Vision; 10tr AA/K Paterson; 10ctr AA/K Paterson; 10cr AA/K Paterson; 10l K Russell; 10cbr K Russell; 10br AA/C Sawyer.

LIVING MALLORCA

11 AA/K Paterson; 12/3bg AA/K Paterson; 12tl AA/K Paterson; 12tr AA/K Paterson; 12c AA/P Baker; 12b AA/P Baker; 13tl AA/P Baker; 13tr AA/K Paterson; 13ct AA/K Paterson; 13cr AA/C Sawyer; 13cb AA/K Paterson; 13cl AA/C Sawyer; 14/5bg AA/K Paterson; 14t The Joan Miro Foundation; 14cl AA/C Sawyer; 14cr AA/K Paterson (© Successio Miro, DACS, 2004); 14b AA/K Paterson; 15tl AA/K Paterson; 15tr AA/P Baker; 15cr AA/K Paterson; 15c AA/K Paterson; 15cl Corbis/Christopher Felver; 16/7bg AA/J Cowham; 16tl AA/J Cowham; 16tr AA/P Baker; 16c AA/K Paterson; 16b Fomento Del Turismo de Mallorca; 17tl Corbis; 17cbl Penguin Books Ltd; 17ctl Getty Images/Carlos Alvarez; 17c Costa Nord; 17tr Corbis; 17cr AA/K Paterson; 18/9bg AA/J Cowham; 18tl AA/K Paterson; 18tr AA/J Cowham; 18cr AA/C Sawyer; 18cl AA/C Sawyer; 18b AA/C Sawyer; 19t AA/C Sawyer; 19cr Getty Images; 19cl AA/J Cowham; 19ct AA/C Rose; 19c AA/C Sawyer; 19cb AA/A Kouprianoff; 19tr AA/K Paterson; 20/1bg AA/K Paterson; 20cr Balearic Pictures/Alamy; 20cl AA/K Paterson; 20bl AA/P Baker; 20tr AA/K Paterson; 20tl IBATUR/Manuela Munoz; 21ct Getty Images/ Nicholas Hernandez; 21tr AA/K Paterson; 21cl AA/K Paterson; 21c AA/J Cowham; 21cr AA/K Paterson; 21b AA/P Baker; 22t AA/K Paterson; 22cl AA/C Sawyer; 22cr R Barton; 22br AA/K Paterson; 22bg AA/K Paterson; 22tr Getty Images; 22bl AA/K Paterson.

THE STORY OF MALLORCA

23 AA/K Paterson; 24/5bg AA/P Baker; 24t AA/K Paterson; 24cr AA/K Paterson; 24bl AA/K Paterson; 24br AA/K Paterson; 24bc Illustrated London News; 25cl AA/P Baker; 25c AA/K Paterson; 25cr AA/K Paterson; 25bl AA/P Baker; 25br AA; 26/7bg AA/J Cowham; 26t AA/W Voysey; 26cr AA/K Paterson; 26bc AA/K Paterson; 26bl Saint Jordi Altarpiece, detail showing the conquest of the City of Majorca by the army of James 1, 1229, Nisart, Pedro (15th century)/Museuo Dioecesano de Mallorca, Spain, Credit: Index/Bridgeman Art Library; 26br Mary Evans Picture Library; 27cl AA/P Baker; 27c AA/P Baker; 27cr AA/K Paterson; 27bc AA/W Voysey; 27br AA/K Paterson; 28/9bg AA/K Paterson; 28t AA/P Baker; 28btl AA; 28bl AA; 28cr AA/C Sawyer; 29bl Mary Evans Picture Library; 29cc AA/W Voysey; 29tr AA; 29cl AA/C Sawyer; 29cb AA/K Paterson; 29cr AA/K Paterson; 28/9b Map of Palma, from 'Civitates Orbis Terrarum' by Georg Braun (1541-1622) and Frans Hogenburg (1535-90), c.1572 (coloured engraving), Hoefnagel, Joris (1542-1600) (after)/Private Collection, CREDIT: The Stapleton Collection:/Bridgeman Art Library; 29r AA; 30/1bg AA/W Voysey; 30tl AA/P Baker; 30cr AA/K Paterson; 30bl AA/J Cowham; 30br AA/W Voysey; 31cl AA/P Baker; 31ccl AA/K Paterson; 31ccr Fomento Del Turismo de Mallorca; 31cr Illustrated London News; 31br

Bettmann/Corbis; 31b AA/J Cowham; 32/3bg Illustrated London News; 32t Illustrated London News; 32c Corbis; 32bl AA/K Paterson; 32br AA/K Paterson; 33cl AA/K Paterson; 33br Getty Images; 33ccl AA/K Paterson; 33ccr AA/C Sawyer; 33bl AA/K Paterson; 33cr AA/W Voysey; 34btl AA/C Sawyer; 34btr AA/C Sawyer; 34bl AA/C Sawyer; 34br AA/K Paterson; 34bg AA/K Paterson.

ON THE MOVE

35 AA/C Sawyer; 36t Digital Vision; 36cr AA/C Sawyer; 36br AA/C Sawyer; 37t Digital Vision; 37br AA/C Sawyer; 38t AA/C Sawyer; 38cr AA/K Paterson; 38bl AA/K Paterson; 39t AA/C Sawyer; 39bl AA/P Baker; 40t AA/P Baker; 40cl AA/K Paterson; 40br AA/K Paterson; 41t AA/J Cowham; 41cr AA/C Sawyer; 42t AA/K Paterson; 42cr AA/P Baker; 42cl AA/K Paterson; 42br AA/K Paterson; 43t AA/K Paterson; 44t AA/K Paterson; 44cl AA/P Baker; 44cr AA/P Baker; 44bl AA/K Paterson; 45t AA/P Baker; 45cl AA/K Paterson; 45br AA/C Sawyer; 46t AA/K Paterson; 46cr AA/C Sawyer.

THE SIGHTS

47 AA/K Paterson; 49tl AA/P Baker; 49tc AA/K Paterson; 49tr AA/C Sawyer; 50t AA/P Baker; 50cl AA/K Paterson; 50c AA/K Paterson; 50cr AA/K Paterson; 51 AA/K Paterson; 52t AA/K Paterson; 52cl AA/K Paterson; 52c AA/K Paterson; 52cr AA/K Paterson; 53 AA/J Cowham; 54t AA/K Paterson; 54cl AA/K Paterson; 54c AA/K Paterson; 54cr AA/P Baker; 55 AA/K Paterson; 56 AA/K Paterson; 57t AA/P Baker; 57c AA/K Paterson; 58t AA/K Paterson (©Successio Miro, DACS, 2004); 58b Corbis; 59tl AA/P Baker; 59tc AA/P Baker; 59tr AA/K Paterson; 60t AA/K Paterson; 60c AA/K Paterson; 60b AA/K Paterson; 61tl AA/P Baker; 61tc AA/K Paterson; 61tr AA/K Paterson; 61b AA/K Paterson; 60/1 AA/W Voysey; 62t AA/P Baker; 62cl AA/K Paterson; 62c AA/K Paterson; 62cr AA/K Paterson; 63 AA/P Baker; 64ct AA/C Sawyer; 64c AA/C Sawyer; 66tl AA/K Paterson; 66tr AA/P Baker; 67t AA/K Paterson; 67c AA/K Paterson; 68t AA/K Paterson; 68c AA/K Paterson; 69t AA/P Baker; 69c AA/K Paterson; 69b AA/K Paterson; 70 AA/P Baker; 71t AA/K Paterson; 71cl AA/P Baker; 71c AA/P Baker; 71cr AA/K Paterson; 71b AA/J Cowham; 72 AA/K Paterson; 73tl AA/J Cowham; 73tr AA/J Cowham; 73cl AA/C Sawyer; 73c AA/J Cowham; 73cr AA/P Baker; 73b K Russell; 74tl AA/K Paterson; 74tc AA/K Paterson; 74tr AA/J Cowham; 75t AA/K Paterson; 75c Spanish Tourist Board; 76t AA/K Paterson; 76cl AA/K Paterson; 76c AA/K Paterson; 76ct AA/K Paterson; 77tl AA/K Paterson; 77tr AA/K Paterson; 77cr AA/W Voysey; 78 AA/K Paterson; 79t AA/P Baker; 79cl AA/K Paterson; 79c AA/K Paterson; 79cr AA/W Voysey; 80t AA/K Paterson; 80cl AA/P Baker; 80c AA /K Paterson; 80cr AA/P Baker; 80cb AA/P Baker; 80b AA/P Baker; 81tl AA/K Paterson; 81tr AA/K Paterson; 83ct AA/K Paterson; 83c AA/J Cowham; 84t AA/J Cowham; 84cl AA/P Baker; 84c AA/P Baker; 84cr AA/C Sawyer; 85 AA/K Paterson; 86tl K Russell; 86tc AA/K Paterson; 86tr AA/K Paterson; 87t Courtesy of Coves de Campanet Agua; 87c Courtesy of Coves de Campanet Escalera; 88t AA/P Baker; 88c AA/K Paterson; 89tl AA/K Paterson; 89tr AA/P Baker; 89b AA/C Sawyer; 88/9 AA/W Voysey; 90t AA/P Baker; 90cl AA/K Paterson; 90c AA/P Baker; 90cr AA/P Baker; 91 AA/K Paterson; 92 AA/K Paterson; 93tr AA/P Baker; 93l AA/K Paterson; 93c AA/J Cowham; 93r AA/K Paterson; 95tc AA/P Baker; 95tr AA/C Sawyer; 95tl K Russell; 96t AA/K Paterson; 96c AA/K Paterson; 97tl AA/P Baker; 97tr AA/P Baker; 97b AA/C Sawyer; 98t AA/P Baker;

98cl AA/K Paterson; 98c AA/K Paterson; 98cr AA/K Paterson; 99 Courtesy of Cuevas Dels Hams; 100tl AA/P Baker; 100tc AA/K Paterson; 100tr AA/P Baker; 100b AA/K Paterson; 101t AA/J Cowham; 101c AA/K Paterson; 101b AA/C Sawyer; 102ctl AA/K Paterson; 102ctr AA/P Baker.

WHAT TO DO

103 AA/C Sawyer; 104/5 AA/C Sawyer; 104c AA/C Sawyer; 105cl AA/K Paterson; 105cr AA/C Sawyer; 106t AA/K Paterson; 106cl Digital Vision; 106cr AA/K Paterson; 107t AA/K Paterson; 107cl AA/K Paterson; 107cr AA/K Paterson; 108/9t AA P Baker; 108b R Barton; 109cl AA/K Paterson; 109cr AA/K Paterson; 110t AA/J Cowham; 110cl AA/K Paterson; 110cr Photodisc; 111t IBATUR; 111cl AA/K Paterson; 111cr Photodisc; 111b Photodisc; 112t AA/K Paterson; 112cl AA/K Paterson; 112b AA/K Paterson; 113t AA/K Paterson; 113cr AA/K Paterson; 113b AA/K Paterson; 114/5 AA/C Sawyer; 114b AA/J Cowham; 115c AA/P Baker; 116/7 AA/C Sawyer; 116c Digital Vision; 117c AA/K Paterson; 118/9t AA/C Sawyer; 118c AA/C Sawyer; 119c AA/K Paterson; 120t AA/C Sawyer; 120c AA/P Baker; 121t AA/P Baker; 121b AA/K Paterson; 122/3t AA/P Baker; 122c AA/K Paterson; 123c Spanish Tourist Board; 124t AA/P Baker; 124c AA/P Baker; 125t AA/K Paterson; 125b AA/K Paterson; 126/7t AA/K Paterson; 126c R Barton; 127c R Barton; 128/9t AA/K Paterson; 128c AA/C Sawyer; 129c AA/C Sawyer; 130/1 AA/K Paterson; 130c AA/C Sawyer; 131c AA/K Paterson; 132/3 AA/K Paterson; 132c AA/C Rose; 133c AA/P Baker; 134t AA/K Paterson; 134c AA/K Paterson.

OUT AND ABOUT

135 AA/W Voysey; 136bl AA/P Baker; 136br AA/K Paterson; 137tl K Russell; 137tr AA/C Sawyer; 138tl AA/K Paterson; 138tr AA/C Sawyer; 139tr AA/C Sawyer; 139b AA/C Sawyer; 140 AA/C Sawyer; 141tl AA/C Sawyer; 141tr AA/C Sawyer; 142 AA/K Paterson; 143tl AA/K Paterson; 143tr AA/K Paterson; 143b AA/K Paterson; 144t AA/C Sawyer; 144b AA/C Sawyer; 145tl AA/C Sawyer; 145tr AA/K Paterson; 146 AA/P Baker; 147t T Kelly; 147b AA/P Baker; 148 AA/K Paterson; 149t AA/P Baker; 149b AA/C Sawyer; 150 T Kelly; 151tl AA/C Sawyer; 151tr AA/C Sawyer; 151b T Kelly; 152t AA/C Sawyer; 152b AA/C Sawyer; 153tl AA/K Paterson; 153tr AA/C Sawyer; 154 AA/C Sawyer; 155tl AA/C Sawyer; 155tr AA/C Sawyer; 155c AA/c Sawyer; 155b AA/C Sawyer; 156t R Barton; 156b R Barton; 157tl AA/C Sawyer; 157tr R Barton.

EATING

159 Read's Hotel; 160tc Photodisc; 160tr AA/J Edmanson; 161tr AA/C Sawyer; 161b AA/K Paterson; 162tl AA/J Cowham; 162tr AA/K Paterson; 163tl AA/K Paterson; 163tc AA/C Sawyer; 163tr AA/S McBride; 164bl AA/C Sawyer; 164tr AA/C Sawyer; 164cr AA/C Sawyer; 165bl AA/C Sawyer; 165tr AA/C Sawyer; 166bl AA/C Sawyer; 166tr AA/C Sawyer; 166cr AA/C Sawyer; 167tc AA/C Sawyer; 167bc AA/C Sawyer; 168tl AA/T Oliver; 169tl R Barton; 169bl AA/C Sawyer; 170cl AA/C Sawyer; 170bc AA/C Sawyer; 170cr AA/C Sawyer; 171bl AA/C Sawyer; 171bc AA/C Sawyer; 171br R Barton; 172r AA/K Paterson; 173l AA/C Sawyer; 173c AA/C Sawyer; 173r AA/C Sawyer; 174l R Barton; 174c AA/C Sawyer; 175tc R Barton; 175b R Barton; 175r R Barton; 176l AA/P Baker; 176tc R Barton; 176bc R Barton.

STAYING

177 Maricel Hotel; 178tc AA/C Sawyer; 179b AA/J Cowham; 180r AA/C Sawyer; 181tl AA/C Sawyer; 181c AA/C Sawyer; 181tr AA/C Sawyer; 182l AA/C Sawyer; 183r AA/C Sawyer; 184l AA/C Sawyer; 184c AA/C Sawyer; 185l AA/C Sawyer; 185c AA/J Cowham; 186bl AA/C Sawyer; 186tr AA/C Sawyer; 187l AA/C Sawyer; 187c AA/C Sawyer; 187r AA/C Sawyer; 188tl AA/C Sawyer; 188tc AA/C Sawyer; 188b AA/C Sawyer; 189c AA/C Sawyer; 189tr AA/C Sawyer; 189br AA/C Sawyer; 190l AA/C Sawyer; 190c AA/C Sawyer; 190b AA/C Sawyer; 191l AA/C Sawyer; 191c AA/C Sawyer; 191br AA/C Sawyer; 192l AA/C Sawyer; 192c AA/C Sawyer.

PLANNING

195 AA/K Paterson; 197 AA; 198 AA/C Sawyer; 200 AA/C Sawyer; 201cr AA/S McBride; 201c AA/K Paterson; 201b AA/C Sawyer; 202tl AA/K Paterson; 202tr AA/M Chaplow; 202b Photodisc; 203t AA/K Paterson; 203c AA/C Sawyer; 203b AA/C Sawyer; 204 AA/C Sawyer; 205 AA/K Paterson.

Project editor
Robin Barton

AA Travel Guides design team
David Austin, Glyn Barlow, Kate Harling, Bob Johnson,
Nick Otway, Carole Philp, Keith Russell

Additional design work
Katherine Mead, Jo Tapper

Picture research
Paula Boyd-Barrett, Carol Walker

Internal repro work
Susan Crowhurst, Ian Little, Michael Moody

Production
Lyn Kirby, Helen Sweeney

Mapping
Maps produced by the Cartography Department of AA Publishing

Authors
Robin Barton, Tony Kelly

Copy editor
Rebecca Snelling

Published by AA Publishing, a trading name of Automobile Association Developments Limited,
whose registered office is Southwood East, Apollo Rise, Farnborough, Hampshire, GU14 0JW.
Registered number 1878835.

A CIP catalogue record for this book is available from the British Library.

ISBN-10: 0-7495-4512-7
ISBN-13: 978-0-7495-4512-3

Binding style with plastic section dividers by permission of AA Publishing.
Key Guide is a registered trademark in Australia and is used under license.

Colour separation by Keenes
Printed and bound by Leo, China

Find out more about AA Publishing and the wide range of travel publications and services
the AA provides by visiting our website at www.theAA.com

A02004

Maps in this title produced from mapping © KOMPASS-Karten GmbH, A-6063 Rum/Innsbruck

Relief map images supplied by Mountain High Maps® Copyright © 1993 Digital Wisdom, Inc

Weather chart statistics supplied by Weatherbase © Copyright 2004 Canty and Associates, LLC

We believe the contents of this book are correct at the time of printing.
However, some details, particularly prices, opening times and telephone numbers
do change. We do not accept responsibility for any consequences arising from the use
of this book. This does not affect your statutory rights. We would be grateful if readers would
advise us of any inaccuracies they may encounter, or any suggestions they might like to make to
improve the book. There is a form provided at the back of the book for this purpose, or you can
email us at Keyguides@theaa.com

COVER PICTURE CREDITS
Front cover and spine: AA/Clive Sawyer
Back cover, top to bottom: AA/Clive Sawyer, AA/Ken Patterson, Read's Hotel, AA/Ken Patterson

Dear Key Guide Reader

●

Thank you for buying this Key Guide. Your comments and opinions are very important to us, so please help us to improve our travel guides by taking a few minutes to complete this questionnaire.

You do not need a stamp (unless posted outside the UK). If you do not want to cut this page from your guide, then photocopy it or write your answers on a plain sheet of paper.

Send to: Key Guide Editor, AA World Travel Guides
FREEPOST SCE 4598, Basingstoke RG21 4GY

Find out more about AA Publishing and the wide range of
travel publications the AA provides by visiting our website at
www.theAA.com/bookshop

ABOUT THIS GUIDE

Which Key Guide did you buy? _____

Where did you buy it?_____

When? _ _ month/ _ _ year

Why did you choose this AA Key Guide?
- ❏ Price ❏ AA Publication
- ❏ Used this series before; title _____
- ❏ Cover ❏ Other (please state) _____

Please let us know how helpful the following features of the guide were to you by circling the appropriate category: very helpful (**VH**), helpful (**H**) or little help (**LH**)

Size	**VH**	**H**	**LH**
Layout	**VH**	**H**	**LH**
Photos	**VH**	**H**	**LH**
Excursions	**VH**	**H**	**LH**
Entertainment	**VH**	**H**	**LH**
Hotels	**VH**	**H**	**LH**
Maps	**VH**	**H**	**LH**
Practical info	**VH**	**H**	**LH**
Restaurants	**VH**	**H**	**LH**
Shopping	**VH**	**H**	**LH**
Walks	**VH**	**H**	**LH**
Sights	**VH**	**H**	**LH**
Transport info	**VH**	**H**	**LH**

What was your favourite sight, attraction or feature listed in the guide?

Page _____ Please give your reason _____

_____

Which features in the guide could be changed or improved? Or are there any other comments you would like to make?

_____

_____